Emerging Bond Markets

The bond market is a key securities market and emerging economies present exciting, new investment opportunities. This timely book provides insights into these emerging bond markets through empirical models and analytical databases, i.e. Bloomberg, Eikon Refinitiv and the Russian Cbonds.

The book looks at the dynamics of the development of emerging bond markets, their competitiveness, features and patterns using macro and micro level data. It also takes into consideration various securities type i.e. government, corporate, sub-federal and municipal bonds, to identify respective challenges and risks. The book also analyses factors that may inhibit or stimulate a well-balanced financial market. It includes case studies of Asian, Latin American and Russian bond markets, as well as cross-country comparisons.

It will be a useful reference for anyone who is interested to learn more of the bond market and the modelling techniques for critical data analysis.

Tamara Teplova joined HSE (Moscow, Russia) in 1993. HSE is one of the top-300 universities in the world. Dr Teplova is the head of the master program 'Financial markets and institutions' and the author of 11 papers in impact factor Scopus journals. She is the head of research projects initiated by government agencies and investment companies.

Tatiana V. Sokolova is a senior lecturer of HSE. Her research interest is financial economics. Dr Sokolova has published some papers in reputable Scopus journals. She is the co-author of two monographs on bond markets (in Rus.). She successfully participated in research projects initiated by the Ministries of the Russian Federation.

Qaiser Munir is a Professor and Director, Center for Business and Economic Research (CBER) at IBA Karachi, Pakistan. He is also a member of the Research Studies Evaluation and Review Committee, Ministry of Planning Development and Reform. Prior to joining IBA, he was associated with Universiti Malaysia Sabah (UMS) for ten years as a faculty member.

Routledge Studies in the Modern World Economy

Wealth, Inclusive Growth and Sustainability
Edited by Shunsuke Managi

The Korean Economy
From Growth to Maturity
You-il Lee and Richard Lee

North Korea and Economic Integration in East Asia
Yeongseop Rhee and Patrick Messerlin

Health and Education Reforms in Rural China
Li Li
With contributions from Haoming Liu, Yun Xiao and Liqiu Zhao

International Trade and Sustainable Development
Economic, Historical and Moral Arguments for Asymmetric Global Trade
Bob Milward

Ageing, Long-term Care Insurance and Healthcare Finance in Asia
Sabrina Ching Yuen Luk

What Made Korea's Rapid Growth Possible?
Jungho Yoo

Economic Growth, Inequality and Crony Capitalism
The Case of Brazil
Danilo Rocha Limoeiro

Emerging Bond Markets
Shedding Light on Trends and Patterns
Tamara Teplova, Tatiana V. Sokolova and Qaiser Munir

For more information about this series, please visit: www.routledge.com/Routledge-Studies-in-the-Modern-World-Economy/book-series/SE0432

Emerging Bond Markets

Shedding Light on Trends and Patterns

Tamara Teplova, Tatiana V. Sokolova and Qaiser Munir

Routledge
Taylor & Francis Group
LONDON AND NEW YORK

First published 2020
by Routledge
2 Park Square, Milton Park, Abingdon, Oxon OX14 4RN

and by Routledge
52 Vanderbilt Avenue, New York, NY 10017

Routledge is an imprint of the Taylor & Francis Group, an informa business

British Library Cataloguing in Publication Data
A catalogue record for this book is available from the British Library

Library of Congress Cataloging in Publication Data
A catalog record for this book has been requested

ISBN: 978-0-367-50397-0 (hbk)
ISBN: 978-1-003-04981-4 (ebk)

Typeset in Galliard
by Newgen Publishing UK

Contents

Figures

Tables

Preface

The global economy is growing at a slower pace, the population is ageing, the stratification of the population by wealth and access to resources is growing, which leads to a drop in consumer demand. There are fewer breakthrough technologies and products on the market that could fundamentally spur consumer activity.

The analysis of situation during the global financial crisis of 2007–2008 (the subprime problem led to $3 tn of debt write-offs), the euro-debt crisis of 2010, and the subsequent recession of 2010–2011 in the global economy, shows that the initial problems were associated with the accumulation of imbalanced debt (by maturity, currency, income structure, etc.) in many developed and developing economies, especially at the household level and in the financial sector. The governments of the United States and a number of large countries had to take unprecedented measures in order to maintain financial and political stability. It would seem that the post-crisis period should be characterized by a significant easing of the debt burden, a revision of the borrowing policy, both at the level of governments and at the level of firms and households. However, statistics show the opposite. In this monograph we consider trends in the debt market through the prism of bonds.

We note three characteristic features of the global financial system by the beginning of 2020: 1) an ultra-soft monetary policy or a 'money helicopter' by the central banks and governments of most countries and a high level of liquidity in the financial system; 2) the ongoing process of increasing debt, especially in emerging capital markets; 3) the risk of behaviour of major market agents.

In December 2019, the global debt reached the record levels of $256 tn ($182 tn in 2018), or 230% of the global GDP (IIF, according to the Institute of International Finance), the growth over 20 years was more than 3.2 times (in nominal dollar terms from $81 tn in 1999). China's total debt at the end of 2019 exceeded $40 tn (303% of domestic GDP). At near-zero rates, there is no catastrophe with debt growth. But the share of high-risk debts is high. In the monograph, we consider the features of the formation of the recovery rate in emerging markets, the determinants of defaults and the ability to reduce risks through portfolio building (ETFs).

In the total debt about $70 tn is the government debt, $50 tn is the debt of households ($15.3 tn in 1999), $80 tn is the debt of non-financial companies ($22 tn in 1999)[1]. The global bond market exceeded $118 tn in 2019 ($115 tn in 2018). The largest weight in bond debt is held by the US ($41.9 tn), followed by China ($13.6 tn), Japan ($12.4 tn), France ($4.6 tn) and Germany ($3.5 tn). In the structure of the global bond market, the share of government, corporate and municipal bonds is 61%, 36% and 3%, respectively. In Russia, Brazil, and S. Korea, corporate non-financial debt significantly exceeds government debt. Therefore, our monograph focuses on the corporate debt of emerging markets, and special attention is paid to the growing countries of Asia.

Potentially problematic corporate debt of the global market can be estimated at the beginning of 2020 at $5 tn as the sum of $1.2 tn of leveraged loans, $1.2 tn in sub-investment corporate bonds and $2.5 tn of 'frontier bonds' with a BBB rating (70% IG bond matured in the next 5 years falls on this group). In case of rising inflation and interest rates in the market, this debt can create big problems in the financial market. In the event of recession and the downgrade of credit ratings even by one notch, 'frontier bonds' will be thrown into the market by pension and insurance companies that are forbidden to hold sub-investment securities.

Excessive liquidity and ignoring risk led to paradoxical distortions of the 'risk–return rate' ratios, to a deformation of risk perception. The spread between corporate bonds with a minimum investment (BBB) and speculative (BB) ratings has fallen in the global market to 38 basis points (bp), which is the minimum value since 1994 (i.e. the beginning of the collection of these statistics by Bloomberg). Yield spreads of RUSSIA'29[2] and RUSSIA'47 at the end of 2019 were at the minimum levels against UST10: 110 bp and 170 bp, respectively. RUSSIA'47 shows a 20 bp yield less than the higher-rated Indian bonds INDON'47 (YTM 3.9%), while the RUSSIA'29 yield is equal to INDON'29 of the same maturity (YTM 2.9%) and is 30 bp lower than yield of Mexican sovereign bonds MEX'29 (YTM 3.2%).

On average, corporate bonds of emerging markets (estimated by ICE Bofa EM Corporate Bonds indices) provided investors with a total return rate of 12.4% per annum in 2019 against a negative total return on investment in 2018 (minus 1.3%). EM corporate bonds of the BB rating provided 15% of the total yield for the year, and high-yield bonds (with CCC ratings and lower) even higher (24.9%). EM highly reliable bonds (AAA – A ratings) showed the yield of 9.5%.

Economic problems amid the coronavirus epidemic and government promises to help businesses and the public (in the US, the promised aid exceeds $2 tn in 2020, the Fed's balance increased by $1 tn over several weeks of March due to the purchase of government bonds and mortgage securities, which led to even greater decrease in yields on US government bonds) forced companies to attract additional loans. Issuing bonds in March, 2020 turned out to be a record: investment-rated non-financial companies around the world issued bonds totalling $244 bn, wrote the Financial Times (FT), citing estimates from the research company Dealogic. Taking into account bank bonds, the total amount of bond issuance in March, 2020 alone exceeded $400 bn.

It is important for investors and regulators to understand the logic of the functioning of bond markets, the principles of pricing and specific factors of influence that are formed in emerging markets for both sovereign and municipal bonds and corporate bonds. In recent years, a number of trends have appeared in emerging bond markets: the role of foreign capital has grown, especially in the local sovereign bond market, including local currency bonds; public participation in the securities market has increased.

Our monograph reveals trends and interdependencies, observed anomalies in pricing, which will allow investors to correctly make decisions in the bond market.

Notes

1 Bank for International Settlements. www.bis.org/statistics/totcredit.htm?m=6%7C380%7C669

2 Russia's sovereign rating at 2019 from т S&P was BBB-. National rating agency ACRA evaluated it as AAA.

Acknowledgements

The publication was prepared within the framework of the Academic Fund Program at the National Research University Higher School of Economics (HSE) in 2018–2019 (grant №18-05-0007) and within the framework of the Russian Academic Excellence Project '5–100'.

Part 1

Trends and determinants of bond market development

1 Change in tendencies in the global debt market

Specifics of development of emerging markets

Introduction

By the end of the first quarter in 2019, the world's total debt had reached $184 tn. (238% of the world GDP), out of which sovereign debt makes $65 tn, $47 tn comes from households and $72 tn comes from non-financial sector companies.[1] A catastrophically huge amount of debt had been observed in Netherlands (325% of GDP), Japan (378% of GDP), Portugal (303% of GDP), Belgium (339% of GDP), Spain (263% of GDP), China (259% of GDP), and Italy (254% of GDP) at the beginning of 2019.[2] A number of countries have abnormal amounts of total debt (Luxembourg, Ireland and the UK lead in terms of debt-to-GDP ratio).

The year 2018 was one of the most unsuccessful for investors around the world. According to Deutsche Bank, from the beginning of the year till mid-November of 2018, 90% of 70 asset classes showed a synchronous decline in returns in dollar terms. The previous anti-record was in 1920 – 84% out of 37 asset classes which existed in the past dropped in value. For comparison, in 2017, only 1% of asset classes were unprofitable. Low results were also present in the bond market (indices and index funds). According to *The Economist*, global corporate debt grew from 84% of global GDP in 2009 to 92% in 2019 (IIF data), and 39% of bonds of non-financial companies have a rating below the investment level.

At the same time, the emerging bond markets during 2018–2019 demonstrated positive levels of real returns. For example, in the Russian market, the OFZ total return index in RUB grew by 8.01% from January to September 2019, and the indices of corporate and sub-federal bonds also showed a strong growth (8.4% and 9.97% accordingly). For the nine months of 2019, RUB appreciated by 6.49%, which is one of the best results among the countries of CIS.

The tasks of a statistical analysis of the global debt market and an identification of current trends forming in the market after the global financial crisis of 2007–2009, understanding the role of the bond markets, the risks faced by the sovereign and corporate debt holders and the realities faced by the issuers remain relevant.

Comments on the global debt market statistical data

Until a certain moment, the debt paradigm did not indicate its risks. But investors' and financial intermediaries' desire to earn increased returns, backed by the connivance of regulators (especially in the US), led to an almost rampant growth of securitizing various assets, including real estate. Banks issued securities with the next level of reliability on unlimited loans and mortgage bonds by composing assets according to their risk levels, which allowed them to further reduce the requirements for the credit quality of borrowers. The scale of the pyramid scheme that was forming in the US can be assessed by the CDO market (collateralized debt obligations, which combined various assets, primarily mortgage bonds). From 2004, the CDO market in the US had increased more than sevenfold, and by the end of August 2007, it had exceeded $180 bn. Such a situation could not continue indefinitely, and defaults were increasing on highly risky mortgage loans (for example, the share of default loans in May 2005 was 5.37% in the US, and by August 2007 it reached 20%). In 2006, when residential property prices stopped growing (in fact, both high-quality and low-quality mortgage borrowers had already ended), the refusal of loan payments and putting up houses for sale created an excess of supply over demand in the housing market. Since the second half of 2007, housing prices in the US began to decline. As a result, demand for mortgage securities declined, and financial analysts recognized their inability to fairly price assets as a collateral (on August 9, 2007, French bank BNP Paribas closed three funds because of this). This was a signal for the reversal of the stock market, which before then had grown rapidly. A number of analysts on August 9, 2007 recorded the beginning of the financial crisis, although more dramatic events took place at the end of 2007 (the largest financial companies were forced to write off at least $500 billion as a result of the collapse of the CDO pyramid) and in early 2008.

A feature of the global financial market development in the post-crisis period from 2010 to 2019 is the high level of liquidity in the financial system: the total balance of the three leading central banks in the world (Fed, ECB and Bank of Japan) amounted to $14.2 tn in September 2019 (by the end of 2015 – $10.7 tn).[3] The process of increasing debt were ongoing, especially in emerging capital markets (source: IMF), both for sovereign borrowings and for the corporate sector. In 2019, the total debt-to-GDP ratios of emerging and developed markets are about 120% and 165%, respectively (source: IMF).

In connection with the decision of the ECB to launch an asset purchase programme in March 2015 (in 2018 the programme was reduced, but assets were bought up by €15 bn each month), investors' increased demand for bonds in the European market, as in the US market, intensified, which gave rise to a situation where the yields of an increasing number of government and corporate bonds in the European developed countries decreased to negative values. This trend continues till today: for example, the US Federal Reserve lowered the rate twice in 2019.

As a response to the high liquidity generated by the quantitative easing (QE) programme pursued by the US Fed and the largest central banks since 2009 (the ECB and the Bank of Japan), the market for assets, primarily stocks and bonds, of developed countries had been actively growing till 2015–2016. In 2015, the US primary market amounted to $7.1 tn, but in 2018, it fell to $6.86 tn.[4]

Country statistics allows us to compare stock and corporate bond markets. In the US in mid-2018, the stock market was $32 tn, and the bond market was $4.8 tn. In Western Europe, the stock market was $14 tn, and the bond market was $2.6 tn. In Russia, the stock market was $0.6 tn, and the secondary corporate bond (CB) market was $0.198 tn. For comparison, according to JP Morgan at the beginning of 2018, the total value of corporate and sovereign bonds of emerging markets exceeded $2 tn. The volume of CB primary issues in the US market amounted to more than $1.1 tn. in 2018, and $542.3 bn for the nine months of 2019 (IPOs on the stock market reached $42.5 bn. for the nine months of 2019). Initial offerings for the nine months of 2019 in the US bond market exceeded $5.9 tn.

Inside the structure of the global bond market as of September 2019 ($120.9 tn – the bond market), the share of government bonds was 62%, corporate bonds 35%, municipal bonds 3% (Figure 1.1). We note that 92–97% of government bonds in developed and emerging markets are issued in local currency. In emerging markets, the share of corporate bonds in local currency was 72%. The structure of the global bond market is shown in Figure 1.1.

Analysis of the situation during the global financial crisis of 2007–2008, the euro debt crisis of 2010, and the subsequent recession of 2010–2011, shows that in the global economy, the initial problems were associated with the accumulation of misbalanced debt (by timing, currency, income structure, etc.) in many developed and developing countries, especially at the household level and in the financial sector of the economy. The governments of the US and a number of major countries had to take unprecedented support measures in order to maintain the financial and political stability of the system. It would seem that the post-crisis period should be characterized by a significant easing of the debt burden, a revision of the borrowing policy both at the level of governments and at the level of firms and households. However, statistics show the opposite.

By the beginning of 2019, global debt reached $184 tn., or 238% of global GDP. From pre-crisis 2007 to 2018, global debt grew by $68 tn., and half of this growth was provided by emerging markets. Since 2007, China's total debt has grown six times ($5.3 tn), reaching $33 tn. In 2018, out of $68 tn in global debt increment, China's contribution amounted to $27.8 tn. In the global debt structure (238% of global GDP), non-financial corporate sector debt is 94% of GDP, that of the government is 84% of GDP, and that of households is 60% of GDP (Table 1.1).

In developed economies (USA, Australia, Germany, France, Great Britain, Canada, Japan, South Korea, and the Netherlands) during the post-crisis period,

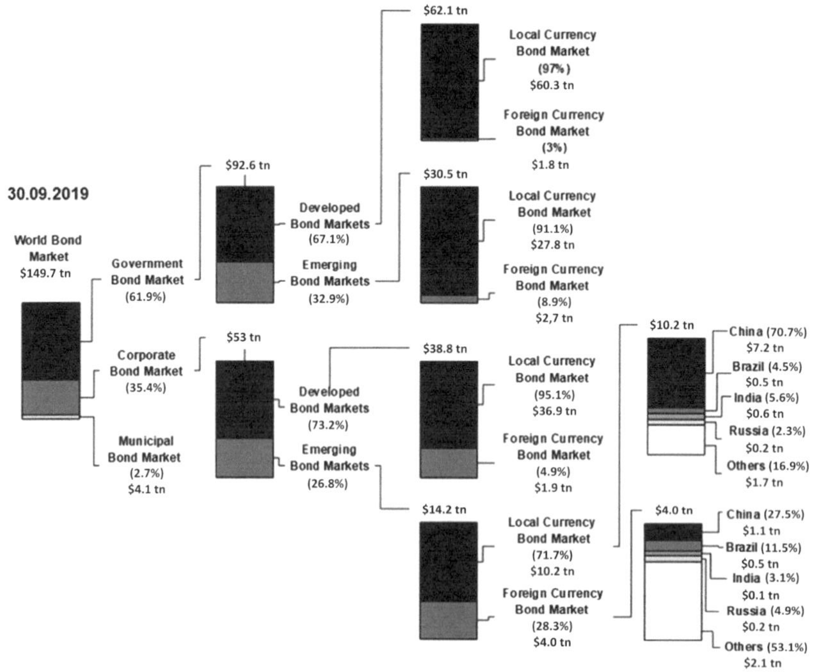

Comparison of 31.12.2006 and 30.09.2019

	World Bond Market, $tn	Share of Government Bonds, %	Share of Corporate Bonds, %	Share of Municipal Bonds, %
2006	62.4	57.0	40.3	2.7
2019	149.7	61.9	35.4	2.7

	Corporate Bond Market, $tn	Share of Developed Corporate Bond Markets, %	Share of Emerging Corporate Bond Markets, %
2006	25.1	88.8	11.2
2019	53	73.2	26.8

	Emerging Corporate Bond Markets, $tn	Share of Local Currency (LCY) Bonds, %	Share of Foreign Currency (FCY) Bonds, %
2006	2.8	52.4	47.6
2019	14.2	71.7	28.3

	LCY Corporate Bond Markets of Emerging Countries ($ tn)	China, $tn	Brazil, $tn	India, $tn	Russia, $tn
2006	1.5	0.12	0.5	0.1	0.03
2019	10.2	7.2	0.5	0.6	0.2

Figure 1.1 The global bond market (bonds outstanding as of September 30, 2019).
Source: Authors' calculations based on the Bloomberg database.

we observe a decrease in bank loans, securitized forms of attracting capital and strengthening of the role of bond loans for the non-financial companies. For households, the situation is reversed: the share of bank loans has been growing since 2007 and the weights of other forms of borrowing have been decreasing. The proportions in the stock and bond markets at the end of the 1990s are shown in Table 1.2.

Global debt market trends in the post-crisis period

We reveal the following interesting trends in the global debt market during the post-crisis period.

Table 1.1 Total debt of Asian countries in % of GDP (government, non-financial companies and households), Q1 2019

Country	*Total debt, % of GDP*	*Structure of debt in % of GDP (the share in total debt, %), Q1 2019*		
		Government	*Corporate (financial and non-financial sectors)*	*Households*
Japan	378	203 (55.7)	103 (28.3)	58 (16)
S. Korea	228	39 (17)	97 (42.6)	92 (40.4)
Malaysia	190	53 (28)	68 (36.1)	68 (35.9)
China	259	51 (19.7)	155 (59.6)	54 (20.6)
Thailand	150	34 (22.4)	48 (31.8)	69 (45.8)
Indonesia	70	30 (43.2)	23 (32.6)	17 (24.2)

Source: Bank for International Settlement.

Table 1.2 Volume of stock markets, government and corporate bonds (% of GDP) in a number of developed and developing countries by the end of the 1990s

Country	*Stock market*	*Bank credit to the private sector*	*Government and corporate bond market*	*Share of corporate bonds, %*	
				in the total volume of the stock market, bank credit to the private sector and the bond market	*in the total volume of the bond market*
USA	158.0	63.6	164.2	18.20	42.75
Japan	65.9	133.3	137.7	11.87	29.05
Germany	51.5	125.9	94.5	19.75	56.83
United Kingdom	169.7	120.8	61.0	7.91	45.57
S. Korea	35.7	82.5	86.5	15.10	35.72
India	28.3	26.6	29.3	5.23	15.02
Thailand	30.9	127.8	18.6	1.75	16.67
Hungary	29.2	17.2	25.1	0.70	1.99
Poland	13.0	19.5	8.0	8.00	0.00

Source: Endo, 2000, World Bank Database.

1. US government bonds had demonstrated low interest rates until the end of 2015. The yield on the bonds with the longest duration did not exceed 2.6% per annum in mid-2015. The increase in rates at the end of 2015 was associated with an increase in the Fed base rate (the first increase in the last 9 years took place on December 18, 2015 from 0–0.25% to 0.25–0.5% and marked the beginning of the cycle of rate hikes).

From 2011 to 2015, most central banks in emerging markets (EM) also lowered their key rates. The period from 2013 to 2014 can be described as a period of conditional tightening monetary policy in EM, but from the end of 2015 to the beginning of 2018, we can talk about the return to monetary easing. In the spring of 2018, problems began not only in Russia, but also in a number of EMs. Outflow of capital, devaluation of currencies, and increase in expected inflation again resulted in tightening monetary policy for most EMs.

The policy of the US Fed is a key factor in determining the dynamics of the global market yield levels in the long run. By September 2019, the 10-year US Treasury bonds rates reached a maximum for the last 8 years (1.75–2%). At the same time, the US negatively impacts EMs in two ways by decreasing its dollar liquidity: 1) by increasing the yields and volume of borrowing (in 2018 and 2019, the volume of new issues of US Treasuries will exceed $1 tn), 2) by reducing the balance. According to the Bloomberg forecast, until the end of 2019, the Fed key rate will remain at 2%. The yield on sovereign bonds of emerging countries in Euro-Cbonds Sovereign EM YTM eff is 3.67% as of October 2019 (Cbonds estimate). The strengthening of the dollar leads to the depreciation of national currencies: for example, the Turkish lira fell by 11% from January to October 2019 (the spread of sovereign bonds amounted to 494.7 bp in October 2019), the Brazilian real fell by 5%.

The policy of quantitative easing in European countries has led to a situation of low, often negative, interest rates on GBs. In March 2019, Germany issued 10-year GBs worth EUR 2.4 billion with a yield of –0.05%. In October 2019, Greece issued 13-week bonds worth € 487.5 million with a –0.02% yield. Note that in a deflationary situation, negative nominal rates turn into positive real ones.

2. The post-crisis debt market of developed countries has become the corporate bond market (CB). By 2013, total demand for the US corporate debt was higher than for Treasuries (valued by research firm Lipper).

   In the US, the largest bond issues are placed by banks. The average size for corporate sector borrowing is $17.35 bn. Among non-financial borrowers, we highlight General Electric, Verizon Communications and CVS Health. General Electric is actively borrowing both in national currency (USD) and in EUR. The average coupon rate on 70 negotiable bonds of Apple is 2.661% per annum. For Microsoft, the average rate is higher: 3.328% per annum (39 issues in circulation as of October 2019). Among municipalities, Texas and California are leading by volume. The average coupon for US municipal bonds is 4.21% per annum (source: Bloomberg database). US government bonds have an average issue size of approximately $300 bn. For corporate borrowing in foreign currencies (euros, pounds sterling), the average volume of issues is $5.3 bn (typical securities: Federal Home Loan Mortgage CorpFHLMC, Fannie Mae Discount Notes).
3. The correlation between the stock and bond markets is of research interest, and this relationship is conditional. There was a positive correlation between the movements of stocks and bonds from the 1970s till the end of the 1990s.

After the collapse of the dotcoms (since the beginning of the 2000s), investor attitudes toward bonds (fixed income assets) have changed: bonds began to be regarded as a hedging instrument. Investors began to include GBs in their portfolios as an insurance against the risk of falling stocks. Models with a stochastic discount factor explain well the low risk premium for bonds and the high risk premium for stocks through the covariance of the risk premium and turbulent periods of development of the financial market. However, in recent years, the connection between the segments of the financial market has again changed its direction.

A study of the factors influencing the relationship between the stock market and the bond market showed that the key drivers were uncertainty about the expected interest rate, real interest rates, covariance between interest rates, dividends and real interest rates, as well as uncertainty about the stock market risk premium. Inflation affects the correlation sign between stocks and bonds depending on the phase of the business cycle. Macroeconomic dynamics tend to fluctuate from periods of anticyclic expected inflation – stagnation – to periods of procyclical expected inflation. During stagnation, good (bad) news of future cash flows is usually accompanied by news of a lower (higher) expected return. Thus, we returned to the situation of the 1970s–1990s that when stock prices rise (fall), bond prices also rise (fall). The procyclical shocks of expected inflation as a result create a negative correlation, for example, during the period of the Great Recession. This is the conclusion of Pericoli (2018). An interesting conclusion is made by Campbell et al. (2018) that the covariance between inflation and the productivity gap is unstable over time, and its conditional nature may explain the change in the direction of correlation between the bond and stock markets. Such a conclusion becomes a good explanation of the observed dependencies: a positive correlation between 1979 and 2001 and a negative correlation between 2001 and 2011.

4. The agiotage around the CB market of developed countries attracted issuers with low credit ratings and changed the financial policies of many companies. Even companies that traditionally focused on growth at the expense of equity capital (IT companies and Internet search engines) entered the debt market. So, in 2013, Apple and Microsoft issued debt securities with a maturity of 2023 (yield 3.488% and 3.366%, respectively). In early 2014, for the first time in three years, Google entered the bond market (Aa2 rating at Moody's, AA at S&P) to refinance previously issued bonds and implement share repurchase plans (Google issued ten-year bonds worth $1 bn. with a yield of 3.377%). The prospectus indicates[5], that these funds will be used for 'general corporate expenses, including the possible payment of the $1 bn main debt of bonds with a yield of 1.25% and maturity in 2014'.

The paradox of the post-crisis debt market is a violation of the relationship between the level of debt burden on the US non-financial companies and the share (percentage) of defaults of high-risk bond issuers. Figure 1.2 shows the dynamics of the level of defaults (in %) from the end of 1986 to the third

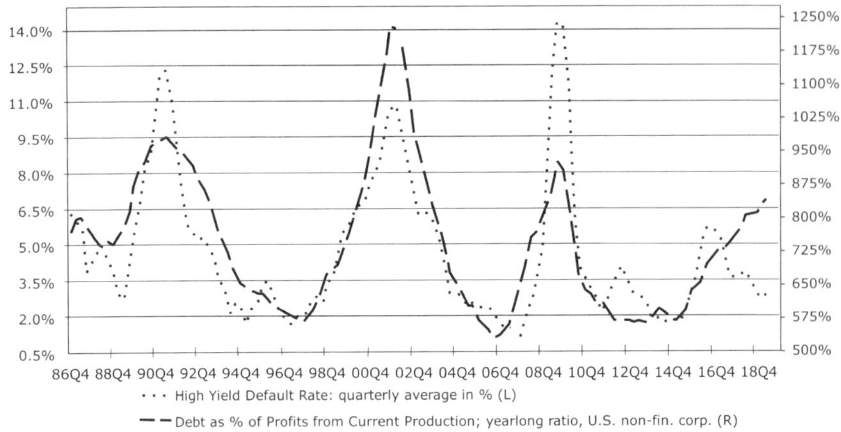

Figure 1.2 The debt burden of US companies in explaining the dynamics high-yield bond defaults.

quarter of 2019 and the dynamics of the US corporate debt (as a percentage of GDP, Moody's data). Until 2011, there was a fairly clear synchronicity, which clearly disappears since 2016 (Figure 1.2[6]).

What is the reason behind this desynchronization? Firstly, due to globalization and increasing international trade, it is more relevant to correlate corporate debt with global GDP; this significantly changes the ratio and narrows the spread. Secondly, due to the fact that until recently, the cost of debt was at a very low level, large corporate debt did not create a high risk of default. With an increase in the cost of funding, which directly depends on the Fed monetary policy, the default rate on high-yield bonds will increase, which will cause sales in all markets, and will most probably affect developing markets.

5. Low rates of return were demonstrated not only by GBs, but also by CBs. In the US bond market, borrowers with high credit ratings raised debt at record low rates (1–1.5% per annum). For example, the yield on three-year Nissan Motor Acceptance bonds maturing in 2018 was 1.5%. In the European market, even low-quality issuers with a CCC rating made attempts to issue Eurobonds. The year 2018 also demonstrated high growth rates of the market for corporate bonds of developed countries.

   In 2019, there was an IPO boom in the US bond market. From January to September 2019, more than 120 companies went IPO with a volume of $42.5 bn.
6. Strengthening regulation in the banking system has led to a change in the traditional proportion of market and bank financing in the US and EU markets. Traditionally, American companies were leaders in attracting market (bond) financing: about 70% of the necessary financing was attracted through bonds

and 30% from bank loans. For European companies, the opposite proportion existed until 2013: 30% – bonds and 70% – bank loans. In 2013, statistics for the first time showed a breakdown of the traditional proportion, and 2014 estimates confirmed this trend. Through the issue of bonds, US companies attracted about 30% of financing, in Europe – about 40%.

This change in proportions can be explained by several reasons. Apparently, the main reason is associated with low economic growth in the EU and the difficult financial situation of European banks, which have not recovered from the global crisis of 2008–2009 and the 2010 European debt crisis. As a result, the EU's regulated banking sector continues to experience major problems in performing its traditional lending functions to companies. They were followed by an increase in the US lending and a slowdown in the EU. If in 2013 in the US banks had a record level of lending (exceeding the 2007 volume by 10%), then European banks, even considering some surge in activity in 2013, reached only 50% of the lending period of 2005–2007. In the Eurozone 2012–2013 banks reduced lending by two trillion euros.

7. Another emerging trend is that non-banking institutions (asset managers, insurance companies, private equity funds, hedge funds and professional associations, industry cooperatives) began to actively lend money to borrowers. To a large extent, this trend is emerging due to the tightening of banking regulation after a series of crisis years 2008–2010. In the USA, assets of industrial cooperatives reached $1.4 trillion by 2014, an increase of 60% since 2008.

   According to *The Economist*, in March, 2020 about 7% of corporate bonds (CBs) in the global market belong to travel companies, airlines and hotels and about 8% of CBs to oil companies. These sectors are seriously affected by the coronavirus and drop of oil prices below $30 / barrel, so 15% of global corporate debt is at risk.

8. Since 2011, we have observed a growing interest in debt instruments of developing countries, not only in sovereign debts, but also in the corporate sector. In 2012, the yield spread between corporate and government bonds decreased to 223 basis points (bp) compared to 351 bp at the end of 2011. Such a low return on developed countries means that in fact institutional investors, primarily insurance and pension companies, invested in 'depreciating assets'. The average return fell to 3.34% in 2011 and dropped to 3% by 2014. Investors were forced to look for higher returns in emerging markets, which until mid-2014 (before the fall in oil prices and the devaluation processes in a number of markets) showed quite acceptable levels in the ratio 'risk–profitability'.

   Since 2012, the interest of global investors in emerging bond markets is evidenced by the dynamics of the index EMBI plus Composite, which showed an increase of 17.4% in 2012. The highest growth rate over the past 15 years was recorded twice in 1999 and in 2009, and these estimates are overstated due to the low comparative base of the previous year, when there was a catastrophic drop in the index of the previous crisis year. By 2014, nine of the

Figure 1.3 Growth of five-year sovereign spreads (CDS) of developing countries in 2018–Q1 2020.

Source: Cbonds.

16 largest US pension funds made strategic investments in the national bond market of developing countries (Arslanalp & Tsuda, 2014).

The peculiarity of mid-2018 and the first quarter of 2020 is the growth of country risks in emerging capital markets, which is shown in Figure 1.3 on sovereign spreads for five-year US bonds.

Since 2012, global investors began to pay attention to bonds in the national currency of countries that demonstrated the stability of their currency, a strong surplus budget and high nominal rates in the domestic market. The ratios of the levels of country credit risk, nominal and real returns are shown in Table 1.3. The liberalization of access of foreign capital to domestic markets (for example, to the markets of Russia and China) also played a positive role. The bond markets of developing countries showed significant growth due to the 'demand for real positive returns', while investors had been faced with extremely low rates in developed capital markets.

The average volume of new issues of corporate bonds in national currency (for comparison, the volumes were converted into USD) in January–September 2019 amounted to \$85.65 m for Brazil, \$142.76 m for Singapore, \$78.98 m for Russia, and mainland China \$232.84 m. Smaller volumes on average attract companies in India (\$56.83 m), Poland (\$55.35 m), Hong Kong (\$43.08 m).

The numbers of bond issues and their nominal volume for emerging markets and for individual geographical regions are shown in Tables 1.4 and 1.5. Bonds of the financial and non-financial sectors of the economy are highlighted.

Table 1.3 Yield levels in emerging capital markets (10-year GBs). October 2019

	Rating S&P / Moody's / Fitch	*Yields of 10-year GBs, %*	*Inflation rate, %*	*Real return rate, %*	*Key rate of the central bank, %*
Russia	BBB-/Baa3/BBB	6.66	3.46	3.20	7.0
S. Africa	BB/Baa3/BB+	8.92	5.46	3.46	10.0
Turkey	B+/B1/BB-	14.1	3.58	10.52	16.5
Brazil	BB-/Ba2/BB-	6.66	2.83	3.83	5.5
Mexico	BBB+/A3/BBB	6.74	3.24	3.50	7.75
India	BBB-/Baa2/BBB-	6.51	3.1	3.41	5.15
Indonesia	BBB/Baa2/BBB	7.2	3.1	4.10	5.25
Columbia	BBB-/Baa2/BBB	6.0	1.46	4.54	4.25
Philippines	BBB+/Baa2/BBB	4.71	3.0	1.71	4.0
Chile	A+/A1/A	2.14	0.29	1.85	2.0
Peru	BBB+/A3/BBB+	4.4	2.5	1.90	2.5

Source: Bloomberg Database, World Bank.

Table 1.4 Dynamics of EM bond market segments in 2017–2019. Asian region

	Emerging debt markets, total				*Incl. Asian region*			
	2019 January–September	*2018*	*2017*	*Change*	*2019 January-September*	*2018*	*2017*	*Change*
Volume in m USD	567 105	652 865	806 967	-19%	297 459	322 888	379 329	-15%
Number of issues	1 571	1 767	1 827	-3,3%	922	1 124	1 060	6%
Volume in m USD								
Government	124 721	159 654	208 474	-23%	12 841	22 469	24 779	-9%
Municipal	11 000	1 432	15 155	-91%	-	-	-	
Corporate	431 384	491 779	583 338	-16%	284 618	300 419	354 550	-15%
Volume in m USD								
financial sector	180 949	202 979	250 123	-19%	117 942	127 790	164 477	-22%
non-financial sector	250 434	288 800	333 215	-13%	166 676	172 629	190 073	-9%

Source: Bloomberg, authors' calculations.

The growth of yields in the bond markets gave rise to discussions about possible problems with economic growth (previously, the credit market often acted as an indicator of future problems in the economy). Economists have

Table 1.5 Dynamics of EM bond markets by region in 2017–2019. Eastern Europe and the Middle East

	Eastern Europe				*Middle East*			
	2019 January–September	*2018*	*2017*	*Change*	*2019 January–September*	*2018*	*2017*	*Change*
Volume in m USD	35 933	40 769	57 049	-29%	86 876	100 509	98 620	2%
Number of issues	53	75	113	-34%	234	227	187	21%
Volume in m USD								
Government	24 178	23 998	30 591	-22%	30 341	42 191	50 671	-17%
Municipal	-	-	-		11 000	1 317	10 000	-87%
Corporate	11 756	16 772	26 457	-37%	45 534	57 001	37 950	50%
Volume in m USD								
Financial sector	5 610	9 927	18 274	-46%	26 659	28 686	25 299	13%
Non-financial sector	6 146	6 844	8 183	-16%	18 875	28 315	12 651	124%

Source: Bloomberg, authors' calculations.

Table 1.6 The share of borrowings in various currencies in the global market (%)

Currency	*2008*	*2009*	*2010*	*2013*	*2014*	*2019*
Dollar	47.5	44	52	50	46.7	34.78
Euro	21.6	25	15	17	18.8	17.23
Yuan	5.1	9	9	15	18.7	19.33

Source: Bloomberg, authors' calculations.

traditionally tracked the spreads between speculative-rated corporate bonds and government bonds (in the run-up to crises, as well as during periods of market downturns, spreads increase dramatically). In 2018, the yields of high-risk CBs (without an investment credit rating) increase with increasing yields on government bonds, but spreads are in an acceptable range and do not signal a pre-crisis state.

9. The role of the US dollar as a bond issue currency returned to its pre-crisis level in 2014 (Table 1.6). In the 1990s the share of USD-denominated bonds increased and reached 49.5% in 2000. By 2008, the weight of dollar borrowings dropped to 47.5% with a slight surge in 2010–2011. By 2015, it returned to the level of 46%. The Japanese government's policy of reducing

external debt has led to a decrease in the share of yen-denominated financial instruments to 2.5%. The share of bond issues in the currencies of other developed countries (Swiss francs, Canadian and Australian dollars) are also at a low level. The emerging trend in the global debt market is the growth of borrowings in the Chinese yuan.

There is a trend for an increase in the share of euro-denominated bonds with a floating interest rate in the total debt. The share of bonds with floating rates in the total bond market volume increased from 23.8% in 2000 to 28% in 2005 and 29% in 2011. At the same time, the share of convertible bonds decreased (at the level of 1–2% of the total volume of bonds market).

10. With the growing volume of debt in EMs, the share of foreign investors in this segment of the financial market increased. According to Arslanalp and Tsuda (2014), in 2013 global investors owned 13% of the debt of 21 emerging market (EM) countries. The highest share of investments – 51% – is in Peru, while the relative share of foreign investors in China and India is lower than 2%, which is associated with strict government regulation of foreign capital inflows (Table 1.7). At the beginning of 2012, the nominal volume of Russian OFZs owned by foreign investors amounted to no more than 3.7% (about 107 bn RUB) of the total volume of the OFZ market (total amount of about 2903 bn RUB). For comparison, at the beginning of 2012, foreign investors held about 11% of Brazilian GBs. Until 2018, the share of foreign investors in the Russian bond market grew precisely in the national currency. The share of non-residents in the OFZ market increased from 3% until 2012 to 33% in March 2018 (local maximums were observed in December 2014 at 32% and in April 2013 at 28.1%). Since April 2018 (introducing of the US sanctions), the share of foreign investors in the OFZ market began to decrease and in November 2018 it was at no more than 24%. But in 2019 it increased and consisted 32% in March, 2020 (source: Moscow Exchange).
11. The Chinese market creates a 'new reality' for market participants. An analysis of bond issues by developing countries in 2019 shows that the Asian market is the leader. China and Hong Kong account for almost a third of the total volume of new issues in developing debt markets (24.6% and 11%, respectively). Latin American countries (Brazil, Mexico, Argentina) have a significant proportion in the developing countries debt structure.

After the 'big landslides' in the Chinese stock market in 2015, 2016 was marked for the Chinese regulator by the need to introduce new rules of the game. In the summer of 2015, the Securities Market Regulatory Commission suspended the rule to stop trading when the index fell by 7%. A six-month moratorium on the sale of minority shareholders with a package of more than 5% ended, which significantly affected China's stock indices, since minority shareholders entered the market. The regulator was forced to introduce a new rule: sales for large shareholders are limited to 1% of their package, and large shareholders are required to publish plans for the sale of shares 15 days before entering the market. This created a situation of declining market participants' confidence in the regulator and

Table 1.7 The share of foreign investors in sovereign debt in national currency

Country	*The volume of sovereign debt in national currency ($bn)*			*Share of foreign investors (% of sovereign debt in national currency)*	
	December 2006	*December 2013*	*December 2013, % GDP*	*December 2006*	*December 2013 (December 2019)*
China	448.09	1340.27	14.50	0.02	1.68 (8.0)
Brazil	511.84	859.48	38.27	2.88	16.10 (11.0)
India	337.46	680.49	36.26	0.26	1.23 (3.0)
Mexico	157.08	379.80	30.12	7.57	36.87
Poland	120.55	191.17	36.94	21.25	34.92
Turkey	153.15	189.78	23.14	13.84	21.53
Malaysia	56.20	146.27	46.82	8.40	29.40
Russia	39.05	120.57	5.75	2.55	24.75 (32.0)
S. Africa	63.89	114.34	32.61	8.59	37.85
Thailand	48.78	104.04	26.87	2.73	17.41
Philippines	43.48	84.08	30.91	0.00	14.44
Columbia	37.87	82.35	21.78	0.00	6.43
Indonesia	46.55	77.22	8.89	13.12	30.01
Egypt	18.62	65.43	24.06	18.57	0.21
Hungary	53.52	57.61	44.32	28.81	40.36
Argentina	32.74	37.20	6.10	16.80	3.20
Ukraine	-	30.06	16.94	0.00	4.83
Romania	-	27.12	14.30	0.00	22.30
Peru	3.70	12.81	6.33	27.21	51.08
Lithuania	1.42	3.30	7.19	1.26	16.09
Bulgaria	1.44	3.16	5.95	0.00	0.98

Source: International Monetary Fund.

increased volatility in different segments of China's financial market. In April–May 2018, China announced a reform in the field of regulation of the debt market. The problem for the global market is that the Chinese market is so large that professionals say: 'when China sneezes, the whole world gets sick'.

12. The increase in US Fed rates has led to an outflow of capital from both the equity markets of developing countries and the bond market. Prices of the major emerging market indices plummeted. Since 2014, there has been a slowdown in the inflow of capital from foreign investors into the bond markets of the BRICS countries.

Since 2015, there has been a tendency to reduce Russian investments in the US public debt. If in 2010, Russian investments in US bonds were $175 bn, then in September 2019 they were only \$8.5 bn. For comparison: China's investments were \$1110 bn, Japan \$1131 bn, Brazil \$310 bn.

Problems and recommendations on development of emerging government bond markets

Since 1988, analysts have distinguished emerging markets. We focus on the largest emerging bond markets in Asia, Latin America and Eastern Europe: China (also the third largest in the world by volume after the US and Japan), India, Brazil and Russia. The volume of outstanding government bonds (GBs) of Russia in relation to GDP is relatively low (10.6% in 2019), but the Russian market has specifics: first, unlike China and India, where the share of over-the-counter trading is high (about 80–90%), 97% of transactions in the Russian bond market are performed in the Moscow stock exchange. Secondly, under the conditions of sanctions from the US and the EU and low oil prices, the Russian government strictly controlled the level of public debt, so by the beginning of 2020 there was a situation that reserves exceed the volume of public debt. Therefore in Russia there is a significant potential for increasing public debt without loss of financial stability. Third, the share of non-residents in Russian GBs is high: 32% on March 19, 2020. This forces the regulator (Bank of Russia) to take into account the interests of non-residents and the problem of possible capital outflows when setting the key rate which affects the rouble exchange rate.

In this chapter, we consider the relatively favourable period of development of bond markets until 2020. Starting in January 2020, there has been an outflow of capital from emerging bond markets due to the coronavirus epidemic and low oil prices. According to Bloomberg estimates, from the beginning of January 2020 to March 20, 2020, the capitalization of the bond markets of developing countries decreased by \$5 tn[7] In Brazil, the regulator faced a difficult situation: from March 1, 2020 to March 16, 2020, trading in the stock exchange was automatically stopped six times. The Brazilian real fell by 9% from March 1, 2020 to March 16, 2020. Overcoming the problem of hyperinflation in recent years facilitated the entry of retail investors into the stock market, and for them the 2020 crisis is the first. Brazil is forced to strictly control the state budget balance, and decreasing the interest rate to stimulate the economy will contribute to further devaluation of the national currency. The situation in Russia is more favourable, but the Russian rouble took second place in terms of the exchange rate volatility against the US dollar since the beginning of 2020 (after the Mexican peso), which became an additional motivation for the inclusion of Brazil and Russia in our consideration.[8]

The government bond (GB) markets of a number of large developing countries (China, India, Russia, Brazil) have investment attractiveness for global investors: on the one hand, they are characterized by positive real interest rates, on the other hand, they offer opportunities for risk diversification. For example, in China, Policy Bank bonds have historically low correlation with the key global debt market indices (about 0.2), which allows an external investor to take

Table 1.8 Average annual nominal and real interest rates (in brackets) on 10-year government bonds

	China	*India*	*Russia*	*Brazil*
2017	3.63	6.75	7.77	10.26
	(2.01)	(4.15)	(3.94)	(6.59)
2018	3.62	7.72	7.89	10.48
	(1.51)	(2.73)	(4.87)	(6.57)
2019	3.20	6.92	7.42	7.80
	(0.30)	(–0.69)	(2.82)	(3.93)

Source: Investing.com, authors' calculations.

Table 1.9 The volumes of the secondary GB markets (in % GDP)

	China	*India*	*Russia*	*Brazil*
Volume of the secondary GB market				
2012	32.6	84.6	7.22	55.09
2018	53.7	89.3	9.94	85.14
2019	54.9	88.9	10.57	80.20
Share of internal GB market, %	99.3	100	77.6	93.7
Average annual growth rate in 2012–2019, %	7.7	0.8	5.6	5.5

Source: Bloomberg, Asian Bonds Online, authors' calculations.

advantage of the diversification.[9] In 2019, we note a trend towards a decrease in real interest rates on 10-year GB denominated in local currency compared to 2017–2018 (Table 1.8).

Among the BRIC countries, in 2012–2018, the GB markets of China grew at the fastest pace (in % of GDP): on average, by 7.7% per year, respectively (Table 1.9). The factors of rapid growth of the Chinese GB market were high GDP growth and investment in long-term infrastructure projects, as well as the process of market liberalization for global investors. The volume of the secondary GB market of India has not practically changed: its average annual growth rate was only 0.9%. The Russian GB market is the least developed (by the volume in GDP) among the BRIC countries: the volume of outstanding GB at the end of 2018 was only 9.9% of GDP (Table 1.9), which is due to the control of debt level under conditions of low oil prices and anti-Russia sanctions. In all the markets under consideration, the internal government debt prevails (Table 1.9).

We highlight the following problems that impede the development of emerging GB markets:

1. Relatively short terms for attracting loans, which is caused by the instability of the macroeconomic environment in many emerging economies. The latter is especially pronounced in the case of Russia, which was characterized in

2013–2019 by low economic growth, high volatility of the exchange rate, as well as the negative effects of anti-Russian sanctions by the US and the EU. For China, the relatively short terms for attracting loans (3–4 years) are associated with a slowdown in the growth rate of long-term capital investments. On average, in emerging markets, the average maturity of GBs was 7.3 years in 2018[10].

2. In a number of developing countries, the vast majority of outstanding bonds are directly or indirectly related to the public sector. The direct share of GBs and regional bonds in China, India and Russia is 38.7%, 52.4% and 65.7% of the total volume of outstanding bonds (source: Bloomberg). But according to the ACRA-Ratings estimates, in China and Russia, about 80% of bonds are issued either by government or by large companies with state participation in the ownership structure. This raises the problem of implicit state guarantees in the event of a potential default on bonds of state-owned companies. This problem is especially relevant for China, due to an increase in the number of defaults on corporate bonds in 2018–2019.
3. Most GB markets in developing countries are characterized by low liquidity; the reasons are a narrow investor base, low confidence of retail investors in the financial market, and investors' choice of buy-and-hold strategies. Since the GB market performs a benchmarking function, the absence of a liquid bond market at different maturities leads to the use of indicative yields instead of market indicators.
4. The volume of GB markets in China, Russia, Brazil and India (Table 1.9) is much smaller than in a number of developed countries (US, Japan). Typical problems of emerging bond markets are insufficient investor confidence, market infrastructure problems, and also the narrow spectrum of debt instruments (often the only differences in conditions of bond issues are the coupon size and maturity). As shown in Table 1.9, Russia has the lowest level of public debt in relation to GDP, because low oil prices and anti-Russian sanctions forced the government to increase reserves and strictly control the debt level. A negative consequence is the lack of fiscal incentives for economic development. The positive trends include the development in Russia of the GB segment with a variable coupon, depending on inflation. A unique feature of the Russian bond market is a high share of exchange trading (about 97%).
5. A not so high (compared with developed countries) sovereign credit rating, which is typical for some developing countries. As of March, 2020, Moody's long-term foreign currency ratings of India is Baa2, China is A1, Brazil is Ba2, Russia is Baa3. In India, the planned deficit of the state budget for the fiscal year 2020 is 3.5%, and according to the forecasts of the Fitch rating agency, the forecast of the ratio of government debt to GDP should not exceed 70% by 2022. Against the background of slowing economic growth, a budget deficit does not allow India's credit rating to exceed Baa2, despite the weakening of barriers to foreign capital inflows, as well as lowering corporate taxes. In Brazil, starting in 2015, there has been a downward trend in the ratings of Moody's, S&P and Fitch. Since 2016, Brazil's long-term sovereign credit

rating has been Ba2 according to Moody's and BB according to S&P and Fitch (i.e., sub-investment rating; source: Eikon). The creation of incentives for domestic investment in financing the budget deficit increased the yields of GBs. In 2018, over 1.8 m brokerage accounts were registered in the Brazilian debt market, while in the stock market only 0.6 m accounts were registered.

6. Problems of regulation of bond markets and liberalization of international capital flows. The share of LCY GB held by non-residents in China and Russia in 2019 was about 8% and 30–33%, respectively[11], and in India and Brazil in 2019 was about 3% and 11%, respectively[12]. In OFZs with debt amortization and OFZs with the float coupon rate, there are practically no non-residents holdings. In inflation-linked OFZs 52001 and 52002 the share of non-residents was 2.95% and 9.30% on March 18, 2020. The maximum share of non-residents in the OFZ bond issue is 81%, one of the minimums is 7–8%. In the total volume of OFZs at the beginning of March 2020 the share of non-residents was 32% (source: Moscow Exchange).

   The high share of foreign investors can greatly affect the exchange rate, especially during periods of turmoil in financial markets. The regulator is forced to consider the possible outflow of capital when pursuing a policy of changing the key rate and foreign exchange interventions (Bank of Russia, mid-March 2020).

   In China, the process of bond issuance is regulated by different agencies: China Banking and Insurance Regulatory Commission, People's Bank of China, National Development and Reform Commission, and China Securities Regulatory Commission.[13] China's bond market is highly segmented, and each segment has its own legal regulations.

7. Insufficient financial literacy of the retail investors that impedes the development of GB markets, as well as the underdevelopment of the segment of institutional investors (mutual funds, private pension funds, and insurance companies). For example, in Russia, the population prefers to save money on bank deposits (about $460 bn at January, 2020). Both the Moscow Exchange and the regulator (Bank of Russia) are interested in that the savings of retail investors are redirected to the stock or bond market. In Russia, there is implemented a project to create a single market place, and in 2017–2019 the largest banks organized placement of OFZs for the population (OFZ-N).

Dominant holders of bonds in the internal bond markets of many emerging countries are commercial banks. For example, in China and Russia their share in bond holdings is 56% and 67%, respectively[14]. The exception is Brazil where the share of funds, pension funds and insurance companies in GBs is 55.8% in 2019 (Source: Brazil National Treasury).

In connection with the identified problems, the following recommendations can be made on the development policy of GB markets in developing countries:

1. Since one of the important factors determining the development of the GB market is the stability of the macroeconomic environment, it is necessary to

pursue appropriate policies aimed at stimulating economic growth and reducing inflation, as well as monitoring and optimizing the ratio of public debt to GDP in order to reduce risks. A stable macroeconomic environment will also increase the term for raising funds in the bond market, as investor confidence will increase.

2. In order to increase the investment attractiveness of the GB markets of developing countries in the eyes of global investors, an institutional environment should be developed that focuses on protecting the rights of investors, including equalizing the rights of internal and external investors. The latter is especially relevant for China, where it can be recommended to allow external investors to participate in repo transactions in order to diversify their portfolios[15].

   Optimization of complicated legislation in the field of regulation of capital markets can attract a larger number of external investors. For China, unification of the rules for bond issuing and trading, as well as the choice of a single regulator are recommended. Since a large number of individual investors participate in the debt market, their interests should be protected. According to IMF recommendations, the legal framework should protect investors from insolvency and inappropriate behaviour of custodians.

   Another aspect important for the development of the GB market is the liberalization of international capital flows in order to attract foreign investors. According to the IMF survey[16], foreign investors pay attention to the ease of access to the public sector, foreign exchange and tax regimes, the liquidity of the bond market, and the organization of market infrastructure.

3. Due to the high share of the public sector among bond issuers, hedging instruments should be developed, including the market of derivative financial instruments. It is also necessary to increase the diversity of fixed income instruments issued, especially regarding inflation-linked bonds. It is necessary to take measures aimed at limiting risks taken by municipalities or major state-owned companies.
4. We recommend the development of technical systems and the stock exchange infrastructure in order to ensure financial stability and prevent the risks of sharp price changes as a result of manipulations or negative practices of high-frequency trading. It is important to introduce and develop electronic trading platforms, which will increase the transparency of pricing in the bond market. IT platforms used by stock exchanges should provide the necessary capacity to handle trade transactions with large volumes and be cyber-secure.
5. One of the instruments for increasing liquidity in the bond market is benchmark building programmes, including setting reliable yields curve, planning of public offerings in the primary GB market, and revisions of primary dealer agreements. According to IMF recommendations[17], one important aspect is the development of the money market, including REPO transactions with GBs as collateral and derivatives market. For the market for outstanding bonds, market makers (financial intermediaries) providing GBs trade play the key role.

6. It is necessary to increase the financial literacy of the population, to clarify the principles of working with various financial instruments, and also to stimulate the development of banking products, which, in addition to traditional deposits, can be used to redirect part of the savings of investors to investment accounts. In parallel, an impetus will be given to the development of a new financial intermediation market.

To ensure the possibility of raising funds in the bond market for the long term, it is important to develop pension funds and insurance companies. One bad practice, used in Russia, is a continuous change of the scheme of a pension system, because this decreases public confidence in institutional investors. We recommend establishing a long-term moratorium on the change of the rules of a pension system.

Another promising area is the development of the bond ETF segment, which allows investors to pay lower fees compared to mutual funds. ETFs can improve the liquidity situation and expand the investor base.

The object of further research is the crisis in emerging bond markets which began in 2020 due to the epidemic of coronavirus and a sharp drop of oil prices.

The Fourth Industrial Revolution in financial markets

The Fourth Industrial Revolution in financial markets means innovative products and technological advances including robots and artificial intelligence. Pieterse-Bloem (2019)[18] highlights the important role of exchange-traded products (ETPs) which allow investors access to a broad segment of the market in 'one transaction' and at a low cost. In 2018, the volume of the global ETP market was about $5 tn. Bond ETPs constituted only 18% of the total volume, but this segment is the most rapidly growing. ETPs contribute to increasing liquidity in different market segments.

In recent years, there has been an expansion and strengthening of the influence of algorithmic trading (AT) on the financial markets of developed and developing economies. Based on a review of research papers, we consider the positive and negative aspects of the impact of AT on the volatility of return rates of securities, liquidity indicators, and market efficiency. Our focus is on high-frequency trading (HFT), which means the submission of a significant number of trade orders per second using robots. This type of trade poses risks to market stability. Currently, the share of HFT in the US stock market is about 50% (Breckenfelder, 2019). In 2017, the global market of AT was $9.3 bn, and it is forecasted that its volume in 2026 will be about $21.7 bn, i.e. the average annual growth rate will be about 10.1% (source: Bloomberg[19]).

HFT allows investors to achieve high return rates, but O'Connell (2019) notes a decrease in HFT profitability since 2015. The first reason is increased competition: the number of investment companies using HFT, modern information technologies and hardware has rapidly grown. The second reason is increased market regulation and surveillance aimed at preventing manipulations and fraud via HFT.

The influence of HFT on volatility in financial markets. One of the classic cases is the Flash Crash which occurred on May 6, 2010 in the US market. Due to price manipulations based on HFT, the decline of the market index was 10% in 36 minutes (O'Connell, 2019). At the end of the day, the situation had stabilized.

The results of previous studies are ambiguous. On the one hand, Hasbrouck and Saar (2013) reveal that low-latency trading (i.e., the execution of trade orders with a faster speed) contributes to a decrease in short-term volatility, even if the financial market is under pressure. Hagstromer and Norden (2013) divide HF traders into market makers (their share at NASDAQ-OMX Stockholm in the total HFT volume is from 63% to 72%) and 'opportunistic' HF traders. The authors reveal that market-making HFTs decrease intraday volatility while Breckenfelder (2019), based on the analysis of trades at the Stockholm Stock Exchange, shows that competition among HFT traders leads to increased speculative trading, and as a result, intraday volatility grows. HFT does not significantly change interday volatility, since most HFT trading positions close at the end of the day.

Gianluca (2016) performs two simulations showing different results. If there is no stress in the financial market and the price movement can be described by a random walk model, then HFT traders do not affect volatility. But if there is a clear upward or downward trend in the financial market, then HFT significantly increases volatility. Trade orders of 'slow' market participants are executed with a time delay in comparison with HFT traders, and this leads to greater market uncertainty.

The influence of HFT on liquidity in financial markets. The results of previous studies are also ambiguous. On the one hand, Moriyasu et al. (2018) analyze data on 1302 stocks traded on the Tokyo Stock Exchange from 2007 to 2012 and show that AT increases liquidity: bid-ask spreads decrease, while market depth increases. The authors explain this effect by the reduction in monitoring costs. If volatility in the stock market grows, the positive effect of AT on liquidity weakens. Mestel et al. (2018) reveal that AT reduces the relative quoted and effective spreads in the Austrian stock market. The authors highlight the role of algorithmic traders as market makers.

On the other hand, Breckenfelder (2019) reveals that competition among HFT traders causes a decrease in liquidity: Amihud's illiquidity measure, bid-ask spreads and Kyle's price impact measure increase. Jiang et al. (2015) study the impact of HFT on the liquidity and pricing of US Treasuries at the time of publication of macroeconomic news. The sample includes 2223 publications of macroeconomic news in 2006–2011. The authors reveal that the activity of HFT traders worsens liquidity indicators, as it leads to a widening of the spread in the pre-announcement period and a decrease in depth at the best quotes and behind the best quotes.

The influence of HFT on the risks and returns of securities. Liu et al. (2013) test the hypothesis that government bonds more exposed to HFT are characterized by increased risks and, therefore, should demonstrate higher yields. The research sample includes 416 US Treasuries; the analysis period is from 2003 to 2011. Based on the regression analysis, the authors find that the participation of HF traders in US Treasuries trades significantly increases their yields. A trading strategy based on opening long positions on Treasuries with a high share of HFT and short positions on Treasuries with low HFT activity is profitable.

The influence of HFT on the efficiency of financial markets. HFT allow investors to react instantly to stock prices changes, supply and demand changes, so they increase the efficiency of financial markets[20]. Chaboud et al. (2013) investigate the influence of AT on price efficiency in the foreign exchange market. The authors find a beneficial effect of AT due to a decrease in arbitrage opportunities. They also note that AT contributes to a faster reflection of new information in prices.

Nevertheless, there is a risk that some information, especially if not presented in a unique systematized form (company financial reports and news), is not taken into account by trading systems and, therefore, is not adequately reflected in prices. This could potentially increase information asymmetry. Gider et al. (2015) reveal that HFT negatively affected fundamental price efficiency in the US stock market from 1990 to 2014.

The influence of HFT on price manipulations and market anomalies. One common manipulation is spoofing, i.e. the practice of creating an order with a large volume and cancelling it microseconds before the execution. This practice distorts balance of supply and demand and is aimed at misleading traders (O'Connell, 2019). There is also a problem of the unpremeditated generation of a great number of trade orders which leads to an excessive burden on the IT infrastructure of stock exchanges. For example, during the IPO of Facebook, a lot of trade orders were not executed in time which caused losses for some investors (Jones, 2013).

HFT regulation issues. O'Connell (2019) states that regulation measures include minimum quoting requirements to market makers regarding benchmark securities which should be quoted, minimum secondary market volume, quotation size, maximum spread limits and minimum continuous quoting periods. These recommendations were basically developed by the US Securities and Exchange Commission (SEC) and US Commodity Futures Trading Commission (CFTC) as a response to the Flash Crash of May, 2010. Other measures are penalties for rapid cancellations of trade orders to prevent spoofing. There are also restrictions on co-location, i.e. the placement of computers of HF traders in the environment of the stock exchange servers, because this practice lets HF traders influence prices before other investors.

In some emerging markets, a lot of attention is paid to risk-management regarding HFT strategies. For example, in India and Thailand each strategy has to be audited and approved by the stock exchange before use[21].

Recommendations on HFT regulation. Based on the literature review, we conclude that HFT have positive effects which are opportunities for investors to obtain higher return rates, lowering bid-ask spreads and increasing the efficiency of the financial market. Negative effects of HFT (for example, price manipulations and increasing volatility) are primarily due to the activity of speculative HF traders.

It is necessary to distinguish between market-making and speculative HFT traders. Regulations should not be aimed at increasing competition among speculative traders (Breckenfelder, 2019), because this can cause a liquidity deterioration. It is recommended to provide lower commissions for market makers if they comply with minimum quoting requirements.

It can be recommended to implement and develop risk-management practices, including auditing and monitoring, to minimize the risks of applying HFT strategies. Possible measures are the certification of HFT strategies and limiting the number of trade orders from one account per time period. In emerging markets, it is advisable to stimulate the development of stock exchange IT infrastructure and to implement sophisticated technologies to monitor and audit trades at the same speed as HFTs.

It can also be recommended to provide a unique location point for traders to solve the potential problem of co-location giving preferences to HFTs. HFTs also take additional advantage from proprietary direct data feeds (Klaus and Elzweig, 2017), so it is reasonable to limit this channel.

An important issue is the worldwide coordination of regulators, because HFT provides opportunities for cross-exchange arbitrage strategies. Exchanges and regulators should collaborate in unifying existing rules and implementing best practices regarding HFT.

Finally, we note that the problems of HFT are less relevant for bond markets than for the stock markets, because bond markets are characterized by a high share of OTC trades.

Conclusion

A feature of the post-crisis period of development of the global financial market is the ongoing process of increasing debt. The crisis did not significantly cool the appetite of earning on borrowed cheap money. Low rates did not create a high risk of defaults, even for companies with low credit ratings. However, with the tightening of monetary policy and rising rates, and with the growth of geopolitical conflicts, in 2019 the situation is changing. We note the following trends in the global debt market in 2014–2019:

a) low interest rates on government and corporate bonds of developed countries associated with the implementation of quantitative easing until 2017. An increase in interest rates in the global debt market since 2018 due to the US Fed policy on increasing the key rate;
b) the interest of global investors in bonds of emerging markets, due to the low yields on bonds in developed markets and the liberalization of capital flows in a number of emerging markets, and, as a result, the high growth rate of the CB segment of developing countries. But in 2018, there has been a flow of capital from emerging markets to developed ones. This process is supported by a change in the US Federal Reserve's policy of raising interest rates (the Fed Rate grew from 2017 to mid-2019), as well as high instability

in the investment market due to crises in Argentina, Turkey and Venezuela, increased sanctions against Russia and Iran, ongoing pickets and trade wars of the US and China (termination agreement signed only at the G20 summit in early December 2018), the EU and NAFTA. From the third quarter of 2019, the Fed rate declined. In the first quarter of 2020 quantitative easing began due to the epidemic of the COVID-2019 and a sharp increase of volatility in the global financial market. Increased risks caused an outflow of funds from the emerging bond market;

c) the high growth rates of the CB segment with speculative ratings began to slow down in 2018. This is due to an increase in US Treasuries rates and an increase in the yields of high-rating borrowers. Yield of high-yield bonds in the Bloomberg Barclays index (EM) reached 8.32%; in the Bloomberg Barclays index (US high-yield bonds), the yield rose to 6.23% per annum;
d) an increase in the share of corporate bonds in the structure of debt financing for companies in the USA and EU countries, which arose in connection with the tightening of regulation in the banking sector;
e) an increase in the share of funds raised by companies of developed countries from non-banking organizations;
f) outstripping growth of GB and CB segments of developing countries denominated in national currency;
g) the struggle for the environment and the implementation of sustainable development policies have reached the bond market. Indonesia became the first sovereign borrower to place green sukuk bond (issue volume amounted to $3 billion) in the global capital market in the first quarter of 2018;
h) if in 2015–2017 Russia was interested in the rouble carry trade due to high real interest rates, it was one of the leaders in attracting investors to the rouble assets market (first of all, OFZ). In mid-2018, the real interest rate was greater than 2% in Turkey (6.7%), Mexico (4%), Russia (3%) and Brazil (2.3%) (Source: Cbonds Review, No. 3, 2018).

Notes

1 Bank for International Settlements. www.bis.org/statistics/totcredit.htm?m=6%7C380%7C669
2 Haver Analytics
3 Haver Analytics
4 SIFMA Factbook 2019
5 www.investing.com/equities/google-inc-financial-summary; http://investor.google.com/pdf/20141231_google_10K.pdf
6 www.moodysanalytics.com/-/media/article/2019/weekly-market-outlook-abundant-liquidity-suppresses-defaults.pdf
7 Leite, J., Oyamada, A. (2020). Emerging Markets Are in the Fastest Collapse in a Generation. URL: www.bloomberg.com/news/articles/2020-03-19/emerging-markets-are-in-the-fastest-collapse-in-a-generation?sref=cus85deZ
8 Leite, J., Oyamada, A. (2020). Emerging Markets Are in the Fastest Collapse in a Generation. URL: www.bloomberg.com/news/articles/2020-03-19/emerging-markets-are-in-the-fastest-collapse-in-a-generation?sref=cus85deZ

9 Barlow, M., Shu, Y. (2019). Chinese Bonds. The Case for an Increased Allocation. State Street Global Advisors. www.ssga.com/investment-topics/emerging-markets/2019/chinese-bonds-the-case-for-an-increased-allocation.pdf
10 IMF. Staff Note for the G20 International Financial Architecture Working Group (IFAWG). January, 2020.
11 Lin, F., Kulikov, D. (2019). What do the Chinese and Russian bond markets have in common? And how do they differ? URL: www.acra-ratings.com/research/1109
12 IMF (2020). Staff note for the G20 International Financial Architecture Working Group (IFAWG).
13 Lin, F., Kulikov, D. (2019). What do the Chinese and Russian bond markets have in common? And how do they differ? URL: www.acra-ratings.com/research/1109
14 Lin, F., Kulikov, D. (2019). What do the Chinese and Russian bond markets have in common? And how do they differ? URL: www.acra-ratings.com/research/1109
15 Schipke, A., Rodlauer, M., Zhang, L. (2019). The future of China's bond market.
16 Lin, F., Kulikov, D. (2019). What do the Chinese and Russian bond markets have in common? And how do they differ? URL: www.acra-ratings.com/research/1109
17 IMF (2020). Staff note for the G20 International Financial Architecture Working Group (IFAWG).
18 Pieterse-Bloem (2019). Financial market integration: Risks and opportunities. Inaugural Lecture 28 June 2019. Erasmus School of Economics.
19 Shah (2019). Global Algorithmic Trading Market to Surpass US$ 21,685.53 Million by 2026. URL: www.bloomberg.com/press-releases/2019-02-05/global-algorithmic-trading-market-to-surpass-us-21-685-53-million-by-2026
20 Levine (2014). Michael Lewis Doesn't Like High-Frequency Traders. URL: www.bloomberg.com/opinion/articles/2014-03-31/michael-lewis-doesn-t-like-high-frequency-traders
21 Gupta, A. (2019). Algorithmic trading in India: History, regulations, platforms and future.

References

Arslanalp, S., Tsuda, T. (2014). Tracking global demand for emerging market sovereign debt, IMF. Working paper 14/39. DOI: 10.5089/9781484326541.001

Breckenfelder, J. (2019). Competition among high-frequency traders, and market quality. European Central Bank. Working Paper Series №2290.

Campbell, J. Y., Pflueger, C., Viceira, L. M. (2018). Macroeconomic drivers of bond and equity risks. Working paper. University of Notre Dame. URL:https://economics.nd.edu/assets/290442/campbellpfluegerviceira_20180827_final.pdf

Chaboud, A., Chiquoine, B., Hjalmarsson, E., Vega, C. (2013). Rise of the machines: Algorithmic trading in the foreign exchange market. *Journal of Finance*, 69(5): 2045–2084. DOI: http://dx.doi.org/10.2139/ssrn.1501135

O'Connell, K. (2019). Has regulation affected the high frequency trading market? *Catholic University Journal of Law and Technology*, 27(2): 145–172. URL: https://scholarship.law.edu/jlt/vol27/iss2/7

Gianluca, V. (2016). The impact of high-frequency trading on market volatility. *The Journal of Trading*, 11(2):55–63. DOI: https://doi.org/10.3905/jot.2016.11.2.055

Gider, J., Schmickler, S. N., Westheide C. (2015). High-frequency trading and fundamental price efficiency. Working paper. URL: http://firn.org.au/wp-content/uploads/2016/05/High-frequency-trading-adn-fundamental-price-efficiency-Gider-Schmickler-Westeide.pdf

Hagstromer, B., Norden, L. (2013). The diversity of high-frequency traders. *Journal of Financial Markets*, 16(4): 741–770. DOI: https://doi.org/10.1016/j.finmar.2013.05.009

Hasbrouck, J., Saar, G. (2013). Low-latency trading. *Journal of Financial Markets*, 16(4): 646–679. DOI: https://doi.org/10.1016/j.finmar.2013.05.003

Jiang, G. J., Lo, I., Valente, G. (2015). High-frequency trading in the U.S. Treasury market: Liquidity and price efficiency around macroeconomic news announcements. Working Paper. www.uts.edu.au/sites/default/files/FDG_Seminar_151215.pdf

Jones, C. (2013). What Do We Know About High-Frequency Trading? Columbia Business School Research Paper, №13-11. http://papers.ssrn.com/sol3/papers.cfm?abstract_id=2236201## DOI: https://dx.doi.org/10.2139/ssrn.2236201

Klaus, T., Elzweig, B. (2017). The market impact of high-frequency trading systems and potential regulation. *Law and Financial Markets Review*, 11(1): 13–19. DOI: https://doi.org/10.1080/17521440.2017.1336397

Liu, X., Lo, I., Nguyen, M., Valente, G. (2013). High frequency trading and Treasury bond returns. Working Paper. https://editorialexpress.com/cgi-bin/conference/download.cgi?db_name=AMES2014&paper_id=215

Mestel, R., Murg, M., Theissen, E. (2018). Algorithmic trading and liquidity: Long term evidence from Austria. Finance Research Letters, 26: 198–203. DOI: https://doi.org/10.1016/j.frl.2018.01.004

Moriyasu, H., Wee, M., Yu, J. (2018). The role of algorithmic trading in stock liquidity and commonality in electronic limit order markets. *Pacific-Basin Finance Journal*, 49: 103–128. DOI: https://doi.org/10.1016/j.pacfin.2018.04.004

Pericoli, M. (2018). Macroeconomics determinants of the correlation between stocks and bonds. Temi di discussione (Economic working papers) 1198, Bank of Italy, Economic Research and International Relations Area

2 Asian bond markets

Potential benefits for global investors

Introduction

Investment in countries with developing capital markets has undergone significant changes over the last 20 years. The financial markets of these countries have become more integrated into the global system and their financial depth has increased. New segments of asset classes comprising sovereign bonds in local currency have been created, the direct interest of global investors has widened. In the 1990s, investment in emerging markets primarily implied the acquisition of equity instruments through funds specializing in these countries. Since the beginning of the 2000s, the role of funds investing in bonds has increased, especially those investing in bonds in local currencies. Depositors in countries with developed markets increasingly allocate their capital through global mutual funds which invest in both developed and emerging markets.

The global financial crisis of 2008–2009, the policy of quantitative easing in the US and the EU, and the European debt crisis that started in 2010 generated greater attention to emerging markets, particularly to Asian ones, as they became leaders by volume and growth rate.

Prior to the global financial crisis (2006–2008) the capital allocation of foreign investors in various emerging markets was relatively proportional, and exposure was moderate. During the crisis of 2008–2009 investment became much more differentiated as risk sensitivity increased, and some countries experienced significant capital outflow. The share of Asia in global foreign capital inflows is growing; it increased from 11.7% in 2007 to 36.4% in 2018 (Table 2.1).

Foreign investors' attention to emerging bond markets in the post-crisis period represents a search for higher profitability due to low interest rates in the developed markets. Global investors have been increasingly attracted to Asian bond markets which demonstrate the liberalization of capital movements, positive real yields, and the absence of significant risk factors of economic deceleration. The growth of cross-country capital inflows is also facilitated by the low levels of volatility measured on the basis of the Chicago Exchange's VIX index.

The volume of the world bond market increased from $62.4 tn in 2006 to $149.7 tn in September, 2019 (source: authors' calculations based on the Bloomberg database). LCY emerging corporate bond markets are the most rapidly growing

Table 2.1 Foreign capital inflows

Year	*Global foreign capital flows, $ tn*	*Foreign capital flows to Asian countries, $ tn*	*Share of Asian countries in foreign capital flows, %*
2007	12.8	1.5	11.7
2008	2.6	0.3	11.5
2010	6.3	1.5	23.8
2012	4.6	1.3	28.3
2014	5.9	1.6	27.1
2016	4.7	1.1	23.4
2018	4.4	1.6	36.4

Source: McKinsey[1].

segment of the global bond market: their share increased from 2.2% in 2006 to 6.8% in September, 2019, i.e. a threefold increase (source: authors' calculations based on the Bloomberg database). According to the Asian Development Bank[2], the volume of LCY government and corporate bonds of emerging East Asian countries was $15.2 tn in September, 2019 (or 83.7% of the regional GDP), which is 13% more than in September, 2018. The share of the Chinese bond market in this volume is 75.4%, but S. Korea and Malaysia are leaders by the bond market volume to GDP. The volume of LCY outstanding corporate bonds was $5.8 tn in September, 2019, which is 15.3% more than in September, 2018 (source: Asian Development Bank). In 2019, LCY corporate bond markets of China, Indonesia, S. Korea and Malaysia demonstrated higher bond turnover ratios than in 2018 (source: Asian Bonds Online).

As risks to the development of the Asian LCY bond markets, Asian Development Bank considers lack of credit risk hedging mechanisms, the low diversity of investor profiles due to the difficulties foreign investors have in assessing the credit risk of LCY corporate bonds, a slowdown in developed economies and trade wars between the US and China.[3]

An urgent problem in the Chinese market is the high debt-to-GDP ratio and the growing volume of corporate defaults. The volume of defaults on corporate bonds in 2019 reached $19.7 bn (source: Bloomberg database). The share of Chinese companies with an interest coverage ratio of less than 1.5% was 37% in 2018. For comparison, the share of such companies in the US market was only 17%, in S. Korea 20%, in Japan 2% (source: McKinsey[4]).

Our study analyzes the trends in nine Asian LCY bond markets from 2005 to 2019 and identifies the determinants of their growth. We distinguish two groups of Asian bond markets: those developed and well known to global investors (Japan, S. Korea, Singapore) and rapidly growing ones (China, Malaysia, Philippines, Indonesia, Vietnam, Thailand). The group of developed bond markets can be considered as a benchmark for an analysis of the attractiveness of emerging bond markets. In addition, we analyze and compare the attractiveness of the Asian bond markets from the perspective of global investors. As key indicators of investment attractiveness we use the 'real return to volatility' ratio, the level of liquidity (measured by the bond market turnover ratio), duration and the level of liberalization (measured by Heritage Foundation Economic Freedom Index and on the base of surveys by Asian Bonds Online).

Literature review

We analyze the determinants of the growth of LCY bond markets and their relative investment attractiveness. Unlike previous papers, we consider a long time period from 2005 to 2019, which is characterized by high turbulence in the world economy and global financial markets: the global financial crisis of 2007–2008, the European sovereign debt crisis, the slowdown of economic growth in China in 2013–2015, and the drop in oil prices in 2014–2016.

Studies on Asian bond markets began in the early 2000s and covered the changes since the 1990s. Some papers analyze trends and differences in the development of Asian bond markets. Sharma (2001) investigated constraints to the development of the corporate bond market in East Asian countries (Thailand, Malaysia and Indonesia) in the 1990s. The author found that the major constraints were the strong relationships among banks, governments and leading companies. Asian companies relied heavily on bank financing, so their debt/equity ratios increased. As a result, companies preferred to issue stocks instead of bonds. Some measures of financial liberalization in East Asian countries in the 1990s also led to the growth of equity markets, while the growth of corporate bond markets was far slower. The size of the corporate bond markets (% GDP) differed significantly in the countries considered: in 1995 Malaysia had the most developed corporate bond market (10.3% GDP) and Indonesia the least (0.7% GDP).

Due to the removal of barriers and restrictions for foreign investors, Asian government bond markets in 1998–2008 grew faster than those of corporate bonds (Bhattacharyay, 2012).

Eichengreen and Luengnaruemitchai (2004) revealed a positive correlation between the volume of Asian bond markets and the size of economies, the strength of institutions, the competitiveness of banking systems, and the negative correlation between the volume of bond markets and the exchange rate volatility. Burger and Warnock (2006) and Eichengreen et al. (2006) compared the bond markets of Asia and Latin America. The authors concluded that Asian countries rely more on bank financing than Latin American countries. Batten et al. (2012) revealed that despite the significant growth of the domestic bond markets of the Asia and Pacific region from 1997 to 2009, these markets remain underdeveloped relative to the region's share in the world economy. Bhattacharyay (2012) found that significant factors for bond market development are the size of the economy, the level of economic development, trade openness, the size of the banking system, and the variability of interest rates.

Rethel and Sinclair (2014) analyzed the emerging bond markets of ten East Asian countries from 2001 to 2011. They focused on institutional innovations and considered them as determinants of development.

Mizen and Tsoukas (2014) analyzed the development of Asian corporate bond markets from 1995 to 2007. They revealed that participation in ABMI and ABF initiatives also positively influenced the bond issuance volume.

Like previous papers, we consider the influence of traditional factors: GDP growth, domestic credit to the private sector, and the Moody's sovereign credit rating. We also analyze the influence of some original factors: the level of stock market development, foreign direct investment, and the level of economic liberalization. In this chapter, for the first time, we compare Asian bond markets by investment attractiveness (measured by the 'risk-real return' ratio, liquidity and duration).

The development of the LCY Asian bond markets: descriptive statistics, the macroeconomic context and imbalances

In this section, we analyze the macroeconomic situation and the development of LCY bond markets of nine Asian countries. We also identify the imbalances in the development of Asian bond markets.

Table 2.2 shows the major macroeconomic indicators for the nine Asian countries under consideration. In terms of GDP per capita in 2019, the group of emerging Asian countries (especially Indonesia, Vietnam, the Philippines) are considerably behind the group of developed countries (Japan, S. Korea, Singapore). For the vast majority of countries in 2010–2019 a slowdown of economic growth took place, in contrast to the period before the global financial crisis of 2007–2008. Japan was characterized by the lowest growth rate of real GDP, while China, Vietnam and the Philippines were the leaders. Vietnam and Indonesia demonstrated relatively high inflation rates before 2014, but in 2015–2019 the inflation rates in all the considered countries are moderate or low (Table 2.2).

In all the countries under consideration, debt burden growth took place from 2007 to 2018: the volume of domestic credit to the private sector in the GDP increased (Table 2.3). The most impressive growth of this indicator (2.3 times more) occurred in the Philippines, while Vietnam occupied second place (1.6 times more). Japan, Singapore and Malaysia have the highest ratios of stock market capitalization to GDP (more than 100% of the GDP). In the period after the global financial crisis of 2007–2008, in many countries the stock market capitalization to the GDP decreased substantially. China became the leader by market capitalization decrease: it changed from 126.2% of GDP in 2007 to 46.5% of GDP in 2018. Vietnam, however, demonstrated a substantial growth of market capitalization: from 25.2% of GDP in 2007 to 54.1 % of GDP in 2018 (Table 2.3).

Many Asian countries are deeply engaged in globalization. The absolute leader in attracting foreign direct investment (FDI) is Singapore (in 2005–2018 FDI inflow constituted 21–25% of the GDP), while S. Korea and Japan are far behind (in 2005–2018, FDI inflows were not more than 1.1% of GDP; Table 2.4).

According to the sovereign credit rating (Table 2.5) Indonesia, Thailand, Vietnam and the Philippines are behind both the developed countries (Japan,

Table 2.2 Key macroeconomic indicators

Country	*Average annual real GDP growth, %*				*GDP per capita, $*				*Average annual inflation rate, %*			
	2005–2007	*2010–2013*	*2014–2015*	*2016–2019*	*2007*	*2013*	*2015*	*2019*	*2005–2007*	*2010–2013*	*2014–2015*	*2016–2019*
China (mainland)	12.7	8.8	7.1	6.5	2651	6807	8280	10098	2.7	3.5	1.7	2.0
Japan	1.7	1.9	0.3	1.1	34095	38634	32481	40847	0.01	-0.2	1.7	0.6
S.Korea	4.9	3.9	3.0	2.7	23101	25977	27513	31431	2.5	2.6	1.0	1.2
Singapore	8.5	6.9	2.6	2.6	39224	55182	53224	63987	1.2	3.7	0.5	0.3
Malaysia	5.7	5.7	5.3	4.9	7218	10538	10073	11136	2.9	2.2	2.8	2.0
Indonesia	5.8	6.2	4.9	5.1	1871	3475	3416	4163	10.0	5.3	6.6	3.4
Thailand	4.9	4.3	1.7	3.6	3738	5779	5426	7791	3.8	3.1	0.5	0.7
Vietnam	7.2	5.8	6.2	6.6	919	1911	2171	2740	8.0	10.8	3.1	3.5
Philippines	5.5	6.3	6.0	6.4	1681	2765	2951	3294	5.0	3.7	3.0	3.0

Source: World Bank Database, IMF, authors' calculations.

Table 2.3 Key indicators of stock market and banking sector development

Country	*Market capitalization, % GDP*				*Domestic credit to the private sector, % GDP*			
	2007	*2013*	*2015*	*2018*	*2007*	*2013*	*2015*	*2018*
China (mainland)	126.2	41.3	74.3	46.5	105.8	134.3	153.2	161.1
Japan	95.9	88.1	111.5	106.5	161.7	162.4	162.2	168.8
S.Korea	100.0	94.6	89.0	87.3	134.9	134.9	140.1	150.3
Singapore	298.0	242.0	207.8	188.7	85.4	124.1	122.4	121.9
Malaysia	168.1	154.8	127.1	111.0	101.6	119.9	123.1	120.4
Indonesia	49.0	38.0	41.0	46.7	25.5	36.1	39.1	38.8
Thailand	75.0	84.3	86.9	99.2	106.4	142.4	149.4	144.6
Vietnam	25.2	26.4	30.4	54.1	85.6	96.8	111.9	133.1
Philippines	68.9	79.9	81.6	78.0	28.9	35.9	41.8	66.3

Source*:* World Bank Database.

Table 2.4 Average annual FDI inflow, % GDP

Country	*2005–2007*	*2010–2013*	*2014–2015*	*2016–2018*
China (mainland)	4.6	3.4	2.4	1.5
Japan	0.2	0.1	0.3	0.6
S.Korea	1.1	0.9	0.5	1.0
Singapore	21.9	21.1	22.2	24.6
Malaysia	3.7	3.8	3.2	3.3
Indonesia	2.0	2.1	2.6	1.5
Thailand	4.6	2.6	1.7	1.7
Vietnam	5.3	5.8	5.5	6.3
Philippines	1.9	1.0	2.0	3.0

Source: World Bank Database, authors' calculations.

Table 2.5 Long-term LCY sovereign credit rating and Heritage Foundation Index of Economic Freedom

Country	*Moody's rating (at year-end)*			*Index of Economic Freedom*		
	2007	*2015*	*2019*	*2007*	*2015*	*2019*
China (mainland)	A1	Aa3	A1	53.1	52.0	58.4
Japan	A1	A1	A1	73.0	73.1	72.1
S.Korea	A2	Aa2	Aa2	68.6	71.7	72.3
Singapore	Aaa	Aaa	Aaa	87.3	87.8	89.4
Malaysia	A3	A3	A3	63.9	71.6	74.0
Indonesia	Ba3	Baa3	Baa2	53.2	59.4	65.8
Thailand	Baa1	Baa1	Baa1	62.3	63.9	68.3
Vietnam	Ba1	Ba1	Ba3	50.4	54.0	55.3
Philippines	B1	Baa2	Baa2	56.0	63.1	63.8

Source: Heritage Foundation, Moody's.

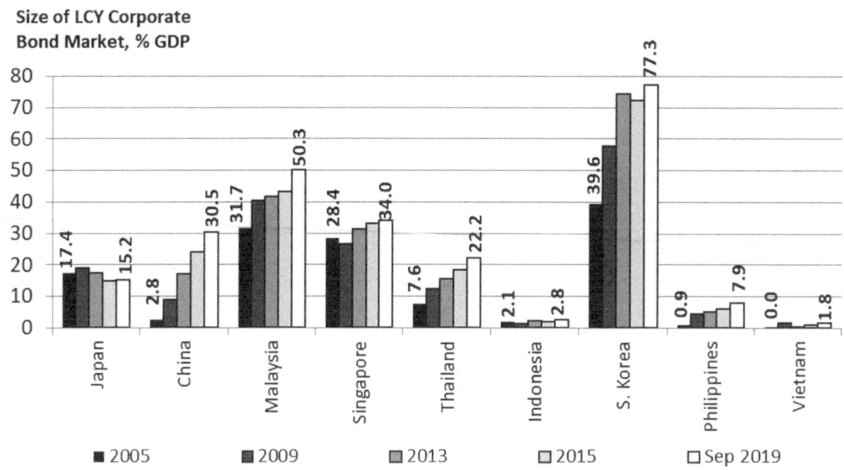

Figure 2.1 The size of LCY corporate bond markets (outstanding bonds, % GDP) in 2005–September, 2019.

Source: Asian Bonds Online.

S. Korea, Singapore) and a number of developing ones (China, Malaysia). Vietnam and China hold the lowest positions on Index of Economic Freedom from the Heritage Foundation.

In September 2019, the largest markets of corporate bonds in national currencies (relative to GDP) among the Asian countries considered were the markets of S. Korea (the volume of bonds outstanding was 77.3% of the GDP), Malaysia (50.3% of the GDP) and Singapore (34% of the GDP); the least developed ones were the markets of Indonesia and Vietnam (2.8% and 1.8% of the GDP respectively). A significant increase in the volume of the corporate bond market from 2005 to 2019 was observed in China, the Philippines, and Thailand (Figure 2.1). The rise was most noticeable in China where the volume of outstanding corporate bonds denominated in yuan increased from 2.8% in 2005 to 30.5% of the GDP in September, 2019.

Figure 2.2 compares the volumes of outstanding government and corporate bonds in LCY (as a percentage of GDP) as at September 30th, 2019. In almost all cases the volume of the LCY government bond market greatly exceeds that of the corporate bond market – the only exception is S. Korea. The most developed market for government bonds in the local currency is in Japan (the market volume is 199.5% of the GDP).

The high share of LCY corporate bonds in the total volume of corporate bonds outstanding is specific to the countries considered, except for Indonesia (Figure 2.3). For the Asian countries with the most developed markets of corporate bonds (Table 2.6), i.e. Japan, China, Malaysia, Singapore, and S. Korea,

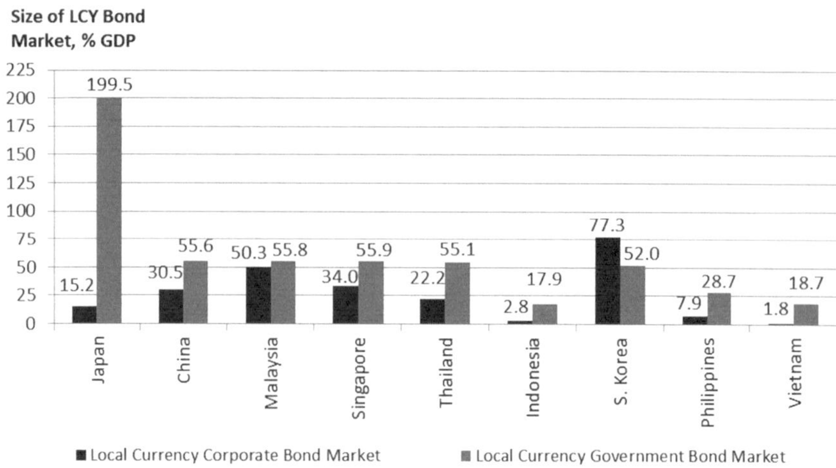

Figure 2.2 The size of LCY government and corporate bond markets (outstanding bonds, % GDP), September, 2019.

Source: Asian Bonds Online.

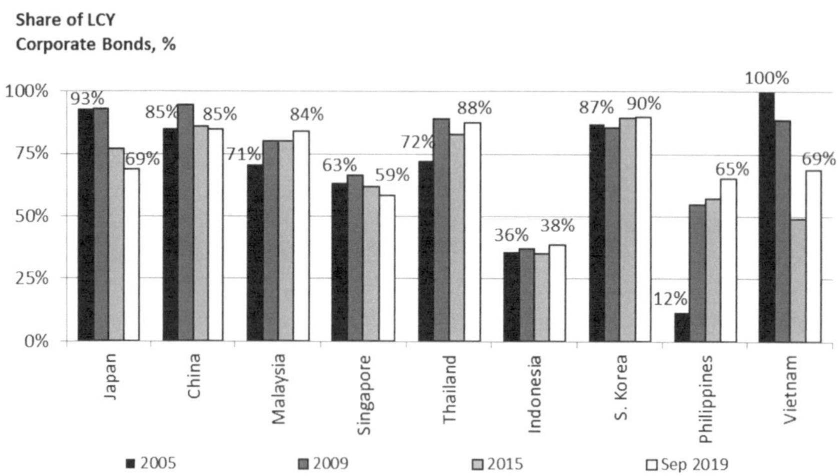

Figure 2.3 The share of LCY corporate bonds in the total volume of corporate bonds outstanding (2005–September 2019).

Source: Asian Bonds Online.

Table 2.6 The size of the Asian bond markets (September 2019)

Country	*LCY corporate bond market*		*Foreign currency corporate bond market*		*Government and corporate bond market (local and foreign currency)*	
	$ bn	*% GDP*	*$ bn*	*% GDP*	*$ bn*	*% GDP*
Japan	778.02	15.20	352.46	6.89	11401.15	222.74
China (mainland)	4057.33	30.48	721.68	5.42	12239.47	91.95
Malaysia	168.92	50.25	32.19	9.58	399.93	118.97
Singapore	122.00	34.01	86.43	24.09	408.88	113.98
Thailand	121.31	22.18	17.25	3.15	442.34	80.88
Indonesia	30.82	2.80	49.46	4.49	352.49	32.02
S. Korea	1184.25	77.28	135.15	8.82	2147.31	140.13
Philippines	27.90	7.91	14.89	4.22	176.37	50.00
Vietnam	4.54	1.79	2.06	0.81	55.99	22.08

Source: Asian Bonds Online, authors' calculations.

the share of corporate bonds in national currency is from 59% (Singapore) to 90% (S. Korea) in the total volume of the corporate bonds outstanding (as at September 2019).

The major investors in the LCY government bonds market are banks, insurance companies and investment funds. For example, in 2018, their total share in China was 84%, in Japan 77%, in S. Korea 66% (source: Asian Bonds Online). But in the government bond markets of Indonesia and Malaysia there was a high share of foreign investors (38% and 33% respectively; source: Asian Bonds Online).

The Asian countries are characterized by imbalances in the debt market. The prevailing funding source in the domestic market in Asian countries in 2018 (Figure 2.4) was either bank credit (China, S. Korea, Japan, Malaysia, Thailand, Vietnam) or stock capital (Indonesia, Philippines, Singapore). The share of LCY corporate bonds outstanding constituted from 1% (Vietnam) to 24% (S. Korea). A specific challenge in the Chinese debt market is the high share of off-balance liabilities of companies and municipalities, and the high share of credit provided by the shadow banking sector. According to Sun (2019), the volume of shadow banking in September, 2018 was 23% of Money Supply (M2). Shadow banking increases risks to financial stability by impeding the efficiency of risk regulation. Sun (2019) reveals the reasons for this situation. First, local governments are trying to increase regional GDP and need funds to invest in infrastructure projects, but the policy of credit tightening hinders them from attracting additional bank loans. Second, banks are also interested in providing shadow loans, because they are characterized by higher rates, a relatively low credit risk (local governments are supported by the central government) and low operating costs.

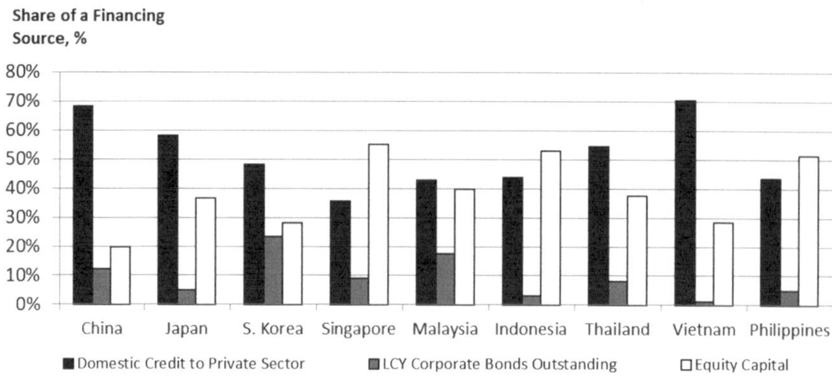

Figure 2.4 Financing sources structure in the internal markets of Asian countries, 2018.
Source: Asian Bonds Online.

Table 2.7 Household debt-to-GDP ratio in different countries, 2019

Country/Region	*Household debt-to-GDP, %*
US	75
Euro Area	57.8
S. Korea	92.9
Thailand	68.5
Malaysia	67.8
Japan	58.7
China	54.6
Singapore	53.3
Indonesia	17

Source: Trading Economics.

In S. Korea the household debt-to-GDP ratio exceeds the traditionally high level of the US (Table 2.7). In Thailand, Malaysia and Japan the household debt-to-GDP ratio is less than in the US, but higher than in the Euro Area.

The Chinese debt market is a specific case. The debt-to-GDP ratio increased from 120% in 2007 to 253% in 2018 (McKinsey[5]). Due to the policy of investment-led growth, almost half of the total debt of China (40–45%; estimates by McKinsey Global Institute, 2017) is directly[6] or indirectly[7] linked with the real estate market. As the Chinese economy is decelerating, the high over-indebtedness may cause problems with debt servicing. According to Bloomberg, the volume of corporate defaults in 2018 and 2019 dramatically increased to $19.7 bn and $17.8 bn, respectively. For comparison, the annual volume of corporate defaults in 2015–2017 did not exceed $4.3 bn (source: Bloomberg).

As shown in Schipke et al. (2019), there is a trend to gradually strengthen the integration of the Chinese financial market into the global financial system. Despite the leading role of the banking sector as a source of financing for corporations, the government is pursuing a policy of developing the stock and bond markets, opening them to foreign investors in order to increase the role of financial markets in the distribution of savings and investments.

In 2016, the yuan was added to the basket of major currencies in SDRs regulated by the IMF, after which the Chinese authorities opened the domestic bond market for foreign investors. In April 2019, China's LCY sovereign bonds were included in the Bloomberg Barclays Global Bond Index.

In 2017, a policy was announced to reduce the debt-to-GDP ratio in the long term in order to ensure the stability of the financial sector. One of the priorities is to reduce shadow banking.

Given that the Chinese bond market is the third largest in the world by volume of outstanding bonds, it is important for investors to understand its features. The share of trading in the interbank bond market is 90% (Schipke et al., 2019). Large institutional investors dominate the interbank market, and trades are conducted as bilateral transactions. Smaller institutional investors and individuals participate in exchange trading.

One of the problems decreasing the investment attractiveness of the Chinese bond market is the low liquidity, caused by the narrow base of investors. In the investor structure, banks and collective investment funds prevail, and these institutions usually hold bonds until maturity. The share of non-residents in the bond market does not exceed 2% of the total volume of outstanding bonds. The participation of long-term investors (pension and insurance funds) is about 6% (Schipke et al., 2019). Low liquidity limits the function of government bonds as a benchmark for the risk-free return rate. Short-term bonds are more liquid. The second problem is the strong market segmentation, because different segments are characterized by different regulatory organizations and regulations, trading platforms and depositories. The third problem is the lack of adequate hedging instruments for investors, due to the undeveloped derivative market.

The sovereign bond segment is about 20% of the total volume of the bond market. The segment of municipal bonds is developing rapidly. Until 2015, severe restrictions were imposed on municipalities to attract loans (which were practically prohibitive). To overcome these restrictions, municipalities were actively engaged in off-balance sheet lending through local government financing vehicles (LGFV), which increased the risks to financial stability. In 2015, a debt exchange programme was initiated by the government, and municipalities were allowed to issue bonds. In 2017, the market of municipal bonds reached 23% of GDP (Schipke et al., 2019).

Borrowers in the Chinese corporate bond market are mainly enterprises with state participation in the ownership structure (their share reaches 80% of bond issuers). The yield on such bonds is approximately 100 bp lower than for bonds issued by private companies with similar financial indicators (Schipke et al., 2019).

Corporate bonds can be traded on both the interbank and exchange markets. Bond issuance requires approval by the National Development and Reform Commission.

The government policy of liberalizing foreign portfolio investments and opening the Chinese bond market was based on the use of quotas on bond acquisitions and targeting specific groups of investors. The launch of Bond Connect in 2017 allowed foreign investors to trade bonds of Chinese (mainland) and Hong Kong issuers. At the end of 2018, investment by foreign institutional investors in Chinese bonds was exempted from taxes for three years.

A rating system has been developing in the Chinese bond market. The licensing of three international rating agencies in 2018 is an important step. Existing bond ratings do not look very adequate, as over 95% of corporate bonds have a rating of AA or higher (for comparison, in the USA, their share is only 6%; Schipke et al., 2019), i.e. the share of high-yield bonds is extremely small, and bond prices do not reflect risks correctly. Such ratings are based on implicit guarantees in China, and the strict standards for issuing corporate bonds, including the procedure of preliminary approval of bond issues. In 2017, the rules for rating agencies in the interbank and exchange markets were unified.

For the successful development of the Chinese bond market, it is necessary to narrow implicit guarantees, increase information transparency, improve the quality of corporate governance, provide opportunities for hedging risks and unify the regulations for different segments of the bond market.

To eliminate implicit guarantees, inefficient state-owned enterprises should leave the market, and government participation in the economy should be reduced. Although the share of employees in state-owned enterprises is lower than 15%, they attract about 40% of bank loans and 80% of corporate bond loans (Schipke et al., 2019).

An important measure for the development of the bond market may be to encourage the placement of bonds by small private firms.

An analysis of the determinants of Asian corporate bond market growth

We present a cross-country analysis of the relationship between the volume of LCY corporate bonds outstanding (% of GDP) and GDP growth, the development of the banking sector and the stock market, Moody's sovereign credit rating, and the level of economic liberalization.

The investigation of key determinants is an important research task, because there is no statistically significant relationship between the market volume of corporate bonds in national currency to GDP or the average annual growth of real GDP. The direction of this relationship is negative. We explain this by the fact that emerging countries are characterized by higher rates of GDP growth and a lower level of the development of bond markets. The fast growth of GDP is not accompanied by an identical growth of the corporate bond market. National companies of Asian countries prefer bank borrowing.

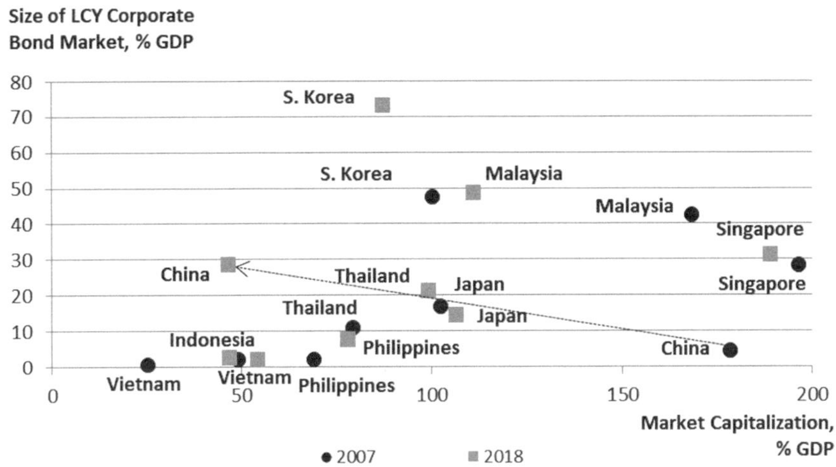

Figure 2.5 The size of LCY corporate bond market (% GDP) and the stock market capitalization (% GDP) in 2007 and 2018.

Source: Asian Bonds, World Bank Database, authors' calculations.

Countries with the lowest GDP per capita are also characterized by comparatively small bond markets in national currency (Philippines, Indonesia, Vietnam). Asian countries leading in per capita GDP (Singapore and Japan) are not the leaders in LCY corporate bond market size (the latter include S. Korea and Malaysia). The correlation between the volume of corporate bonds outstanding and GDP per capita is positive, but not statistically significant.

For the sample of countries for a given year (for example, 2007 or 2018), there is a positive relationship between the development of stock markets and LCY corporate bond markets (Figure 2.5). S. Korea, Singapore and Malaysia are characterized by the highest volumes of corporate bond and stock markets (in regard to GDP), while the markets of Vietnam and Indonesia are far behind the leaders. If we compare the period before the global financial crisis of 2007–2008 and 2018, we note decreasing market capitalization and an increasing volume of corporate bond markets (Figure 2.5). China is characterized by the greatest increase in corporate bond market volume.

In the countries with relatively moderate volumes of domestic credit to the private sector, the markets of corporate bonds in national currency are also the least developed (Indonesia, Philippines; Figure 2.6). In the countries with developed debt markets (Japan, Singapore, Malaysia, S. Korea) various ratios between the volumes of borrowings in bonds markets and the volumes of bank credit are possible, but for all these countries the volumes of bank credit was several times (at least twice or threefold) the markets of corporate bonds in national currency. In 2007–2018, we note increases in both the volume of the corporate bond market

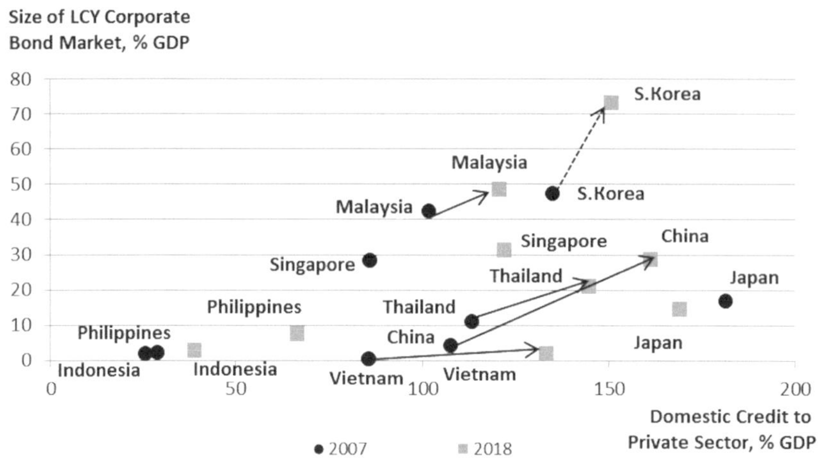

Figure 2.6 The size of LCY corporate bond market (% GDP) and the domestic credit to the private sector (% GDP) in 2007 and 2018.

There is a clear positive linear relationship between Moody's sovereign credit rating (in national currency) and the size of LCY corporate bond market (Figure 2.7). The same is true with the Index of Economic Freedom from the Heritage Foundation.

Source: Asian Bonds, World Bank Database, authors' calculations.

and bank credit (Figure 2.6). China is characterized by the highest growth of these two segments of the debt market.

Comparative analysis of investment attractiveness of the Asian corporate bond markets

An analysis of investment attractiveness of the Asian bond markets is performed taking into account the return rate and the 'return rate–volatility' of LCY corporate bond indices, duration of corporate bonds, liquidity and evaluation of different barriers by market participants. The average annual real yield of S&P LCY Corporate Bond Index of China, Malaysia, Singapore, Thailand, Philippines and S. Korea in the period of 2011–2019 was from 2.0% to 3.2% (Table 2.8). For the Indonesian corporate bond market, the average annual real return rate was a significantly higher 5.4%. On the contrary, the Japan corporate bond market demonstrated the lowest annual return rate of 0.3%. In China, Malaysia, Indonesia and S. Korea the average annual real return rate of bond index exceeded that of the stock index.

Note. Real return rates are given in brackets. Real return rates are calculated by Fisher's formula:

$$Real\ return\ rate = \frac{1 + Nominal\ return\ rate}{1 + Inflation} - 1 \qquad (2.1)$$

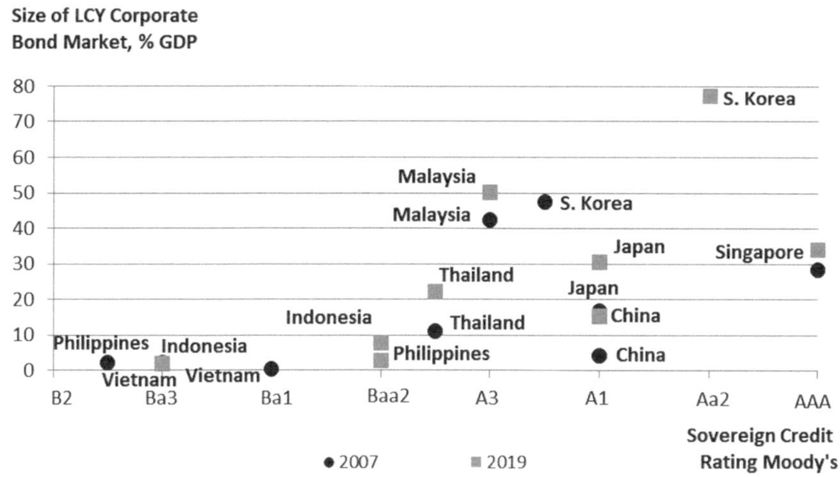

Figure 2.7 The size of LCY corporate bond market (% GDP) and Moody's LCY sovereign credit rating (2007 and 2019).

Source: Asian Bons Online, Moody's.

We compare the average monthly return rate to its volatility for the corporate bond and stock indices and exchange rates of the Asian countries (Table 2.9). In 2011–2019, in China, Malaysia and Indonesia the average monthly return rate of the corporate bond indices was higher than that of the stock indices, while the volatility of the return rate of the bond indices was lower. Consequently, the bond markets of these countries in the short-term period under consideration had higher investment attractiveness than the stock markets.

Among the countries considered, Japan and S. Korea were characterized by the highest volatility of national currency rate in 2011–2019 (Table 2.9). In China, on the contrary, the volatility of the currency rate was the lowest. The national currencies of the most Asian countries were depreciating against the US dollar in the period under consideration (Thailand and S. Korea were the exceptions).

To compare investment attractiveness of LCY bond markets, we also make cross-country comparison of real returns and return-volatility of the Asian corporate bond indices (Table 2.10). For each year from 2011 to 2019 we calculate the 'real return–volatility' ratio (by analogy with the Sharpe coefficient):

$$r = \frac{\bar{R} \cdot 12 - \mathit{Inflation}}{\sqrt{12} \cdot \sigma(R)} \qquad (2.2)$$

Table 2.8 Nominal and real return rates of S&P LCY corporate bond indices and stock indices of Asian markets, % (2011–2019)

Year	*China*	*Japan*	*Malaysia*	*Singapore*	*Thailand*	*Philippines*	*Indonesia*	*S.Korea*
Return rates of LCY corporate bond indices								
2011	3.6	-0.5	7.5	5.1	4.5	7.5	15.8	5.3
	(-1.9)	(-0.2)	(4.2)	(-0.1)	(0.6)	(2.7)	(10.0)	(1.2)
2012	5.9	2.0	4.5	5.0	4.9	8.6	12.1	5.3
	(3.2)	(2.1)	(2.8)	(0.4)	(1.9)	(5.4)	(7.5)	(3.0)
2013	1.2	1.8	3.5	1.4	4.1	7.9	1.6	2.8
	(-1.4)	(1.4)	(1.4)	(-1.0)	(1.9)	(5.1)	(-4.5)	(1.5)
2014	10.3	2.0	4.5	4.6	6.2	4.7	10.4	6.0
	(8.2)	(-0.7)	(1.3)	(3.5)	(4.2)	(1.1)	(3.7)	(4.7)
2015	8.9	0.4	4.5	2.0	4.6	5.6	10.2	3.7
	(7.4)	(-0.4)	(2.3)	(2.6)	(5.6)	(4.9)	(3.6)	(2.9)
2016	2.2	0.8	4.7	1.4	3.0	6.3	12.1	1.9
	(0.2)	(0.9)	(2.6)	(1.9)	(2.8)	(5.0)	(8.3)	(0.9)
2017	0.6	0.7	5.1	6.3	4.7	4.7	13.4	1.1
	(-1.0)	(0.2)	(1.2)	(5.7)	(4.0)	(1.8)	(9.3)	(-0.8)
2018	5.7	0.6	4.9	0.8	2.2	-3.9	4.2	3.9
	(3.6)	(-0.3)	(4.0)	(0.4)	(1.1)	(-8.6)	(1.0)	(2.4)
2019	3.4	0.4	6.6	5.6	6.1	13.9	13.0	3.3
	(1.1)	(-0.6)	(5.6)	(4.8)	(5.2)	(11.1)	(9.5)	(2.8)
Average annual returns in 2011–2019	4.7	0.9	5.1	3.6	4.5	6.1	10.3	3.7
	(2.2)	(0.3)	(2.8)	(2.0)	(3.0)	(3.2)	(5.4)	(2.1)
Return rates of stock indices								
Average annual returns in 2011–2019	3.2	13.7	0.7	4.3	9.5	7.7	8.3	3.5
	(0.9)	(13.0)	(-1.5)	(2.8)	(7.9)	(4.6)	(3.5)	(1.9)

Source: S&P, Eikon Refinitiv, authors' calculations.

Table 2.9 Average monthly return rates and the 'return–volatility' ratio of LCY bond indices, stock indices and exchange rates in 2011–2019

Country	*S&P LCY Corporate Bond Index*		*Stock index*		*Exchange rate (USD per LCY unit)*	
	Average monthly return rate, %	*Volatility of return rate, %*	*Average monthly return rate, %*	*Volatility of return rate, %*	*Average monthly percentage change*	*Volatility of return rate, %*
China	0.38	0.63	0.27	6.24	-0.05	1.07
Japan	0.08	0.19	1.06	4.85	-0.24	2.55
Malaysia	0.41	0.32	0.07	2.49	-0.23	2.36
Singapore	0.29	0.46	0.36	3.65	-0.03	1.66
Thailand	0.37	0.49	0.76	4.04	0.02	1.62
Philippines	0.50	0.92	0.63	3.83	-0.13	1.46
Indonesia	0.82	0.97	0.71	4.25	-0.38	2.06
S.Korea	0.30	0.37	0.30	3.80	0.003	2.47

Source: Eikon Refinitiv, authors' calculations.

where $\overline{R}$ is the monthly average return (for a chosen year), *Inflation* is the annual inflation rate, and $\sigma(R)$ is the standard deviation of the monthly return rates (for the chosen year).

In 2017 and 2019 the bond markets of Singapore was the leader by the 'real return–volatility' ratio, whereas in 2018 the leader was Malaysia (Table 2.10).

We calculate the integral 'real return–volatility' ratio for the whole 2011–2019 period (Table 2.10):

$$r' = \frac{\overline{R}_{real}}{\sigma(R)} \qquad (2.3)$$

where $\overline{R}_{Real}$ is the annual average real return, and $\sigma(R)$ is the volatility of the annual return rates.

In 2011–2019 the bond markets of Malaysia and Thailand were the leaders by the integral 'real return–volatility' ratio (Table 2.10, their ratios are equal to 2.3 and 2.35 respectively), and they were followed by S. Korea and Indonesia. All the Asian LCY corporate bond markets under consideration demonstrated a positive annual average real return.

Another indicator of investment attractiveness of a domestic bond market is average annual bid-ask spreads of LCY bonds (Table 2.11). In the period of the global finance crisis of 2007–2008 in the Philippines, China, Vietnam, Malaysia, Singapore there was a significant increase in bid-ask spreads. In the large Asian markets of government bonds in national currency (S. Korea, Singapore, China) bid-ask spreads are sufficiently lower than in the less

Table 2.10 The 'real return–volatility' ratio for LCY bond indices of the Asian countries, 2011–2019

Year	*S&P LCY corporate bond indices*							
	China	*Japan*	*Malaysia*	*Singapore*	*Thailand*	*Philippines*	*Indonesia*	*S.Korea*
2011	-0.6	-0.2	3.0	-0.2	0.3	0.7	3.8	1.2
2012	1.9	3.4	3.3	0.2	0.8	2.6	1.9	2.0
2013	-0.6	1.9	0.6	-0.3	1.0	1.3	-0.8	1.2
2014	2.6	-2.7	1.5	3.7	2.3	0.3	2.0	4.8
2015	3.5	-1.2	3.0	2.6	3.6	1.5	1.0	1.7
2016	0.1	1.2	1.9	0.8	1.5	1.4	2.4	0.6
2017	-0.9	0.4	2.6	7.8	5.3	1.3	5.4	-1.0
2018	3.6	-0.9	10.9	0.3	1.7	-3.3	0.3	2.6
2019	1.3	-0.7	6.8	9.4	3.3	6.8	5.2	2.2
Integral ratio, 2011–2019	0.65	0.3	2.3	0.95	2.35	0.67	1.18	1.27

Source: S&P, authors' calculations.

Table 2.11 LCY government bonds: average annual bid-ask spreads in 2007–2019 (basis points)

	S. Korea	*Singapore*	*Malaysia*	*Philippines*	*China*	*Indonesia*	*Thailand*	*Vietnam*
2007–2008	3.1	11.7	6.9	14.9	17.5	5.1	8.1	47.8
2009–2013	0.8	3.1	2.9	4.5	3.6	5.5	3.1	24.9
2014–2015	0.6	2.2	2.1	3.4	4.4	7.6	1.7	13.4
2016–2019	0.5	2.6	2.3	4.5	1.3	4.5	2.3	6.5

Source: Asian Bonds Online.

developed markets (Indonesia, Vietnam, Philippines). In 2014–2015 the Indonesian bond market demonstrated an increase in bid-ask spreads due to the drop in oil prices. A moderate increase in bid-ask spreads in 2014–2015 was also observed in China.

Table 2.12 presents data on liquidity of corporate and government bond markets of Asian countries. Surprisingly, the undeveloped corporate bond market of Indonesia demonstrates higher turnover ratio (0.82 in 2018) than the developed markets of Japan and S. Korea (0.11 and 0.48, respectively) and the rapidly growing market of China (0.3 in 2018). The same is true for government bond markets: in Thailand and Indonesia turnover ratios (2.12 and 2.25, respectively) are higher than in Japan, S. Korea and China (1.05, 1.96 and 1.66,

Table 2.12 Bond market turnover ratio in the Asian countries

	LCY corporate bond market				*LCY government bond market*			
	2007	*2013*	*2015*	*2018*	*2007*	*2013*	*2015*	*2018*
Japan	0.19	0.13	0.1	0.11	2.67	1,71	1,53	1,05
China (mainland)	2.29	1.91	1.03	0.3	1.46	1,14	2.1	1,66
Malaysia	0.53	0.34	0.25	0.18	2.35	2,17	1,36	0,93
Singapore			no data			1.84	1.17	0.99
Thailand	0.15	0.26	0.33	0.34	3.04	2,96	2,61	2,12
Indonesia	0.98	0.91	0.79	0.82	2.86	2,07	2,55	2,25
S. Korea		0.59	0.46	0.48	2.13	4,05	2,74	1,96
Vietnam			no data			1.01	1.24	1.3

Source: Asian Bonds Online.

respectively). We also reveal a trend to decreasing liquidity after the global financial crisis of 2007–2008. For most bond markets, turnover ratios in 2018 are lower than in 2013 and 2015. We find that the correlation between the size of LCY corporate bond market and the turnover ratio is negative, while the correlation between the size of LCY government bond market and the turnover ratio is positive. In the both cases the statistical significance is not high.

We also compare the duration of LCY corporate bonds (Table 2.13). We note that in the less developing corporate bond markets of Thailand, Philippines, Vietnam and Indonesia short-term bonds (with maturity 1–3 years) prevail. The same is true for the developed market of S. Korea. On the contrary, the markets of Singapore and Malaysia are characterized by a large share of long-term bonds (with maturity more than 5 years; Table 2.13).

Asian Bonds Online evaluates investment attractiveness of Asian corporate bond markets based on the opinion of market participants. Surveys include different projections: FX regulation, diversity of investor profiles, market access, information transparency. China, Indonesia, S. Korea, Singapore demonstrate trends to liberalization of FX regulation, while Malaysia, Thailand and Vietnam show the opposite trends (Table 2.14). The most liberalized markets are those of S. Korea and Singapore: in 2019, their scores are 3.7 and 3.5, respectively (the scale is from 1 to 4).

Note. In Tables 2.14–2.18, the score of 4 corresponds to the best value (i.e. respondents consider the market to be developed) and the score of 1 corresponds to the worst value (i.e. respondents consider the market to be undeveloped).

All the considered corporate bond markets demonstrate a trend of decreasing the diversity of investor profiles. The scores in 2019 are lower than in 2013 and 2015 (Table 2.15). In 2019, the scores of all the countries vary from 2 (Vietnam) to 2.8 (China). According to the Asian Development Bank, it is one of the important structural issues, which requires an adequate regulation policy[8].

Table 2.13 Distribution of LCY corporate bonds outstanding by duration

Country	*Year*	*Percentage of bonds with duration*			
		1–3 years	*3–5 years*	*5–10 years*	*More than 10 years*
China	2010	21.70	30.19	35.49	12.62
	2015	36.39	26.42	26.97	10.31
	Sep 2019	No data			
Singapore	2010	22.07	17.76	36.35	23.82
	2015	28.25	21.37	28.93	21.44
	Sep 2019	23.42	21.04	24.44	31.09
Thailand	2010	41.19	25.51	26.78	6.51
	2015	39.63	21.27	34.54	4.56
	Sep 2019	44.59	20.67	28.36	6.39
Philippines	2010	27.25	39.63	33.11	0
	2015	11.17	34.89	51.12	2.82
	Sep 2019	42.21	34.06	22.07	1.66
Vietnam	2010	53.39	19.67	25.35	1.59
	2015	40.45	47.87	10.85	0.83
	Sep 2019	No data			
Indonesia	2010	33.01	24.74	37.33	4.91
	2015	57.11	26.34	15.19	1.35
	Sep 2019	53.49	26.15	16.87	3.49
S. Korea	2010	55.76	24.59	15.74	3.91
	2015	45.72	21.74	18.83	13.71
	Sep 2019	50.55	21.91	15.74	11.81
Malaysia	2010	21.64	18.76	30.77	28.82
	2015	14.28	15.03	37.75	32.93
	Sep 2019	18.40	17.79	32.44	31.37

Source*:* Asian Bonds Online.

Table 2.14 Corporate bond market: survey data on FX regulation

	2010	*2013*	*2015*	*2019*
China	2	2.8	3	3.3
Indonesia	2	3	2.9	3.3
S. Korea	2.8	3.3	3	3.7
Malaysia	n/d	3.2	3.7	2.8
Philippines	3.5	3.1	2.8	2.7
Singapore	3	3.2	3	3.5
Thailand	3.2	3.3	3.5	2.8
Vietnam	3.7	2.8	3.5	2.2

Source: Asian Bonds Online

Table 2.15 Corporate bond market: survey data on greater diversity of investor profile

	2010	*2013*	*2015*	*2019*
China	3.7	3.5	3.3	2.8
Indonesia	3.3	3.7	3.6	2.5
S. Korea	3.3	3.1	3.7	2.7
Malaysia	n/d	3.5	3.6	2.5
Philippines	3.8	3.7	3.8	2.4
Singapore	4	3.6	4	2.6
Thailand	3.3	3.6	3.5	2.7
Vietnam	3.3	3.5	3.5	2

Source: Asian Bonds Online.

Table 2.16 Corporate bond market: survey data on market access

	2010	*2013*	*2015*	*2019*
China	2.6	3	3.2	3
Indonesia	2.6	2.9	3.3	3.1
S. Korea	2.8	2.4	3.2	3.6
Malaysia	n/d	2.8	2.9	3
Philippines	3.3	3	3.8	2.6
Singapore	3.2	2.8	3.5	3.3
Thailand	3.2	2.6	3.5	2.5
Vietnam	3.2	2.5	2.5	1.8

Source: Asian Bonds Online.

China made access to the bond market easier for investors from 2010 to 2013, but in 2014–2019 accessibility is stable (about 3–3.2; Table 2.16). Indonesia and S. Korea show trends to making the access to the bond market easier, while Thailand, Philippines and Vietnam demonstrate the opposite trends (Table 2.16). In 2019, market participants find that the accessibility of the Korean bond market is the highest (its score is 3.6) and that of Vietnam the lowest (1.8).

From 2010 to 2015, information transparency of the bond markets under consideration grew (Table 2.17). But in 2019, for most countries (China, Indonesia, Singapore, Thailand) it decreased to the levels of 2010. S. Korea and Malaysia demonstrated a stable trend to growth of information transparency. In Vietnam information transparency significantly decreased (Table 2.17).

According to the opinion of market participants, in 2019 all the LCY corporate bond markets under consideration demonstrated a significant decrease by the criteria of presence of hedging mechanisms in comparison with 2013 or 2015 (Table 2.18). Therefore lack or limited access to hedging is one of the major risks in the Asian bond markets from the investors' point of view. China and Vietnam took the last place by this criteria, while Malaysia was the leader.

Table 2.17 Corporate bond market: survey data on transparency

	2010	*2013*	*2015*	*2019*
China	2.6	3	3.5	2.8
Indonesia	2.7	3.2	3.3	2.8
S. Korea	2.5	3	3.2	3.4
Malaysia	n/d	2.6	2.8	3.8
Philippines	3.4	3.1	3.8	3
Singapore	2.8	2.9	4	2.7
Thailand	2.7	3.1	3.5	2.7
Vietnam	3.7	3	3.5	2

Source: Asian Bonds Online.

Table 2.18 Corporate bond market: survey data on hedging mechanisms

	2010	*2013*	*2015*	*2019*
China	3.0	3.5	3.0	1.5
Indonesia	3.4	3.1	3.0	2.0
S. Korea	2.5	3.3	3.0	2.0
Malaysia	n/d	3.7	2.9	2.4
Philippines	3.3	2.5	2.3	2.0
Singapore	3.0	3.1	3.0	1.9
Thailand	2.6	3.3	3.0	1.8
Vietnam	2.7	2.5	4.0	1.5

Source: Asian Bonds Online.

Conclusions

The LCY bond markets of Asian countries take an important place in the global bond market. The volume of LCY outstanding government and corporate bonds of emerging East Asian countries reached $15.2 tn in September, 2019, i.e. 83.7% of the regional GDP and 10.2% of the global bond market.

We aim to identify the determinants of development of LCY corporate bond markets and compare these markets by investment attractiveness (the 'real return–risk' ratio, liquidity, duration and the barriers for market participants).

We analyze both traditional (GDP growth, sovereign credit rating, development of banking sector) and original factors (stock market capitalization, foreign direct investment, the level of economy liberalization). The key factors directly or indirectly influencing emerging Asian markets of LCY corporate bonds are domestic credit to the private sector, the level of economic freedom and Moody's sovereign credit rating. The volume of LCY bond markets depends on the economy size, but their growth rates show an inverse relationship: if GDP growth decreases, the size of the LCY bond market (as % GDP) increases. In 2007–2019, growth of LCY corporate bond markets in many Asian was accompanied by a decrease in stock market capitalization. We can assume that capital flows moved from the stock market to the bond market.

S. Korea and Malaysia have the most developed LCY corporate bond markets (as % GDP), whereas Indonesia and Vietnam are characterized by the lowest financial depth. The Chinese LCY bond market is the biggest in the East Asia by absolute volume.

We reveal essential imbalances by the segment of debt markets of Asian countries. In all the nine Asian countries considered, bond markets as a source of finance do not exceed bank credit. The most significant gap between bank credit and relatively less developed bond markets is observed in Vietnam and Indonesia. In China, despite the rapid growth of the LCY corporate bond market, the banking sector prevails, and the share of shadow banking is high. Singapore, Philippines and Indonesia demonstrate the prevalence of the stock market over the bond market and bank lending. As the Chinese economy is decelerating, the high over-indebtedness may cause problems with debt servicing. According to Bloomberg, the volume of corporate defaults in 2018 and 2019 dramatically increased.

We show that in 2011–2019 in China, Malaysia, Indonesia and S. Korea the average annual real return rate of LCY corporate bond index exceeded that of the stock index. All the considered Asian LCY corporate bond markets demonstrated a positive annual average real return in 2011–2019. We highlight Malaysia's and Thailand's bond markets due to the highest 'real return–risk' ratios in this period. The corporate bond market of Malaysia is also characterized by a large share of long-term bonds and by a stable trend to growth of information transparency, which increases its attractiveness for foreign investors.

There are a number of risks of investing in Asian LCY corporate bond markets: lack of credit risk hedging mechanisms, low diversity of investors' profiles and trade wars between China and the US.

Notes

1 Signs of stress in the Asian financial system. McKinsey and company. July 2019.
2 Asia Bond Monitor. November 2019. Asian Development Bank. www.adb.org/sites/default/files/publication/538066/asia-bond-monitor-november-2019.pdf
3 Asia Bond Monitor. November 2019. Asian Development Bank. www.adb.org/sites/default/files/publication/538066/asia-bond-monitor-november-2019.pdf
4 Signs of stress in the Asian financial system. McKinsey and company. July 2019.
5 China Brief: The state of the economy. McKinsey. March 2019. www.mckinsey.com/featured-insights/china/china-brief-the-state-of-the-economy
6 Mortgage, bonds of development companies, government funding for social housing projects.
7 Related sectors – construction materials, metal structures, etc.
8 Asia Bond Monitor. November 2019. Asian Development Bank. www.adb.org/sites/default/files/publication/538066/asia-bond-monitor-november-2019.pdf

References

Batten, J. A., Hogan, W., Szilagyi, P. (2012). Foreign bond markets and financial market development: International perspectives. In *Implications of the global financial crisis for financial reform and regulation in Asia*. Eds. M. Kawai, D.G. Mayes, and P. Morgan, 248–269. Cheltenham UK: Edward Elgar Publishing. DOI: https://doi.org/10.4337/9780857934727

Bhattacharyay, B. N. (2012). Modes of Asian financial integration: financing infrastructure. In *Infrastructure for Asian Connectivity*. Eds. B. N. Bhattacharyay, M. Kawai, and R. M. Nag, chapter 10, 349–401. Edward Elgar Publishing.

Bhattacharyay, B. N. (2013). Determinants of bond market development in Asia. *Journal of Asian Economics*, 24: 124–137. DOI: https://doi.org/10.1016/j.asieco.2012.11.002

Burger, J. D., Warnock, F. E. (2006). LCY bond markets. *IMF Staff Papers*, 53: 133–146. DOI: https://doi.org/10.2307/30036026

Eichengreen, B., Borensztein, E., Panizza, U. (2006). A tale of two markets: Bond market development in East Asia and Latin America. Hong Kong Institute for Monetary Research.

Eichengreen, B., Luengnaruemitchai, P. (2004). Why doesn't Asia have bigger bond markets? NBER Working Paper No. 10576. Cambridge.

Mizen, P., Tsoukas, S. (2014). What promotes greater use of the corporate bond market? A study of the issuance behaviour of firms in Asia. *Oxford Economic Papers*, 66(1): 227–253. DOI: https://doi.org/10.1093/oep/gpt005

Rethel, L., Sinclair, T. J. (2014). Innovation and the entrepreneurial state in Asia: Mechanisms of bond market development. *Asian Studies Review*, 38(4): 564–581. DOI: https://doi.org/10.1080/10357823.2014.956685

Schipke, A., Markus, R., Zhang, L., eds. (2019). *The future of China's bond market*. Washington, DC: International Monetary Fund. DOI: http://dx.doi.org/10.5089/9781484372142.071

Serkan, A., Tsuda, T. (2014). Tracking global demand for advanced economy sovereign debt. *IMF Economic Review*, 62(3): 430–464. DOI: https://doi.org/10.1057/imfer.2014.20

Sharma, K. (2001). The underlying constraints on corporate bond market development in Southeast Asia. *World Development*, 29(8): 1405–1419. DOI: https://doi.org/10.1016/S0305-750X(01)00043-2

Sun, G. (2019). China's shadow banking: Bank's shadow and traditional shadow banking. BIS Working Papers №822. URL: www.bis.org/publ/work822.pdf

3 National currency weakness and collective investment as determinants of development of domestic corporate bond markets

Introduction

The relevance of studying the development of national bond markets is due to a number of new trends in recent years: an aggravation of geopolitical tensions in 2017–2018, the aggressive policy of the US Federal Reserve on raising interest rates, causing strengthening of the dollar and exacerbating problems with servicing and repaying the external USD-denominated debt of some developing countries (especially Turkey and Argentina in 2018). In particular, regulators of emerging markets face a dilemma: to rely on national debt markets to finance companies belonging to the real sector or to continue the policy of liberalization of capital flows and not limit borrowing in foreign markets. Strengthening the regulation of the banking sector (Basel 3) leads to the search for alternative channels for funding national companies. The interest of both investors and borrowing companies is shifting to the bond market, which has grown substantially in recent years.

The aim of our paper is to reveal tendencies and determinants of growth of local currency corporate bond markets in the period from 2006 to 2018. This period is characterized by macroeconomic and financial shocks: the 2008–2009 global financial crisis, the European crisis of 2010 and the difficult financial situation in oil-exporting countries after the drop in oil prices since mid-2014 (Russia, Brazil, Indonesia).

For a long time developing countries' debt with fairly long maturity (five to seven years) which was available for global investors has been denominated in foreign (USD) rather than national currencies. Bonds issued in developing countries and denominated in USD were especially attractive for global investors since such bonds demonstrated higher yield compared to those issued by US issuers. As a result, some issuers from developing countries attracted excessive amounts of loans in foreign currency, thus disturbing the currency mismatch between their assets and their liabilities. These imbalances are minor in periods of fixed or stable exchange rates, in times of rapid economic growth, but under devaluation of national currencies the debt of borrowers from developing countries grows substantially, which leads to defaults and bankruptcies.

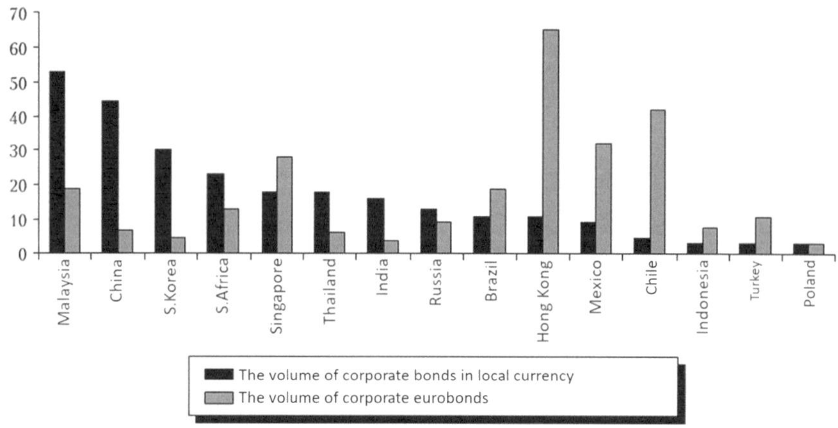

Figure 3.1 The volume of LCY corporate bonds outstanding and corporate Eurobonds, December 31, 2017 (% GDP).

Sources: Bloomberg, authors' calculations.

Our analysis of bond markets demonstrates that the main reason for imbalance in proportions between assets and cash flows, as well as in debt obligations in foreign currency connected with these disproportions of currency risks, has been the weakness of national bond markets and the abundance of foreign investors on these markets. Actually, in the 1990s, bond markets in national currencies were so weak that many analysts doubted their growth potential. By the mid-2000s, the situation began to change and by 2018 emerging bond markets became quite important in the financial market sphere (see Chapter 1).

The ratio of the volume of LCY domestic and Eurobond corporate bond markets is shown in Figure 3.1. As follows from country comparisons, Russia does not lead either in terms of LCY corporate bond market or in the corporate Eurobond market. The Russian LCY corporate bond market is characterized by a high degree of public bond issues, although liquidity is low. For example, most bond issues in China are non-market. Next, we will try to identify the drivers of the LCY corporate bond market development.

For Russia, India, Brazil and China in the first quarter of 2018, the share of LCY corporate bonds with a maturity of less than three years dominated in the total volume of outstanding bonds (Table 3.1). Foreign markets allow national companies to attract debt financing through Eurobonds for longer periods. As of the first quarter of 2018, in Russia, Brazil, India and South Africa corporate Eurobonds with duration from 3 to 7 years prevailed in the total volume of outstanding Eurobonds (according to Bloomberg).

Local corporate bond markets, especially of developing countries, after the crisis of 2008–2009 began to attract global investors by relatively high yields,

Table 3.1 Distribution of shares of LCY corporate bonds in the total volume of corporate bonds outstanding by the time to maturity, March, 2018 (in %)

Country	*Time to maturity (years)*							
	<1	*1–2*	*2--3*	*3–5*	*5–7*	*7–10*	*10–15*	*>15*
Russia	5.6	24.8	15.7	12.9	14.8	8.7	4.7	13.1
India	5.0	13.7	64.1	8.1	2.1	2.9	1.2	3.0
Brazil	11.6	34.6	21.2	14.5	12.3	0.8	4.1	0.8
China	19.3	37.2	23.9	10.5	6.7	0.6	1.1	0.7
S.Africa	5.3	27.5	15.5	10.5	12.5	11.0	6.5	11.1

Source: Bloomberg; authors' calculations.

the opportunity to participate in faster economic growth of these countries, the improvement of issuers' credit ratings and the quality of corporate governance. The depreciation of most national currencies of developing countries, as well as their high volatility, motivated many issuers to pay attention to raising capital in the national currency. A significant factor in the growth of the share of bonds in national currency since 2014 was the fall in oil prices. The oil-exporting countries (Brazil, Mexico, Venezuela, Russia, the Philippines, Indonesia) faced a depreciation of their national currency and a decline in economic growth. In these countries, the effect of currency depreciation on the currency structure of the corporate bond market is most evident.

This paper makes an empirical contribution to the analysis and clarification of determinants of the development of the local currency bond markets. Unlike previous studies (Bhattacharyay (2013); Claessens, Klingebiel and Schmukler (2007); Fidora, Fratzscher and Thimann (2007)), we consider a wide range of macroeconomic and institutional factors, and the focus of our study is on indicators of financial sector development. Most previous studies are based only on multi-factor linear regression analysis, and do not take into consideration that the bond data may be endogenous to the macroeconomic data. We apply not only multi-factor linear regressions, but also the generalized method of moments (GMM), allowing us to overcome this problem.

In our research we analyze a balanced panel of 24 countries from 2006 to 2018 by means of linear panel regressions and GMM (1248 country-quarter observations). We consider two dependent variables: 1) the share of LCY bonds in the total issue volume of corporate bonds and 2) the volume of LCY bonds outstanding to GDP. The explanatory variables include macroeconomic factors and institutional quality of the countries under consideration. Our sample includes the top-15 developing countries by issue volume of corporate bonds, as well as representatives of the groups G7, New Industrial Countries (NIC) and Next 11 (the list of countries is given in Appendix 2).

Earlier research of determinants of the structure of the corporate bond market

Crisis events in the economy bring to light disproportions in the financial sphere, especially for emerging markets, where some market segments may be developing. For instance, the Asian crisis of 1997–1998 aggravated the position of Asian companies and banks in a situation of national currency devaluation and affected their ability to service debts in foreign currency (Rose and Spiegel (2012)). This leads to appeals to put more effort into developing national markets, especially the local currency corporate bond market (Burger, Warnock and Cacdac (2012); Goldberg and Ronn (2013)). Certain efforts aimed at improving infrastructure through establishing the Asian Bond Market Initiative (ABMI) were made with the support of Asian Development Bank for ASEAN group of countries.

Cross-country comparisons of bond markets are widely presented in literature (Batten, Hogan and Szilagyi (2012); Burger and Warnock (2006)). Burger and Warnock (2006) on the basis of one-year results in a sample of 41 countries (2001) demonstrate the ability to implement foreign and domestic policy instruments, as well as institutional development, to successfully build up the public debt market. Countries with a more stable inflation rate (as a result of creditor-friendly national policy) have better developed domestic bond markets (Fidora, Fratzscher and Thimann (2007)), represented both by government and corporate bonds, and a smaller market of foreign borrowings. Burger and Warnock (2006) show that legislation is of importance here (more lucid legislative rules for protecting creditors' rights correspond to a bigger local bond market, including bonds in national currency).

Cross-country comparative research on government bonds is also given in various papers (Claessens et al., 2007; Eichengreen and Luengnaruemitchai, 2004).

The role of institutional factors is investigated by Eichengreen and Luengnaruemitchai (2004) for the sample of Asian markets. They consider such institutional determinants as accounting standards, legislation, and the level of corruption and bureaucracy.

The conclusions of previous research efforts are: countries with a large economy, historically lower inflation rates and less volatile exchange rates have better developed national government and corporate bond markets and issue fewer bonds in foreign currency. Moreover, an important role is played by creditor-friendly legislative and regulatory factors (as a rule, law supremacy is related to larger national bond markets, and countries that protect investors' rights better are able to issue larger share of bonds in national currencies).

Most previous studies analyze the period before the global financial crisis of 2008–2009. We make an attempt to investigate whether the factors revealed in previous studies retain influence during the period from 2006 to 2018. This period is characterized by high turbulence on the global financial market. Furthermore, we first consider the domestic corporate bond markets of BRICS countries and other developing countries worldwide rather than the markets of one region (Asia or Latin America). Earlier papers conclude that stronger protection of investors' rights and openness of the economy stimulate the growth of the domestic bond market. We assume that it is not definitely obvious, because in some cases the limitations on international capital movements could promote the issuance of local currency bonds. For example, under the sanctions of the EU and US, the Russian rouble corporate bond market grew in 2014–2015 from 7.8 to 10.0 percent of GDP. Finally, it is doubtful if a well-developed banking sector or a stock market positively influences the domestic corporate bond market, because different sources of funding can compete with each other.

Following most previous studies, we use linear panel regressions in order to reveal factors which influence the development of a bond market. We also test GMM models (difference and system estimators) in order to deal with the problem of likely endogeneity between the development of bond markets and macroeconomic and financial indicators.

Within the framework of our research we check whether such factors as national economy size and growth, macroeconomic stability (low inflation volatility), investors' rights protection, and currency stability retain their importance for the bond markets of emerging economies (including corporate bond markets) in the mid-2000s and after the 2008–2009 crisis. Unlike Claessens et al. (2007) and Eichengreen and Luengnaruemitchai (2004), Teplova, Sokolova and Galenskaya (2019) we introduce into our consideration new factors of financial market development and stability that, in our opinion, may influence the volume of local currency bonds. We analyze the influence of the return rate of the stock market index and its volatility, the VIX index, and the PMI index. To account for national specifics and to reflect the economic cycle stage we introduce in our model country dummies and a dummy of the global financial crisis of 2008–2009. Compared to Teplova et al. (2017, 2018), we consider an extended cross-country sample (24 developed and developing countries).

Hypotheses of our research: determinants of LCY bond market development

The use of quarter data allows us to increase the number of observations and to improve the reliability of models. Moreover, we consider the period from 2006 to 2018 which is characterized by macroeconomic and financial shocks, dramatic changes in economic growth, inflation and exchange rates for many developed and emerging countries. The use of quarter periods allows us to capture these changes. We consider 52 time periods from the first quarter of 2006 to the fourth quarter of 2018. The analysis is conducted on the base of linear panel regressions and the GMM.

We empirically test the following hypotheses:

Hypothesis 1. The share of LCY corporate bonds in the total volume of new issues of corporate bonds significantly depends on macroeconomic factors, development and stability of the financial market and institutional indicators.

Hypothesis 2. The volume of LCY corporate bonds outstanding in GDP depends on the same indicators.

Following Eichengreen and Luengnaruemitchai (2004), we consider the influence of macro-indicators and indicators of institutional development. We assume that devaluation of national currency can stimulate the issuance of local currency corporate bonds, because servicing of foreign debt becomes more expensive (Rose and Spiegel, 2012). For developing countries under consideration the behaviour of national currencies in 2006–2018 was quite unstable. The same effect on the bond market can be produced by an acceleration of inflation (CPI).

According to Fink et al. (2003) we expect that there is a positive relationship between economic growth and the LCY bond market development, because GDP growth increases firms' demand for funding.

Following Eichengreen and Luengnaruemitchai (2004), Burger and Warnock (2006), and Bhattacharyay (2013), we assume that stronger institutions and protection of creditors' rights, openness of the economy and financial markets promote the development of the domestic bond market. But in some cases introducing limitations on international capital movement can lead to a rapid growth of local bond markets. For example, under the sanctions of the US and EU (2014–2018), the size of the Russian LCY corporate bond market increased from 7.8 to 12 percent of GDP. Therefore the relationship between institutional factors and the issue volume of LCY bonds is not clear. Our model includes the following indicators of institutional development: investment climate (protection of investors' and creditors' rights) and conditions of doing business (economic freedom). We also analyze the dynamics of sovereign credit ratings and assume that a rating improvement can give impetus to the domestic bond market.

In emerging countries there is often a problem of competition among different sources of funding in local currency.[1] One of the peculiarities of our model is the inclusion of variables characterizing the development of different segments of the financial market: the banking sector and the stock market, as well as indicators of financial stability; VIX, yield, overall volatility and downside volatility of the stock market index. We assume that in emerging countries a relatively developed equity market or a hypertrophied banking sector can limit the growth of the domestic bond market. Bhattacharyay (2013) showed that the size of the banking system positively influences the government bond market, but negatively influences the corporate bond market. At the same time, Hawkins (2002) revealed that a competitive and large banking sector can promote the development of a liquid bond market because banks can play the role of dealers. A more detailed description of variables selection is given in Table 3.2.

Table 3.2 Variables of the Multi-Factor Models

Explained variables		*Expected sign*	*Description of variable selection (previous studies)*	*Data source*
dom_cur_bonds	Share of LCY corporate bonds in total corporate LCY and FCY bond issuance (per cent)	-	-	Bloomberg database
bondmarket	ln [1 + Volume of LCY corporate bond outstanding (% GDP)]	-	-	Bloomberg database
Explanatory variables				
Yield	The return rate of the LCY stock index for the current quarter, %	-	Teplova et al. (2017) conclude that the development of the equity market has a negative effect on the corporate bond market in developing countries: these markets are competing sources of financing.	TR Eikon
Volat	The volatility of the stock index daily return rate for the current quarter	+	We assume that an increase in the volatility of returns in the stock market encourages investors to invest in more conservative instruments – corporate bonds	TR Eikon
Downside	The downside volatility of the stock index' daily return rate for the current quarter: $downside = \sqrt{\frac{\sum_{i=1}^{n}(\min(r_i,0))^2}{n-1}}$			
Vix	The country volatility index VIX at the beginning of the quarter	+		
PMI	The country Purchasing Managers Index (PMI) at the beginning of the quarter	+	We assume that higher indicators of business activity contribute to the fact that issuers attract funding for growth through the corporate bond markets	TR Eikon

(*continued*)

Table 3.2 Cont.

Explained variables		*Expected sign*	*Description of variable selection (previous studies)*	*Data source*
cur_usd	Change in the exchange rate (USD per LCY Unit) over the current quarter, per cent.	Negative	Based on conclusions by Teplova et al. (2017), Rose, Spiegel (2012), we assume that devaluation of the national currency contributes to the development of the LCY corporate bond markets (service of LCY-denominated debt becomes cheaper)	Bloomberg database
Domestic_credit	Domestic Credit to Private Sector (percent of GDP).	Positive / Negative	Eichengreen and Luengnaruemitchai (2004) stated that banks can serve as dealers and market makers to promote the development of bond markets. Bhattacharyay (2013) concludes that the size of banking sector limits the development of the corporate bond market and promotes the development of government bond market.	World Bank database
GDP	Annual growth rate of real GDP in the current quarter, per cent	Positive	Burger, Warnock (2006), Fink et al. (2003) reveal a positive effect of GDP growth on the development of corporate bond markets	Trading Economics database
inflation	Inflation rate based on CPI, per cent (calculated as the monthly average of the annual growth rates of CPI over the same months in the previous year)	Positive	Teplova et al. (2017) conclude that the acceleration of the inflation stimulates national companies to increase the share of loans in national currency (as servicing of LCY-denominated debt becomes cheaper)	Trading Economics database
inflation_stab	Change in inflation rate over the previous period	Positive		Trading Economics database

ln_MC	Natural logarithm of domestic market capitalization	Negative	Teplova et al. (2017) reveal a negative impact of market capitalization on the development of the bond market, due to the fact that in developing countries equity and corporate bond markets act as competing sources of financing	World Federation of Exchanges
rating_SP rating_Fitch rating_Moodys	Changes in S&P's / Fitch / Moody's long-term sovereign credit rating respectively: 0 – no changes, 1 – the rating increased, -1 – the rating decreased	Negative	Teplova et al. (2017) show that an increase in sovereign credit ratings negatively affects the share of LCY corporate bonds, since the attractiveness of FCY loans for global investors increases	Bloomberg database
rating	Changes in Any of Long-Term Sovereign Credit Ratings (S&P, Moody's or Fitch)			
dcrisis	Dummy of the global financial crisis of 2008–2009	Positive	In the crisis periods the ability of borrowers to access international markets is limited. Mizen and Tsoukas (2012) reveal that the dummy of the 1997-1998 Asian crisis had a significant influence on the external finance premium.	
next11	Dummy indicating if a country belongs to the Next 11 group (1 — yes, 0 — no)	Positive	We assume that LCY corporate bond markets of the Next11 and NIC countries have more incentives to development, since these countries are characterized by relatively high rates of economic growth	
nis	Dummy indicating if a country belongs to the Next 11 group NIC (1 — yes, 0 — no)			
c1 – c23	Country dummies		Mizen and Tsoukas (2014) reveal cross-country differences regarding the policy of bond issues.	

(*continued*)

Table 3.2 Cont.

Explained variables		*Expected sign*	*Description of variable selection (previous studies)*	*Data source*
Economic Freedom Indicators				
IPR	Heritage Foundation's Index of Property Rights (Score: 0 – minimum, 100 – maximum)	Positive / Negative	Teplova et al. (2017) reveal a negative influence of institution quality on the share of LCY corporate bonds in the total issuance volume, since an improvement of the quality of institutions contributes to the entrance of bond issuers to foreign markets. On the contrary, Burger and Warnock (2006), Eichengreen and Luengnaruemitchai (2004) reveal a positive influence of quality of institutions on LCY corporate bond markets development. We assume that influence of institutions may be different for different country groups.	Heritage Foundation
IEF	Heritage Foundation's Index of Economic Freedom (Score: 0 – minimum, 100 – maximum)			
Multiplicative variables				
ipr_nis	ipr*nis	Positive / Negative		Authors' calculations
ief_nis	ief*nis			
ipr_next11	ipr*next11			
ief_next11	ief*next11			

Source: Authors' research.

Methodology of econometric research and descriptive statistics

We analyze a balanced panel of 24 countries and 52 quarter periods. To test hypotheses 1 and 2, we apply multi-factor regressions and GMM models on panel data. The variables are described in Table 3.2. The specifications of the models with random and fixed effects are the following:

$$y = \alpha + \sum \beta_{1,k} \cdot Macrofactor_k + \sum \beta_{2,l} \cdot Institution_l + \sum \beta_{3,n} \cdot FinMarket_n + u + \varepsilon \tag{3.1}$$

where y is the explained variable (*lcy_new_bonds* or *bondmarket*, Table 3.2), $Macrofactor_k$ is a macroeconomic factor, $Institution_l$ is an institutional factor, and $FinMarket_n$ is an indicator of the financial market development or stability. Factors are included in the regression, taking into account the collinearity matrix.

Due to potential endogeneity of variables, we also test dynamic models on the basis of the GMM introduced by Holtz-Eakin et al. (1990), Arellano and Bond (1991), and Arellano and Bover (1995):

$$y_{i,t} = \alpha \cdot y_{i,t-1} + \beta_0 \cdot X_{i,t} + \mu_i + \varepsilon_{i,t} \tag{3.2}$$

$$y_{i,t} - y_{i,t-1} = \alpha \cdot (y_{i,t-1} - y_{i,t-2}) + \beta_0 \cdot (X_{i,t} - X_{i,t-1}) + \varepsilon_{i,t} - \varepsilon_{i,t-1} \tag{3.3}$$

The moment conditions are the following:

$$\begin{aligned} &E[y_{i.,t-s}(\varepsilon_{i,t} - \varepsilon_{i,t-1})] = 0,\ for\ s \geq 2;\ t = 3,\ldots,T \\ &E[X_{i,t-s}(\varepsilon_{i,t} - \varepsilon_{i,t-1})] = 0,\ for\ s \geq 2;\ t = 3,\ldots,T \end{aligned} \tag{3.4}$$

$$\begin{aligned} &E[(y_{i.,t-s} - y_{i,t-s-1})(\mu_i + \varepsilon_{i,t})] = 0,\ for\ s = 1 \\ &E[(X_{i,t-s} - X_{i,t-s-1})(\mu_i + \varepsilon_{i,t})] = 0,\ for\ s = 1 \end{aligned} \tag{3.5}$$

where $y_{i,t}$ is a dependent variable, i and t are country and time period respectively, $X_{i,t}$ is a vector of explanatory variables (see Table 3.2), μ_i is an observed country-specific effect, and $\varepsilon_{i,t}$ is the error term.

The descriptive statistics on the sample is shown in Table 3.3. The list of Next11 and NIC countries is given in Table 3.4.

Table 3.3 Descriptive statistics on the sample

Variable	*Obs*	*Mean*	*Std.Dev.*	*Min*	*Max*
y1share	1248	0.63007	0.3058	0	1
y2ln	1248	2.68741	1.1196	0.00832	4.6074
yield	1248	0.01849	0.10783	-0.44246	0.6376
volat	1248	0.01172	0.00612	0.00269	0.05105
downside	1248	0.00697	0.0039	0.0014	0.02819
vix	522	21.426	8.2827	9.51	60.46
pmi	794	51.383	4.2745	30.8	73.2
pmichange	793	-0.00182	0.06707	-0.35902	0.464
cur_usd	1248	-0.00301	0.05061	-0.3408	0.2392
dom_credit	1248	4.4591	0.60386	2.83	5.45
gdpgr	1248	0.03448	0.03504	-0.144	0.189
infl	1248	0.03697	0.03409	-0.03027	0.2775
infl_stab	1248	-0.00016	0.01191	-0.09111	0.08091
lnmc	1248	4.3325	0.856	2.4776	7.15
rating_sp	1248	-0.01362	0.17632	-1	1
rating_fitch	1248	-0.00881	0.20983	-1	1
rating_moodys	1248	0.01202	0.22445	-1	1
rating	1248	0	0.32781	-1	1
ief	1248	66.531	10.8137	48.7	90.2
ipr	1248	60.457	23.731	10	98.4
dcrisis	1248	0.11538	0.31961	0	1
c2-c24	1248	0.04167	0.19991	0	1
next11	1248	0.25	0.43319	0	1
nis	1248	0.5	0.5002	0	1
ief_next11	1248	15.192	26.53418	0	74.3
ipr_next11	1248	10.603	20.53669	0	79.4
ipr_nis	1248	29.542	32.91892	0	98.4
ief_nis	1248	33.78	34.77296	0	90.2

Table 3.4 List of Next11 and NIC countries from our sample

Next11	*Vietnam, Indonesia, Mexico, Turkey, Philippines, S.Korea*
NIC	Brazil, Hongkong, India, Indonesia, Malaysia, Mexico, Singapore, Thailand, Turkey, Philippines, Chile, S.Korea

Results of the empirical research

The results of the econometric analysis are given in Tables 3.5–3.8.

We obtained an original conclusion about a significant positive effect of volatility, downside volatility of return rate of the stock market index and the VIX index on the share of LCY corporate bonds in the total issuance volume for both RE and FE models and GMM models. Thus, instability on the stock market encourages investors to invest in more conservative instruments – corporate

Table 3.5 The results for the share of LCY corporate bonds in the total issuance volume. Random effects (RE) and fixed effects (FE) models

	1	*2*	*3*	*4*	*5*	*6*	*7*
Model	RE	RE	RE	RE	FE	FE	FE
Wald	102.82	103.66	138.8	122.38			
F-statistics					6.72	16.3	14.95
_cons	1.3134*** (0.2711)	1.3088*** (0.271)	0.5511*** (0.182)	1.1529*** (0.2336)	1.0026*** (0.2667)	1.3231*** (0.2964)	1.2352*** (0.1219)
cur_usd	-0.2565** (0.1178)	-0.2632** (0.1176)	-0.4221*** (0.1125)	-0.2167* (0.1162)	-0.4726*** (0.1459)	-0.2058* (0.1147)	-0.4052*** (0.117)
dcrisis	0.0759*** (0.0295)	0.0769*** (0.0295)	0.0251 (0.0201)	0.0718*** (0.0264)	0.0537 (0.0347)	0.0591** (0.0262)	0.0811*** (0.019)
dom_credit	-0.1485*** (0.0533)	-0.1488*** (0.0532)					
downside			10.7821*** (1.7481)	7.5042*** (1.9608)		7.125*** (1.9369)	
gdpgr	0.3394 (0.3477)	0.363 (0.3482)					
ief			0.0066*** (0.0024)	0.001 (0.0031)		0.0132*** (0.0046)	
ief_next11			0.0019 (0.0016)	-0.0011 (0.0017)			
ief_nis						-0.0392*** (0.0084)	
infl			0.2273 (0.2435)	0.6718** (0.3326)		0.8051** (0.3333)	
infl_stab					0.5814 (0.8575)		1.6664*** (0.4876)
ipr					0.0033* (0.0018)		-0.0021* (0.0013)
ipr_next11					-0.0048 (0.0086)		
ipr_nis							0.0028 (0.0021)
lnmc			-0.1103*** (0.0229)	-0.168*** (0.0284)	-0.1874*** (0.0498)	-0.1838*** (0.0309)	-0.1302*** (0.0251)
pmi	-0.0015 (0.0019)	-0.0014 (0.0019)		0.0022 (0.0017)	0.004 (0.0025)	0.0022 (0.0017)	
rating		-0.0447** (0.0189)					
rating_fitch				-0.0213 (0.0277)			
rating_moodys	-0.0615** (0.0279)				-0.0623* (0.0362)		
rating_sp			-0.0192 (0.0319)			-0.0223 (0.0301)	-0.0128 (0.0322)
vix					0.0026* (0.0015)		
volat	7.4092*** (1.4451)	7.5215*** (1.4449)					
yield	0.0915 (0.0706)	0.091 (0.0705)			0.059 (0.0984)		-0.2071*** (0.0555)
Number of obs	794	794	1248	794	421	794	1248

Significance levels: * $p < 10\%$, ** $p < 5\%$, *** $p < 1\%$

Table 3.6 The results for the share of LCY corporate bonds in the total issuance volume. GMM models

	1	*2*	*3*	*4*	*5*	*6*	*7*
Wald	89	76.41	89.87	131.7	54.04	68.31	130.22
L1,	-0.1732*** (0.0364)	-0.2846*** (0.0452)	-0.3159*** (0.0448)	-0.2084*** (0.0361)	-0.3152*** (0.0616)	-0.3129*** (0.0603)	-0.2017*** (0.0362)
_cons	-0.1927 (1.4598)	1.068 (2.1503)	-0.5865 (1.1074)	1.7316* (1.0227)	0.1992 (0.7751)	0.7433 (0.7707)	1.9745* (1.0509)
cur_usd	-0.3158** (0.1258)	-0.1474 (0.1249)	-0.2252* (0.1246)	-0.4984*** (0.1244)	-0.3679** (0.1753)	-0.352** (0.1723)	-0.4987*** (0.1245)
dcrisis	-0.0214 (0.0437)	-0.0046 (0.0537)	-0.0033 (0.0517)	-0.0389 (0.0414)	0.0544 (0.0673)	0.0574 (0.0661)	-0.0392 (0.0414)
dom_credit	0.1967 (0.3274)	-0.0713 (0.4721)					
downside			3.3564 (2.5254)	5.75*** (2.174)			5.9228*** (2.1777)
gdpgr	-1.0931** (0.4707)	-1.423** (0.6236)					
ief			0.0359** (0.0166)	0.0116 (0.017)			0.021 (0.019)
ief_next11			0.0084 (0.0436)	-0.0178 (0.0348)			
ief_nis							-0.0346 (0.0303)
infl			1.5472* (0.8604)	2.2754*** (0.676)			2.2874*** (0.6766)
infl_stab					0.0348 (1.2204)	0.462 (1.203)	
ipr					0.0293*** (0.0087)	0.0407*** (0.009)	
ipr_next11					-0.0213 (0.0325)		
ipr_nis						-0.0778*** (0.0219)	
lnmc			-0.2745*** (0.0756)	-0.3679*** (0.0555)	-0.3234*** (0.1141)	-0.3059*** (0.112)	-0.3624*** (0.0555)
pmi		0.0008 (0.0026)	0.0001 (0.0025)		0.0038 (0.004)	0.0051 (0.0039)	
rating		-0.0231 (0.0205)					
rating_fitch	-0.0822*** (0.0276)		-0.0536** (0.0274)	-0.0801*** (0.0269)			-0.082*** (0.027)
rating_ moodys						0.0215 (0.0384)	
rating_sp					0.0052 (0.0436)		
vix					0.0014 (0.0022)	0.0027 (0.0022)	
volat	7.7962*** (1.6356)	6.5209*** (1.8917)					
yield	0.0956 (0.0732)	0.1524* (0.0846)			-0.0118 (0.1321)	-0.0555 (0.13)	
Number of obs	624	400	400	624	209	209	624

Source: Authors' calculations.
Significance levels: * $p<10\%$, ** $p<5\%$, *** $p<1\%$

Table 3.7 The results for the volume of LCY corporate bonds outstanding to GDP. GMM models

	1	*2*	*3*	*4*	*5*	*6*	*7*
Wald	3355.4	909.99	927.07	3404.65	902.93	3670.49	3581.3
L1	0.9055*** (0.0176)	0.8135*** (0.0322)	0.859*** (0.0296)	0.9077*** (0.0161)	0.8595*** (0.0299)	0.9027*** (0.0156)	0.9115*** (0.0157)
_cons	0.0399 (0.1381)	-0.4869* (0.2882)	0.2419 (0.1716)	0.1282 (0.1034)	0.2022 (0.1757)	0.1419*** (0.0515)	0.0829 (0.0507)
cur_usd	0.0638*** (0.0121)	0.0845*** (0.0169)	0.0937*** (0.0172)	0.0736*** (0.0122)	0.0962*** (0.0173)	0.0726*** (0.0119)	0.069*** (0.012)
dcrisis	-0.0005 (0.0042)	0.0048 (0.0073)	0.0128* (0.0071)	0.0036 (0.004)	0.0129* (0.0072)	0.0031 (0.0039)	0.0027 (0.0039)
dom_credit	0.0513 (0.0335)	0.238*** (0.0685)					
downside			0.4056 (0.3446)	0.3761* (0.2086)	0.3412 (0.3487)		
gdpgr	-0.0288 (0.0466)	-0.1091 (0.085)					
ief			0.0025 (0.0023)	0.0021 (0.0016)	0.0001 (0.0024)		
ief_next11			-0.0083 (0.006)	-0.0054 (0.0034)			
ief_nis					0.0045 (0.0048)		
infl			0.532*** (0.119)	0.2598*** (0.0658)	0.4984*** (0.1202)		
infl_stab						-0.1092** (0.0534)	-0.1208** (0.0539)
ipr						0.0003 (0.0005)	0.0032*** (0.0005)
ipr_next11						0.0054*** (0.0009)	
ipr_nis							-0.0029*** (0.0009)
lnmc			0.0328*** (0.0102)	0.0147*** (0.0053)	0.0308*** (0.0103)	0.0136*** (0.0051)	0.014*** (0.0052)
pmi		-0.0002 (0.0003)	-0.0006* (0.0003)		-0.0006* (0.0003)		
rating		0.0071** (0.0028)			0.0058** (0.0028)		
rating_fitch				0.0068** (0.0026)			
rating_ moodys			0.0101*** (0.0038)				
rating_sp	0.0101*** (0.0032)					0.0125*** (0.0032)	0.0089*** (0.0032)
volat	-0.0124 (0.155)	-0.2109 (0.2557)					
yield	-0.0118* (0.0069)	-0.011 (0.0115)				-0.0107* (0.0063)	-0.0112* (0.0064)
Number of obs	624	400	400	624	400	624	624

Source: Authors' calculations.

Significance levels: * p <10%, ** p <5%, *** p <1%

Table 3.8 The results for the volume of LCY corporate bonds outstanding to GDP. RE and FE models

	1	*2*	*3*	*4*	*5*	*6*
Model	FE	RE	RE	RE	FE	RE
Wald		162.79	290.52	158.55		109.05
F-statistic	88.96				11.25	
_cons	-2.096*** (0.355)	2.4686*** (0.4508)	-0.0085 (0.3582)	2.3789*** (0.4541)	2.2587*** (0.2832)	2.6868*** (0.2638)
cur_usd	-0.0353 (0.136)	-0.2639 (0.1714)	-0.4614*** (0.1641)	-0.265 (0.1716)	-0.0821 (0.1558)	-0.2762 (0.1808)
dcrisis	-0.2341*** (0.0343)	-0.2226*** (0.039)	-0.1176*** (0.0295)	-0.2239*** (0.039)	-0.1212*** (0.037)	-0.2034*** (0.0294)
dom_credit	1.2412*** (0.072)					
downside		-11.6657*** (2.8931)	-13.9583*** (2.5538)	-11.634*** (2.8955)		
gdpgr	-2.9386*** (0.4095)					
ief		0.0187*** (0.0055)	0.0509*** (0.0043)	0.0202*** (0.0058)		
ief_next11		-0.0152*** (0.0059)	-0.0042 (0.0053)			
ief_nis				-0.0088* (0.0051)		
infl		-2.4841*** (0.4966)	-0.5265 (0.3572)	-2.4681*** (0.4974)		
infl_stab					-1.6408* (0.9145)	-1.2202 (0.7517)
ipr					0.0137*** (0.0019)	0.0113*** (0.0019)
ipr_next11					-0.0193** (0.0092)	
ipr_nis						-0.0088*** (0.0028)
lnmc		0.115** (0.0452)	-0.1156*** (0.0353)	0.1256*** (0.0454)	0.151*** (0.0532)	-0.0919** (0.0389)
pmi	-0.0056** (0.0022)	-0.0188*** (0.0026)		-0.0191*** (0.0026)	-0.0075*** (0.0026)	
rating						-0.0727*** (0.0276)
rating_fitch					-0.1362*** (0.0392)	
rating_sp	-0.0205 (0.0354)	-0.0649 (0.0449)	-0.13*** (0.0466)	-0.0655 (0.045)		
vix					0.0002 (0.0016)	
volat	-10.2108*** (1.6757)					
yield	-0.3719*** (0.0817)				0.034 (0.1048)	-0.2187** (0.0856)
Number of obs	794	794	1248	794	421	1248

Source: Authors' calculations.
Significance levels: * p <10%, ** p <5%, *** p <1%

bonds. At the same time, a similar pronounced effect on the volume of LCY corporate bond outstanding is not observed: there are multidirectional effects in different models, and for most calculations the statistical significance is not high. We explain this by greater inertia of the indicator of the volume of outstanding bonds; perhaps, effects of instability on the stock market can be revealed when longer periods are under consideration.

We do not reveal a significant effect of the return rate of the stock market index on the issuance of LCY corporate bonds. For the volume of outstanding LCY corporate bonds to GDP, most calculations reveal a significant negative impact: a high return rate in the stock market encourages investors to invest in stocks, rather than bonds of national companies.

Regarding the index of business activity PMI, we have obtained unstable results: in different models, and the direction of influence is opposite.

Depreciation of the national currency against the US dollar stimulates national companies to issue more LCY corporate bonds, as debt servicing costs decrease. For the volume of outstanding LCY corporate bonds, we reveal the opposite direction of influence for different model specifications: in many calculations, statistical significance is low. The volume of outstanding LCY corporate bonds is a rather inert indicator, so the result is expected. Our results coincide with those of Teplova et al. (2019).

The impact of the crisis on the issuance of LCY corporate bonds for the FE and RE models is consistently positive: in conditions of instability, the market for LCY corporate bonds receives incentives for development. We explain this by the fact that during the 2008–2009 financial crisis global investors were fleeing from emerging capital markets and national companies were forced to attract funds in domestic markets. The flight of foreign investors from the Russian market was observed in 2018. This result coincides with the findings by Teplova et al. (2019). At the same time, in GMM models, the direction of influence changes to the opposite, but the statistical significance is not high. The same is true for the volume of outstanding LCY corporate bonds: the influence is unstable.

Regarding issuance of LCY corporate bond, stock market capitalization shows a steady negative effect; we explain this by the replacement effect in emerging markets. A relatively weak financial market leads to competition between the two sectors – bonds and stocks. This result coincides with the findings by Teplova et al. (2019). For the volume of outstanding bonds we reveal a change in the direction of influence. The growth of market capitalization (i.e. stock prices) allows firms to reduce the cost of equity. Such growth indicates an increase in risk appetite and reduces the attractiveness of raising debt in the public market.

We find a significant negative impact of the GDP growth rate on both the issuance of LCY corporate bonds and the volume of LCY corporate bonds outstanding to GDP. We explain this by the fact that in our sample there is a large share of developing countries, where bond and equity markets are competing sources of financing. When GDP growth slows down, investors prefer more conservative instruments – bonds; during periods of growth, on the contrary, they prefer to invest in riskier instruments – stocks. This contradicts the results of Burger and Warnock (2006) who revealed a positive relationship between these indicators.

If inflation and instability of inflation increase, national companies receive more incentives for issuing LCY bonds. We explain this by the fact that for many bond issues the coupon rate is fixed or set by the issuer, which allows issuers to win with an increase in yields on the market (loan servicing becomes cheaper). This conclusion coincides with that obtained by Teplova et al. (2019). At the same time, for the volume of outstanding LCY corporate bonds to GDP, no sustained effect of inflation is revealed. This contradicts the results of Burger and Warnock (2006) that revealed a positive correlation between inflation stability and the size of the domestic corporate bond market, but Burger and Warnock (2006) did not analyze directly the influence of inflation stability on the share of local currency bonds in the total issuance volume. This also does not coincide with the results of Claessens, Klingebiel and Schmukler (2007) who revealed that countries with low inflation have larger local currency bond markets; however, Claessens, Klingebiel and Schmukler (2007) analyzed government bond markets whereas we focus on corporate bond markets.

We identify a positive impact of bank credit to private sector on the volume of LCY corporate bond outstanding circulating. This coincides with the results by Teplova et al. (2019), and Eichengreen and Luengnaruemitchai (2004) who also revealed a positive relationship between the size of the banking sector and the bond market.

If sovereign credit ratings increase, the likelihood of advanced development of LCY corporate bond markets decreases: national issuers prefer the global financial market and attracting debt in foreign currency (due to lower interest rates). The statistical significance of the credit ratings is low, and the stability of the influence is observed only for issuance volume. This result coincides with the conclusions by Teplova et al. (2019). This contradicts the results of Böninghausen and Zabel (2015) who revealed spillover effects in government bond markets in response to changes in sovereign credit ratings, but the focus of our paper is on corporate bonds.

For institutional factors – the Index of Economic Freedom and Protection of Investors' Rights – we reveal a positive sign of the impact on the LCY corporate bonds issuance and on the volume of LCY corporate bonds outstanding for the entire sample of countries. This coincides with the results of Teplova et al. (2019), Burger and Warnock (2006), and Eichengreen and Luengnaruemitchai (2004) who also revealed the positive influence of stronger institutions. The country's membership in the Next 11 or NIC groups does not have a significant effect on the LCY corporate bonds share in the total issuance volume. The multiplicative variables *ief_next11* and *ipr_nis* demonstrate a sustained negative impact on the volume of LCY corporate bonds outstanding to GDP. We explain this by the fact that with a low quality of institutions, their improvement does not contribute to the development of the national bond market, and issuers tend to enter global markets.

We conclude that the key determinants of the development of emerging corporate bond markets are: instability in the stock market, devaluation of the local currency, inflation and inflation stability, quality of institutions, and market capitalization. The direction of their influence does not change.

Conclusions

Local currency corporate bond markets are rapidly growing and prospective considering high local risk premiums (markets demonstrate high bond yields and growth in these yields in periods of financial instability). Given increasing issue and outstanding volumes of developing corporate bond markets, further understanding of them is of importance for regulators and private investors.

In our study we applied not only linear multi-factor regressions, but also the GMM to deal with the problem of endogeneity of the bond data to the macroeconomic data. We first consider such factors as volatility and downside volatility of the return rate of the stock market index, as well as VIX index, the return rate of the stock market index and the index of business activity PMI.

The key determinants of the share of LCY corporate bonds in the total issuance volume are the volatility and downside volatility of the return rate of the stock market index, inflation and its stability, market capitalization, currency devaluation and the Index of Economic Freedom. We conclude that in emerging countries there is competition in the national debt and equity markets. In periods of economic growth and respective growth in the stock market, capital flows to the stock market and development of the LCY corporate bond market slows down. On the contrary, in crisis periods, capital flows to the bond market because investors prefer more conservative instruments. In periods of currency devaluation and inflation acceleration firms also tend to issue a higher share of LCY bonds. A high level of economic freedom increases the investment attractiveness of LCY corporate bonds in investors' eyes.

The key determinants of the volume of LCY corporate bonds outstanding to GDP are domestic credit to private sector, the index of property rights and belonging to the group of NIC countries. A more developed banking sector stimulates development of corporate bond markets: banks act as market makers and issue a large share of corporate bonds. Better investor rights protection increases the investment attractiveness of national bond markets. But belonging to the NIC group decreases the volume of LCY corporate bonds outstanding. In NIC countries the quality of institutions is relatively low, and its improvement does not contribute to the development of the national bond markets. Issuers tend to enter global markets.

Note

1 According to: Economic Importance of the Corporate Bond Markets. International Capital Market Association. 2013; Local Currency Bond Markets – A Diagnostic Framework. IMF, World Bank, EBRD, OECD. July 2013.

References

Arellano, M., Bond, S. (1991). Some tests of specification for panel data: Monte Carlo evidence and an application to employment equations. *Review of Economic Studies*, 58: 277–297. DOI: https://doi.org/10.2307/2297968

Arellano, M., Bover, O. (1995). Another look at the instrumental-variable estimation of error-components. *Journal of Econometrics*, 68: 29–52. DOI: http://dx.doi.org/10.1016/0304-4076(94)01642-D

Batten, J. A., Hogan, W., Szilagyi, P. (2012). Foreign bond markets and financial market development: International perspectives. In *Implications of the Global Financial Crisis for Financial Reform and Regulation in Asia*. Eds. M. Kawai, D. G. Mayes and P. Morgan, 248–269. Cheltenham UK: Edward Elgar Publishing. DOI: https://doi.org/10.4337/9780857934727.00024

Bhattacharyay, B. N. (2013). Determinants of bond market development in Asia. *Journal of Asian Economics*, 24: 124–137. DOI: https://doi.org/10.1016/j.asieco.2012.11.002

Blundell, R., Bond, S. (2000). GMM Estimation with persistent panel data: An application to production functions. *Econometric Reviews*, 19(3): 321–340. DOI: https://doi.org/10.1080/07474930008800475

Böninghausen, B., Zabel, M. (2015). Credit ratings and cross-border bond market spillovers. European Central Bank. Working Paper 1831.

Burger, J. D., Warnock, F. E. (2006). Local currency bond markets. IMF Staff Papers, 53, Special Issue: 133–146. DOI: https://doi.org/10.2307/30036026

Burger, J. D., Warnock, F. E., Cacdac, V. (2012). Emerging local currency bond markets. *Financial Analysts Journal*, 68(4): 73–93. DOI: https://doi.org/10.2469/faj.v68.n4.4

Claessens, S., Klingebiel, D., Schmukler, S. L. (2007). Government bonds in domestic and foreign currency: The role of institutional and macroeconomic factors. *Review of International Economics*, 15(2): 370–413. DOI: https://doi.org/10.1111/j.1467-9396.2007.00682.x

Eichengreen, B., Borensztein, E., Panizza, U. (2006). A Tale of two markets: Bond market development in East Asia and Latin America. Hong Kong Institute for Monetary Research Occasional Paper 3.

Eichengreen, B., Luengnaruemitchai, P. (2004). Why doesn't Asia have bigger bond markets? NBER Working paper series, Cambridge, Working Paper 10576.

Fidora, M., Fratzscher, M., Thimann, C. (2007). Home bias in global bond and equity markets: The role of real exchange rate volatility. *Journal of International Money and Finance*, 26(4): 631–655. DOI: https://doi.org/10.1016/j.jimonfin.2007.03.002

Fink, G., Haiss, P., Hristoforova, S. (2003). Bond markets and economic growth. Working paper 49. Vienna: Research Institute for European Affairs, University of Economics and Business Administration.

Goldberg, R. S., Ronn, E. I. (2013). Quantifying and explaining the new-issue premium in the post-Glass-Steagall corporate bond market. *The Journal of Fixed Income*, 23(1): 43–55. DOI: https://doi.org/10.3905/jfi.2013.23.1.043

Hawkins, J. (2002). Bond markets and banks in emerging economies. BIS papers 11, June–July. DOI: http://dx.doi.org/10.2139/ssrn.1187575

Holtz-Eakin, D., Rosen, H. (1990). Federal deductibility and local property tax rates. *Journal of Urban Economics*, 27(3), 269–284. DOI: https://doi.org/10.3386/w2427

Holtz-Eakin, D., Newey, W., Rosen, H. (1988). Estimating vector autoregressions with panel data. *Econometrica*, 56: 1371–1395. DOI: https://doi.org/10.2307/1913103

Mizen, P., Tsoukas, S. (2012). The response of the external finance premium in Asian corporate bond markets to financial characteristics, financial constraints and two financial crises. *Journal of Banking & Finance*, 36(11), 3048–3059. DOI: https://doi.org/10.1016/j.jbankfin.2012.07.005

Rose, A. K., Spiegel, M. M. (2012). Dollar illiquidity and central bank swap arrangements during the global financial crisis. *Journal of International Economics*, 88(2): 326–340. DOI: https://doi.org/10.1016/j.jinteco.2012.02.014

Spiegel, M. M. (2012). Developing Asian local currency bond markets: Why and how? In *Implications of the Global Financial Crisis for Financial Reform and Regulation in Asia*. Eds. M. Kawai, D. G. Mayes and P. Morgan, 221–227. Cheltenham UK: Edward Elgar Publishing. DOI: https://doi.org/10.4337/9780857934727

Teplova T. V., Sokolova T. V. (2018). Market development determinants for corporate bonds in national currencies: Emerging markets review. *Journal of East-West Business*, 24(1): 50–80. DOI: https://doi.org/10.1080/10669868.2017.1340387

Teplova T. V., Sokolova T. V., Galenskaya K. V. (2019). Drivers and brakes on the development of corporate bond markets of developed and developing countries. *Voprosy Ekonomiki*, 3: 1–24 (In Russian). DOI: https://doi.org/10.32609/0042-8736-2019-3-77-100

Teplova T. V., Sokolova T. V., Teplov A. S. (2017). Quality of institutions and import substitution of capital: Cross-country research on the corporate bond markets. *Journal of Institutional Studies*, 9(2): 97–118. (In Russian). DOI: https://doi.org/10.17835/2076-6297.2017.9.2.097-118

Part 2

Pricing in bond markets

4 The determinants of government bond yields in emerging markets

Introduction

Since 2010, developed countries have started to increase their public debt. The median estimate of the debt-to-GDP (for a sample of 12 countries: USA, Japan, Germany, Great Britain, France, Italy, Australia, Canada, Netherlands, Sweden, Spain, Switzerland) reached 70%, which is the maximal value after the Second World War. In 1870 it was 69%, after the Great Depression it dropped to 41%, and in the 1940s it reached the peak of 125% and then decreased to 20% in the 1970s. Then the debt-to-GDP ratio was 53% at the beginning of the 2000s and fell to 40% in 2008 (Source: Deutsche Bank).

The increasing debt of developed economies and the vigorous efforts to avoid a recession since 2018 put emerging markets in a difficult position. Several countries voiced the financial goal of de-dollarizing their national economy and self-reliance. These processes became especially relevant at the beginning of the U.S. and China trade war in 2019. We see the relevance of studying the formation of yields in the domestic bond markets of developing countries.

As of October 1, 2019, the nominal and real yields of sovereign bonds in local currency for emerging markets are shown in Table 4.1. Interest rates in developing countries are attracting global investors, and there are ongoing capital flows and betting on carry trade. Several countries decided to develop their government bond market in local currency (GBLC). For example, Russia and Turkey decided to stimulate the issue of debt securities in domestic markets in local currency. In this regard, it is important to understand the factors that determine the dynamics of interest rates in the bond markets of developing countries.

The purpose of this study is to analyze the determinants of the nominal yield of sovereign bonds in the large GBLC markets of Brazil, Russia, and China after the global financial crisis of 2008. We consider the impact of both global and national factors and rank the factors by the significance of their impact.

Edwards and Khan (1985) present a theoretical model explaining the nominal interest rate of a financial asset in a country based on inflation and interest rates in other markets. The model is empirically tested on data from Colombia (from 1968 to 1982) and Singapore (from 1976 to 1983).

Table 4.1 Nominal and real yield of GBLC in emerging markets as of October 1, 2019

Country	*Rating*	*Nominal yield, %*	*Current inflation, %*	*Real yield, %*	*Rate of the Central Bank, %*
Russia	BBB-/Baa3/BBB	7.0	4.6	2.4	7.0
S. Africa	BB/Baa3/BB+	8.4	4.0	4.4	6.5
Turkey	B+/B1/BB-	16.0	16.7	-0.7	16.5
Brazil	BB-/Ba2/BB-	7.1	3.2	3.9	5.5
Mexico	BBB+/A3/BBB	6.9	3.8	3.1	7.75
India	BBB-/Baa2/BBB-	6.8	3.2	3.6	5.4
Indonesia	BBB/Baa2/BBB	7.3	3.4	3.9	5.25
Columbia	BBB-/Baa2/BBB	5.8	3.8	2.0	4.25
Philippines	BBB+/Baa2/BBB	4.7	2.4	2.3	4.25
Chile	A+/A1/A	2.9	2.8	0.1	2.0
Peru	BBB+/A3/BBB+	4.1	1.9	2.3	2.5

Source: Authors' calculations.

Most authors identify factors of the global market (Fed rates, US Treasuries yields, S&P 500 returns, etc.), and factors of the national market (inflation rate, debt-to-GDP, government budget surplus to GDP, etc., see Table 4.2). The research question is about how the correlation of these groups of factors has changed since the global financial crisis of 2008 and several regional crises of 2014–2015, caused by a drop in oil prices.

Literature review

Most current papers focus on the yield determinants in the secondary GB markets (Silvapulle et al., 2016; Izadi and Hassan, 2018; Boysen-Hogrefe, 2017; Senga et al., 2018; Capelle-Blancard et al., 2019; Boubaker et al., 2019). One of the problems in secondary GB markets is low liquidity since most issues can be held by institutional investors. Primary GB markets are less studied (Edwards, 1986; Min, 1998).

As the dependent variables, researchers often use the nominal GB yields (Senga et al., 2018; Boubaker et al., 2019) and the spreads of the GB yield on national market to the benchmarks – the yields of the US or German GBs (Silvapulle et al., 2016; Boysen-Hogrefe, 2017; Izadi and Hassan, 2018). In other papers, the determinants of real GB yield are studied (Ardagna et al., 2007; Segura-Ubiergo, 2012).

Numerous studies have been devoted to the determinants of dollar- and euro-denominated GBs (Hartelius et al., 2008; Siklos, 2011; Silvapulle et al., 2016; Izadi and Hassan, 2018; Boysen-Hogrefe, 2017; Senga et al., 2018; Capelle-Blancard et al., 2019; Boubaker et al., 2019). The determinants of GBLC are less studied (Rodionova, 2014; Moreno, 2008; Peiris, 2010; Jaramillo, Weber, 2013).

Table 4.2 Traditionally considered determinants of government bond yields

Global market factors	*National market factors*
Fed rates (Boubaker et al., 2019)	GDP growth rate (Boysen-Hogrefe, 2017; Senga et al., 2018; Boubaker et al., 2019)
US Treasuries rates (Senga et al., 2018)	Industrial growth rate (Izadi and Hassan, 2018)
US corporate and government bond spread (Izadi and Hassan, 2018)	Inflation rate (Izadi and Hassan, 2018; Boubaker et al., 2019; Capelle-Blancard et al., 2019)
S&P500 index return (Silvapulle et al., 2016)	National exchange rate (Senga et al., 2018)
VIX volatility index (Silvapulle et al., 2016; Izadi and Hassan, 2018)	Debt-to-GDP (Boysen-Hogrefe, 2017; Senga et al., 2018; Capelle-Blancard et al., 2019)
Commodity prices, including oil prices (Min, 1998; Senga et al., 2018)	Government budget balance to GDP (Boysen-Hogrefe, 2017; Senga et al., 2018; Capelle-Blancard et al., 2019)
LIBOR, EIBOR rates (Silvapulle et al., 2016)	Economy openness (Edwards and Khan, 1985)
Conference Board US lagging leading Economic indicator (Izadi and Hassan, 2018)	Change in money supply (Dua and Raje, 2010)
Chicago Fed's NFCI (Boubaker et al., 2019)	Sovereign credit rating (Silvapulle et al., 2016; Izadi and Hassan, 2018; Boubaker et al., 2019; Capelle-Blancard et al., 2019)
	Returns of the local stock index (Silvapulle et al., 2016; Afonso, 2010)
	Current account on the Balance of Payments to GDP (Boysen-Hogrefe, 2017)
	International reserves to GDP (Senga et al., 2018; Capelle-Blancard et al., 2019)
	Total bank loans to GDP (Boubaker et al., 2019)
	Share of foreign participation in the government bond market (Peiris, 2010)
	Nonfinancial factors – environmental, social, and governance (Capelle-Blancard et al., 2019)
	Event factors – changes in economic policy, statements by national leaders, elections (Bellas et al., 2010)

Source: Compiled by authors.

The hypotheses depend on the research objects. Since the 1990s, the countries of the former Eastern Bloc and many developing countries in Asia have undergone economic liberalization. Market factors affected interest rates in the domestic bond markets of these countries. Distinguishing of the BRICS countries generated research interest in these countries.

The debt crisis of 2010–2012 in the Eurozone stimulated research on the 'domino effect'. Silvapulle et al. (2016) study the 'domino effect' in the Eurozone sovereign bond market. Using the ARMA-EGARCH model, as well as the robust semiparametric copula method, the authors conclude that the financial markets of Italy and Spain behaved independently during the crisis, while Portugal, Ireland, and Greece were exporters of the 'domino effect'.

Boysen-Hogrefe (2017) also explores the problem of the yield spread determinants in European countries in the period from 2005 to 2014. The dependent variable is the spread of the respective country's GB yield over the yield of German sovereign bonds. The author concludes that during the 2007–2008 crisis the role of the debt-to-GDP ratio in explaining the GB yield spreads increased, but in the following years the predictive power of traditional macroeconomic indicators declined, while the role of the quality in public administration in GB yields in the Eurozone markets increased.

Izadi and Hassan (2018) consider a wide sample of developed countries from three regions and investigate sovereign bond yield determinants. They conclude that global factors play a more significant role than national factors in the pricing of sovereign bonds in the three regions under study. The negative relationship hypothesis is confirmed for CPI, the standard deviation of the inflation rate and the ADSI index, and the positive relationship hypothesis is confirmed for the yield spread of US corporate and government bonds, Conference Board US lagging leading Economic indicator and VIX.

Senga et al. (2018) analyze the sovereign Eurobond yield determinants on the secondary market of Sub-Saharan Africa. They conclude that internal factors are no less important than global factors on the secondary Eurobonds market of Sub-Saharan African countries. The authors find that the Bloomberg commodity index and GDP growth rate are negatively correlated with GB revenues, while VIX, the yield of 10-year US GBs, the debt-to-GDP and inflation rate are positively correlated.

Boubaker et al. (2019) consider a long period from 1999 to 2015 and a wide sample of 28 developed and developing countries. They study the influence of the national financial market development level on the yield of outstanding GBs, subject to market conditions. They conclude that the effect of national financial market development on the yield of sovereign bonds depends on market conditions and differs significantly between developed and developing countries. For developed countries, the effect of financial development is positive and significant only in favourable market conditions, while for developing countries the effect of financial development is positive in favourable and negative under adverse market conditions.

A number of research papers pay attention to the impact of environmental, social, and managerial factors (ESG factors) on the yields of sovereign bonds. Capelle-Blancard et al. (2019) construct an original ESG index based on World Development Indicators. They reveal a strong correlation between ESG factors and the yield of sovereign bond markets. The correlation between the yield spread and the GDP growth rate, the debt-to-GDP are positive. The yield spread and S&P sovereign credit rating, the ratio of the Balance of Payments to GDP and the inflation rate are negatively correlated.

The hypotheses of our study

We perform our research for the largest emerging bond markets of China, Brazil and Russia.

The first group of hypotheses concern *national market factors.*

> Hypothesis 1.1. The level of domestic market interest rates has a significant positive effect on the GBLC yields.

As proxy variables of the interest rate level, we choose the inflation rate and the Central Bank key rate. With a key rate increase, bondholders start to demand a higher rate of return on borrowed capital. With an increase in the inflation rate, firstly, investors' expectations increase with the forthcoming tightening of monetary policy by the regulator, and secondly, investors demand higher rates due to the depreciation of funds, as a result of which the yield on GBLC also increases. Senga et al. (2018) reveal a positive effect of inflation on the yield of GBLC in Sub-Saharan Africa.

> Hypothesis 1.2. Depreciation of the LCY against the US dollar raises the GBLC yields.

In the case of the depreciation of the LCY against the US dollar, bondholders expect inflation to increase and require a higher yield. When the exchange rate of the local currency increases, the reverse process takes place: inflationary expectations are reduced, and GBLC holders benefit from investments in instruments denominated in the local currency (compared to investments in dollar-denominated securities). As a result, we can expect a decrease in the GBLC yield. Sun et al. (2011) find that for several developing countries from 1999 to 2008, the expected depreciation of the LCY had a positive effect on the yield spreads of outstanding GBs.

> Hypothesis 1.3. The growth of the Purchasing Managers' Index (PMI) and the growth of industrial production significantly affect the GBLC yields.

The business activity index and industrial production growth are proxies of the business cycle stage. We assume that the impact of these indicators can be both negative and positive. On the one hand, an increase in business activity and an increase in production show a favourable situation in the country's economy and, thereby, reduce the risk of default and the rate of return on GBLC. Boysen-Hogrefe (2017) reveals an inverse relationship between the GDP growth rate and the yield of sovereign bonds of the Eurozone countries, which happened during the 2011–2012 debt crisis.

On the other hand, in the context of increasing production volumes, companies increase their demand for money to finance this growth, and the return on borrowed capital may increase. Izadi and Hassan (2018) show that the growth of the Conference Board US lagging leading Economic indicator has a positive effect on the yield of sovereign bonds of 24 developed countries. Capelle-Blancard et al. (2019) reveal a similar positive effect of GDP growth rate on the yield of sovereign bonds of 20 OECD countries.

Hypothesis 1.4. Government debt-to-GDP significantly affects rates of return on GBLC.

We assume that the effect of government debt-to-GDP is ambiguous. If the level of government debt is high, its further increase reveals an increase in credit risk, and GBLC holders start to demand a higher yield. If the level of government debt is low, its increase gives positive signals about increasing liquidity and the depth of the financial market. As a result, GBLC yields decrease. Rodionova (2014) reveals an inverse relationship between the level of government debt and the GBLC yields for China, due to the low volume of public debt. Boysen-Hogrefe (2017) studies the sovereign bond yield determinants of Eurozone countries and reveals a positive influence of government debt-to-GDP, which sharply intensified during the debt crisis of 2011–2012. Senga et al. (2018) also find a positive effect of this factor for government Eurobonds in Sub-Saharan African countries.

Hypothesis 1.5. The higher the budget surplus, the lower the GBLC yields.

An increase in the budget surplus is a positive signal for investors, as it reveals a decrease in credit risk. As a result, interest rates decrease. On the contrary, an increase in the budget deficit shows a decrease in the government's ability to service its debt, which leads to an increase in bond yields. Boysen-Hogrefe (2017) reveals the negative impact of the government budget balance on the GB yields of Eurozone countries before the debt crisis of 2011–2012.

Hypothesis 1.6. The greater the increase in the money supply, the lower the GBLC yield.

According to the IS-LM macroeconomic model, an increase in the money supply leads to an increase in the real money supply in the short term, and therefore the level of interest rates in the economy decreases. Dua and Raje (2010) reveal a significant effect of money supply growth on the short-term and long-term yields in India, and the significance level is greater for short-term bonds compared to long-term ones.

The second group of factors concern the *global market factors*.

Hypothesis 2.1. The higher the VIX volatility index in the US market, the higher GBLC yields in developing countries.

VIX is a proxy indicator of the implied volatility of the S&P500 index. The growth of the VIX index indicates an increase in risks in the US financial market, and as a result, the potential emergence of 'infection' effects, manifested in increased volatility in the financial markets of developing countries, and the subsequent flight of global investors from emerging markets. As a result, we expect an increase in GBLC yields in developing countries. Piljak (2013) shows that increasing uncertainty in the global bond market raises government bond yields. Silvapulle et al. (2016) find that the VIX index of the US market has a positive impact on the GB yield spreads in European countries.

Hypothesis 2.2. GBLC yields on emerging markets decrease with an increase in the US stock market index S&P 500.

We assume that the growth of the US stock market index indicates an improvement in global macroeconomic conditions and a phase of growth in the global business cycle. The growth of the S&P 500 index is viewed positively by GBLC holders in developing countries and signals a decrease in credit risks; therefore, GBLC yields decrease. Silvapulle et al. (2016) reveal a significant negative impact of the S&P 500 index on the GB yield spreads in Portugal, Ireland, and Greece.

Hypothesis 2.3. Oil price significantly affects the yield.

We suggest that the impact of oil prices may be ambiguous. On the one hand, with rising oil prices in exporting countries, revenues of oil producers and government budget revenues increase, which reduces GBLC credit risks and yields. On the other hand, eventually, inflationary pressures increase in exporting countries, and as a result, bond yields increase. Rodionova (2014) reveals this positive effect of 'oil inflation' on the Brazilian market. For importing countries, rising oil prices are an unfavourable factor that could slow down economic growth. As a result, GBLC yields are growing.

Hypothesis 2.4. With rising interest rates for U.S. GBs, GBLC yields also rise in emerging markets.

According to the theory of interest rate parity, an increase in interest rates abroad causes an outflow of capital from investors in the country, the demand for GBLC decreases, and their yields grow. In contrast, lower yields abroad increase interest in GBLC, their prices start to rise, and yields fall (Hartelius et al., 2008). Yields for long-term U.S. Treasuries serve as a benchmark of the global risk-free rate and reflect the situation with liquidity in the global capital market, and therefore a change in the U.S. Treasury yields causes a change in GBLC yields in emerging markets. Silvapulle et al. (2016) show that a one-month rate in the German money market has a positive effect on the GB yields in Portugal, Ireland, and Greece. Senga et al. (2018) show that the yield on ten-year US Treasuries has a significant positive effect on the GB yields of Sub-Saharan African countries.

Research methodology

At the first stage of our study, we check the series of the daily nominal GBLC yields for stationarity by Dickey–Fuller and Philips–Perron tests, as well as for cointegration. The test results are presented in Appendix 2. We find that for all markets and maturities, the series of GBLC nominal yields is non-stationary. In this regard, the first differences in the GBLC nominal yield are taken as the dependent variables. These series are stationary (see Appendix 2).

We test the dependent and explanatory variables for cointegration using the Engle–Granger test (Appendix 3). The cointegration is revealed over the initial time series of GBLC nominal yields and some explanatory variables (debt-to-GDP, the yield on three-month US Treasury bills). For the first differences in the GBLC nominal yields and explanatory variables, cointegration is absent (Appendix 3).

At the second stage of our research, to test the hypotheses on the influence of factors on the yields of government bonds, we apply the following linear multifactor regression models:

$$y = \alpha + \sum_i \beta_{1,i} \cdot national\_factor_i + \sum_j \beta_{2,j} \cdot global\_factor_j + \varepsilon \qquad (4.1)$$

where y is the dependent variable (first differences of yields of government bonds of different time to maturity), $national\_factor_i$ is one of the country macroeconomic indicators, and $global\_factor_j$ is one of the global factors (see Table 4.3).

Explanatory variables are included in model (1) with an account of the correlation matrix. We perform Dicky–Fuller and Philips–Perron tests for stationarity of time series of GB yields. We also perform tests for heteroscedasticity, and, if necessary, evaluate models with robust errors.

In order to check the robustness of results, we evaluate models with nominal and real yields of GB. We also test models with and without the inclusion of year dummies.

Sample descriptive statistics

We take the monthly series on the GB yields of Brazil, China, and Russia with different maturities (from 1 to 10 years) from January 2007 to July 2019, as well as the monthly series of explanatory factors (see the list of variables and sources of data in Table 4.3). In total, the sample includes 151 observations. Descriptive statistics are presented by country in Tables 4.4–4.6.

Table 4.3 Dependent and explanatory variables

Variable	*Description*	*Direction of influence*	*Source*
Dependent variable			
y1_gb_ytm	Nominal yield to maturity (YTM) of one-year government bonds in local currency		investing.com
y3_gb_ytm	Nominal YTM of a three-year GBLC		
y5_gb_ytm	Nominal YTM of a five-year GBLC		
y10_gb_ytm	Nominal YTM of a ten-year GBLC		
D1.y1_gb_ytm	The first difference of y1_gb_ytm		
D1.y3_gb_ytm	The first difference of y3_gb_ytm		
D1.y5_gb_ytm	The first difference of y5_gb_ytm		
D1.y10_gb_ytm	The first difference of y10_gb_ytm		
Explanatory variables – national market factors			
budget_to_gdp	The government budget balance to the nominal GDP ratio	-	Eikon Refinitiv
debt_to_gdp	Debt-to-GDP ratio	+ / -	Eikon Refinitiv
inflation	Three-month moving average value of CPI (with three lags)	+	
keyrate	The key rate, set by the country's central bank at the end of previous month	+	CB websites of countries under consideration
m2_change	Monthly percentage change in M2 money supply in the local currency	+	EikonRefinitiv
output_change	Monthly industrial growth rate (year-over-year)	+ / -	
pmi	Purchasing Managers' Index (PMI), calculated by Markit Economics for Russia and Brazil and by National Bureau of Statistics for China	+ / -	investing.com
usd_lcyreturn	Monthly percentage change in the currency pair US dollar / local currency	-	Eikon Refinitiv
Explanatory variables – global factors			
brentreturn	Monthly percentage changes of Brent oil market price	+ / -	investing.com
cboe_vix_return	Monthly percent change in VIX Volatility Index	+	investing.com
sp500_return	S&P 500 Stock Index monthly returns	-	Eikon Refinitiv
usa_10y_ytm	Nominal yield to maturity on ten-year US Treasuries	+	investing.com
usa_3m_ytm	Nominal yield to maturity of three-month US Treasury bills	+	investing.com

Table 4.4 Sample for the GBLC of Brazil

Variable	*Obs*	*Mean*	*Std.Dev.*	*Min*	*Max*
y1_gb_ytm	151	10.649	2.563	5.45	15.8
y3_gb_ytm	151	11.329	2.124	6.18	16.77
y5_gb_ytm	151	11.646	1.955	6.82	17.38
y10_gb_ytm	151	11.844	1.762	7.25	17.33
inflation	151	5.647	1.856	2.6	10.56
output_change	150	-0.119	6.660	-15.37	18.4
pmi	133	49.502	3.437	39	58
debt_to_gdp	150	60.703	8.646	51.27	79.05
budget_to_gdp	150	-4.219	2.750	-9.32	-0.23
usd_lcyreturn	151	0.492	4.697	-11.01	18.24
m2_change	150	0.999	1.452	-3.13	6.36
keyrate	151	10.495	2.493	6	14.25
usa_3m_ytm	151	0.855	1.278	0	5.11
usa_10y_ytm	151	2.733	0.837	1.45	5.03
Brentreturn	151	0.445	8.819	-33.46	28.98
cboe_vix_return	151	2.757	24.654	-38.49	134.57
sp500_return	151	0.585	4.268	-16.94	10.77

Table 4.5 Sample for the GBLC of China

Variable	*Obs*	*Mean*	*Std. Dev.*	*Min*	*Max*
y1_gb_ytm	151	2.729	0.724	1	4.12
y3_gb_ytm	151	3.076	0.613	1.43	4.43
y5_gb_ytm	151	3.303	0.534	1.72	4.49
y10_gb_ytm	151	3.616	0.458	2.74	4.63
inflation	151	2.736	1.961	-1.6	8.3
output_change	151	10.448	4.498	3.8	20.7
pmi	151	51.432	2.576	38.8	59.2
debt_to_gdp	66	15.632	0.716	14.25	16.62
budget_to_gdp	151	-1.894	1.647	-4.94	1.78
usd_lcyreturn	151	-0.079	0.905	-3.35	3.29
m2_change	151	1.148	1.068	-1.27	4.72
keyrate	151	5.530	0.981	4.35	7.47
usa_3m_ytm	151	0.855	1.278	0	5.11
usa_10y_ytm	151	2.733	0.837	1.45	5.03
brentreturn	151	0.445	8.819	-33.46	28.98
cboe_vix_return	151	2.757	24.654	-38.49	134.57
sp500_return	151	0.585	4.268	-16.94	10.77

Table 4.6 Sample for the GBLC of Russia

Variable	*Obs*	*Mean*	*Std.Dev.*	*Min*	*Max*
y1_gb_ytm	151	7.462	2.150	3.53	15.57
y3_gb_ytm	151	8.117	2.169	5.66	15.85
y5_gb_ytm	151	8.296	2.019	6.09	15.63
y10_gb_ytm	151	8.380	1.641	6.27	14.09
inflation	151	8.146	3.786	2.3	16.45
output_change	151	1.822	5.343	-18.3	9.7
pmi	133	50.024	3.153	34.8	55.8
debt_to_gdp	150	9.999	2.339	5.49	13.18
budget_to_gdp	151	1.123	4.128	-7.37	15
usd_lcyreturn	151	0.697	4.836	-11.25	23.17
m2_change	150	1.155	2.864	-11.91	11.33
keyrate	151	8.126	2.106	5	17
usa_3m_ytm	151	0.855	1.278	0	5.11
usa_10y_ytm	151	2.733	0.837	1.45	5.03
brentreturn	151	0.445	8.819	-33.46	28.98
cboe_vix_return	151	2.757	24.654	-38.49	134.57
sp500_return	151	0.585	4.268	-16.94	10.77

Results

Determinants of Brazilian GBLC yields

The most significant variables that affect Brazil's GBLC yields for all considered maturities are the local currency exchange rate against the US dollar and the yield of 10-year US Treasuries (Table 4.7). The depreciation of the Brazilian real against the US dollar leads to an increase in yield to maturity of Brazilian GBLC. In most model specifications, this factor is significant at the 1% or 5% level. Sun et al. (2011) reveal a similar trend for other emerging markets.

With an increase in the yields of the 10-year US Treasuries, the yields on Brazil's GBLC increase for all maturities. For most model specifications considered, the factor is significant at the 1% level (Table 4.7). We attribute this to the fact that the 10-year US Treasuries yield to maturity serve as a proxy for the global risk-free rate, and its increase leads to an increase in the GBLC yields on the Brazilian market. Senga et al. (2018) obtain a similar conclusion for the impact of the US Long-term Treasury yields in African countries. At the same time, the influence of the three-month US Treasury bills yield is not significant for the sample (Table 4.7).

The impact of changes in the VIX volatility index on Brazil's GBLC yields is positive. In several model specifications, the factor is significant at the 10% level (Table 4.7). This conclusion is consistent with the results of Piljak (2013) and Silvapulle et al. (2016). We conclude that an increase in volatility in the US market leads to increased risks in the Brazilian GBLC market and contributes to the outflow of the capital of global investors.

Table 4.7 Determinants of yields of GBLC of Brazil

	1	*2*	*3*	*4*	*5*
Dependentvariable	y1_gb_ytm	y3_gb_ytm	y5_gb_ytm	y5_gb_ytm	y10_gb_ytm
R^2	0.417	0.380	0.351	0.389	0.368
Number of obs	132	132	149	132	149
_cons	-4.0816*** (0.7465)	-5.7084*** (2.0865)	-5.4241** (2.4117)	-5.3864** (2.2828)	-3.5 (2.3166)
brentreturn	0.0009 (0.0058)	0.0074 (0.0078)	0.0167 (0.0118)	0.0067 (0.0086)	0.0141 (0.0116)
budget_to_gdp	-0.0198 (0.0666)				
cboe_vix_return		0.004* (0.0023)	0.0034 (0.0023)	0.0029 (0.0025)	0.004* (0.0021)
debt_to_gdp		0.0389 (0.0394)	0.0597 (0.0469)	0.0402 (0.0431)	0.025 (0.0451)
inflation			0.0641 (0.0987)		0.0761 (0.1026)
keyrate			-0.0421 (0.0838)		-0.0394 (0.077)
m2_change	0.0543 (0.0361)	-0.0013 (0.0489)	0.0083 (0.041)	-0.0121 (0.0535)	0.0243 (0.0347)
output_change			0.006 (0.0268)		0.012 (0.0263)
pmi	0.0536*** (0.0173)	0.0233 (0.0234)		0.0094 (0.0256)	
sp500_return	0.006 (0.0111)				
usa_10y_ytm	0.2879** (0.1228)	0.4605*** (0.1712)	0.4978* (0.2962)	0.5452*** (0.1874)	0.4868* (0.2737)
usa_3m_ytm	-0.0488 (0.2177)				
usd_lcyreturn	0.0165* (0.0098)	0.0558*** (0.0132)	0.0768*** (0.0158)	0.0781*** (0.0144)	0.0764*** (0.0158)

Significance levels: * $p < 10\%$, ** $p < 5\%$, *** $p < 1\%$

The original conclusion is set by the PMI business activity index and the industrial production growth rate: their impact on the GBLC yields for all maturities is positive (Table 4.7). Statistical significance at the 1% level is observed only between the PMI index and the yield of one-year GBLC. This conclusion contradicts the results of Boysen-Hogrefe (2017) on GBs of Eurozone countries but coincides with the conclusions of Capelle-Blancard et al. (2019) for OECD countries. Our explanation is that in the case of favourable macroeconomic conditions, the demand for funds grows in order to finance investment projects and production expansion, so interest rates increase. Investors prefer riskier strategies by transferring funds from GBLC to other instruments.

The government debt-to-GDP ratio has a stable positive effect on the Brazilian GBLC yields (Table 4.7), although the statistical significance is not high. Similar relationships are observed by Rodionova (2014) in the Brazilian market, Boysen-Hogrefe (2017) in the Eurozone markets, and Senga et al. (2018) in African markets. The government debt-to-GDP ratio for Brazil increased from 58% in 2014 to 78% in 2018 (source: World Bank). A further increase in public debt is a signal of increased risks and is perceived negatively by investors.

The higher the balance of the government budget to GDP, the lower Brazil's GBLC yield (Table 4.7). A budget surplus indicates a decrease in credit risks for GBLC, and thus bondholders require less yields. This conclusion coincides with the results of Rodionova (2014) for Brazil, and Boysen-Hogrefe (2017) for the countries of the Eurozone.

The influence of the inflation on the yield of GBLC is steadily positive, which corresponds to our assumptions, despite their low statistical significance. The conclusion is consistent with the results of Senga et al. (2018) for the countries of Sub-Saharan Africa, and of Rodionova (2014) for Brazil.

Changes in oil prices have a steady positive impact on the yields of Brazilian GBLC (Table 4.7). Rodionova (2014) reveals the effect of 'oil inflation' on Brazil before the 2014–2015 crisis, when rising oil prices led to a change in the balance of payments, an influx of money into the economy and an increase in inflation. We conclude that under the conditions of low oil prices this effect remains valid, although the statistical significance is not high.

We note the low statistical significance and instability in the direction of influence of the Brazilian money supply and the S&P 500 index returns on Brazil.

Determinants of Chinese GBLC yields

The most significant factor determining GBLC yields in the Chinese market is the inflation rate, followed by the percentage change in the money supply and the yield of US Treasuries (Table 4.8).

The inflation rate has a positive effect on the yields of GBLC in China for all maturities. In most specifications, the factor is significant at the 1% or 5% level (Table 4.8). The conclusion is consistent with the results of Senga et al. (2018) for African countries.

Table 4.8 Determinants of yields of GBLC of China

	1	*2*	*3*	*4*	*5*
Dependent variable	y1_gb_ytm	y3_gb_ytm	y3_gb_ytm	y5_gb_ytm	y10_gb_ytm
Adjusted R^2	0.1805	0.2527	0.2464	0.2211	0.1587
R^2	0.2960	0.3580	0.3476	0.3257	0.2717
Number of obs	150	150	150	150	150
_cons	-1.1861* (0.6173)	-0.9988** (0.4963)	-0.7351 (0.533)	-0.4422 (0.4364)	0.1661 (0.4307)
brentreturn	0.0009 (0.0027)	0.0033 (0.0023)	0.0041* (0.0021)	0.003 (0.0021)	0.0029* (0.0017)
budget_to_gdp				0.0018 (0.0451)	
cboe_vix_return	0.0004 (0.0009)		0.0012* (0.0007)	0.0007 (0.0007)	0.0 (0.0006)
inflation	0.0667** (0.0269)	0.0432** (0.0217)	0.0473* (0.0265)	0.0594*** (0.0215)	0.0366* (0.0214)
keyrate			-0.0668 (0.0803)		-0.0998 (0.0649)
m2_change	-0.0444** (0.0202)	-0.0275* (0.016)	-0.0239 (0.0161)	-0.0046 (0.0155)	-0.0056 (0.013)
output_change	-0.0082 (0.0153)	-0.0145 (0.0121)			
pmi	0.0037 (0.0115)	0.0101 (0.0095)	0.0161* (0.0096)	-0.0007 (0.0087)	0.0042 (0.0077)
sp500_return		-0.0034 (0.0046)			
usa_10y_ytm	0.1209* (0.0667)	0.0467 (0.0531)	0.056 (0.0513)	0.0791 (0.0503)	0.0524 (0.0415)
usa_3m_ytm	0.1138 (0.0735)	0.1139* (0.0582)			
usd_lcyreturn	-0.0219 (0.0252)	-0.0104 (0.0199)	-0.0144 (0.0202)	-0.0098 (0.0194)	-0.0164 (0.0163)

Significance levels: * $p < 10\%$, ** $p < 5\%$, *** $p < 1\%$

The influence of the percentage change in the money supply on the yields of GBLC is consistently negative. A statistical significance of 5–10% is observed only for one-year and three-year GBLC (Table 4.8). A similar negative effect is revealed by Rodionova (2014) on the GBLC market in China, and by Dua and Raje (2010) on the Indian GB market, and the significance of the influence of money supply growth is higher for the short and medium-term GB segments compared to the long-term one. We conclude that the effect of increasing liquidity is significant for China's emerging bond market.

The effect of yield to maturity on 10-year Treasuries and three-month US Treasury bills is steadily positive. In several model specifications, the significance of these factors reaches 5%. A similar beneficial effect is identified by Silvapulle et al. (2016) on GB markets in Portugal, Ireland, and Greece, and by Senga et al. (2018) on government Eurobond markets of African countries.

An increase in oil prices leads to an increase in GBLC yields in China. In some specifications, the factor is significant at the 10% level (Table 4.8). This conclusion is consistent with the results of Rodionova (2014) on the Chinese market until 2013. We explain the positive direction of the influence by the fact that the Chinese economy is much less focused on oil exports compared to Russia and Brazil. The increase in oil prices leads to higher spending by corporations and a larger government budget. As a result, the level of interest rates in the domestic market is growing.

The influence of the change in the VIX volatility index is positive, but the statistical significance of this factor is not remarkably high; only in one of the specifications it is significant at the 10% level (Table 4.8). This conclusion is consistent with the results of Piljak (2013), Silvapulle et al. (2016).

The strengthening of the US dollar against the Chinese yuan has a stable and negative effect on the yields of GBLC, and the statistical significance of this factor is not high (Table 4.8). It contradicts the findings of Sun et al. (2011) for emerging markets. Rodionova (2014) reveals an insignificant effect of the national currency exchange rate on the yield of Chinese GBLC. We attribute this to the fact that the yuan is not a freely convertible currency, and its exchange rate is artificially overvalued.

Government debt-to-GDP has a persistent negative impact on the yields of GBLC for all maturities. This conclusion contradicts the results of Rodionova (2014) on the Chinese market, and Boysen-Hogrefe (2017) on the markets of the Eurozone countries. We explain that in China, the ratio of government debt-to-GDP is not so high: 16% in 2018 (according to the World Bank). In these conditions, the increase in public debt due to the issuance of GBLC serves as a positive signal for investors and indicates the development of the national financial market, and the increase in its depth and liquidity.

The influence of such factors as the government budget balance to GDP, S&P 500 index returns, PMI business activity index, and industrial production growth is not significant, and the direction of influence is unstable (Table 4.8).

Determinants of Russian GBLC yields

The most significant factors determining the dynamics of Russian GBLC yields are the change in the exchange rate of the Russian rouble against the US dollar and the key rate of the Bank of Russia (Table 4.9). The higher the dollar exchange rate, the higher the yields of rouble government bonds. In most model specifications, this factor is significant at the 1% level. A similar conclusion about the effect of the depreciation of the local currency is obtained by Sun et al. (2011) for emerging markets, including Russia, and by Rodionova (2014) for the Russian market.

The higher the Bank of Russia's key rate, the higher the GBLC yields (Table 4.9). The conclusion about the positive effect of the proxy interest rates coincides with the results of Senga et al. (2018).

The effect of public debt-to-GDP on GBLC yields is positive. In several models, the factor is significant at the 10% level (Table 4.9). With an increase in government debt, the credit risks of bondholders grow. Boysen-Hogrefe (2017) reaches a similar conclusion on the bond markets for the Eurozone countries, and Senga et al. (2018) for African markets.

We observe a significant negative impact of the industrial production growth rate on three-year GBLC and the index of business activity PMI on ten-year GBLC. For five-year GBLC, the influence of these factors is negative, but their statistical significance is not high (Table 4.9). Boysen-Hogrefe (2017) reveals a negative influence in the GB markets of the Eurozone countries. An increase in business activity indicates a favourable situation in the country's economy and the risk of default on GBLC decreases.

With an increase in the S&P 500 stock market returns, the yields on Russian GBLC decrease. For three-year GBLC, this factor is significant at the 5% level. We attribute this to the fact that the growth of the S&P 500 index indicates a decrease in global credit risks and is positively perceived by holders of rouble government bonds. The conclusion is consistent with the results of Silvapulle et al. (2016) for the GB markets in Portugal, Ireland, and Greece.

Substantial risk in the financial markets (volatility index VIX) has a steady positive impact on the Russian GBLC yields of all maturities, but in only one of the specifications the factor is significant at a 10% level. This conclusion is consistent with the results of Piljak (2013) and Silvapulle et al. (2016).

Foreign market factors affect the yield of Russian sovereign bonds. A positive impact (significant for several specifications at the 5–10% level) is exerted by the yields of ten-year US Treasuries (Table 4.9). Yield to maturity for ten-year US Treasuries is a proxy of the global risk-free rate, and its increase leads to an increase in the Russian GBLC yields. Senga et al. (2018) obtain a similar conclusion about the impact of the US Long-term Treasuries yield in African countries. The relationship between the yield of three-month US Treasury bills and the yield of Russian GBLC for the sample is negative. On the one hand, in 2016–2019, the yields of three-month US Treasury bills are steadily increasing, and they currently exceed the yields of 10-year US Treasuries. On the other hand, the

Table 4.9 Determinants of yields of GBLC of Russia

	1	*2*	*3*	*4*	*5*
Dependentvariable	y1_gb_ytm	y1_gb_ytm	y3_gb_ytm	y5_gb_ytm	y10_gb_ytm
Adjusted R^2	0.3093	0.3647			0.3928
R^2	0.4120	0.4714	0.4771	0.4889	0.4948
Number of obs	149	132	149	132	132
_cons	-3.1092** (1.2383)	-5.2624*** (1.7153)	-2.9374 (1.8194)	-2.9844 (3.2212)	-1.5362 (1.5696)
brentreturn		-0.0044 (0.0081)	-0.0051 (0.0067)		0.0103 (0.0074)
budget_to_gdp	0.025 (0.0315)	0.0337 (0.0343)	0.0804 (0.0345)	0.1086 (0.0642)	0.0318 (0.0314)
cboe_vix_return		0.0038* (0.0022)		0.0029 (0.0029)	0.0022 (0.002)
debt_to_gdp	0.1871* (0.0976)	0.2051* (0.1067)	0.217 (0.1443)	0.0681 (0.1814)	0.0942 (0.0976)
inflation	0.0678 (0.055)	0.0342 (0.0568)	-0.0534 (0.0517)	-0.037 (0.0803)	0.0095 (0.052)
keyrate	0.188*** (0.0486)	0.1935*** (0.0492)	0.2203* (0.1142)	0.1847 (0.1211)	0.1228*** (0.045)
m2_change	-0.0103 (0.0228)	-0.0154 (0.025)	0.0267 (0.0191)	-0.0037 (0.0275)	-0.0207 (0.0229)
output_change	0.0047 (0.0194)		-0.0352* (0.0187)		
pmi		0.0131 (0.0297)		0.0012 (0.0447)	-0.0469* (0.0272)
sp500_return	-0.0071 (0.0138)		-0.0321** (0.0162)		
usa_10y_ytm	0.1974 (0.1779)	0.1671 (0.1815)	0.2673 (0.1716)	0.3615* (0.1984)	0.1803 (0.1661)
usa_3m_ytm	-0.2707 (0.1982)	-0.0455 (0.3086)	-0.3249** (0.1509)	-0.1835 (0.2534)	0.4556 (0.2824)
usd_lcyreturn	0.025* (0.0128)	0.0153 (0.0141)		0.0603*** (0.0196)	0.0605*** (0.0129)

Significance levels: * p <10%, ** p <5%, *** p <1%

crisis in the Russian economy during 2016–2019, caused by the action of anti-Russian sanctions and a sharp decline in oil prices, is gradually smoothing out, and interest rates are decreasing. Further, the carry trade has a bearish effect on Russian GBLC yields.

It is interesting to note that despite the high dependence of the Russian economy on oil prices, the influence of this factor on the yields of GBLC depends on their maturity, and the statistical significance is not high (Table 4.9). While there is a negative relationship between the yields and oil prices for one- and three-year GBLC, for ten-year GBLC the relationship is positive. We explain that in favourable economic conditions there is a higher demand for riskier financial instruments compared to long-term GBLC. In the segment of short-term GBLC, the prevailing role is played by the signal of an increase in government budget surplus and a reduction in credit risk.

We observe that the effect of money supply growth is unstable and not significant.

Conclusion

For the first time we conduct an analysis of the GBLC yield determinants for a sample of three large emerging markets – Russia, China, and Brazil from 2007 to 2019, covering the global financial crisis of 2008–2009 and regional crises of 2014–2015 caused by a sharp drop in oil prices on the global market. We investigate the influence of a wide range of national and global factors by testing multivariate linear regression models.

We find that the set of key determinants of GBLC yields differ among the three markets. The most significant factors determining the yield dynamics in the Brazilian market are the Brazilian real to the US dollar rate and the 10-year US Treasuries yields. For the Chinese market, the inflation rate, the percentage change in the money supply and the US Treasuries yields are the most significant factors. For the Russian market, the US dollar to rouble rate and the Bank of Russia's key rate have a decisive impact.

Among global factors, the yield to maturity on long-term US Treasuries (a proxy of the global risk-free rate) is the most significant and positive factor for all three markets. The remaining global determinants lose their importance to national factors. We note that the most important national factor is the exchange rate for the economies of Brazil and Russia, which are characterized by a high dependence on oil exports, a relatively weak pace of economic growth, and sharp jumps in the exchange rate during crisis periods from 2007 to 2019. For the Chinese market, the exchange rate is less significant, but inflation (as a proxy for the level of interest rates in the economy) and the dynamics of the money supply prevail.

We have obtained two original conclusions. For the Brazilian market, the PMI index and the industrial production growth rate have a positive impact on the GBLC yields. We attribute this to an increased demand for cash in the face of favourable macroeconomic conditions. For the Chinese market, we note that the public debt-to-GDP has a steady negative effect on GBLC yields. We attribute this to the fact that in China the ratio of debt to GDP is relatively low, and the increase in debt due to issuing GBLC serves as a signal for the development of the national financial market, and an increase in its depth and liquidity.

References

Afonso, A. (2010). Long-term government bond yields and economic forecasts: Evidence for the EU. *Applied Economics Letters*, 17(15): 1437–1441. DOI: https://doi.org/10.1080/13504850903049627

Ardagna, S., Caselli, F., Lane, T. (2007). Fiscal discipline and the cost of public debt service: Some estimates for OECD countries. *The B.E. Journal of Macroeconomics*, 7(1): 1–35. DOI: https://doi.org/10.2202/1935-1690.1417

Bellas, D., Papaioannou, M. G., Petrova, I. (2010). Determinants of emerging market sovereign bond spreads: Fundamentals vs financial stress. *IMF Working Paper* 10(281). International Monetary Fund. DOI: https://doi.org/10.1596/978-0-8213-8483-1

Boubaker, S., Nguyen, D. K., Piljak, V., Savvides, A. (2019). Financial development, government bond returns, and stability: International evidence. *Journal of International Financial Markets, Institutions and Money*, 61: 81–96. DOI: https://doi.org/10.1016/j.intfin.2019.02.006

Boysen-Hogrefe, J. (2017). Risk assessment on Euro area government bond markets: The role of governance. *Journal of International Money and Finance*, 73(A): 104–117. DOI: https://doi.org/10.1016/j.jimonfin.2017.01.005

Capelle-Blancard, G., Crifo, P., Diaye, M. A., Oueghlissi, R., Scholtens, B. (2019). Sovereign bond yield spreads and sustainability: An empirical analysis of OECD countries. *Journal of Banking & Finance*, 98: 156–169. DOI: https://doi.org/10.1016/j.jbankfin.2018.11.011

Dua, P., Raje, N. (2010). Determinants of weekly yields on government securities in India. Working Paper №. 187.

Edwards, S., Khan, M. S. (1985). Interest rate determination in developing countries: A conceptual framework. National Bureau of Economic Research. Working paper 1531.

Hartelius, K., Kodres, L. E., Kashiwase, K. (2008). Emerging market spread compression: Is it real or is it liquidity? International Monetary Fund. Working Paper No. 08/10.

Izadi, S., Hassan, M. K. (2018). Impact of international and local conditions on sovereign bond spreads: International evidence. *Borsa Istanbul Review*, 18(1): 41–51. DOI: https://doi.org/10.1016/j.bir.2017.08.002

Jaramillo, L., Weber, A. (2013). Bond yields in emerging economies: It matters what state you are in. *Emerging Markets Review*, 17: 169–185. DOI: https://doi.org/10.1016/j.ememar.2013.09.003

Kaufmann, D., Kraay, A., Mastruzzi, M. (2005). Governance Matters Indicators for 1996–2004. Washington, DC: World Bank. DOI: https://doi.org/10.1596/1813-9450-3630

Min, H. G. (1999). Determinants of emerging market bond spread: Do economic fundamentals matter? World Bank Publications, №1899. DOI: https://doi.org/10.1596/1813-9450-1899

Moreno, R. (2008). Monetary policy transmission and the long-term interest rate in emerging markets. BIS Papers, № 35: 61–80.

Peiris, S.J. (2010). Foreign participation in emerging markets' local currency bond markets. International Monetary Fund. DOI: http://dx.doi.org/10.5089/9781451982602.001

Piljak, V. (2013). Bond markets co-movement dynamics and macroeconomic factors: Evidence from emerging and frontier markets. *Emerging Markets Review*, 17: 29–43. DOI: https://doi.org/10.1016/j.ememar.2013.08.001

Segura-Ubiergo, A. (2012). The puzzle of Brazil's high interest rates. *IMF Working Papers*, 12(62). Washington, DC: International Monetary Fund.

Senga, C., Cassimon, D., Essers, D. (2018). Sub-Saharan African Eurobond yields: What really matters beyond global factors? *Review of Development Finance*, 8(1): 49–62. DOI: https://doi.org/10.1016/j.rdf.2018.05.005

Siklos, P.L. (2011). Emerging market yield spreads: Domestic, external determinants, and volatility spillovers. *Global Finance Journal*, 22(2): 83–100. DOI: https://doi.org/10.1016/j.gfj.2011.10.001

Silvapulle, P., Fenech, J.P., Thomas, A., Brooks, R. (2016). Determinants of sovereign bond yield spreads and contagion in the peripheral EU countries. *Economic Modelling*, 58: 83–92. DOI: https://doi.org/10.1016/j.econmod.2016.05.015

Sun, E.W., Tenengauzer, D., Bastani, A., Rezania, O. (2011). Identification of driving factors for emerging markets sovereign spreads. *Economics Bulletin*, 31(3): 2584–2592.

Rodionova, A.V. (2014). Factors of the formation of government bond returns in the BRIC countries. PhD thesis. National Research University Higher School of Economics, Moscow, Russia. In Rus.

5 Regional bond yields

Debt burden and liquidity are the key factors

Introduction

The regional bond market is a separate subject of research, because the risk of these bonds and yields depend on the development of federalism and the 'power vertical' in the country. If for the US the situation of defaulting on debt obligations of a region or city is normal, then for a number of countries with centralized financial resources (for example, for Russia) sub-federal bonds have practically the same level of risk as sovereign bonds. In this chapter, we identify the determinants of yields on regional bonds of Russia and India.

Most papers on this subject are focused on developed markets and on government bonds (Beck et al., 2017; Padovani et al., 2018; Sola and Palomba, 2016; Schuknecht et al., 2008).

Figure 5.1 shows the classification of quasi-government bonds used in the current paper. We distinguish two subgroups – regional bonds and bonds of corporations where the state has a controlling stake. Regional bonds we divide into two groups – sub-federal and municipal bonds. Pinna (2015) analyzes the Italian municipal bond market, characterized by different levels of issuers (cities, provinces and regions) and inherent sovereign risk. The author concludes that the pricing of bonds issued by regions is different from bonds issued by cities and provinces. In particular, the creditworthiness and the risk of issuer default do not significantly affect the bond spreads of cities and provinces (as opposed to sub-federal bonds), which is explained by the dependence of local budgets on federal subsidies.

This study identifies the determinants of the yields of Russian and Indian LCY regional bonds (RB). For the first time, we test the hypotheses of the impact of the regional economic indicators and bond issue characteristics on the yields of LCY Russian and Indian RBs in primary and secondary markets. Due to low liquidity levels of bonds in emerging markets, we also pay attention to the impact of liquidity indicators on the yield.

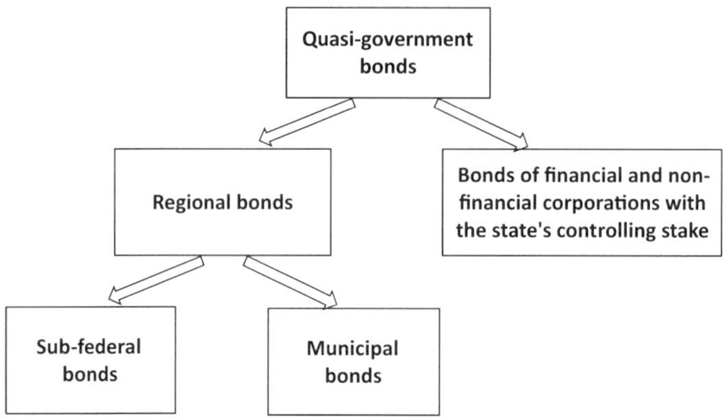

Figure 5.1 Classification of quasi-government bonds.

Literature review

In order to explain the difference between the yields of government and regional bonds, researchers traditionally study a wide range of factors that can be separated into several groups: macroeconomic, economic and social indicators of regions, and bond issue characteristics (Beck et al., 2017; Padovani et al., 2018; Table 5.1). In some cases they study a dummy-variable to account for event-factors: country elections, calendar effects, phases of business cycles, etc.

A number of research papers analyze developed bond markets and consider traditional macroeconomic factors. Cebula (2014) for US municipal bonds from 1960 to 2011 concludes that the growth of the federal budget deficit causes an increase in the costs of the borrowing of regions and states, and it can have a negative impact on their economic activities. Cebula and Nair-Reichert (2018) reveal a positive correlation between municipal bond yields and budget deficit levels and the yields of 3- and 10-year US Treasuries. Yields of municipal bonds are inversely related to federal income tax rates. Expected inflation has a positive influence on the yields of municipal bonds.

The impact of credit rating in the US municipal bond market in 2000–2015 is revealed by Kriz and Xiao (2017). The authors conclude that changes in ratings influenced investors' perceptions of risk and led to an increase in the spread of municipal bonds rated A and higher. Changes in the rating did not have a significant effect on bond issues with Baa rating.

Padovani et al. (2018) consider determinants of spreads of sub-federal bonds in the primary Italian market. They reveal that the bond spreads increase significantly in the case of a high financial dependence of the regional budget on transfers, a high level of criminal activity and low operating income.

Bellot et al. (2017) analyze factors influencing the market spreads of sub-federal European bonds and conclude that the government bond spread, the

Table 5.1 Factors traditionally considered in research papers

Factor	*Research papers*
Regional economical indicators	
Budget deficit to GRP	Cebula (2014)
Budget revenues	Espinosa and Moreno (2014)
GRP	Espinosa and Moreno (2014), Beck et al. (2017)
GRP per capita	Pinna (2015)
Debt burden	
Transfers from the federal budget	Beck et al. (2017)
Bond issue characteristics	
Volume of a bond issue	Espinosa and Moreno (2014)
Time to maturity	Espinosa and Moreno (2014), Pinna (2015)
Coupon	Pinna (2015)
Credit rating	Kriz and Xiao (2017)
Macroeconomic and global factors	
S&P 500 index	Cebula (2014)
US Treasuries yields	
Real GDP growth rate	
Income tax rate	Cebula and Nair-Reichert (2018)
Money market rates	Bellot et al. (2017)
VIX	Beck et al. (2017)

regional debt and the total debt of the issuer country are the most important determinants of sub-federal bond spreads.

Beck et al. (2017) investigate the role of the tax burden and transfer expectations in determining the yield of sub-federal bonds in European markets. The ratio of debt to GRP is the most significant factor in the yield spread of sub-federal bonds. Significant determinants also include the tax deficit to GRP, and the GRP growth rate. The global risk appetite significantly affects the spread. Receiving state support reduces the influence of fundamental factors: such practice increases the role of expectations of its receipt in the future. Regions with a large economy pay a higher premium on bonds, as it is more difficult for the federal government to render assistance to a larger region.

Sola and Palomba (2016) analyze markets of developed countries and demonstrate that a high debt burden and budget deficit increase the yield spreads of sub-federal bonds in the secondary market. With the availability of financial assistance (transfers from the federal budget), the relationship between fundamental factors and the yield spread on sub-federal bonds disappears.

Schuknecht et al. (2008) find that sub-federal bond spreads positively correlate with government debt and the budget deficit in the regions of the EU and Canada. Before joining the EU, the yield spreads on German sub-federal bonds in the event of financial assistance from the federal government did not depend on the budget deficit. After joining the EU, this effect is levelled, that is, monetary union contributed to the improvement of tax discipline. A significant positive effect of maturity on the yield spread is also identified. The influence of short-term interest rates is positive, but the statistical significance is not high.

Some papers consider developed and developing markets. Espinosa and Moreno (2014) analyze the determinants of the yield spread of sub-federal bonds of Mexico and the United States. Studying Mexican sub-federal bond issues, they find that the characteristics of bond issues, the socio-economic conditions of the region and its geographical location have a significant impact on yield spreads, whereas factors that reflect the issuer's financial state are not statistically significant for Mexico's sub-federal bonds.

The determinants of government bond yields in the Indian market are investigated by Krishna and Nag (2018). Our research focuses on a different research object: the regional bond market of India.

The novelty of our paper is that we identify the determinants of the Russian and Indian RB yields with an emphasis on the liquidity indicators of bond issues and the debt burden of the regions.

Hypotheses regarding the determinants of RB yields

We put forward several hypotheses regarding the impact of the bond issue characteristics and regional economic indicators on the yield-to-maturity of RBs and its spread to the yield of GBs, as well as on the yield of their initial placement.

The first group of hypotheses is about the impact of regional economic and macroeconomic indicators:

Hypothesis 1.1. The higher the debt burden of the region, the higher the RB yield (yield spread).

We assume that a higher level of debt burden, expressed as the debt of the region to GRP, entails a higher risk of default on the RB. Accordingly, RB yields of these regions will be higher. A similar relationship is found in Beck et al. (2017) for the RB markets in European countries, Greenwood and Vayanos (2014) for US Treasuries, Schuknecht et al. (2008) for RB of the EU and Canada, and Bellot et al. (2017) for the European market of sub-federal bonds.

Hypothesis 1.2. The higher the budget revenues and the lower the budget spending of the region (in % GRP), the lower the RB yield (yield spread).

We assume that higher revenues and lower expenditures, and accordingly, a higher budget surplus of the region, indicates a greater possibility of debt repayment by the issuer and, thus, reduces the risks of default on bonds. We consider the following factors: a) the ratio of non-transfer income to GRP, b) ratio of budget expenditures to GRP, c) investments to GRP, d) the region's budget surplus (deficit) to the GRP. Similar relationships are revealed by Beck et al. (2017) for the RB markets of European countries, by Padovani et al. (2018) for the

Italian RB market, by Krishna and Nag (2018) for the Indian government bond market, and by Cebula (2014) and Cebula (2018) for the US market.

Hypothesis 1.3. The higher the GRP per capita, the lower the RB yield.
Our explanation is that higher GRP per capita indicators imply a more favourable economic situation in the region; thus, the risk of default is lower. Pinna (2015) shows that the yield spreads of sub-federal Italian bonds negatively depend on GRP per capita.

Hypothesis 1.4. The higher the interest rates in the market (expressed by a risk-free rate or inflation rate), the higher the RB yield.
Krishna and Nag (2018) find that short-term interest rates and the rate of inflation have a consistently positive and significant impact on the yield of Indian government bonds. Cebula and Nair-Reichert (2018) find a positive impact of the US Treasuries yields on US municipal bond yields.

The second group of hypotheses concerns the influence of the bond issue characteristics:

Hypothesis 2.1. The higher the RB liquidity, the lower the RB yield.

As a proxy for liquidity indicators, we consider the trading volume and bid-ask spread for outstanding RB, as well as the volume of the bond issue for initial RB placements. We assume that a higher liquidity reduces investors' risks and, thereby, reduces the levels of RB yield.

The positive impact of the bid-ask spread and the negative impact of the issue volume on the US corporate bond yield spreads are revealed by Chen et al. (2007). Favero et al. (2010) reveal that liquidity indicators are significant factors affecting the yield of EU government bonds.

Hypothesis 2.2. The longer the duration, the higher the yield on RB, since a long duration is equivalent to greater risk.

Schuknecht et al. (2008) reveal a significant and positive effect of maturity on the yield spread of sub-federal bonds of the EU and Canada.

Methodology of our research

To test the hypotheses on the influence of factors on the yield spread of outstanding RB, we apply the following regression models:

– pool linear multifactor regression:

$$y1 = \alpha + \sum_i \beta_{1,i} \cdot bond\_characteristic_i + \sum_j \beta_{2,j} \cdot region\_indicator_j + \varepsilon \quad (5.1)$$

– regressions with random and fixed effects:

$$y1 = \alpha + \sum_i \beta_{1,i} \cdot bond\_characteristic_i + \sum_j \beta_{2,j} \cdot region\_indicator_j + u + \varepsilon \qquad (5.2)$$

where $bond\_characteristic_i$ is one of the characteristics of the bond issue, and $region\_indicator_j$ is one of the economic indicators of the subject of the Russian Federation. More detailed description of the variables is presented in Table 5.2. Explanatory variables are included in models (1) and (2) with an account of the correlation matrix (see Appendix 1).

To test the hypotheses about the influence of factors on RB yields at the initial placement, we apply the following models of linear multifactor regression:

$$y2 = \alpha + \sum_i \beta_{1,i} \cdot bond\_characteristic_i + \sum_j \beta_{2,j} \cdot region\_indicator_j + \beta_3 \cdot risk\_free + \varepsilon \qquad (5.3)$$

Explanatory variables are included in the model (5.3) with an account of the correlation matrix.

Trends and descriptive statistics on rouble RBs

An important task for many federal subjects of the Russian Federation is to improve the mechanisms of debt management. In December 2019, the debt-to-budget revenue ratio for 27% of Russian federal subjects exceeded 60%, and for 1% of the subjects this ratio was higher than 100% (estimated by the authors according to the data of Ministry of Finance of the Russian Federation).

Cross-country differences in the development of RB markets are significant. The RB market in Russia is much smaller than in a number of developed and developing countries. In China, the RB market volume is 21.2% of GDP, in the USA 18% of GDP, and in India 15.3% (see Fig. 3). The size of the RB market in Russia is close to that of France (0.8% of GDP), South Korea (1.3% of GDP), and Mexico (0.4% of GDP; Figure 5.2).

The number of RB issued between 2010 and 2018 increased from 91 to 129 and the number of their issuers increased from 34 to 51. In December 2019, there were 125 issues of sub-federal bonds trading in the market, issued by 47 Russian subjects (from the total of 85 subjects).

Despite the crisis of the Russian economy during 2014–2016 caused by a decrease in oil prices and an imposition of anti-Russian sanctions, during 2014–2018 there were no defaults on RB (source: Cbonds).

The weighted average yield-to-maturity of the outstanding RB included in the Cbonds-Muni index was 0.8–0.9 p.p. higher than the yield of OFZ with corresponding maturity (source: Cbonds).

Table 5.2 Description of the variables

Variable	*Description*	*Expected sign*	*Source*
y1	Dependent variable: Z-spread of the yield of an outstanding RB to the yield of a GB with the same maturity, averaged for the first quarter of each year (2015–2018)		Cbonds, Eikon Refinitiv
y2	Dependent variable: yield of primary placement of RB, %		Cbonds, Eikon Refinitiv
debt_GRP	Debt of the region, in % of GRP	+	Ministry of Finance of the Russian Federation, Reserve Bank of India
income_GRP	Non-transfer budget revenues of the region, in % of GRP	-	Rosstat, Reserve Bank of India
expense_GRP	Budget spending of the region, in % of GRP	+	
invest_GRP	Investment in fixed assets in the region, in % of GRP	+	
proficit_GRP	Budget surplus (deficit) of the region, % GRP	-	
gov_grants	State subsidies to the budget of the region, % GRP	-	
risk_free	Yield-to-maturity on 5-year GBs, at the beginning of the quarter of issuance of a RB	+	Cbonds, Eikon Refinitiv
cpi	Inflation rate in the region (% per annum)	+	Rosstat, Reserve Bank of India
ln_dur	The logarithm of duration (years), at the beginning of each year for outstanding RB, or at the date of RB issuance	+	Cbonds, Eikon Refinitiv
bidask_spr	Bid-ask spread, at the first quarter of each year (2015–2018)	-	Cbonds, Eikon Refinitiv
ln_volume	Logarithm of issue volume	-	Cbonds, Eikon Refinitiv
d1, d2, d3	Dummy years: 2015, 2016 and 2017 respectively (2018 is considered as basic)	+ / -	

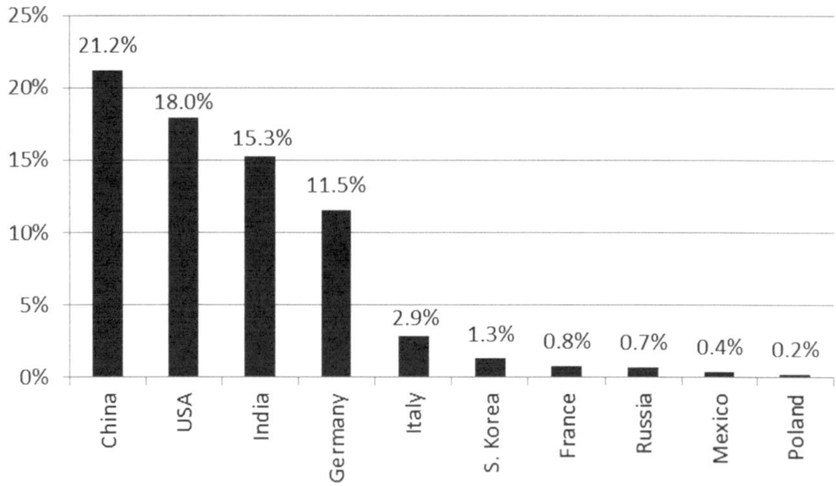

Figure 5.2 The volume of the outstanding RB (% GDP) in some developed and developing countries.

Source: Bloomberg database, estimated by authors.

Investors in sub-federal and municipal bonds have tax benefits like investors in OFZ: they are exempt from income tax on coupon interest. As for capital gains tax, resident individuals pay 13% and resident enterprises pay 20%. For corporate bonds, the exemption from coupon tax applies only to the bonds issued after 2017. As a result, RB take an intermediate position between corporate bonds and OFZ in terms of risk and return: risks in RB are lower than in corporate bonds, while the yields are higher than in OFZ.

The crisis of 2014 negatively affected duration of municipal bonds: it decreased from 2.9 to 1.9 years. We note a trend to growth of duration from 2016 to 2019, and in June 2019 it was 3.1 years (Source: Cbonds). From 2013 liquidity decreases (Figure 5.3).

From 2013 to 2016, the debt of the RF subjects increased from 2.4 to 2.7% of GDP (Source: authors' calculations based on Cbonds). This growth was due to the following factors: a) a decrease in economic growth due to the fall in oil prices and the imposition of sanctions, which caused a decrease in budget revenues, including tax revenues, b) the growth of social expenditures due to the execution of the President's May orders from 2012. From 2016 to 2018, on the contrary, there was a decrease in government debt to 2.1% of GDP (source: Ministry of Finance). According to the Ministry of Finance, foreign debt of Russian subjects decreased to zero levels. Nonetheless, for several regions there is an acute problem of financing the budget (Figure 5.4).

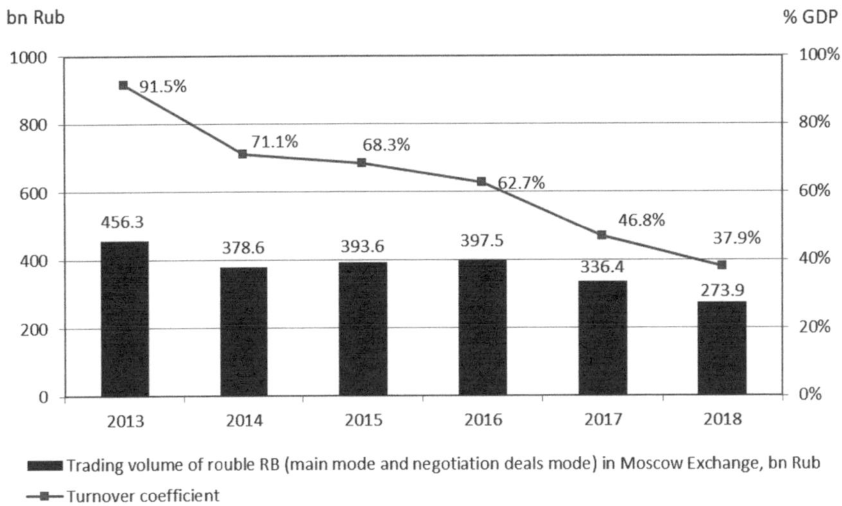

Figure 5.3 The trading volume of RB and turnover coefficients, 2014–2018.

Source: Cbonds, estimates by the authors.

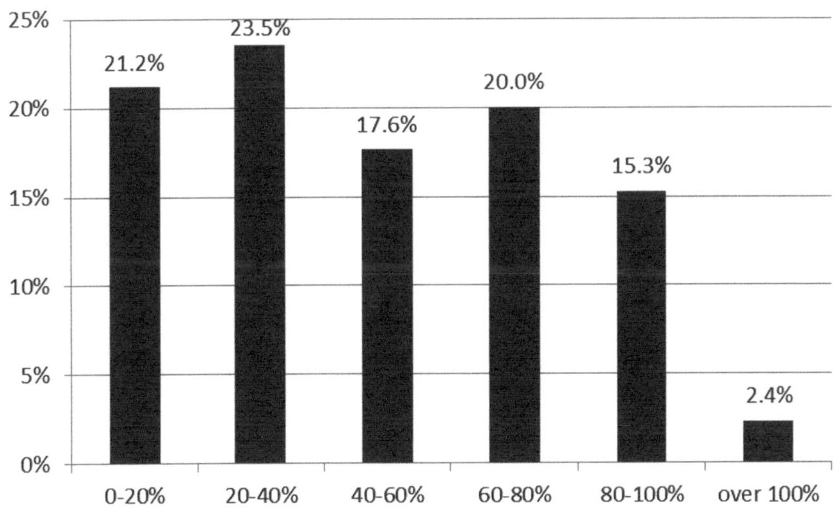

Figure 5.4 The distribution of Russian subjects by levels of debt burden: the ratio between government debt-to-budget revenues (%), 2018.

Source: Authors' estimations based on RIA Rating data, URL: http://vid1.rian.ru/ig/ratings/gosdolg_01_2019.pdf.

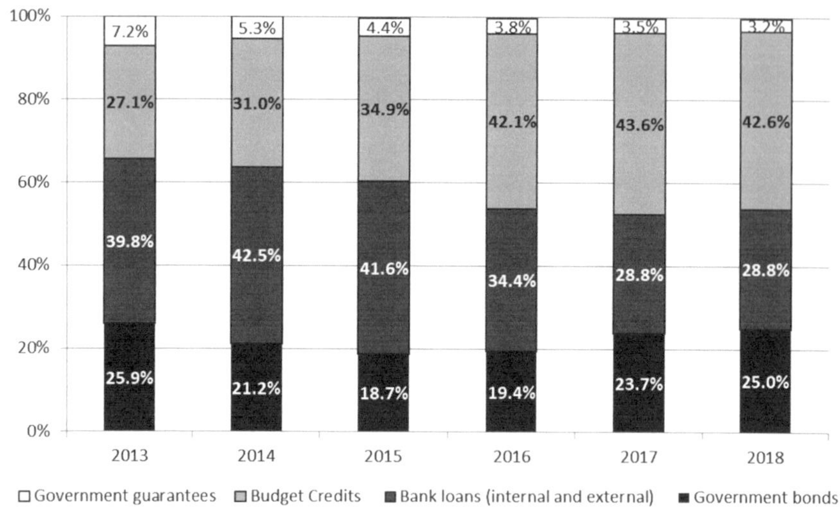

Figure 5.5 The structure of the subjects government debt by sources of funding, 2013–2018.

Source: The Ministry of Finance of the Russian Federation, www.minfin.ru/ru/perfomance/public_ debt/subdbt/, estimates by the authors.

The share of RB in the debt structure of the subjects was 25% at the end of 2018. The key fund sources are shown in Figure 5.5. The paradigm of budget relations in Russia is the concentration of fund flows in the centre with transfers to the regions through grants and budget loans. Thus, in the presence of a growing recession in the economy and an increase in the budget deficit, budget credits, which were offered at 0.1% interest by the Ministry of Finance to the subjects, crowded out bank loans.

As a result, RB can be interesting for investors from the point of risk-return optimization and investment period. The issues for the further growth of this market segment are low liquidity, non-market mechanisms of financing regional budget spending, the high debt burden for some regions and the impossibility of issuing bonds for specific purposes.

Our empirical research is based on two samples of rouble RB: a) outstanding in the Russian market in the first quarter of 2015–2018 and b) having initial placements during 2016–2019.

Data on yields and spreads, and the characteristics of bond issues are obtained from the Cbonds database and economic indicator data on the subjects of the Russian Federation is collected from the Federal Statistics Service (Rosstat) and the Ministry of Finance database (Tab. 2). In order to expand the sample, we consider both sub-federal and municipal bonds. We align the economic indicators of the cities – issuers of municipal bonds with the indicators of the subjects of the RF which the cities belong to.

Table 5.3 Russia: descriptive statistics on the sample for analyzing the determinants of the outstanding RB yield spread

Variable	*Obs*	*Mean*	*Std. Dev.*	*Min*	*Max*
y1	135	4.74	0.57	2.52	6.25
tr_volume	135	14.4	7.4	2.7	109.4
ln_dur	135	0.75	0.80	-0.96	1.77
bidask_spr	135	284.45	153.49	11.76	2 223.86
debt_GRP	135	60.15	55.03	4.58	234.38
income_GRP	135	0.15	0.14	0.07	0.32
GRP_per_capita	135	564.19	388.52	160.24	6 283.75
CPI	135	105.76	104.40	101.10	113.90
expense_GRP	135	0.16	0.14	0.07	0.32
invest_GRP	135	0.23	0.22	0.11	0.56

Table 5.4 Russia: descriptive statistics on the sample for analyzing the determinants of the yield of the RB initial placement

Variable	*Obs*	*Mean*	*Std. Dev.*	*Min*	*Max*
y2	83	9.18	1.31	7.19	14.75
Debt_GRP	83	8.37	1.07	3.91	10.31
Proficit_GRP	83	8.03	0.49	7.02	9.21
Ln_dur	83	1.81	0.32	0.85	2.30
Ln_volume	83	5.50	2.72	0.38	19.98
Risk_free	83	-0.67	0.80	-4.90	0.78

Before testing the regressions, observations with extreme values on the yield-to-maturity spread and the yield on the initial placement are excluded from the two samples. Based on the analysis of the spread distribution by separate years, bond issues with extremely high Z-spread values are removed from the sample. At the next step, we take the logarithm of the Z-spread, and by doing so, we remove outliers from the final distribution. We also check the Z-spread for heterogeneity.

For several bond issues of the same region in the same year, the three largest issues by volume are left in the samples. This is done to solve the problem of potential bias of the samples under consideration. The final sample includes 135 observations of outstanding RB and 83 observations on RB initial placement.

In Table 5.3 we present descriptive statistics on the sample of outstanding rouble RB, and in Table 5.4 we provide statistics for the sample of RB initial placement.

Descriptive statistics on Indian RBs

We analyze data on 371 Indian RB outstanding in 2015–2019. These bonds were issued by 30 regions. We note that the debt burden of Indian regions is less than that of Russian regions: in 2018, the debt of each region with outstanding bonds

Table 5.5 India: descriptive statistics on the sample for analyzing the determinants of the outstanding RB yield spread

Variable	*Obs*	*Mean*	*Std. Dev.*	*Min*	*Max*
y1	371	0.503	0.180	0.194	0.847
ln_dur	371	1.859	0.204	0.598	2.358
bid_ask	371	0.0049	0.0005	0.0016	0.0061
ln_GRP	346	28.686	1.400	25.743	30.814
debt_GRP	344	24.944	8.492	10.854	48.116
proficit_GRP	346	1.425	1.959	-6.318	11.02
invest_GRP	346	55.952	38.799	5.308	373.017
expense_GRP	346	74.450	44.045	20.496	418.199
grants_GRP	346	5.761	6.924	0.402	39.569
ln_grants	346	1.244	0.975	-0.912	3.678

Table 5.6 India: descriptive statistics on the sample for analyzing the determinants of the yield of the RB initial placement

Variable	*Obs*	*Mean*	*Std. Dev.*	*Min*	*Max*
y2	371	6.872	0.344	5.354	8.066
risk_free	371	7.396	0.388	6.645	7.832
ln_dur	371	1.895	0.1978	0.604	2.344
ln_volume	371	22.683	1.102	19.133	24.818
ln_GRP	346	28.686	1.400	25.743	30.814
debt_GRP	344	24.944	8.492	10.854	48.116
proficit_GRP	346	1.425	1.959	-6.318	11.02
invest_GRP	346	55.952	38.799	5.308	373.017
expense_GRP	346	74.450	44.045	20.496	418.199
grants_GRP	346	5.761	6.924	0.402	39.569
ln_grants	346	1.244	0.975	-0.912	3.678

did not exceed 45% of GRP, and for 75% of regions their debt did not exceed 30% of GRP. In 2018, the average budget proficit of the regions with outstanding bonds was 1.05% of GRP, and only 6% of regions were characterized by budget deficit (source: authors' calculations based on Reserve Bank of India data).

In Table 5.5 we present descriptive statistics on the sample of outstanding Indian RB, and in Table 5.6 we provide statistics for the sample of Indian RB initial placement.

Results

Results for the Russian RB market

In Table 5.7 we demonstrate the results of regression model tests (pool regression, with fixed and random effects) with respect to the factors determining the yield spread of traded RB.

Table 5.7 Regression results: determinants of the Russian outstanding RB yield spreads

	(1)	*(2)*	*(3)*	*(4)*	*(5)*
constant	-4.948** (1659)	-6.573*** (1556)		-5.004** (1662)	
bidask_spr	0.0016*** (0.0002)	0.0014*** (0.0002)	0.0009*** (0.0003)	0.0017*** (0.0002)	0.0010*** (0.0003)
cpi	0.080*** (0.016)	0.095*** (0.015)	0.122*** (0.016)	0.079*** (0.016)	0.119*** (0.017)
debt_GRP	0.0073*** (0.0017)	0.007** (0.0019)	0.0095 (0.009)	0.007*** (0.0018)	0.0101 (0.0095)
income_GRP	1.449 (1.650)	2.235 (1.799)	19.087* (8.019)	2.451 (2.048)	20.035* (8.341)
invest_GRP	-0.778 (0.796)	-0.744 (0.853)	-1.204 (1.887)	-0.651 (0.811)	-1.157 (1.898)
gov_grants				-0.007 (0.008)	-0.003 (0.005)
R^2 adjusted	0.460	0.504	0.299	0.458	0.292
Number of obs	135				
Type of regression model	Pool	Random Effects	Fixed Effects	Pool	Fixed Effects

Significance levels: * p <10%, ** p <5%, *** p <1%

We note that the sign and the direction of influence of the most significant factors – bid-ask spread, inflation rate and debt burden –coincide in all types of models (Table 5.7). Bid-ask spread has a significant positive impact on the yield spread for outstanding RB: investors consider the low liquidity characteristic of the Russian bond market and demand a risk premium. The significance level of this factor is 1%. In previous studies on sub-federal bond markets, the impact of this factor is not investigated. The results coincide with the findings of Chen et al. (2007) and Favero et al. (2010) on government and corporate bond markets of developed countries.

We consider the inflation rate as a proxy indicator of the levels of interest rates and crisis phenomena in the Russian economy. From Table 5.7 we see that a higher rate of inflation has a significant at 1% level and positive effect on the RB yield spreads. This result corresponds to the conclusion of Krishna and Nag (2018) on the Indian market.

The impact of debt burden is significant and positive: the higher the relative debt levels of the subject of the Russian Federation, the higher the RB spread (Table 5.7). Our explanation is that investors demand a premium for increased risk of default. The result is same as that of Beck et al. (2017), Greenwood and Vayanos (2014), Schuknecht et al. (2008) and Bellot et al. (2017) for developed countries.

There is a steady negative impact of investments to GRP (although the statistical significance is not high): investors perceive a higher level of investment as a positive signal. As far as we know, this relationship has not been studied in previous works.

The impact of the subject's budget revenues on the yield spread is positive and in the two regressions the significance level is 10% (Table 5.7). We explain this by the high correlation between budget revenues and expenditures (the correlation coefficient is 0.97).

Receiving government support has a negative impact on the spread: such support is a positive signal for investors and is seen as a guarantee in the event of a possible default, although the statistical significance is not high. Inclusion of the *gov_grant* variable in the model (Table 5.7) does not change the previous results: a high debt burden, inflation rate and bid-ask spread remain significant determinants of the RB yield spread. This conclusion on the Russian market contradicts the results obtained by Sola and Palomba (2016) and Schuknecht et al. (2008) for the markets of developed countries, in which it is shown that in the presence of transfers from the federal budget, the relationship between the fundamental indicators and the yield spread on sub-federal bonds disappears.

Breush–Pagan test results (chi-square 8.7695, p-value 0.003) indicate the superiority of the random-effects model over the pooled regression. The results of the Hausman test (chi-square 61.2, p-value < 0.001) show that the hypothesis of uncorrelated individual effects and errors can be rejected. Thus the fixed-effects model performs better than the pooled regression models and the random-effects model in terms of the validity and effectiveness of the estimates.

The results of testing the hypotheses on the determinants of RB initial placement yields are presented in Table 5.8. Like an outstanding RB yield spread, debt burden plays a significant role in forming RB initial placement yield: the

Table 5.8 Regression results: determinants of Russian RB initial placement yields

	(1)	*(2)*	*(3)*	*(4)*
Constant	-4.94**	-3.60**	-3.38*	-1.80
	(2.00)	(1.79)	(1.90)	(1.70)
ln_volume	-0.07		-0.06	
	(0.10)		(0.09)	
risk_free	1.76***	1.70***	1.58***	1.51***
	(0.21)	(0.20)	(0.20)	(0.19)
ln_dur		-0.79**		-0.83***
		(0.31)		(0.29)
debt_GRP	0.11***	0.10***		
	(0.04)	(0.04)		
proficit_GRP			-0.54***	-0.54***
			(0.12)	(0.12)
R^2adjusted	0.52	0.56	0.58	0.61
Number of obs	83			

Significance levels: * p <10%, ** p <5%, *** p <1%

higher the subject's debt (in relation to GRP), the higher the spread. The result coincides with the results of Beck et al. (2017), Greenwood and Vayanos (2014), and Schuknecht et al. (2008).

The higher the budget surplus, the lower the yield of RB initial placement. The result is significant at 1% level and is consistent with the findings of Beck et al. (2017) and Padovani et al. (2018).

A positive correlation (at 1% level) is found between the RB initial placement yield and the risk-free rate, i.e. the yield of 5-year OFZs. This result is consistent with the findings of Krishna and Nag (2018).

The logarithm of the duration has a significant negative effect on the RB initial placement yield. We explain this relationship by the fact that the period under consideration includes crisis years, when the Russian market experienced an inverted term structure of interest rates.

The logarithm of the issue volume negatively affects the RB initial placement yield, but the statistical significance is not so high. Our explanation is that the volume of the issue represents one of the liquidity indicators, and investors require a lower risk premium for higher liquidity.

Results for the Indian RB market

The results of calculations for the Indian RB secondary and primary markets are given in Tables 5.9 and 5.10, respectively.

As for the Russian market, bid-ask spread significantly (at the 1% level) and positively impacts on the yield spread of outstanding RB: investors demand a risk premium for the low liquidity in the Indian bond market (Table 5.9).

The higher the relative debt levels of the Indian region, the higher the RB yield in the secondary and primary markets (Tables 5.9, 5.10). This factor is significant at the 5% level. So, investors demand a premium for increased risk of default, which is same as the Russian market.

Unlike the Russian market, the impact of investments to GRP is positive and significant at the 5–10% level (Tables 5.9, 5.10). Our explanation is that the capital investment-to-GDP in India (31.1% in 2015–2018 on average; source: World Bank) is much higher than in Russia (23.2% in 2015–2018 on average; source: World Bank). Therefore investors in Indian RBs perceive an increase in investment as a risk factor. Budget proficit also increases RB yields spreads. We explain this by the fact that the balance between savings (budget surplus) and high investment activity is important.

The impact of the region budget expenditures on the yield and its spread is positive (Tables 5.9, 5.10), and this coincides with the Russian RB market. The higher the budget surplus, the lower the cost of debt. This factor is significant at the 5–10% level.

As for the Russian market, receiving government support has a negative impact on the yield and its spread: such support is seen by investors as a guarantee in the event of a possible default (Table 5.9, 5.10). The statistical significance is not high.

Table 5.9 Regression results: determinants of the Indian outstanding RB yield spreads

	(1)	*(2)*	*(3)*	*(4)*
_cons	0.3536***	-0.2514	-0.06	0.2824***
	(0.059)	(0.1654)	(0.061)	(0.0778)
bid_ask		62.6704***	61.1862***	
		(11.6674)	(11.6565)	
debt_GRP	0.0018**	0.0018**	0.0014*	0.0026**
	(0.0008)	(0.0008)	(0.0008)	(0.0012)
expense_GRP	0.0003*		0.0002	(0.0002)
	(0.0002)		(0.0002)	(0.0002)
grants_GRP	-0.0005			-0.0040***
	(0.0012)			(0.0014)
invest_GRP		0.0003*		
		(0.0002)		
ln_dur	-0.063**			0.0741*
	(0.0284)			(0.0409)
ln_grants			-0.0016	
			(0.0081)	
ln_GRP		0.0061		
		(0.0049)		
proficit_GRP	-0.0063**	-0.0063**	-0.0067**	-0.0087*
	(0.0032)	(0.003)	(0.003)	(0.0045)
cpi				0.1328***
				(0.0778)
year dummies	yes			no
Adjusted R^2	0.6279	0.6524	0.6512	0.2451
Number of obs	344	344	344	326

Significance levels: * p <10%, ** p <5%, *** p <1%

We also note that the larger the size of the region economy, the higher spread of outstanding RB (Table 5.9). Our explanation is that investors consider it more difficult for the state to help large regions.

The logarithm of the issue volume positively affects the RB initial placement yield, but the statistical significance is not high (Table 5.10).

Conclusions

In this chapter we reveal the determinants of Russian and Indian RB yields in both primary and secondary markets for the first time. Emphasis is placed on the debt burden indicators of the regions and the liquidity of bond issues. Hypothesis testing is carried out based on models of pooled regression and regressions with fixed and random effects.

We reached an interesting conclusion regarding RB yields and spreads. In a rapidly growing economy, investors pay much attention to the quality of money management: too large savings are the signal of inefficiency. In an economy with low GDP growth, there is no such effect.

Table 5.10 Regression results: determinants of Indian RB initial placement yields

	(1)	*(2)*	*(3)*	*(4)*
_cons	3.8386***	3.8291***	3.9904***	3.852***
	(0.222)	(0.222)	(0.227)	(0.0827)
debt_GRP	0.0028**	0.0027**	0.0023**	0.0029***
	(0.0011)	(0.0011)	(0.0011)	(0.0011)
expense_GRP		0.0005**		
		(0.0002)		
grants_GRP	-0.0003	-0.0008		
	(0.0017)	(0.0017)		
invest_GRP	0.0005**		0.0005**	0.0006**
	(0.0002)		(0.0002)	(0.0002)
ln_dur	1.3969***	1.3969***	1.3956***	1.3959***
	(0.0397)	(0.0397)	(0.0397)	(0.0397)
ln_grants				-0.0055
				(0.0107)
ln_GRP			-0.0044	
			(0.0068)	
ln_volume	0.0005	0.0007		
	(0.0089)	(0.0089)		
proficit_GRP	-0.0074*	-0.0073*	-0.0078*	-0.0075*
	(0.0043)	(0.0043)	(0.0042)	(0.0042)
Year dummies	yes			
Adjusted R^2	0.8236	0.8240	0.8244	0.8243
Number of obs	344	344	344	344

Significance levels: * p <10%, ** p <5%, *** p <1%

We conclude that in both emerging markets the most significant factors are liquidity and debt burden. The budget proficit is also a significant factor reducing the cost of debt.

Receiving state subsidies negatively affects the spread of outstanding RBs, but the significance of this factor is not very high. For the initial bond placement, duration plays an important role.

References

Beck, R., Ferrucci, G., Hantzsche, A., Rau-Göhring, M. (2017). Determinants of sub-sovereign bond yield spreads: The role of fiscal fundamentals and federal bailout expectations. *Journal of International Money and Finance*, 79(1): 72–98. DOI: https://doi.org/10.1016/j.jimonfin.2017.08.003

Bellot, N. J., Selva, M. M., Menendez, L. G. (2017). Spreads of bonds issued by sub-sovereign European governments. *Journal of Innovation and Knowledge*, 2: 146–154. DOI: https://doi.org/10.1016/j.jik.2016.10.002

Cebula, R. J. (2014). An exploratory analysis of the impact of budget deficits and other factors on the ex post real interest rate yield on tax-free municipal bonds in the United States. *Applied Financial Economics*, 24(19): 1297–1302. DOI: https://doi.org/10.1080/09603107.2014.925057

Cebula, R. J., Nair-Reichert, U. (2018). Impact of federal income tax rates and government borrowing on nominal interest rate yields on tax-free municipal bonds. *Journal of Financial Economic Policy*, 10(3): 342–350. DOI: https://doi.org/10.1108/JFEP-10-2017-0104

Chen, L., Lesmond, D. A., Wei, J. (2007). Corporate yield spreads and bond liquidity. *Journal of Finance*, LXII(1): 119–149. DOI: https://doi.org/10.1111/j.1540-6261.2007.01203.x

Chionis, D., Pragidis, I., Schizas, P. (2016). The determinants of Greek bond yields: An empirical study before and during the crisis. *Journal of Economic Studies*, 43(3): 504–519. DOI: https://doi.org/10.1108/JES-12-2014-0197

Espinosa, S., Moreno, J. O. (2014). Regional development and cross-border infrastructure finance comparing the yield-spread determinants of Mexican and U.S. sub-sovereign government bonds. *Journal of Structured Finance*, 20(1): 64–75. DOI: https://doi.org/10.3905/jsf.2014.20.1.064

Favero, C., Pagano, M., Thadden, E. -L. (2010). How does liquidity affect government bond yields? *Journal of Financial and Quantitative Analysis*, 45(1): 107–134. DOI: https://doi.org/10.1017/S0022109009990494

Greenwood, R., Vayanos, D. (2014). Bond supply and excess bond returns. *The Review of Financial Studies*, 27(3): 663–713. DOI: https://doi.org/10.1093/rfs/hht133

Krishna, G. D., Nag, B. (2018). Long-run determinants of sovereign bond yields. *Money, Banking and Finance*, 53(13): 111–119.

Kriz, K. A., Xiao, Y. (2017). The impact of rating recalibration on municipal bond yield spreads. *Public Budgeting and Finance*, Summer 2017: 83–101. DOI: https://doi.org/10.1111/pbaf.12151

Padovani, E., Rescigno, L., Ceccatelli, J. (2018). Municipal bond debt and sustainability in a non-mature financial market: The case of Italy. *Sustainability*, 10: 3249–3273. DOI: https://doi.org/10.3390/su10093249

Pinna, M. (2015). An empirical analysis of the municipal bond market in Italy: Sovereign risk and sub-sovereign levels of government. *Public Budgeting and Finance*, Fall 2015: 68–94. DOI: https://doi.org/10.1111/pbaf.12061

Schuknecht, L., Von Hagen, J., Wolswijk, G. (2008). Government risk premiums in the bond market: EMU and Canada. *European Journal of Political Economy*, 25(3), 371–384. DOI: https://doi.org/10.1016/j.ejpoleco.2009.02.004

Silvapulle, P., Fenech, J. P., Thomasa, A., Brooksa, R. (2016). Determinants of sovereign bond yield spreads and contagion in the peripheral EU countries. *Economic Modelling*, 58(1): 83–92. DOI: https://doi.org/10.1016/j.econmod.2016.05.015

Sola S., Palomba, G. (2016). Sub-nationals' risk premia in fiscal federations: Fiscal performance and institutional design. *Journal of International Money and Finance*, 63: 165–187. DOI: https://doi.org/10.1016/j.jimonfin.2016.01.009

6 Liquidity metrics in the bond market

Explaining yields in the non-financial and banking sectors

Introduction

It is not trivial to isolate the liquidity effect and calculate its influence on bond yields. The problem is that both liquidity and credit (or country) risks are difficult to measure directly, and it is difficult to distinguish one from the other (Helwege et al., 2014). As a concept, liquidity is too complicated to be measured by a simple indicator in the form of the trading volume. An increase in the trading volume may not reflect increased liquidity, but indicate a policy of dealers in portfolio balancing and active hedging. Speculative demand also infuses significant corrections that increase trading volume before the disclosure of important financial information about the issuer.

Currently there is no widely accepted indicator for measuring liquidity in the analysis of fixed-income instruments (Konstantinovsky et al., 2016; Schestag et al., 2016). There are a few papers in the literature that aim at either creating an original indicator or trying to combine existing instruments to show their effect on the credit spread. In this chapter, we briefly describe the different approaches for building liquidity indicators in the bond market and present recent studies from the last decade that prove the significant influence of liquidity indicators on corporate bond (CB) yields.

The purpose of this study is to identify liquidity indicators that significantly affect yield to maturity (YTM) and the spread of outstanding CBs in India and Russia for the period after the regional crisis of 2014–2015. We consider and compare the determinants of the YTM and the spread on samples of bank and non-financial sector CBs.

The most frequently analyzed liquidity indicators are presented in Table 6.1.

Literature review

Liquidity is a multifaceted concept, but most researchers note a common property: the rapid conversion of an asset into money (Longstaff et al., 2005). An important research question is the creation of a system of indicators or an integrated measure that estimates the liquidity of assets for problem solving. Pastor and Stambaugh (2003) interpret liquidity as a combination of four characteristics

Table 6.1 The liquidity indicators used in research papers

Indicator	*Papers*
Trade volume	Helwege et al. (2014); Shin and Kim (2015); Wang and Wu (2015)
Transaction volume	Kalimipalli et al. (2013); Wang and Wu (2015)
Number of transactions	Kalimipalli et al. (2013); Wang and Wu (2015)
Number (or share) of days with zero/non-zero trade volume during the period	Helwege et al. (2014); Aquilina and Suntheim (2017); Hafner and Walders (2017)
Turnover ratio, i.e. the ratio of the trade volume to the amount of bond issue	Aquilina and Suntheim (2017)
Indicator of liquidity zero costs (zero return method)	Chen et al. (2007)
A liquidity indicator that incorporates transaction costs, based on the LOT model	Amihud and Mendelson (1986); Chen et al. (2007); Febi et al. (2018)
Bid-ask spread	Chen et al. (2007); Boermans et al. (2016); Han and Zhou (2016); Hafner and Walders (2017)
The ratio of the difference between the maximum and minimum price for the period to the average price divided by the trade volume	Kalimipalli et al. (2013)
Inter-quartile range (the ratio of the difference between the 75th and 25th percentiles of price to the average price)	Helwege et al. (2014)
Amihud's illiquidity measure	Amihud (2002); Han and Zhou (2016); Hafner and Walders (2017)
The γ liquidity measure, calculated based on the autocovariance of the asset's price changes during a day	Bao et al. (2011); Helwege et al. (2014); Aquilina and Suntheim (2017); Bai et al. (2019)
Roll's illiquidity measure, based on estimating the covariance between the asset's price changes	Roll (1984), Shin and Kim (2015)
Integral liquidity measures, developed by the authors or investment companies and information-analytical agencies (incl. Thomson Reuters)	Kalimipalli et al. (2013); Boermans et al. (2016); Teplova et al. (2016).
Bond's age	Helwege et al. (2014)
Years to maturity	Shin and Kim (2015)

Source: Compiled by authors.

of an asset (transaction volume, speed of implementation, associated costs and price deviation due to the transaction). Market practitioners are forced to invent ways to separate liquid bonds from weakly liquid and illiquid ones. Thomson Reuters also introduced its own Integrated Liquidity Indices for the Russian bond market.[1]

Most of the papers focus on studying the impact of liquidity indicators on the YTM in developed countries (Chen et al., 2007; Kalimipalli et al., 2013; Helwege et al. 2014; Boermans et al., 2016; Aquilina and Suntheim, 2017; Febi et al., 2018). A much smaller number of papers are devoted to studying this effect in developing countries (Tarek, 2009; Shin and Kim, 2015; Teplova et al., 2016). Typically, authors focus on the study of the US market, underestimating the possible prospects of the analysis in emerging markets. A relevant research question is the identification of key liquidity indicators that influence bond yields and spreads in emerging markets after the global financial crisis of 2008 and regional crises of 2014–2015. Our paper closes the gap in this area on sample of rouble CBs from different sectors.

Shin and Kim (2015) identify and compare the determinants of the CB yield spread in South Korea during (2007–2008) and after the global financial crisis (2009–2011). The authors conclude that liquidity indicators play a more significant role in pricing Korean CBs during the crisis, while during the post-crisis period the credit risk comes to the fore. The Roll measure and the credit rating have a significant positive effect on the CB spread. After the crisis, trading volume has a significant negative effect.

Aquilina and Suntheim (2017) study the role of liquidity in the formation of the yield spread for the UK market. The sample includes more than 6000 bond issues and 3 million exchange transactions for the period 2008–2014. The authors construct an original integrated measure of liquidity based on the principal component analysis. The authors find that the influence of liquidity indicators on the speculative-grade CB yield spread is significantly higher than on the investment-grade CB spread.

Bianchi et al. (2017) investigate the effect of various risk factors: term risk, default risk, and liquidity risk on the yield spreads of Australian CBs. The liquidity risk factor is measured as proposed by Chen et al. (2007), i.e. based on calculating the effective liquidity transaction cost by seller and buyer. The authors conclude that, regardless of the credit rating and duration, the liquidity risk significantly positively affects the CB yield spread.

Febi et al. (2018) assess the effect of liquidity on the spread of corporate European 'green' bond yields to government bond yields in 2014–2016. The results show that green bonds are characterized by higher liquidity compared to plain vanilla bonds, so liquidity risk has a lower effect on their yield spread. Both the LOT and bid-ask spread measures are significant.

Based on the literature review, we can conclude that research papers demonstrate the importance of various liquidity indicators in explaining the differences in CB yields and yield spreads. Lower liquidity ratios positively correlate with the default probability and bond yield spreads (Kalimipalli et al., 2013; Bianchi et al.,

2017; Aquilina and Suntheim, 2017; Bai et al., 2019). An increase in the number of days with no trades increases the credit spread, and bonds with high trading activity show lower credit spreads. The explanatory power of liquidity measures, such as the Amihud measure and the IRC, are high.

Our hypotheses

We put forward the following hypotheses regarding the impact of liquidity indicators on YTM and its spreads for a sample of outstanding Indian and Russian LCY CBs:

Hypothesis 1. The higher the trading volume, the lower the YTM and its spread of LCY CBs.

The higher the trading activity, the faster the execution of a trade within the required volume, and the lower the liquidity risk for bondholders. As demonstrated by Helwege et al. (2014), the accumulated trading volume has a significant negative effect on the CB yield spread in the US market. A similar conclusion is made by Shin and Kim (2015) for the South Korean bond market during the period after the global financial crisis of 2007–2008.

Hypothesis 2. The higher the number of days with non-zero trading volume, the lower the YTM and its spread of LCY CBs.

The more days with non-zero trading volume, the faster the execution of transactions and the lower the liquidity risk. Chen et al. (2007) and Hafner and Walders (2017) reveal a negative impact of this measure on the US bond spreads.

Hypothesis 3. The higher the relative bid-ask spread, the higher the YTM and its spread of LCY CBs.

The bid-ask spread is a measure of transaction costs; therefore, when it increases, bondholders require a premium for the increased liquidity risk, and as a result, the YTM and the bond spreads increase. Han and Zhou (2016) find a significant positive effect of the bid-ask spread on US CB yield spreads; Febi et al. (2018) on the European market of green bonds.

Hypothesis 4. The greater the Amihud illiquidity measure, the higher the YTM and its spread of LCY CBs.

The Amihud illiquidity measure computes the price impact of a transaction based on the trading volume and is one of the measures of the financial depth of a market (Chaikun, 2010). The less the CB price reaction to transactions with a large volume, the lower the liquidity risks. Han and Zhou (2016) and Hafner and Walders (2017) reveal a significant positive impact of the Amihud measure on CB yield spreads in the US market, and Aquilina and Suntheim (2017) in the UK market.

Hypothesis 5. The higher the volume of the CB issue, the higher the YTM and its spread of LCY CBs.

We assume that the higher the volume of CB issue, the higher the number of these CB holders, and, as a result, the higher the volume of trades and the lower the liquidity risk. As demonstrated by Helwege et al. (2014), the CB issue volume significantly affects the CB yield spread in the US market. A similar conclusion is drawn by Shin and Kim (2015) for the South Korean CB market after the global financial crisis of 2008–2009.

In the specification of the regression models, we include several control variables that characterize the credit risks of CBs, including characteristics of CBs, the financial situation of the issuing companies, as well as dummies for periods and industry affiliation of the issuers.

We calculate the following control variables:

- The inclusion of the CB issue in the list of repo-eligible securities. We assume that if the CB issue is included in this list, then YTM and its spreads are lower. A negative direction of influence was previously found by Teplova et al. (2016) for the Russian market.
- The logarithm of the CB issue duration. We assume a positive direction of influence in this explanatory variable. As shown by Bai et al. (2019), the higher the maturity, the higher the CB yield spread on the US market.
- The size of the issuer (revenue for non-financial companies or total assets for banks). For large companies, we assume that the YTM and the spreads are decreasing. As shown in Teplova and Sokolova (2019) for the Russian market, the size of the issuer company has a negative impact on the CB spread.
- The debt burden of the issuer (liabilities to equity for non-financial companies or the volume of deposits to equity for banks). We assume that the higher the leverage, the higher the YTM and the spread. As shown by Casteuble et al. (2013) and Lester and Kumar (2014), higher debt burden indicators (in particular, higher financial leverage) lead to an increase in the CB yield spread.
- Return on equity. We suggest that the influence of this factor may be ambiguous. On the one hand, Lester and Kumar (2014) and Teplova and Sokolova (2019) find that an increase in ROA or ROE leads to a decrease in the yield spreads: higher profitability rates serve as a positive signal for bondholders. On the other hand, Balasubramnian and Cyree (2011) reveal a positive correlation between the spread and the ROA, explaining that investors are confident that additional income is due to taking additional risks.
- The issuer's belonging to public companies. We assume that if the issuer is a public company, then its information transparency for investors is higher, and therefore, the YTM and the spreads are reduced.

Research methodology

To test the hypotheses on the influence of liquidity factors on the CB yields and spreads, we apply the following linear multifactor regression models:

$$y = \alpha + \sum_i \beta_{1,i} \cdot liquidity\_indicator_i + \sum_j \beta_{2,j} \cdot control\_variable_j + \varepsilon \qquad (6.1)$$

where y is the dependent variable (YTM or its spread), $liquidity\_indicator_i$ is one of the liquidity indicators, and $control\_variable_j$ is one of the control variables. A detailed description of the variables is presented in Table 6.2.

Explanatory variables are included in model (1) with an account of the correlation matrix (see Appendix 1). We test model specifications for the non-financial and banking sectors separately.

In order to check the robustness of the results, we evaluate models for the two dependent variables – YTM and its spreads, with and without dummy variables, for the full sample and the sub-samples with non-zero trading volume.

Sample descriptive statistics

We analyze two different LCY corporate bond markets – Indian and Russian – and two different samples for each market: bonds of non-financial companies and banks outstanding in April 2017, 2018, and 2019. The main source of data on LCY Russian CB quotes is the Cbonds database, due to the lack of data on several matured bonds in Eikon Refinitiv (Table 6.2). The main source of data on LCY Indian CB quotes is the Eikon Refinitiv.

We clear the sample of extremal values; we do not take into account 5% of the smallest and 5% of the largest values, both in terms of the YTM and the financial indicators for several companies. For example, for the Russian market the issue of the Agricultural Bank (RU000A0JS6N8) is excluded from our calculations; its YTM in April 2018 was 29.1% compared to a median value of 7.95% for a sample of bank bonds in the considered period. The initial sample of Russian bank CBs includes 614 observations, and CBs of non-financial companies consists of 1209 observations.

To avoid the problem of a sample bias for each company and each year, no more than 5 observations are left with different indicators of the number of non-zero trading days: two CB issues with the highest, two issues with the smallest and one issue with the median number of non-zero trading days. The final sample for the Russian market includes 343 observations for banks and 780 observations for non-financial companies. Descriptive statistics of the final samples in the Russian market are presented in Tables 6.3, 6.4.

A specific of the Indian corporate bond market is that trades are performed in the OTC mode. Eikon Refinitiv and Bloomberg do not contain data on trading volume. Due to the lack of data on trading volume, the variable of non-zero

Table 6.2 Dependent and explanatory variables

Variable name	*Description*	*Sign*	*Source*
Dependent variables			
ln_ytm	The logarithm of the outstanding CB average nominal YTM on April of the corresponding year (2017, 2018, or 2019)		Cbonds, Eikon Refinitiv
ln_spread	The logarithm of the average CB YTM spread to government bond yields with the same duration on April		
Explanatory variables			
ln_trade_ volume	The logarithm of the CB average trading volume on April	-	Cbonds, Eikon Refinitiv
non_zero_days	The number of days with the non-zero trading volume of the CB issue on April	-	
bid_ask	The logarithm of the relative bid-ask spread, calculated as the average value of the CB issue Bid and Ask daily prices in April: $LM = (Ask - Bid) / [(Ask + Bid) / 2]$	+	
illiq	Amihud measure, calculated as: $ILLIQ_{iy} = \frac{1}{D_{iy}} \sum_{t=1}^{Diy} \frac{\lvert R_{iyd} \rvert}{VOLD_{iyd}}$ where: *Diy* is the number of days with non-zero trading volume on April for the CB issue under consideration; *Riyd* is the difference in closing and opening prices of CBs per day *d*; *VOLDiyd* is the trade volume on day *d*	+	Computed by authors based on Cbonds, Eikon Refinitiv
ln_issue_ volume	The logarithm of the CB issue volume (in RUB)	-	Cbonds, Eikon Refinitiv
Control variables			
repo_eligible	A dummy variable characterizing if the bond issue is repo eligible: 1 – yes, 0 – no	-	Cbonds, Eikon Refinitiv
ln_dur	The logarithm of a CB duration (in years)	+	
ln_total_assets	The logarithm of the total assets of a bank which issued CBs (at the end of the previous year)	-	Eikon Refinitiv, issuers financial reports
ln_sales	The logarithm of the revenue of a non-financial company which is the issuer of CBs (as for the previous year)	-	
liabilities_ equity	The ratio of the total liabilities to the equity of a non-financial company which issued CBs (at the end of the previous year)	+	

(*continued*)

Table 6.2 Cont.

Variable name	*Description*	*Sign*	*Source*
deposits_equity	The ratio of the deposits of individuals and legal entities to the equity of a bank which issued CBs (at the end of the previous year)	+	
ln_ROE	The logarithm of the issuer's ROE (for the previous year)	+ / -	
Public	Dummy variable, indicating if the issuer is a public company: 1 – yes, 0 – no	-	
dummy_2018, dummy_2017	Dummy variables for observations in 2018 and 2017, respectively	+	
sectoral dummies	Industry dummies for non-financial companies that are issuers of CBs	+ / -	

Table 6.3 The Russian market: the non-financial company CB sample descriptive statistics

Variable	*Obs*	*Mean*	*Std.Dev.*	*Min*	*Max*
ln_ytm	780	2.308	0.255	1.549	3.211
ln_spread	778	1.387	0.507	-0.373	2.985
ln_trade_volume	780	10.805	6.457	0	21.119
non_zero_days	780	9.644	8.350	0	22
bid_ask	626	0.589	0.361	-1	1.386
illiq	506	7.269	35.450	0	773.196
ln_issue_volume	780	22.325	1.034	17.22	25.89
repo_eligible	780	0.608	0.489	0	1
ln_dur	780	1.563	0.567	0.1	2.7
ln_sales	780	17.661	2.469	7.89	22.66
liabilities_equity	780	5.454	6.380	0.09	20
public	780	0.546	0.498	0	1
dummy_2017	780	0.292	0.455	0	1
dummy_2018	780	0.347	0.476	0	1

trading days was replaced by the number of days in which both bid and ask prices were present. According to this indicator, the majority of bonds were traded on almost all working days of April. The number of observations with a non-zero trading day less than 19 days is only 4.3% of all observations. Descriptive statistics of the final sample for the Indian market are presented in Table 6.5.

Results

For the Russian market, the results for the sample of non-financial companies and banks are presented in Tables 6.6 and 6.7, respectively. The trading volume is the most significant (at the 1% level) liquidity indicator, negatively affecting rouble CB

Table 6.4 The Russian market: the bank CB sample descriptive statistics

Variable	*Obs*	*Mean*	*Std.Dev.*	*Min*	*Max*
ln_ytm	343	2.250	0.225	1.568	2.933
ln_spread	339	1.277	0.454	0.282	2.458
ln_trade_volume	343	9.617	6.393	0	19.583
non_zero_days	343	8.152	8.070	0	22
bid_ask	272	0.069	0.106	0.0002	0.405
illiq	202	19.805	24.462	0	60
ln_issue_volume	343	22.397	0.816	19.34	25.11
ln_dur	343	0.925	0.515	0.046	2.383
repo_eligible	343	0.592	0.492	0	1
ln_total_assets	343	13.151	1.803	9.286	17.253
deposits_equity	343	6.691	3.956	0.368	15
ln_roe	343	3.486	0.532	2.303	4.382
public	343	0.294	0.456	0	1
dummy_2018	343	0.353	0.479	0	1
dummy_2017	343	0.341	0.475	0	1

YTM and spreads of both banks and non-financial companies (Table 6.6, 6.7). The result coincides with the conclusions of Helwege et al. (2014) on the American CB market, and Shin and Kim (2015) on the CB market of the South Korea.

For CBs of non-financial companies, the issue volume is also significant: its effect on YTM and its spread is negative and significant at the 1% level (Table 6.6). This result coincides with the conclusions of Helwege et al. (2014) on the US market, Shin and Kim (2015) on the South Korean market. On the contrary, for bank CBs, the issue volume is statistically insignificant, and the direction of its influence is unstable (Table 6.7).

The influence of Amihud's illiquidity measure on the YTM and its spread for both samples is positive, but the statistical significance at the 10% level is observed only for bank CBs. The conclusion about the positive impact of this indicator coincides with the results of Han and Zhou (2016), Hafner and Walders (2017) for the US corporate market, and Aquilina and Suntheim (2017) for the UK market.

We note a positive, but statistically insignificant effect of the bid-ask spread on the spread of the YTM to the risk-free rate for non-financial companies and banks. A similar positive direction of influence is identified by Han and Zhou (2016) for the US market, and Febi et al. (2018) for the European market of green bonds.

A paradoxical result is that the number of days with a non-zero trading volume positively affects the spread (Table 6.6, 6.7). This finding contradicts the results of Chen et al. (2007) and Hafner and Walders (2017) for the US CB market. We attribute this to the fact that the number of non-zero trading days on the Russian market is a less reliable indicator of liquidity than the trading volume. Huberman and Stanzl (2005) find that in illiquid markets, especially during crises, investors

Table 6.5 The Indian market: the CB sample descriptive statistics

	N	*Mean*	*St. Dev.*	*Min*	*Max*
YTM and spread of CBs					
ytm 2017	8854	8.535	1,015	0.008	20.406
ytm 2018	8854	8.874	5,630	-0.232	18.472
ytm 2019	8854	8.890	2,673	-0.863	19.601
spread 2017	8854	1.681	0.983	-2.236	13.77
spread 2018	8854	2.118	5,922	-6.816	63.403
spread 2019	8854	2.581	2,165	-8.948	93.429
Liquidity indicators of CBs					
bid_ask 2017	8854	0.004	0.004	0.0001	0.169
bid_ask 2018	8854	0.004	0.002	0.0001	0.028
bid_ask 2019	8854	0.003	0.002	-0.004	0.016
non_zero_days 2017	8854	18.51	2.119	1	19
non_zero_days 2018	8854	20.672	2.083	1	21
non_zero_days 2019	8854	18.779	1.650	1	19
Indicators of non-financial companies					
Sales 2016	1109	5 498.2	11 549.7	1.3	62 223.2
Sales 2017	1110	6 126.7	12 899.7	6.6	70 338.2
Sales 2018	1056	7 031.8	14 846.8	1.9	77 331.3
Indicators of banks					
Total Assets 2016	3310	23 411.5	50 710.2	30.8	461 022.5
Total Assets 2017	3305	27 310.9	57 953.6	39.4	533 993.8
Total Assets 2018	3179	31 007.2	61 147.7	36.9	542 465.0
Total Deposits 2016	803	46 099.4	62 633.4	1.6	338 078.6
Total Deposits 2017	789	54 772.9	74 178.0	1.5	402 970.7
Total Deposits 2018	778	57 810.1	75 498.1	1 188.5	408 326.7
Indicators of non-financial companies and banks					
Total Liabilities 2016	1324	8 187.2	10 686.2	7.4	55 116.2
Total Liabilities 2017	1328	9 597.2	12 947.9	9.5	69 537.7
Total Liabilities 2018	1236	10 779.2	14 833.9	14.3	78 426.3
Total Equity 2016	4679	2 832.4	4 795.9	0.0	34 733.4
Total Equity 2017	4679	3 218.6	5 571.9	-1 008.3	40 874.9
Total Equity 2018	4444	3 691.3	6 090.4	-3 907.8	44 025.9
public	10641	0.402	0.49	0	1
ROE 2016, %	2985	11.68	9.35	-33.35	57.90
ROE 2017, %	3017	12.37	9.32	-65.04	76.37
ROE 2018, %	2992	12.95	10.34	-109.13	48.74

seek to increase the number of transactions by breaking a larger deal into several smaller ones to reduce the impact on the price of traded instruments. As a result, the number of trading days for each instrument increases, which is not accompanied by a corresponding increase in trading volume. The domestic Russian market of corporate bonds is characterized by low liquidity indicators, and since 2016, a trend towards a significant increase in the number of transactions has been observed in the rouble CB market, which has not been accompanied by an increase in the trading volume (see Table 6.8).

Table 6.6 The Russian market: the results for the non-financial company CBs

NumCalc	*1*	*2*	*3*	*4*
dependent	ln_ytm	ln_ytm	ln_spread	ln_spread
R^2	0.3647	0.342	0.4741	0.3495
Adjusted R^2	0.3488	0.3264	0.4635	0.3341
Number of obs	780	780	504	778
_cons	3.5836***	2.6971***	3.8215***	2.4768***
	(0.1882)	(0.0821)	(0.3539)	(0.1626)
illiq			0.0001	
			(0.0004)	
liabil_ equity	0.0028**	0.0026*	0.013***	0.0017
	(0.0013)	(0.0014)	(0.0026)	(0.0027)
bid_ask			0.0017	
			(0.0595)	
ln_trade_ volume	-0.0121***	-0.0122***	-0.0269***	-0.0261***
	(0.0017)	(0.0017)	(0.0069)	(0.0034)
ln_dur	0.0384***	0.0288**	0.0225	0.0428
	(0.0136)	(0.0138)	(0.0281)	(0.0273)
ln_issue_ volume	-0.053***		-0.0688***	
	(0.0102)		(0.019)	
ln_sales	-0.0046	-0.0189***	-0.0377***	-0.0526***
	(0.0055)	(0.0048)	(0.0096)	(0.0096)
non_zero_ days	0.0062***	0.0064***	0.0117***	0.014***
	(0.0013)	(0.0014)	(0.0025)	(0.0027)
public	0.0297*	0.0266	0.0077	0.0374
	(0.018)	(0.0183)	(0.0325)	(0.0363)
repo	-0.1419***	-0.1672***	-0.2676***	-0.332***
	(0.0193)	(0.019)	(0.0389)	(0.0377)
dummy_ 2017	0.1422***	0.1376***		0.1051***
	(0.0194)	(0.0197)		(0.039)
dummy_ 2018	-0.0288	-0.0334*		0.118***
	(0.0179)	(0.0182)		(0.0361)
dummy_ machine	0.068**	0.0621*		0.1528**
	(0.0341)	(0.0346)		(0.0693)
dummy_ metals	0.0497	0.043		0.1371**
	(0.0335)	(0.0341)		(0.0675)

Significance levels: * p <10%, ** p <5%, *** p <1%

The expected results are obtained for most of the control variables. For example, the YTM and its spread increase with an increase in the duration. This indicator is significant at the 5% level in most model specifications for CBs of non-financial companies and at the 10% level for bank CBs. The result is consistent with the findings of Bai et al. (2019) for the US market.

The inclusion of a bond issue in the Lombard list of the Bank of Russia has a negative and significant at the 1% level effect on the YTM and its spread, which is consistent with the results of Teplova et al. (2016) for the Russian market.

The larger the size of the issuer (both the non-financial company and the bank), the lower the YTM and its spread (the 'too big to fail' effect). In almost all model specifications, this factor is significant at the 1% level. This conclusion is consistent with the results of Teplova and Sokolova (2019).

Table 6.7 The Russian market: the results for bank CBs

NumCalc	*1*	*2*	*3*	*4*
dependent	ln_ytm	ln_ytm	ln_spread	ln_spread
R^2	0.4902	0.4115	0.3771	0.4362
Adjusted R^2	0.4578	0.392	0.344	0.3966
Number of obs	202	343	199	199
_cons	2.6155***	2.1608***	3.522***	2.7174***
	(0.4457)	(0.3075)	(0.9521)	(0.9423)
bid_ask	-0.1112		0.2838	0.2221
	(0.1894)		(0.4353)	(0.4312)
Illiq	0.001*		0.0021**	0.0015
	(0.0005)		(0.0011)	(0.0011)
ln_dur	0.0207	0.0485**	-0.0211	0.0214
	(0.0268)	(0.0194)	(0.057)	(0.056)
ln_trade_ volume	-0.0125***	-0.0085***		-0.0403***
	(0.0045)	(0.0026)		(0.0116)
ln_roe	0.08***	0.0616***	0.1488**	0.1631***
	(0.0288)	(0.0209)	(0.0613)	(0.0609)
ln_issue_ volume	-0.0042	0.0129	-0.0695	-0.0297
	(0.0207)	(0.0147)	(0.0443)	(0.0439)
ln_total_ assets	-0.0456***	-0.0404***	-0.1153***	-0.1033***
	(0.0088)	(0.0073)	(0.0188)	(0.0184)
non_zero_ days		0.0033	-0.0013	0.0106*
		(0.002)	(0.0047)	(0.0056)
public	0.1044***	0.0781***	0.2749***	0.2458***
	(0.0271)	(0.0232)	(0.0582)	(0.0564)
repo_ eligible	-0.0917***	-0.1263***	-0.1758***	-0.192***
	(0.025)	(0.0219)	(0.0532)	(0.0525)
deposits_ equity	0.0188***	0.015***	0.0477***	0.0413***
	(0.0042)	(0.0029)	(0.0089)	(0.0087)
dummy_ 2017	0.2177***	0.2186***		0.2214***
	(0.0316)	(0.0263)		(0.0669)
dummy_ 2018	0.0088	0.0117		0.162**
	(0.0318)	(0.0244)		(0.0665)

Significance levels: * $p < 10\%$, ** $p < 5\%$, *** $p < 1\%$

Table 6.8 The Russian corporate bond market: the dynamics of the number of transactions and the trading volume (in the main and negotiated mode on the Moscow Exchange and SPEX)

Year	*Number of transactions (thousand)*	*Trading volume, bn Rub.*
2016	486.3	4 650
2017	702.3	5 495
2018	1 000.3	3 331
Jan.–Sept. 2019	1 447.9	1 809

Source: Cbonds.

The issuer's debt burden has a significant positive effect on the YTM and its spread, which is consistent with the findings of Casteuble et al. (2013) and Lester and Kumar (2014).

ROE has a significant positive effect on the YTM and its spread of bank CBs. This finding contradicts the results of Lester and Kumar (2014), and Teplova and Sokolova (2019), but coincides with the conclusions of Balasubramnian and Cyree (2011). Our explanation is that investors interpret the increased return rate on capital as a signal that the issuer is taking additional risks.

Among industry dummies, the dummies of the company's affiliation to the engineering and metallurgical industries are positively significant. We attribute this to the fact that the systematic risk for companies in pro-cyclical sectors is also observed in the bond market. Dummies of 2017 and 2018 have a significant positive effect on CB spreads for non-financial companies and banks. We attribute this to the Bank of Russia's policy of consistently reducing the key rate.

An interesting conclusion is that a higher spread is observed for public companies, although this indicator is statistically significant only for the sample of bank CBs. Our explanation is that due to limited funds, investors in growing emerging markets prefer to invest in the stock market rather than in the bond market. As a result, public company spreads increase. For private companies, investors buy bonds of that company, if the demand for CBs is larger and the yield and spread are lower.

For the Indian bond market, the results are presented in Tables 6.9 and 6.10. For non-financial companies the bid-ask spread significantly positively affects the

Table 6.9 The Indian market: the results for the non-financial company CBs

	ytm	*ytm*	*spread*
	(1)	*(2)*	*(3)*
bid_ask	-4.232		
	(13.366)		
non_zero_days		0.045**	-3.485*
		(0.018)	(2.021)
dur		0.039***	-8.299***
		(0.011)	(1.319)
amount_issued	-0.025	-0.011	0.191
	(0.016)	(0.010)	(1.182)
ln_sales	-0.146***		
	(0.037)		
ln_total_equity		-0.283***	-24.391***
		(0.021)	(2.393)
ROE	-0.015***	-0.010***	-1.161***
	(0.002)	(0.002)	(0.244)
Constant	13.292***	15.438***	949.474***
	(1.081)	(0.714)	(82.161)
Number of obs	678	810	810
R^2	0.488	0.608	0.586
Adjusted R^2	0.468	0.595	0.571

Significance levels: * p <10%, ** p <5%, *** p <1%

Table 6.10 The Indian market: the results for the financial company CBs

	ytm	*ytm*	*spread*
	(1)	*(2)*	*(3)*
bid_ask	56.058***		
	(7.946)		
non_zero_ days		-0.115***	-19.097***
		(0.015)	(1.578)
dur		0.092***	-2.808***
		(0.009)	(0.931)
amount_issued	-0.054***	-0.042***	-3.089***
	(0.008)	(0.009)	(0.949)
ln_total_equity	-0.229***		-24.422***
	(0.019)		(2.200)
ln_total_assets		-0.222***	
		(0.020)	
public	0.332***	0.241***	22.748**
	(0.081)	(0.091)	(9.952)
ROE	-0.007***	-0.005**	-0.025
	(0.002)	(0.002)	(0.202)
Constant	15.299***	17.588***	1263.879***
	(0.494)	(0.649)	(67.544)
Number of obs	2196	1886	1908
R^2	0.165	0.166	0.182
Adjusted R^2	0.161	0.162	0.177

Significance levels: * p <10%, ** p <5%, *** p <1%

YTM which coincides with the results of Han and Zhou (2016) and Febi et al. (2018) for the US and the European market. The number of days with trades significantly decreases the spread on bonds of non-financial and financial companies and the YTM of bonds of financial companies. Our results are in line with Chen et al. (2007) and Hafner and Walders (2017) who reveal a negative impact of non-zero trading volume days for US bond spreads. Amount issued significantly negatively affects the YTM and its spread of bonds of financial companies.

We also conclude that the size of a company and ROE significantly negatively affect the YTM and its spread for both samples (Tables 6.9, 6.10). Investors follow the principle 'too big to fail'. This conclusion is consistent with the results of Teplova and Sokolova (2019) for the Russian bond market. Investors also consider higher ROE as a positive signal.

Conclusion

We analyze the influence of liquidity indicators on the YTM and its spread in the Indian and Russian CB market after the crisis in the oil market of 2014–2015. We use various liquidity indicators: the trading volume, the number of days with non-zero trading volume, the bid-ask spread, Amihud's measure, and the bond issue volume. Multivariate linear regressions are used to test the hypotheses. The sample includes LCY CBs of non-financial companies and banks that were outstanding in the market in April 2017, 2018, and 2019.

For the Russian bond market, we reveal that the set of key determinants of YTM and its spread is different in the samples of non-financial companies and banks. The most significant liquidity indicator that negatively affects the YTM and its spread of rouble CBs in both samples is the trading volume. For CBs of non-financial companies, the issue volume is also negatively significant. We reveal a positive significant effect of Amihud's measure for the bank CBs. The influence of the bid-ask spread for both CB samples is positive, although the statistical significance is not high.

For the Russian bond market, we obtain the original result that the number of days with non-zero trading volume positively affects the CB spread for both samples. We attribute this to the fact that after the crisis of 2014–2015, liquidity in the rouble-denominated market is decreasing, trading volumes are showing a downward trend, and bondholders seek to compensate for this effect by increasing the number of transactions to reduce the impact on the CB prices.

For the Russian bond market, the expected results are obtained for most of the control variables. The higher the duration, the higher the YTM and its spread. The level of debt burden and the issuer's affiliation to cyclical industries has a positive effect on the CB spread. The inclusion of a bond issue in the Bank of Russia's Lombard list and the size of the issuer negatively affect the spread. An interesting result is that the ROE has a significant positive effect on the YTM and its spread of bank CBs. We attribute this to the fact that investors interpret the increased return on capital as an acceptance of additional risk by the issuer.

A specific of the Indian LCY corporate bond market is the high share of OTC trades and lack of data on trading volume. We reveal that for non-financial companies the bid-ask spread significantly positively affects the YTM. The number of days with trades significantly decreases the spread on bonds of non-financial and financial companies and the YTM of bonds of financial companies. Amount issued significantly negatively affects the YTM and its spread of bonds of financial companies. The size of a company and ROE significantly negatively affect the YTM and its spread for both financial and non-financial companies.

Note

1 Testing of these indicators is shown in the monograph by Teplova et al. (2016). Since 2018, the calculation of the Thomson Reuters integrated liquidity indices has been discontinued.

References

Amihud, Y. (2002). Illiquidity and stock returns: Cross-section and time-series effects. *Journal of Financial Markets*, 5(1): 31–56. DOI: https://doi.org/10.1016/S1386-4181(01)00024-6

Amihud, Y., Mendelson, H. (1986). Asset pricing and the bid-ask spread. *Journal of Financial Economics*, 17(2): 223–249. DOI: https://doi.org/10.1016/0304-405X(86)90065-6

Aquilina, M., Suntheim, F. (2017). Liquidity in the U.K. corporate bond market: Evidence from Trade Data. *The Journal of Trading*, 12(4), 67–80. DOI: https://doi.org/10.3905/jot.2017.12.4.067

Aquilina, M., Suntheim, F. (2017). Liquidity in the UK corporate bond market: evidence from trade data. *The Journal of Trading*, 12(4), 67–80. DOI: https://doi.org/10.3905/jot.2017.12.4.067

Bai, J., Bali, T. G., Wen, Q. (2019). Common risk factors in the cross-section of corporate bond returns. *Journal of Financial Economics*, 131: 619–642. DOI: https://doi.org/10.1016/j.jfineco.2018.08.002

Balasubramnian, B., Cyree, K. B. (2011). Market discipline of banks: Why are yield spreads on bank-issued subordinated notes and debentures not sensitive to bank risks?. *Journal of Banking & Finance*, 35(1), 21–35. DOI: https://doi.org/10.1016/j.jbankfin.2010.07.015

Bao, J., Pan, J., Wang, J. (2011). The illiquidity of corporate bonds. *The Journal of Finance*, 66(3), 911–946. DOI: https://doi.org/10.1111/j.1540-6261.2011.01655.x

Bianchi, R. J., Drew, M. E., Roca, E., Whittaker, T. (2017). Risk factors in Australian bond returns. *Accounting and Finance*, 57: 373–400. DOI: https://doi.org/10.1111/acfi.12174

Boermans, M. A., Frost, J., Bisschop, S. S. (2016). European bond markets: Do illiquidity and concentration aggravate price shocks? *Economics Letters*, 141: 143–146. DOI: https://doi.org/10.1016/j.econlet.2016.02.023

Casteuble, C., Nys, E., Rous, P. (2013). Bank Risk-Return Efficiency and Bond Spread: Is There Evidence of Market Discipline in Europe, Working Papers, HAL.

Chaikun, A. N. (2010). Assessment of bond liquidity by the example of corporate and municipal sectors. PhD dissertation. In Russian.

Chen, L., Lesmond, D., Wei, J. (2007). Corporate yield spreads and bond liquidity. *Journal of Finance*, 62(1): 119–149. DOI: https://doi.org/10.1111/j.1540-6261.2007.01203.x

Febi, W. Schäfer, D., Stephan, A., Sun, C. (2018). The impact of liquidity risk on the yield spread of green bonds. *Finance Research Letters*, 27: 53–59. DOI: https://doi.org/10.1016/j.frl.2018.02.025

Hafner, C. M., Walders, F. (2017). Heterogeneous liquidity effects in corporate bond spreads. *Journal of Fixed Income*, 26(4): 73–91. DOI: https://doi.org/10.3905/jfi.2017.26.4.073

Han, S., Zhou, H. (2016). Effects of liquidity on the non-default component of corporate yield spreads: Evidence from Intraday Transactions Data. *Quarterly Journal of Finance*, 6(3): 1–49. DOI: https://doi.org/10.1142/S2010139216500129

Helwege, J., Huang, J. Z., Wang, Y. (2014). Liquidity effects in corporate bond spreads. *Journal of Banking and Finance*, 45: 105–116. DOI: https://doi.org/10.1016/j.jbankfin.2013.08.018

Huberman, G., Stanzl, W. (2005). Optimal liquidity trading. *Review of Finance*, 9(2), 165–200. DOI: https://doi.org/10.1007/s10679-005-7591-5

Kalimipalli, M., Nayak, S., Perez, M. F. (2013). Dynamic effects of idiosyncratic volatility and liquidity on corporate bond spreads. *Journal of Banking and Finance*, 37: 2969–2990. DOI: https://doi.org/10.1016/j.jbankfin.2013.04.019

Konstantinovsky, V., Kwok, Y., Phelps, B. (2016). Measuring bond-level liquidity. The *Journal of Portfolio Management*, 42(4): 116–128. DOI: https://doi.org/10.3905/jpm.2016.42.4.116

Lester, J., Kumar, A. (2014). Do Bond Spreads Show Evidence of Too Big To Fail Effects? *Oliver Wyman Financial Services*. WP

Longstaff, F. A., Mithal, S., Neis, S. (2005). Corporate yield spreads: Default risk or liquidity? New evidence from the credit default swap market. *The Journal of Finance*, LX(5): 2213–2253. DOI: https://doi.org/10.1111/j.1540-6261.2005.00797.x

Pastor, L., Stambaugh, R. (2003). Liquidity risk and expected stock returns. *Journal of Political Economy*, 111(3): 642–685. DOI: https://doi.org/10.1086/374184

Roll, R. (1984). A simple implicit measure of the effective bid-ask spread in an efficient market. *The Journal of Finance*, 39(4): 1127–1139. DOI: https://doi.org/10.1111/j.1540-6261.1984.tb03897.x

Schestag, R., Schuster, P., Uhrig-Homburg, M. (2016). Measuring liquidity in bond markets. *The Review of Financial Studies*, 29(5): 1170–1219. DOI: https://doi.org/10.1093/rfs/hhv132

Shin, D., Kim, B. (2015). Liquidity and credit risk before and after the global financial crisis: Evidence from the Korean corporate bond market. *Pacific-Basin Finance Journal*, 33: 38–61. DOI: https://doi.org/10.1016/j.pacfin.2015.03.003

Tarek, C. (2009). Default, liquidity and credit spread: Empirical evidence from structural model. *IUP Journal of Financial Risk Management*, 6(2): 46–61.

Teplova, T. V. et al. (2016). The Bond Market: Analysis of Trends and Perspectives. Ed. Teplova, T. V. INFRA-M, Moscow, Russia. In Russian.

Teplova, T. V., Sokolova, T. V. (2019). Surprises of corporate governance and Russian firms debt. *Journal of Economics and Business*, 102(March–April): 39–56. DOI: https://doi.org/10.1016/j.jeconbus.2018.10.001

Wang, J., Wu, C. (2015). Liquidity, credit quality, and the relation between volatility and trading activity: Evidence from the corporate bond market. *Journal of Banking and Finance*, 50: 183–203. DOI: https://doi.org/10.1016/j.jbankfin.2014.10.003

7 Determinants of bank bond spreads in Latin America

Introduction

Banks and bank holding companies both lead in terms of the volume of outstanding bonds. Therefore, it is logical that academia has placed considerable interest in the determinants of bond yields for financial sector companies, and in bondholders' risk assessment during the restructuring of financial sector companies. The 2007–2009 global financial crisis raised a whole spectrum of claims towards regulating the banking sectors in the US, EU and several other countries. For the last ten years, the banking sector experienced great changes that reflected on the processes concerning the accumulation of debt financing. Companies started to actively use subordinate instruments, issue securitized assets and impose additional conditions in issuance. However, there are still weak spots that could create new financial and economic crises.

Balasubramnian and Cyree (2011) came to the conclusion that bailing out the LTCM fund in the US had considerably worsened market discipline, especially for the bigger banks. The entry of the state into the banking capital was a necessary measure, and it is important to consistently decrease state intervention, both in decision-making at corporate level, and in the regulation of the banking sector. The authors also stress the importance of regulating the rules of disclosing off-balance sheet assets such as derivatives, in the financial statement, which could improve transparency and investors perception of the issuer's risk.

Our aim is to reveal the determinants of Latin-American bank bonds yield-to-maturity spread. For the first time, we investigate the effect of corporate governance, as well as several original factors – capital expenditure to assets ratio, and share of individual deposits in total liabilities on the spread of bank bonds from developing countries. The paper considers a sample of the 21 largest banks, in terms of market capitalization, with outstanding bonds during the period 2008–2018.

Literature review

Usually, research papers analyze the following groups of determinants of bank bond spreads: the characteristics of bond issues, the financial indicators of banks, macroeconomic indicators, and the introduction of new regulatory standards (Table 7.1).

The first papers were devoted to the US market (Martin, 1977; Jagtiani et al., 2002; Choi et al., 2010). An important factor is the Basel Accords (Resti and Sironi, 2007).

Table 7.1 Factors influencing bank bond spreads

Factor	*Research papers*
Issuer's financial indicators	
Size	Martin (1977), Alanis et al. (2015)
Interest coverage	Martin (1977)
Share of insured deposits	Jagtiani et al. (2002)
ROA	Jagtiani et al. (2002), Balasubramnian and Cyree (2011), Lester and Kumar (2014)
Reserves to loans	Choi et al. (2010)
Financial leverage	Evanoff et al. (2011), Zhang et al. (2014), Casteuble et al. (2013)
Current liquidity ratio	Zhang et al. (2014)
Off-balance accounts	Balasubramnian and Cyree (2011)
MV/BV	Lester and Kumar (2014)
Structure of liabilities: uninsured deposits	Alanis et al. (2015)
Issuer's non-financial indicators	
Participation in M&A and alliances	Hasan et al. (2018)
Bond issue characteristics	
Liquidity	Martin (1977)
Maturity	Martin (1977)
Credit rating	Jagtiani et al. (2002), Resti and Sironi (2007), Zhang et al. (2014), Zaghini (2014)
Subordinated debt	Sironi (2003), Evanoff et al. (2011)
Bid-ask spread	Lester and Kumar (2014)
Macroeconomic factors	
Unemployment rate	Evanoff et al. (2011)
Interest rates (US Treasury bill rates, LIBOR)	Evanoff et al. (2011), Zhang et al. (2014)
Stock index return rate	Zhang et al. (2014)
Stock exchange volatility	Alam (2012)
GDP growth rate	Casteuble et al. (2013)
CDS	Zaghini (2014)
Regulatory standards and institutional factors	
Markets in Financial Instruments Directive	Giudice (2017)
Basel Committee on Banking Supervision reforms	Sironi (2003)
Protection of investors' rights	Giudice (2017)

A lot of papers are devoted to subordinated debt (Balasubramnian and Cyree, 2011; Evanoff et al., 2011). Sironi (2003) concludes that subordinated debt reveals significant information about the issuer, for the investor, and therefore the policy on banks should be aimed at encouraging the issuance of subordinated obligations to improve market discipline, according to Basel.

Zhang et al. (2014) present a study on the UK market during the period 1997–2009. The authors obtain the following conclusions: a) the worse the credit rating, the larger the spread; b) the issuer's financial indicators are insignificant; c) the stock market indices are significant and positively correlate with the spread.

Casteuble et al. (2013) build an efficiency ratio in terms of the ratio of 'risk-return', estimated using the method of Stochastic Frontier Analysis (SFA), for a sample of European banks during the years 2001–2011. Then the authors assess the impact of the efficiency ratio on the bond spread and conclude that for more efficient banks, the spread is lower.

The following features of previous research can be distinguished: most of them are focused on researching the determinants of bank bond yields in developed markets, and there are few papers in which the determinants are analyzed for emerging markets. For several factors (for example, ROA, size of assets, credit rating), the results of previous studies contradict each other.

Unlike previous papers, the sample of our research consists of bank bonds from developing countries in Latin America. As explanatory variables, we consider not only the financial indicators of the issuing banks, but also indicators of the quality of corporate governance. We use both statistical (with fixed and random effects) and dynamic regression models (GMM) and check the results for stability.

Hypotheses regarding the determinants of the yield spread of bonds of Latin American banks

We put forward the following hypotheses regarding the impact of the characteristics of the bond issue and the issuing bank on the yield-to-maturity spread over the rate of inflation:

Hypothesis 1. The higher the bond duration, the higher the yield spread, since a longer period implies greater uncertainty for an investor when buying this bond.

Hypothesis 2. The higher the quality of corporate governance, the lower the yield spread of bank bonds.

The size of the board of directors and the percentage of independent directors are selected as proxy variables of corporate governance quality. We assume that a larger board of directors and a higher proportion of independent directors allow directors to create more effective control over the actions of management and smooth out agency conflicts.

Hypothesis 3. The higher the debt load (measured by the ratio of assets to equity, the share of long-term borrowing in assets, and the ratio of interest payments to liabilities), the higher the yield spread.

We attribute this to the fact that a higher level of debt burden entails a higher risk of default.

Hypothesis 4. Profitability, measured by ROE, has a significant effect on the yield spread of bank bonds.

We assume that the effect of ROE on the spread may be ambiguous. On the one hand, a bank's higher profitability is associated by investors with more risky operations and, accordingly, they require an increased yield on bonds. On the other hand, higher profitability indicates an increase in free cash flow and thus reduces the risk of default on bonds.

Hypothesis 5. The larger the size of the bank (measured by the logarithm of total assets and market capitalization), the lower the yield spread.

We explain this by the fact that a larger bank is more resistant to external risks and can cope with them more effectively, as well as the principle of 'too big to fail'.

Hypothesis 6. The higher the share of term deposits, the lower the yield spread on bank bonds.

We assume that a higher proportion of term deposits contributes to improving the financial stability and liquidity of the bank's balance sheet (by ensuring compliance with the terms of placement and attraction of funds), which reduces the yield spread.

Hypothesis 7. The share of customer deposits in assets has a positive effect on the yield spread of bank bonds.

We assume that a high proportion of customer deposits is a risk factor, since in crisis situations depositors may be prone to panic and try to close deposits at the same time.

Hypothesis 8. The ratio of market capitalization to book value of equity (MVE/BVE) significantly increases the yield spread of bank bonds.

We assume that the effect of the MVE/BVE multiplier may be ambiguous. On the one hand, higher values of MVE/BVE indicate a positive assessment of the bank's financial position and growth prospects by investors which allows a reduction in the yield spread on bonds. On the other hand, high MVE/BVE values may signal that the company is overvalued, and therefore bondholders will demand higher returns for the risk of reducing the enterprise value.

Hypothesis 9. The ratio of capital expenditures to assets decreases the yield spread of bank bonds.

Table 7.2 The description of the variables

Variable	*Description*	*Expected sign*	*Comment*
y	Dependent variable: spread between the weighted average yield to maturity on outstanding bonds of the issuing bank to the inflation rate		
mac_dur	Weighted average duration on bank bonds outstanding	+	As shown by Evanoff et al. (2011), Casteuble et al. (2013), Zaghini (2014), Teplova and Sokolova (2018), the longer the maturity, the higher the yield spread on bank bonds
indep_directors	Share of independent directors (of total board members)	-	As shown by Andres and Vallelado, (2008), a higher percentage of independent directors correlates positively with the financial performance of banks. We assume that a higher proportion of independent directors creates more effective control over the actions of management and smooths out agency conflicts, and consequently, reduces the cost of debt.
board_size	Board size	-	Anderson et al. (2004) revealed a negative correlation between the number of board members and the cost of debt for non-financial companies. We assume that a similar relationship holds for banks.
assets_equity	The ratio of assets to equity of the bank	+	As shown by Martin (1977), Casteuble et al. (2013), Lester and Kumar (2014), higher debt burden indicators (in particular, higher financial leverage) lead to an increase in the yield spread on bank bonds.
interest_liabil	The ratio of interest payments to liabilities	+	
ltborrow_assets	The share of long-term liabilities in assets, %	+	
normalized_roe	Return on equity of the bank, %	+ / -	On the one hand, Jagtiani et al. (2002), Lester and Kumar (2014) found that with an increase in ROA, the yield spread decreases: higher bank profitability rates are a positive signal for bondholders. Teplova and Sokolova (2018) obtained a similar conclusion regarding ROE.

			On the other hand, as shown by Balasubramnian and Cyree (2011), the correlation between spread and ROA is positive, as investors are confident that additional income is possible only by taking additional risks.
marketcap_equity	The ratio of market capitalization to book value of equity	+ / -	On the one hand, Lester and Kumar (2014) found that banks with a higher MVE / BVE ratio are characterized by lower bond spreads. On the other hand, high MVE / BVE values may be a signal that the company is overvalued; therefore, bondholders will demand higher returns.
ln_assets	Logarithm of assets (expressed in millions of dollars)	-	As shown by Martin (1977), Lester and Kumar (2014), Teplova and Sokolova (2018), larger and systemically important banks are characterized by lower spreads on bonds.
ln_marketcap	Logarithm of market capitalization (in millions of dollars)	-	
timedeposit_liabil	The share of term deposits in liabilities, %	-	We assume that a higher proportion of term deposits contributes to improving the financial stability and liquidity of the bank's balance sheet, which reduces the yield spread.
customerdeposits_liabil	The share of customer deposits in liabilities, %	+	Alanis et al. (2015) show that a higher ratio of deposits to assets raises the spread on bank bonds.
capexpend_assets	Capital expenditures to assets, %	+ / -	On the one hand, higher capital expenditures may be associated with a higher risk of investment and reduce the bank's free cash flow, which can be a negative signal for bondholders. On the other hand, higher capital expenditures can be a signal of the expansion of the bank's activities, which, on the contrary, is positively perceived by investors.

We assume that the impact of capital expenditures on the yield spread on bonds may be uncertain. On the one hand, higher capital expenditures may be associated with a higher risk of investment and reduce the bank's free cash flow. Bondholders perceive this fact negatively and demand greater profitability. On the other hand, higher capital expenditures can be a signal of the expansion of the bank's activities; for example, the opening of new branches and offices and the implementation of large-scale investment projects, which is positively perceived by investors.

The description of variables is given in Table 7.2.

The methodology of our study

The specifications of the models with random and fixed effects are the following:

$$y = \alpha + \beta_1 \cdot mac\_dur + \sum \beta_{2,k} \cdot FinIndicator_k + \sum \beta_{3,l} \cdot CorpGov_l + u + \varepsilon \quad (7.1)$$

where y is the explained variable (see Table 7.2), $FinIndicator_k$ is a financial indicator of the bond issuer, and $CorpGov_l$ is an indicator of the quality of corporate governance of the bond issuer.

Due to the potential endogeneity of variables, we also test dynamic models on the basis of the GMM introduced by Holtz-Eakin et al. (1990), Arellano and Bond (1991), and Arellano and Bover (1995):

$$y_{i,t} = \alpha \cdot y_{i,t-1} + \beta_0 \cdot X_{i,t} + \mu_i + \varepsilon_{i,t} \quad (7.2)$$

$$y_{i,t} - y_{i,t-1} = \alpha \cdot (y_{i,t-1} - y_{i,t-2}) + \beta_0 \cdot (X_{i,t} - X_{i,t-1}) + \varepsilon_{i,t} - \varepsilon_{i,t-1} \quad (7.3)$$

The moment conditions are the following:

$$\begin{aligned} &E[y_{i.,t-s}(\varepsilon_{i,t} - \varepsilon_{i,t-1})] = 0, \ for \ s \geq 2; \ t = 3,\ldots,T \\ &E[X_{i,t-s}(\varepsilon_{i,t} - \varepsilon_{i,t-1})] = 0, \ for \ s \geq 2; \ t = 3,\ldots,T \end{aligned} \quad (7.4)$$

$$\begin{aligned} &E[(y_{i.,t-s} - y_{i,t-s-1})(\mu_i + \varepsilon_{i,t})] = 0, \ for \ s = 1 \\ &E[(X_{i,t-s} - X_{i,t-s-1})(\mu_i + \varepsilon_{i,t})] = 0, \ for \ s = 1 \end{aligned} \quad (7.5)$$

where $y_{i,t}$ is a dependent variable, i and t are the company and time period respectively, $X_{i,t}$ is a vector of explanatory variables (see Table 7.2), μ_i is an observed company-specific effect, and $\varepsilon_{i,t}$ is the error term.

In order to correctly construct the specifications of the above regression models, we check for the multicollinearity of the included factors. The choice of regressors for simultaneous inclusion in the model is carried out considering the correlation matrix.

Table 7.3 Descriptive statistics on the sample

Variable	*Obs*	*Mean*	*Std.Dev.*	*Min*	*Max*
y	167	5.2880	1.6036	1.7183	10.2787
indep_directors	152	49.3404	18.5958	10.0000	88.8890
board_size	166	9.4096	2.7171	4.0000	15.0000
normalized_roe	167	18.1332	25.1325	-79.6044	182.4510
assets_equity	167	7.5517	4.0849	1.0581	18.4411
mac_dur	167	3.7654	1.9927	0.0190	8.2160
marketcap_equity	167	2.4032	2.5913	0.2872	18.4501
ln_assets	167	9.7274	1.1932	6.7434	11.2499
ln_marketcap	167	8.5494	0.9947	6.1939	10.1163
interest_liabil	127	0.0296	0.0192	0.0009	0.1107
timedeposit_liabil	102	0.2853	0.0829	0.1106	0.4552
ltborrow_assets	163	0.1573	0.1223	0.0032	0.6163
customerdeposits_liabil	113	0.6906	0.1103	0.4592	0.9141
capexpend_assets	151	-0.0081	0.0297	-0.3446	-0.0001

Descriptive statistics for a sample of Latin American banking bonds

The research sample includes outstanding bonds in national currencies for the 21 largest banks in terms of market capitalization from Latin America (Brazil, Mexico, Colombia, Chile, Argentina, Trinidad and Tobago). To solve the problem of a potential sample bias for each bank, for each year a weighted average yield to maturity for outstanding bonds (as of April–May of each year) and a weighted average duration are calculated. Data on bonds is collected from the database of Refinitiv Eikon. The absence of YTM for several bonds led to a reduction in the final sample to 167 observations.

Data on the financial performance and corporate governance indicators of the issuing banks is collected from the Bloomberg database, due to the wider coverage of financial data in the Bloomberg database compared to Eikon. We consider the period from 2008 to 2018, including the period of the global financial crisis of 2008–2009 and the period of instability in the global commodity markets of 2014–2015.

Before building a regression, observations with extreme values of the YTM-to-inflation spread (over 11%) are excluded from the sample. Table 7.3 shows descriptive statistics for the sample.

Results of testing regression models

The results of testing GMM models are presented in Table 7.4, and models with fixed and random effects are shown in Table 7.5. When identifying different areas of the influence of factors, we prefer GMM models, since they allow for the potential endogeneity of variables to be considered.

Table 7.4 Calculation results. GMM models

	1	*2*	*3*	*4*	*5*	*6*	*7*
Wald	63.37	47.47	85.65	93.77	62.15	65.23	67.15
L1	0.0037 (0.1519)	0.1372 (0.1636)	-0.0167 (0.148)	-0.3249** (0.1627)	-0.1099 (0.1654)	0.1223 (0.144)	-0.0184 (0.1645)
constant	-0.7593 (3.2755)	1.5231 (2.7261)	-1.0881 (3.304)	2.7132 (3.2037)	25.2281*** (5.9853)	14.1994** (6.3604)	-1.9955 (2.1832)
interest_liabil			46.3672*** (17.183)	37.7194** (15.1175)	16.3617 (17.7539)	53.9818** (22.9434)	26.8285* (15.2577)
timedeposit_liabil		5.2609** (2.4395)			2.0547 (2.9075)	-4.3025 (3.1128)	
ltborrow_assets						-2.4509 (2.3386)	
customerdeposits _liabil	7.8522*** (2.7742)		3.8086 (3.046)	5.5835** (2.6855)			5.7749** (2.9526)
capexpend_assets	-50.775 (37.5871)	-29.4717 (38.9656)		-91.6485** (37.1153)			
indep_directors			-0.0029 (0.0113)			-0.0265** (0.0131)	
board_size				-0.2717*** (0.102)	-0.3365*** (0.1024)		
normalized_roe	0.1007*** (0.0286)	0.0957*** (0.0278)	0.089*** (0.0292)	0.0894*** (0.0266)			0.0954*** (0.0285)
assets_equity							0.0288 (0.0707)
mac_dur	0.1266 (0.0791)	0.0351 (0.0812)	0.2317*** (0.0852)	0.2548*** (0.0805)	0.0882 (0.0892)	0.0332 (0.1143)	0.1699** (0.0852)
marketcap_equity					0.1326 (0.1722)	-0.0459 (0.1912)	0.014 (0.1815)
ln_assets					-1.6842*** (0.5025)	-0.7637 (0.5593)	
ln_marketcap	-0.2087 (0.2684)	-0.04 (0.2644)	0.0535 (0.2618)	-0.09 (0.2471)			
Number of obs	79	70	66	76	71	59	79

Significance levels: * p <10%, ** p <5%, *** p <1%

Table 7.5 Calculation results. Models with random and fixed effects

	1	*2*	*3*	*4*	*5*	*6*
Type of model	RE	RE	RE	FE	RE	RE
R^2 within	0.4491	0.3292	0.4434	0.4863	0.2948	0.4495
R^2 between	0.0391	0.4819	0.0014	0.0038	0.7802	0.0216
R^2 overall	0.0559	0.5190	0.0031	0.0248	0.6210	0.0438
constant	7.3235** (3.4494)	3.7598 (4.4473)	7.9978** (3.6562)	29.8254*** (8.2463)	17.512*** (3.3366)	1.8932 (2.5767)
interest_liabil		31.4278** (13.0529)	-5.2641 (14.0547)	-29.9777 (29.6399)	38.6456*** (9.9713)	4.9115 (10.7073)
timedeposit_liabil				0.4875 (4.4458)	-9.9492*** (2.3212)	
ltborrow_assets					-3.5588 (2.6568)	
customerdeposits _liabil	0.1972 (3.2592)	-4.7617** (2.3101)	1.7927 (3.0438)			1.8567 (2.8291)
capexpend_assets	-77.4998* (47.0461)					
indep_directors		0.0283* (0.0162)				
board_size			-0.0952 (0.0962)	-0.2448** (0.0966)		
normalized_roe	0.0825** (0.0339)	0.0872*** (0.0323)	0.0918** (0.0365)			0.0876** (0.0362)
assets_equity						0.1284 (0.1113)
mac_dur	-0.0399 (0.2323)	0.2365* (0.1404)	-0.0569 (0.241)	-0.3642* (0.1844)	-0.3756** (0.158)	-0.053 (0.2345)
marketcap_equity				0.1415 (0.2092)	-0.0546 (0.341)	-0.0378 (0.167)
ln_assets				-1.7187* (0.8394)	-0.7264*** (0.2025)	
ln_marketcap	-0.3662 (0.3415)	-0.0112 (0.405)	-0.3982 (0.4112)			
Year dummies	yes					
Number of obs	109	95	109	99	100	110

Significance levels: * p <10%, ** p <5%, *** p <1%

In our research, for the first time, the influence of the quality of corporate governance on the yield spread of banking bonds in Latin America has been studied. We conclude that a larger size of board of directors and a higher percentage of independent directors contribute to a decrease in the yield spread. The size of the board of directors has a higher statistical significance and a stable direction of influence, regardless of the type of regression model being tested. This conclusion is in line with the results of Andres and Vallelado (2008) and Anderson et al. (2004) for non-financial companies.

The greater the amount of assets and market capitalization of the bank, the lower is the bond yield spread, with a significance level higher for the amount of assets variable. This result is obtained according to both GMM models and FE and RE models, and it is consistent with the findings of Jagtiani et al. (2002), Lester and Kumar (2014), and Teplova and Sokolova (2018).

We also obtain a paradoxical result that banks with higher ROE demonstrate a higher yield spread of bank bonds. We explain this by the fact that, from the viewpoint of bondholders, a higher level of profitability is evidence of highly risky operations carried out by banks. This result contradicts the conclusions of Jagtiani et al. (2002), Lester and Kumar (2014), and Teplova and Sokolova (2018), but coincides with the findings of Balasubramnian and Cyree (2011).

According to GMM models, such indicators of debt burden as the ratio of interest paid to liabilities and the ratio of assets to equity have a significant positive effect on the yield spread. In the FE and RE models, the direction of influence of the variable *interest_liabil* is unstable, but only the coefficients with a positive sign are significant. The variable *assets_equity* has a positive effect, but its statistical significance is low. These results are consistent with the findings of Casteuble et al. (2013), and Lester and Kumar (2014). The impact of the third variable – the share of long-term liabilities in the assets – is not statistically significant; different patterns of influence are revealed in different models.

We conclude that a higher proportion of customer deposits in total liabilities contributes to an increase in the spread of bond yields (according to the GMM models). This result is consistent with the findings of Alanis et al. (2015).

The original conclusion of our research is that the impact of capital expenditure to assets ratio on the yield spread is negative. The direction of influence is stable in various specifications of models. We attribute this to the fact that realization of large investment projects is a welcome signal for investors.

The impact of the share of time deposits in liabilities and the ratio of market capitalization to book value of equity are not significant: the direction of influence varies in different specifications and its significance is not high.

According to GMM models, the greater the duration, the higher is the yield spread of bank bonds. This is consistent with the results of Robbins and Kim (2003), Evanoff et al. (2011), Casteuble et al. (2013), Zaghini (2014), and Teplova and Sokolova (2018). In the case of FE and RE models, this effect is not detected: the sign of the variable *mac_dur* is unstable and mostly negative.

Conclusion

By employing GMM models, as well as models with fixed and random effects, we analyze the determinants of yield-to-maturity spreads on bank bonds of Latin America during the period from 2008 to 2018. For the first time, the impact of corporate governance quality, as well as a number of original factors – the ratio of capital expenditures to assets, and the share of term deposits in liabilities – are investigated for the segment of banking bonds in emerging markets.

Bigger board size and higher percentage of independent directors contribute to reduction in the yield spread of bank bonds.

A higher ratio of capital expenditures to assets leads to a decrease in the yield spread of bank bonds. We explain this phenomenon by the fact that for bondholders the implementation of large-scale investment projects by the bank is a favourable signal.

An unexpected result of our empirical research is that banks with higher profitability (measured by ROE) demonstrate higher yield spread on bank bonds. Our explanation is that from the point of bondholders, higher level of profitability indicates that banks carry out high-risk operations.

It is revealed that indicators of the debt burden, the share of customer deposits in total liabilities, term to maturity, and the amount of the bank assets also are significant determinants of the spread of yield of bank bonds in Latin America. The impact of the share of time deposits in liabilities is insignificant.

References

Alam, N. (2012). Linkage between stock volatility and corporate bond yield spread in Singapore. *International Journal of Financial Management*, 2(2): 1–10.

Alanis, E., Beladi, H., Quijano, M. (2015). Uninsured deposits as a monitoring device: Their impact on bond yields of banks. *Journal of Banking & Finance*, 52(C): 77–88. DOI: https://doi.org/10.1016/j.jbankfin.2014.11.015

Andres, P., Vallelado, E. (2008). Corporate governance in banking: The role of the board of directors. *Journal of Banking and Finance*, 32(12): 2570–2580. DOI: https://doi.org/10.1016/j.jbankfin.2008.05.008

Balasubramian, B., Cyree, K. (2011). Market discipline of banks: Why are yield spreads on bank-issued subordinated notes and debentures not sensitive to bank risks? *Journal of Banking and Finance*, 35(1): 21–35. DOI: https://doi.org/10.1016/j.jbankfin.2010.07.015

Casteuble, C., Nys, E., Rous, P. (2013). Bank risk – return efficiency and bond spread: Is there evidence of market discipline in Europe. <hal-00916717> DOI: 10.2139/ssrn.2232889

Choi, S., Francis, B., Hasan, I. (2010). Cross-border bank M&As and risk: Evidence from the bond market. *Journal of Money, Credit and Banking*, 42(4): 615–645. DOI: https://doi.org/10.1111/j.1538-4616.2010.00301.x

Evanoff, D., Jagtiani, J., Nakata, T. (2011). Enhancing market discipline in banking: The role of subordinated debt in financial regulatory reform. *Journal of Economics and Business*, 63(1): 1–22. DOI: https://doi.org/10.1016/j.jeconbus.2010.07.001

Giudice, A. (2017). Impact of the Market in Financial Instruments Directive (MiFID) on the Italian financial market: Evidence from bank bonds. *Journal of Banking Regulation*, 18: 256–267. DOI: https://doi.org/10.1057/s41261-016-0035-7

Hasan, I., Meslier, C., Taraz, A., Zhou, M. (2018). Does it pay to get connected? An examination of bank alliance network and bond spread. *Journal of Economics and Business*, 95: 141–163. DOI: https://doi.org/10.1016/j.jeconbus.2017.12.003

Jagtiani J., Kaufman, G., Lemieux, C. (2002). The effect of credit risk on bank and bank holding company bond yields: Evidence from the post-FDICIA period. *Journal of Financial Research*, 25(4): 559–575. DOI: https://doi.org/10.1111/1475-6803.00037

Lester, J., Kumar, A. (2014). Do bond spreads show evidence of too big to fail effects? Evidence from 2009–2013 among US bank holding companies. Marsh & McLennan Companies. DOI: https://dx.doi.org/10.2139/ssrn.2422769

Martin, M. (1977). Risk premiums and bank bond investors. *Atlantic Economic Journal*, 5(2): 68–72. DOI: https://doi.org/10.1007/BF02300312

Penas, M., Unal, H. (2004). Gains in bank mergers: Evidence from the bond markets. *Journal of Financial Economics*, 74(1): 149–179. DOI: https://doi.org/10.1016/j.jfineco.2003.05.004

Resti, A., Sironi, A. (2007). The risk-weights in the New Basel Capital Accord: Lessons from bond spreads based on a simple structural model. *Journal of Financial Intermediation*, 16(1): 64–90. DOI: https://doi.org/10.1016/j.jfi.2006.04.002

Robbins, M., Kim, D. (2003). Do state bond banks have cost advantages for municipal bond issuance? *Public Budgeting and Finance*, 23(3): 92–108. DOI: https://doi.org/10.1111/1540-5850.2303005

Sironi, A. (2003). Testing for market discipline in the European banking industry: Evidence from subordinated debt issues. *Journal of Money, Credit and Banking*, 35(3): 443–472.

Teplova, T. V., Sokolova, T. V. (2018). Research fields of bond markets. INFRA-M. Russia, Moscow. (In Rus.)

Zaghini, A. (2014). Bank bonds: Size, systemic relevance and the sovereign. *International Finance*, 17(2): 161–184. DOI: https://doi.org/10.1111/infi.12050

Zhang, Z., Song, W., Sun, X., Shi, N. (2014). Subordinated debt as instrument of market discipline: Risk sensitivity of sub-debt yield spreads in UK banking. *Journal of Economics and Business*, 73: 1–21. DOI: https://doi.org/10.1016/j.jeconbus.2013.11.002

8 Specifics of pricing of corporate bonds with embedded put and call options

Introduction

Callable bonds represent a hedging mechanism for bond issuers. They allow issuers to pay off bonds before maturity, for example, when interest rates are decreasing, thus allowing the issue of bonds with lower coupon rates. Such bonds consist of a non-callable bond and a call option. The seller of the option is the investor, who buys the bond from the issuer.

The possibility of a call by the issuer entails certain risk for the bondholder, since the call date is unknown, while the redemption happens in a market condition which is favourable for the issuer (when interest rates are falling). Therefore these bonds should offer higher coupon rates, or a discount compared to non-callable bonds with similar levels of risk.

Banko and Zhou (2010) review three possible reasons for the popularity of callable bonds among issuers, in line with the hypotheses of information asymmetry, risk-shifting, and underinvestment. The information asymmetry hypothesis predicts that firms issue callable bonds as a signal of its future financial stability and as an opportunity to refinance debt with a lower interest rate. The risk-shifting hypothesis supposes that the presence of callable bonds among investors prevents the issuer from investing in high-risk projects, because in this case the value of a call provision, owned by the shareholders, falls. The underinvestment hypothesis studies the conflict of interest between shareholders and creditors: firms with debt reject potentially profitable investments since the creditors can benefit from it, leaving little profit for the shareholders. All three hypotheses are related to the theory of agency costs.

A holder of corporate bonds (CBs) with an embedded put option has the right to demand a bond repayment before maturity. As a result, a put option serves as a mechanism to hedge investor risks, for example, in case of interest rate hikes or unfavourable economic conditions.

In developed markets, where the investor rights are better protected, CBs with an embedded call option are more popular, but in some developing markets, on the contrary, CBs with an embedded put option are more popular (for example, China and Russia, Table 8.1).

Table 8.1 Primary and secondary market issue statistics of CBs with embedded put and call options in 2016–2018

Country	*Indicator*	*Primary market*			*Secondary market*		
		2016	*2017*	*2018*	*2016*	*2017*	*2018*
China	Number of bond issues	32 069	43 444	45 684	7 923 216	8 226 795	9 025 761
	Share of issues with embedded options (%):						
	Put	5.34	2.46	2.94	4.01	2.07	2.39
	Call	1.39	1.36	1.47	1.83	2.25	2.11
	Call and Put	0.29	0.16	0.13	0.28	0.11	0.10
India	Number of bond issues	5 071	5 038	3 283	624 161	597 401	510 354
	Share of issues with embedded options (%):						
	Put	1.85	1.29	1.74	0.83	0.42	0.45
	Call	9.54	12.35	4.23	1.70	3.09	1.45
	Call and Put	3.10	4.27	6.31	0.88	1.18	1.76
Russia*	Number of bond issues	227	236	252	32 190	49 014	26 335
	Share of issues with embedded options (%):						
	Put	33.04	37.29	26.19	55.25	58.78	31.02
	Call	6.61	2.97	2.78	4.94	0.88	3.6
	Call and Put	0.88	0.00	0.00	0.7	0.00	0.00
S. Korea	Number of bond issues	5 348	5 681	5 341	507 557	537 535	576 899
	Share of issues with embedded options (%):						
	Put	0.95	1.21	0.37	0.31	0.64	0.08
	Call	5.83	2.97	3.88	1.94	1.48	1.75
	Call and Put	0.30	0.25	0.04	0.02	0.01	0.00
USA	Number of bond issues	15 416	14 530	15 007	18 938 959	20 779 389	15 090 301
	Share of issues with embedded options (%):						
	Put	0.05	0.09	0.17	0.00	0.00	0.00
	Call	56.18	46.10	37.92	8.37	8.17	9.12
	Call and Put	0.12	0.27	0.33	0.01	0.01	0.02

Germany	Number of bond issues	33 920	48 915	64 694	1 458 550	1 678 037	1 705 032
	Share of issues with embedded options (%):						
	Put	0.00	0.00	0.02	0.00	0.00	0.01
	Call	2.69	1.39	0.86	4.44	3.74	3.58
	Call and Put	0.01	0.00	0.00	0.00	0.01	0.01
France	Number of bond issues	2 034	2 089	2 367	940 543	946 926	883 252
	Share of issues with embedded options (%):						
	Put	0.15	0.00	0.04	0.10	0.00	0.00
	Call	22.17	22.02	22.01	12.68	9.92	14.40
	Call and Put	0.00	0.00	0.04	0.00	0.00	0.00
Spain	Number of bond issues	266	316	263	354 167	383 251	311 662
	Share of issues with embedded options (%):						
	Put	1.13	0.95	1.52	0.06	0.03	0.04
	Call	11.65	21.20	12.55	3.48	8.70	7.94
	Call and Put	0.75	0.00	0.00	0.24	0.00	0.00

Source: Bloomberg, Cbonds.

* excluding VTB's short-term issues (with a placement period of not more than 1 month)

The goal of this paper is to empirically study the effects of embedded put and call options on CB yield-to-maturity (YTM) and spreads in developing markets. Many papers are devoted to theoretical modelling, which reflects the effect of an embedded option on bond prices and yields (Brennan and Schwartz, 1977; Lim et al., 2012; Dong et al., 2010; Nunes, 2011). Prior empirical research on this topic is rare and it generally focuses on analyzing the effects of an embedded call option (Kim and Stock, 2014; Samet and Obay, 2014; Booth et al., 2014) and in developed markets, predominantly in the US (Kim and Stock, 2014; Booth et al., 2014).

The novelty of our paper is in analyzing the effects of both embedded call and put options on YTM and spread. We focus on the major developing bond markets of South Korea, Russia and India. We study separately the samples of banking and non-financial sector CBs.

Literature review

Within the framework of the topic, we distinguish theoretical and empirical studies.

The first area of research in the field of pricing bonds with embedded options is the development of theoretical models (Brennan and Schwartz, 1977; Ingersoll, 1977; Ho-Pfeffer, 1996; Tsiveriotis and Fernandes, 1998; Andre-Le Pogamp and Moraux, 2004; Lim et al., 2012; Nunes, 2011).

The second area of research is to assess the impact of embedded put and call options on bond YTM and spreads based on empirical regression models (Kim and Stock, 2014). Kim and Stock (2014) examine how interest rate volatility affects yield spreads of CBs with and without a call option. The sample included more than 200 thousand observations on non-callable and callable bonds in the US market for the period 2003–2009. The authors reveal that the presence of an embedded call option increases the yield spread on CBs. There is a positive relationship between the interest rate volatility and the spread, which is most pronounced for low-rated bonds as they have a greater risk. This effect is less pronounced for callable bonds since an increase in the default risk of the issuer reduces the cost of the call option, and hence the spread on the callable bond. Yield spreads on callable bonds with a long maturity are lower than on non-callable bonds.

Booth et al. (2014) analyze the determinants of the issue and yield spread of callable CBs in the US market from 1995 to 2008. The sample includes 5776 observations on the CB initial offering of companies in the financial and non-financial sectors. The authors test two groups of hypotheses. The first group is about the fact that changes in macroeconomic indicators – the level of interest rates, the slope of the yield curve, and the volatility of yield on the bond market – affect the probability of issuing callable bonds and their spreads on the yield of GBs. The second group of hypotheses concerns the significant influence of the information asymmetry problem, which is often faced by small firms, as well as companies with low credit ratings and profitability. The authors consider such model factors as the returns of one-year Treasury bills, the logarithm of bond issue size and nominal issue volume, ROA, etc. To test hypotheses, the authors use the Heckman model.

Booth et al. (2014) show that for CBs in the financial and non-financial sectors, the presence of an embedded call option is negatively related to the level and slope of the interest rate curve and the narrowness of credit spreads, positively to interest rate volatility. The embedded call option has a significant positive effect on the financial sector CB spread. For issuers from the non-financial sector, the authors fail to identify a statistically significant call premium on CBs. The authors also calculate spreads for 270 pairs of callable and non-callable bonds issued on the same day by companies in the same industry. Based on the regression analysis, the authors identify determinants of these spreads. They reveal a positive effect of the interest rate level and volatility, differences in maturity, and a negative effect of differences in the credit rating.

Samet and Obay (2014) study the impact of the issuer and the bond issue characteristics, as well as country factors, on bond yield spreads with and without embedded call options. The study sample includes 13936 bonds issued by 1726 companies from 39 countries for the period 1991–2007. The authors conclude that the call spread was positive (52 to 58 basis points). The call spread is higher for junk bonds than for investment-grade bonds. Bonds of high-leveraged issuers have a greater call spread.

The third area of research is the analysis of the determinants of issuing callable bonds considering the information asymmetry problem (Banko and Zhou, 2010; Tewari et al., 2015; Choi et al., 2013).

We note that there are currently few empirical works that explore the impact of embedded call options on CB yield and its spread (Kim and Stock, 2014; Samet and Obay, 2014; Booth et al., 2014). These papers are mainly focused on the US market. As far as the authors of this study know, there are no papers that empirically analyze the effects of the put option. Our paper closes this gap, as we consider bonds with both embedded call and put options. Our research focuses on large emerging markets for CBs (South Korea, India, Russia).

The hypotheses of our study

We put forward the following key hypotheses:

H1. The presence of an embedded call option has a significant positive effect on YTM and its spread on CBs.

The presence of an embedded call option is a tool for hedging the issuer's risks. The seller of the option is the investor who buys this bond from the issuer. For holders of CBs, the possibility of their early repayment by the issuer imposes a certain risk, due to which we assume that CB holders demand an increased yield on such bonds. Samet and Obay (2014) reveal a positive effect of the embedded call option on the CB yields in 39 emerging and developed markets, and Kim and Stock (2014) do so on the US market.

H2. The presence of an embedded put option significantly affects YTM and its spread on CBs.

The presence of an embedded put option is an instrument for hedging the risk of bondholders, and the issuer is the seller of the option. For the issuer, the possibility of an early repayment to their creditors is a risk factor. Accordingly, we assume that CB holders will accept a reduced yield on such bonds.
We consider the following control variables:

- CB maturity. Bai et al. (2019) show that the higher the maturity, the higher the CB yield spread in the US market. Accordingly, we assume a positive direction of influence in this explanatory variable.
- The debt burden of the issuing company (total debt to equity for all companies, except banks; liabilities to total assets for banks). We assume that the higher the debt burden, the higher the risks to bondholders, and, accordingly, the higher the YTM and the spread. Casteuble et al. (2013), Lester and Kumar (2014) and Kim and Stock (2014) obtain similar results.
- Return on capital and assets (ROE, ROA, ROC). We assume that the influence of these factors on YTM and its spread may be multidirectional. On the one hand, Lester and Kumar (2014) and Teplova and Sokolova (2019) find that an increase in ROA or ROE leads to a decrease in yield spreads: higher profitability rates serve as a positive signal to bondholders. On the other hand, Balasubramnian and Cyree (2011) reveal a positive correlation between the spread and ROA, explaining that investors believe that additional income is due to taking additional risks.
- The yield on short-term (one-year) GBs. We assume that the influence of this indicator on the dependent variables may be multidirectional. On the one hand, since CBs in emerging bond markets are usually characterized by short maturities, the yield on short-term bonds can be a proxy for interest rates and be positively associated with dependent variables. On the other hand, Bao et al. (2011) and Kim and Stock (2014) show that an increase in the short-term (one-month) GB yields leads to a decrease in the YTM and the spread on CBs due to a decrease in the issuer's credit risk.
- The difference between the YTM of long-term (ten-year) and short-term (one-year) GBs. We assume a negative impact of this indicator on the dependent variables. The slope of the interest rate curve reflects investor expectations regarding growth prospects (Kim and Stock, 2014). The higher the slope of the interest rate curve, the higher the growth prospects and the lower the credit risks; therefore, the lower the YTM and its spread. Kim and Stock (2014) show in the US CB market that the slope of the interest rate curve for GBs significantly affects the CB yield spread.
- The yield volatility on the GB market, defined as the standard deviation of the one-year GB YTM. We assume a positive effect of this factor on the dependent variables: the interest rate volatility reflects instability in the financial markets. With its growth, the issuer default risk increases, and

therefore, the YTM and the CB spread increase. Kim and Stock (2014) reveal a significant positive effect of the interest rate volatility on the US market CB spread.

The methodology of our study. The description of variables

To test the hypotheses on the influence of embedded options on the yields and spreads of corporate bonds, we apply the following linear multifactor regression models:

$$y = \alpha + \beta_1 \cdot dummy\_call + \beta_2 \cdot dummy\_put + \beta_3 \cdot maturity + \\ + \sum_i \beta_{4,i} \cdot financial\_indicator_i + \sum_j \beta_{5,j} \cdot macro\_indicator_j + \varepsilon \quad (8.1)$$

where y is the dependent variable (YTM or its spread), $dummy\_call$ and $dummy\_put$ are dummy variables of embedded call and put options respectively, $maturity$ is time to maturity, $financial\_indicator_i$ is one of the issuer's financial indicators, and $macro\_indicator_j$ is one of the characteristics of the financial conditions in the bond market. A detailed description of the variables is presented in Table 8.2.

Explanatory variables are included in model (1) with an account of the correlation matrix. We test model specifications for the non-financial and financial sectors separately.

The sample descriptive statistics

The sample is formed as follows: for the markets of Russia, India and South Korea, we use data from Eikon Refinitiv and Cbonds information and analytical databases on CBs with embedded put and call options, which were issued in the primary market in 2015–2018. If a bond with an embedded option is issued by the SPV issuer and there are no consolidated IFRS statements for the group of companies, then we exclude the bond from the sample.

For each CB with an embedded option which was issued in the primary market in 2015–2018, we select a bond without options by the following criteria: 1) its issue date is within three months from the issue date of the bond with an embedded option; 2) the issuer belongs to the same industry; 3) the revenue (for non-financial companies) or the assets (for banks) of the issuer of the bond without options differ from the revenue or the assets of the issuer of the bond with an embedded option by no more than 50%. If possible, we select CB issue of the same issuer as a pair bond.

The final sample contains 446 issues of CBs in the South Korean market, 544 in the Russian market, and 638 in the Indian market. The descriptive statistics are in Tables 8.3–8.5.

Table 8.2 The description of variables

Name	*Description*	*Sign*	*Source*
ytm	Dependent variable: CB yield at pricing		Eikon Refinitiv
spread	Dependent variable: the difference between the CB yield at pricing and government bond (GB) yield with the corresponding maturity on the date of the CB issue		
Explanatory variables: bond issue characteristics			
dummy_call	Dummies of having an embedded call option: 1 – a call option is present, 0 – otherwise	+	Eikon Refinitiv
dummy_put	Dummies of having an embedded put option: 1 – put option is present, 0 – otherwise	-	
maturity	Maturity of the CB	+	
Issuer's financial indicators			
Debt_Equity	The ratio of total debt to equity. The indicator is calculated for companies in the real sector and financial companies (except banking)	+	Eikon Refinitiv
Liab_Assets	The ratio of the book value liabilities to the total book value assets	+	
ROA	The ratio of net earnings to total assets,%	+ / -	
ROE	The ratio of net earnings to the equity,%	+ / -	
ROC	The ratio of EBIT to the total debt and the book value of equity,%	+ / -	
Conditions in the national bond market			
interest_ rate_vol	The standard deviation of a one-year GB YTM for the previous 12 months at the date of the CB issue	+	ru. investing. com
ST_interest_ rate	The YTM of a one-year GB at the date of the CB issue	+ / -	
slope	The difference between the YTM of a 10-year and a one-year GB at the date of the CB issue	-	

The results

South Korea

The results for the South Korean bond market are in Table 8.6. We observe a positive, significant, at the 1% level, impact of the embedded call option on the YTM and its spread on bank CBs, as well as a persistent negative, significant, at the 1% level, impact of the embedded call option on the YTM and its spread on non-financial sector company CBs, which corresponds to the hypotheses. Kim and Stock (2014), Samet and Obay (2014), and Booth et al. (2014) obtain a similar conclusion about the effect of the embedded call option. An original conclusion is obtained for companies in the non-financial sector: the presence of an embedded

Table 8.3 Descriptive statistics on the CB in the South Korean market

Variable	*Non-financial sector*					*Banking sector*				
	Obs	*Mean*	*Std. Dev.*	*Min*	*Max*	*Obs*	*Mean*	*Std. Dev.*	*Min*	*Max*
ytm	344	3.804	1.190	1.50	6.00	102	3.019	1.166	1.300	5.710
spread	344	2.202	1.245	0.07	4.60	102	1.422	1.186	0.020	4.140
int_rate_vol	344	0.154	0.065	0.064	0.303	102	0.164	0.072	0.064	0.302
st_int_rate	344	1.623	0.181	1.254	2.025	102	1.573	0.182	1.254	2.035
slope	344	0.562	0.212	0.093	0.990	102	0.571	0.227	0.093	0.901
maturity	344	1.584	1.384	0.080	10.00	102	3.116	3.004	0.080	10.010
debt_equity	344	1.609	1.445	0	6.00	-				
ROE	344	0.835	16.171	-25.00	45.00	102	8.289	3.330	4.000	20.000
ROA	344	-1.702	9.631	-25.00	23.00	102	1.083	1.536	-1.000	10.000
ROC	344	2.552	9.862	-27.00	25.00	-				
liab_assets	344	0.625	0.205	0.05	0.95	102	0.867	0.150	0.220	0.940
dummy_call	344	0.410	0.493	0	1.00	102	0.471	0.502	0.000	1.000
dummy_put	344	0.113	0.318	0	1.00	-				

Table 8.4 Descriptive statistics on the CB in the Russian market

Variable	*Non-financial sector*					*Banking sector*				
	Obs	*Mean*	*Std. Dev.*	*Min*	*Max*	*Obs*	*Mean*	*Std. Dev.*	*Min*	*Max*
yield_issue	222	10.534	1.927	6.200	15.030	322	12.487	3.005	5.060	20.110
yield_spread	222	1.198	1.736	-2.000	6.000	322	2.613	2.374	-3.000	8.000
int_rate_vol	222	0.965	0.691	0.400	2.627	322	1.085	0.778	0.397	2.709
st_int_rate	222	9.091	1.381	6.050	11.570	322	9.793	2.415	6.050	16.910
slope	222	-0.268	0.710	-1.510	1.200	322	-0.239	0.712	-1.710	1.840
maturity	222	4.572	2.710	0.440	10.000	322	4.139	4.239	0.060	24.810
debt_equity	222	1.155	1.463	0.100	7.000	-				
roe	222	13.506	17.180	-10.00	50.000	322	4.283	16.364	-25.000	50.000
roc	222	11.614	10.312	-8.000	40.000	-				
liab_assets	222	0.616	0.230	0.100	1.460	322	0.874	0.081	0.430	0.990
dummy_call	222	0.149	0.357	0.000	1.000	322	0.109	0.312	0.000	1.000
dummy_put	222	0.450	0.499	0.000	1.000	322	0.460	0.499	0.000	1.000

Table 8.5 Descriptive statistics on the CB in the Indian market

Variable	*Non-financial sector*					*Banking sector*				
	Obs	*Mean*	*Std. Dev.*	*Min*	*Max*	*Obs*	*Mean*	*Std. Dev.*	*Min*	*Max*
yield_issue	110	9.795	1.339	7.000	14.200	525	9.186	1.599	6.700	16.900
yield_spread	110	2.466	1.238	0.060	6.000	528	1.931	1.481	0.190	6.000
int_rate_vol	110	0.265	0.080	0.085	0.436	528	0.250	0.081	0.085	0.440
st_int_rate	110	7.159	0.591	6.070	8.300	528	6.917	0.547	6.010	8.270
slope	110	0.309	0.335	-0.429	0.987	528	0.317	0.254	-0.436	1.029
maturity	110	3.279	2.870	0.200	18.000	528	4.850	3.296	0.200	11.400
debt_equity	110	2.528	2.126	0.000	7.000	-				
roe	110	5.818	11.089	-10.00	30.000	528	11.493	8.885	-10.000	30.000
roa	110	2.463	4.515	-5.000	15.000	528	1.304	1.064	-1.000	3.520
roc	110	9.363	6.192	-3.000	22.000	-				
liab_assets	110	0.728	0.154	0.370	1.000	528	0.878	0.084	0.400	0.960
dummy_call	110	0.464	0.501	0.000	1.000	528	0.316	0.465	0.000	1.000
dummy_put	110	0.391	0.490	0.000	1.000	528	0.267	0.443	0.000	1.000

call option reduces YTM and its spread. We attribute this to the fact that the presence of a call option is a favourable signal to investors about the issuer's future financial stability and the quality of the management system: at falling interest rates, the issuer can not only refinance debt, but also pay off bond loans.

For the bank CBs, we reveal a positive dependence of YTM and the spread on maturity. The influence of the factor is stable and significant at the 5% level. This result is consistent with the findings of Bai et al. (2019) for the US market. On the contrary, the dependence of YTM and the spread on maturity is negative for non-financial sector companies. We attribute this to shorter maturities for non-financial sector CBs: 1.6 years on average in the sample (while the average maturity of the bank CBs is 3 years).

For non-financial sector CBs, we find a positive and significant at the 1% level impact of debt indicators, i.e. the ratio of debt to equity and liabilities to assets, on both dependent variables (Table 8.6). This finding is consistent with the results of Casteuble et al. (2013), Lester and Kumar (2014) and Kim and Stock (2014). For bank CBs, we observe an inverse relationship: the share of liabilities in assets has a significant negative effect on both dependent variables. We attribute this to the fact that bank liabilities include deposits from individuals and legal entities, interbank loans, and loans from the Central Bank. There is a deposit insurance system in South Korea (up to KRW 50 m per depositor). The banking sector is more tightly regulated compared to non-financial sector companies, and bank acceptance of risks is limited. Investors view a high share of liabilities in the assets not as high levels of debt burden, but as a proxy for stability.

The returns on capital and assets significantly positively affect YTM and its spread for both the non-financial and the bank CB samples (Table 8.6). The influence of ROA and ROC is most significant (at the 1–5% level) for non-financial sector CBs, and ROA and ROE for the bank CBs. This result is consistent with the findings of Balasubramnian and Cyree (2011): investors associate an increase in ROC with the adoption of additional risks by issuers.

For non-financial sector CBs, we reveal a significant positive effect of interest rate volatility on YTM and its spread (Table 8.6). A similar conclusion is drawn by Kim and Stock (2014) for the US market.

We note a negative impact of the slope of the GB yield curve on YTM and its spread for non-financial sector CBs (Table 8.6). This factor significantly affects only the spread (at the 1% level). The conclusion is consistent with the results of Kim and Stock (2014): an increase in the slope of the interest rate curve for GBs is a signal of favourable economic development prospects. For banks, we observe a different picture: the influence of the slope of the GB yield curve is positive, and for most specifications, the statistical significance is low. We attribute this to the fact that companies in the non-financial sector seek to attract long-term financing, while banks work with shorter loans, and for them, it is more important to balance their assets and liabilities by maturity.

The influence of short-term interest rate levels on the yield spread of bank CBs is negative, which is consistent with the findings of Bao et al. (2011) and Kim and Stock (2014).

Table 8.6 Results for the sample of CBs of the South Korea

Dependent variable	*Non-financial sector*		*Banking sector*	
	ytm	*spread*	*ytm*	*spread*
Adjusted R^2	0.3583	0.4873	0.6571	0.5923
Number of obs	344	344	102	102
_cons	4.11***	2.7909***	3.7475***	3.3275***
	(0.5235)	(0.5124)	(0.7217)	(0.9226)
dummy_call	-0.7642***	-0.9446***	1.4955***	1.4563***
	(0.1362)	(0.1276)	(0.1376)	(0.1527)
dummy_put	-0.9779***	-0.9833***		
	(0.1703)	(0.1597)		
Debt_Equity	0.1059***			
	(0.0387)			
interest_rate_vol	1.8332**	1.8037**	-0.7625	1.2155
	(0.8716)	(0.8168)	(1.0843)	(1.2117)
Liab_Assets		1.935***	-3.9551***	-2.437***
		(0.2695)	(0.5064)	(0.7779)
maturity	-0.5233***	-0.5565***	0.1026***	0.0622**
	(0.0472)	(0.0445)	(0.0251)	(0.0278)
ROA		0.0119**		0.2423***
		(0.0052)		(0.0746)
ROC	0.0202***			
	(0.0056)			
ROE			0.0788***	
			(0.0206)	
slope	-0.4046	-0.7961***	0.208	0.8386**
	(0.3143)	(0.2937)	(0.3671)	(0.4085)
ST_interest_rate	0.4124	-0.1412	0.6543	-1.0258**
	(0.3513)	(0.3293)	(0.461)	(0.5151)

Significance levels: * p <10%, ** p <5%, *** p <1%

Russia

The results for the Russian bond market are given in Table 8.7. We find a negative impact of the embedded put option on YTM and its spread for bank CBs, which is consistent with the hypotheses. As far as we know, no empirical studies have been done on the impact of the put option. For the non-financial sector CBs, the effect of the put option on YTM and its spread is significantly positive. We attribute this to the fact that many Russian borrowers significantly lower the bond coupon rate (to values less than 1% per annum) after the offer date. Investors have to pay a commission to the broker when the bonds are repaid on the offer date. Owners of puttable bonds perceive the presence of such an option as a risk factor and demand an increased premium.

The effect of the call option on YTM and the spread for non-financial and bank CBs is consistently negative, but the statistical significance is not high. This result contradicts the hypothesis and conclusions of Samet and Obay (2014) and Booth et al. (2014). We attribute this to the fact that the presence of a call

Table 8.7 Results for the sample of CBs of Russia

Dependent variable	*Non-financial sector*		*Banking sector*	
	ytm	*spread*	*ytm*	*spread*
Adjusted R^2	0.5861	0.1179	0.4856	0.136
Number of obs	222	222	322	322
_cons	0.937	4.0119***	10.2584***	9.8871***
	(1.1577)	(1.4945)	(1.4526)	(1.4869)
dummy_call	-0.3121	-0.2009	-0.076	-0.1476
	(0.2664)	(0.3512)	(0.3919)	(0.4012)
dummy_put	0.3027*	0.1553	-0.1785	-0.0414
	(0.1834)	(0.245)	(0.2945)	(0.3014)
interest_rate_volatility	0.6232**	0.5481	0.8781***	0.0286
	(0.2597)	(0.3325)	(0.2229)	(0.2281)
Debt_Equity	0.2853***			
	(0.0627)			
Liab_Assets		-0.5337	-5.974***	-8.7302***
		(0.5328)	(1.5889)	(1.6264)
maturity	-0.085**	-0.1996***	-0.0364	-0.1041***
	(0.0383)	(0.0462)	(0.0344)	(0.0352)
ROC	0.0333***			
	(0.0095)			
ROE		0.0222***	-0.0077	-0.0289***
		(0.0074)	(0.0078)	(0.008)
slope	0.3631	-0.5246*	-0.2188	-0.1816
	(0.2231)	(0.2953)	(0.2171)	(0.2222)
ST_interest_rate	0.9543***	-0.284	0.686***	0.089
	(0.1411)	(0.1833)	(0.0804)	(0.0823)

Significance levels: * $p < 10\%$, ** $p < 5\%$, *** $p < 1\%$

option is a favourable signal to investors about the future financial stability and the quality management system of the issuing company.

For the non-financial sector and bank CBs, we reveal a negative dependence of YTM and the spread on maturity. In most specifications, the influence of the factor is significant at the 5% level. This result contradicts the findings of Bai et al. (2019) for the US market. We attribute this to the fact that in the crisis of 2015–2016, there was an excess yield of short-term bonds over long-term bonds in the Russian market.

For the real sector CBs, we find a positive and significant at the 1% level effect of the debt to equity ratio on both dependent variables (Table 8.7). This finding is in line with the results of Casteuble et al. (2013), Lester and Kumar (2014) and Kim and Stock (2014). For bank CBs, we reveal a negative impact of the share of liabilities in assets on YTM and its spread (as for bank CBs in South Korea).

ROE and ROC have a significant positive effect on YTM and its spread on the sample of non-financial sector CBs (Table 8.7), which is consistent with the results of Balasubramnian and Cyree (2011). For bank CBs, on the contrary, the effect of ROE on dependent variables is negative, which is consistent with the findings of Lester and Kumar (2014), and Teplova and Sokolova (2019). We explain this discrepancy in the conclusions for the two subsamples by the fact that due to the strict regulatory policy of the Bank of Russia, measures are taken in the banking sector to control the adoption of risks, and an increase in ROE is a positive signal for investors. Non-financial companies are not provided with the same rigorous standards for risk management, and an increase in ROE and ROC can occur due to the implementation of high-risk projects that increase the likelihood of default, which is negatively perceived by investors.

For non-financial and bank CBs, we find a significant positive effect of interest rate volatility on YTM and its spread (Table 8.7). A similar conclusion is made by Kim and Stock (2014) for the US market.

We note the negative influence of the slope of the interest rate curve on YTM and the spread on non-financial and bank CBs (Table 8.7). This factor significantly affects only the spread (at the 5% level). The result is consistent with the results of Kim and Stock (2014).

The level of short-term interest rates has a significant positive effect on the yield spread on bank and non-financial CBs. We attribute this to the fact that the one-year GB yield serves as a proxy for the interest rate of CBs with 1–3 years maturity. According to the Cbonds database, the average duration of CBs in the MOEX RUCBITR corporate bond index was 2.3 years in 2015–2018.

India

The results for the Indian bond market are in Table 8.8. Following the hypotheses, we observe a positive impact of the embedded call option and the negative impact of the embedded put option on YTM and its spread on bank and non-financial CBs. The influence of these variables is significant at the 1% level only for the sample of bank CBs. Kim and Stock (2014), Samet and Obay (2014), and Booth et al. (2014) obtain similar conclusions on the effect of an embedded call option.

For the bank and non-financial CBs, we reveal a negative dependence of YTM and the spread on maturity, while for most models the statistical significance is low. The result contradicts the findings of Bai et al. (2019) for the US market. We explain this dependence by the flattening of the Indian GB yield curve in 2015–2017.

We find a positive effect of the debt to equity ratio on both dependent variables for the real sector CBs (Table 8.8). This finding is consistent with the results of Casteuble et al. (2013), Lester and Kumar (2014), and Kim and Stock (2014). For bank CBs, we observe a negative impact of the share of assets in liabilities on YTM and its spread (we obtain a similar conclusion above in Russia and South Korea).

ROE and ROC have a significant negative effect on YTM and its spread across the sample of non-financial sector CBs (Table 8.8). For bank CBs, we reveal a significant negative effect of ROE and ROA. Lester and Kumar (2014) and Teplova and Sokolova (2019) reach a similar conclusion: an increase in ROC and ROA is a positive signal for investors, because it indicates the issuer's efficient use of its assets.

We note a negative influence of the slope of the GB interest rate curve on YTM and the spread across non-financial CBs (Table 8.8). The conclusion is

Table 8.8 Results for the sample of CBs of India

Dependent variable	*Non-financial sector*		*Banking sector*	
	ytm	*spread*	*ytm*	*spread*
Adjusted R^2	0.2414	0.0588	0.334	0.3507
Number of obs	110	110	525	528
_cons	3.2523	4.4579**	8.6041***	7.9875***
	(2.0913)	(2.1705)	(1.0641)	(0.9731)
dummy_call	0.1249	0.3045	0.9053***	0.9033***
	(0.3233)	(0.3354)	(0.1351)	(0.1264)
dummy_put	-0.0755	-0.1532	-0.4691***	-0.4115***
	(0.3334)	(0.3506)	(0.1565)	(0.1419)
interest_ rate_vol	-0.732	-1.016	0.3253	-0.3715
	(1.5086)	(1.5185)	(0.7383)	(0.6843)
Debt_ Equity	0.0655			
	(0.0654)			
Liab_ Assets		1.0641	-7.5509***	-7.2285***
		(0.9401)	(0.7351)	(0.6865)
maturity	0.032	-0.0599	-0.0059	-0.0616***
	(0.0453)	(0.0465)	(0.0228)	(0.0207)
ROA			-0.2411***	
			(0.0631)	
ROC		-0.05**		
		(0.0215)		
ROE	-0.0262**			-0.0222***
	(0.0119)			(0.007)
slope	-0.067	-0.7312	0.5606**	0.0438
	(0.4757)	(0.4937)	(0.2508)	(0.2293)
ST_interest _rate	0.9235***	-0.2358	1.0316***	0.1083
	(0.2742)	(0.2929)	(0.1209)	(0.1118)

Significance levels: * $p < 10\%$, ** $p < 5\%$, *** $p < 1\%$

consistent with the results of Kim and Stock (2014). On the contrary, the influence of the slope of the GB yield curve is positive for bank CBs (similar to the bank CBs in South Korea).

The level of short-term interest rates has a significant positive effect on the bank and non-financial CB yields. We explain this dependence by the flattening of the Indian GBs yield curve, as a result of which the one-year GB yield serves as a proxy for the CB interest rates of all maturities.

Conclusion

For the first time, based on empirical methods, the influence of embedded call and put options on YTM and its spread across the large emerging bond markets of South Korea, Russia and India is investigated. We test linear multifactor models for each market separately, and the results for the banking and non-financial sectors are compared. The initial sample includes all CBs with embedded call and put options that were issued in 2015–2018, then a pair bond without options is selected for each CB based on the comparability of the size of the issuer, its industry, and date of issue. The final sample includes 446 observations in the South Korean market, 544 observations on the Russian market, and 638 observations in the Indian market.

Following the hypotheses, we reveal a positive effect of the embedded call option on YTM and spread of bank CBs of South Korea and India and the non-financial CBs of India (for bank CBs, the effect of the call option is significant at the 1% level). Also, we reveal a negative impact of the embedded put option on YTM and its spread of bank and non-financial CBs in South Korea and India (for South Korea, the influence of the put option is significant at the 1% level for all CBs; for India only for bank CBs), as well as of bank CBs in Russia.

We identify several original features of the influence of embedded call and put options. For the Russian non-financial sector CBs, the influence of the put option on YTM and its spread is significant and positive. We attribute this to the fact that many Russian borrowers significantly lower the bond coupon rate after the offer date, and when paying off bonds on the offer date, investors must pay a commission to the broker; thus the risks of the CB holders increase. For non-financial sector CBs of Russia and South Korea, the influence of the embedded call option is negative: borrowers perceive the presence of such an option as a signal about the favourable prospects of the borrower, and its ability to pay off debt while lowering interest rates.

We find the expected conclusions concerning the influence of most control variables, but there are also differences in several markets. For example, for non-financial companies and banks in India, indicators of ROC negatively affect YTM and its spread; that is, bondholders have a positive view of the growth of ROE, ROC, and ROA. On the contrary, in the markets of Russia and South Korea, bondholders associate an increase in ROC with the adoption of additional risks by the issuers, and as a result YTM and its spread increase.

For all three markets, we note the negative impact of the share of liabilities on assets on YTM and its spread of CBs: under the strict regulation of the banking sector and limited risks, bondholders perceive the growth of liabilities as a proxy for stability.

References

Bai, J., Bali, T. G., Wen, Q. (2019). Common risk factors in the cross-section of corporate bond returns. *Journal of Financial Economics*, 131(3), 619–642. DOI: https://doi.org/10.1016/j.jfineco.2018.08.002

Balasubramnian, B., Cyree, K. B. (2011). Market discipline of banks: Why are yield spreads on bank-issued subordinated notes and debentures not sensitive to bank risks?. *Journal of Banking & Finance*, 35(1), 21–35. DOI: https://doi.org/10.1016/j.jbankfin.2010.07.015

Banko, J. C., Zhou, L. (2010). Callable bonds revisited. *Financial Management*, 39(2): 613–641. DOI: https://doi.org/10.1111/j.1755-053X.2010.01086.x

Booth, L., Gounopoulos, D., Skinner, F. (2014). The choice between callable and noncallable bonds. *Journal of Financial Research*, 37(4): 435–460. DOI: https://doi.org/10.1111/jfir.12042

Brennan, M. J., Schwartz, E. S. (1977). Convertible bonds: Valuation and optimal strategies for call and conversion. *Journal of Finance*, 32(5): 1699–1715. DOI: https://doi.org/10.1111/j.1540-6261.1977.tb03364.x

Casteuble, C., Nys, E., Rous, P. (2013). Bank Risk-Return Efficiency and Bond Spread: Is There Evidence of Market Discipline in Europe. Working Papers. hal-00916717, HAL.

Choi, S., Jameson, M., Jung, M. (2013). The issuance of callable bonds under information asymmetry. *Journal of Empirical Finance*, 21: 1–14. DOI: https://doi.org/10.1016/j.jempfin.2012.12.004

Cox, J. C., Ingersoll, J. E., Ross, S. A. (1985). Theory of the term structure of interest rates. *Econometrica*, 53(2): 385–408. DOI: https://doi.org/10.1142/9789812701022_0005

Dong, F., Chiara, N., Vecer, J. (2010). Valuing callable and putable revenue-performance-linked project backed securities. *International Journal of Theoretical and Applied Finance*, 13(5): 751–765. doi: 10.1142/S021902491000598X

Dong, M., Dutordoir, M., Veld, C. (2011). Why do firms issue convertible bonds? Evidence from the field. *Evidence from the Field* (May 2, 2011). Working Paper.

Ho, T., Pfeffer, D. (1996). Convertible bonds: Model, value attribution and analytics. *Financial Analysts Journal*, September/October: 35–44. DOI: https://doi.org/10.2469/faj.v52.n5.2022

Ingersoll, J. (1977). A contingent-claims valuation of convertible securities. *Journal of Financial Economics*, 4: 289–322. DOI: https://doi.org/10.1016/0304-405X(77)90004-6

Kim, D. H., Stock, D. (2014). The effect of interest rate volatility and equity volatility on corporate bond yield spreads: A comparison of noncallables and callables. *Journal of Corporate Finance*, 26: 20–35. DOI: https://doi.org/10.1016/j.jcorpfin.2014.02.005

Kimitoshi, S., Katsushige, S. (2014). The dynamic pricing for callable securities with Markov-modulated prices. *Journal of the Operations Research Society of Japan*, 57(3–4): 87–103. DOI: https://doi.org/10.15807/jorsj.57.87

Lester, J., Kumar, A. (2014). Do Bond Spreads Show Evidence of Too Big To Fail Effects? *Oliver Wyman Financial Services*. WP

Lim, D., Li, L., Linetsky, V. (2012). Evaluating callable and putable bonds: An eigenfunction expansion approach. *Journal of Economic Dynamics and Control*, 36(12): 1888–1908. DOI: https://doi.org/10.1016/j.jedc.2012.06.002

Nunes, J. P. V. (2011). American options and callable bonds under stochastic interest rates and endogenous bankruptcy. *Review of Derivatives Research*, 14(3): 283–332. DOI: https://doi.org/10.1007/s11147-010-9058-x

Pogamp, A. L., Moraux, F. (2004). Valuing callable convertible bonds: A reduced approach. *Applied Financial Economics*, 14: 743–749. DOI: https://doi.org/10.1080/0960310042000243574

Samet, A., Obay, L. (2014). Call feature and corporate bond yield spreads. *Journal of Multinational Financial Management*, 25–26: 1–20. DOI: https://doi.org/10.1016/j.mulfin.2014.06.004

Teplova T. V., Sokolova T. V. (2019). Surprises of corporate governance and Russian firmsdebt. *Journal of Economics and Business*, 102(March–April): 39–56. DOI: https://doi.org/10.1016/j.jeconbus.2018.10.001

Tewari, M., Byrd, A., Ramanlal, P. (2015). Callable bonds, reinvestment risk, and credit rating improvements: Role of the call premium. *Journal of Financial Economics*, 115(2): 349–360. DOI: https://doi.org/10.1016/j.jfineco.2014.09.011

Vasicek, O. A. (1977). An equilibrium characterization of the term structure. *Journal of Financial Economics*, 5(2): 177–188. DOI: https://doi.org/10.1016/0304-405X(77)90016-2

9 Do covenants really reduce the cost of debt in emerging markets?

Review of previous studies

One of the mechanisms for protecting the interests of creditors is the inclusion of covenants in issue documents (Bazzana and Broccardo, 2013), i.e. conditions that oblige the borrower to perform some actions or to refrain from them. In the case of the violation of covenants, the issuer of the debt is obliged to purchase or repay early the issued securities. The main reason for using such an instrument is the need to overcome a possible conflict of interest between owners and creditors, as well as to reduce the agency costs associated with it (Chava and Purnanandam, 2010).

The results of empirical studies on this subject are mixed. On the one hand, a number of authors (Chava and Jarrow, 2004; Reisel, 2004; Ju and Wei, 2005; Bradley and Roberts, 2004), despite the use of various samples (corporate bonds, bank loans, etc.), come to the conclusion that the inclusion of covenants in loan agreements reduces the cost of debt. On the other hand, covenants, especially when they are offered directly by the borrower, can be evaluated by creditors as a signal of a higher level of risk, which will entail a higher required return on debt. Tanigawa and Katsura (2014), studying the data on corporate bonds issued in Japan from January 2000 to December 2011, reveal that the relationship between covenants and the cost of debt depends on the segment determined by the issuer's credit rating. In the class of bonds rated AAA and AA, there is a negative relationship: the more covenants are included in the prospectus, the lower the bond yield spread. At the same time, bonds rated A, BBB, B demonstrate a positive relationship.

Today, there are a large number of different types of covenants. In one early research paper, Porteus and Isern (2005) identify 84 types, 28 of which are financial. Such a variety suggests that covenants are highly dependent on the current market situation. Permanent macroeconomic, institutional and regulatory changes lead to the obsolescence and disappearance of certain types of covenants and the emergence of new ones adapted to the financial conditions of a certain economic period. In a global financial crisis, the inclusion of covenants in the terms of loan agreements is widespread, because the crisis increases the risk of a bank's unawareness of the financial conditions of the borrower, and the use of covenants in loan agreements allows not only the prediction and reduction of credit risks, but also distribution of the responsibility of participants in loan relations.

Covenants are usually divided into several types: active (obligation to perform some actions), passive (obligation not to perform actions), restrictive (close to negative, usually used in mergers and acquisitions), financial (obligation to maintain certain borrower financial indicators at an agreed level) and non-financial.

As mentioned, financial covenants are most widely used: liquidity ratios, profitability indicators and others can serve as examples.

The global market

Descriptive statistics

The list of standard covenants in the global Eurobond market is slightly different from the Russian one; however, many of the components are identical. Considering the markets of the US, the UK, Germany, China, India, South Korea and Poland, the following list of covenants is contained in the Bloomberg database: Negative Pledge, Change of Control, Fundamental Change, Limit of Indebtedness, Cross Default, Certain Sales of Assets, Restriction on Activities, Debt Service Coverage Ratio, Free Cash Flow to Debt Service Ratio, Merge Restrictions, Limitation on Sale-and-Leaseback, Limitation on Subsidiary Debt, Restricted Payments, Ratings Trigger, Collective Action Clause, Material Adverse Change Clause, Force Majeure (Source: Bloomberg).

Table 9.1 Number of issues of corporate Eurobonds with covenants by country for the period January 1, 2014 to January 1, 2019

	US	*Germany*	*India*	*China*	*S. Korea*	*Poland*	*UK*
Total number of issues	2447	3777	194	5000	822	68	6592
Of which: non-financial organizations	656	833	63	109	260	4	662
Total number of issues with covenants	1404	727	114	261	174	11	2997
Of which: non-financial organizations	580	87	58	99	84	0	576
% of issues with covenants of the total issue volume	41%	12%	51%	38%	48%	0%	19%

Source: Bloomberg.

Table 9.2 Number of corporate Eurobonds issued in 2014–2018 with and without covenants

Issuer Sector	*Covenants*	*India*	*S.Korea*	*Germany*	*China*
Financials	no	75	461	2220	4569
	yes	56	101	724	133
Quasi-Government	no	0	0	620	3
	yes	2	0	108	57
Industrials	no	2	17	1	0
	yes	14	19	3	0
Consumer Discretionary	no	0	54	18	5
	yes	3	39	42	16
Communications	no	0	11	0	0
	yes	3	4	9	0
Consumer Stample	no	0	7	0	0
	yes	0	9	8	1
Energy	no	3	9	0	0
	yes	20	2	3	1
HealthCare	no	0	5	1	0
	yes	3	2	0	0
Materials	no	0	22	0	2
	yes	5	14	14	8
Technology	no	0	13	1	0
	yes	2	16	3	1
Utilities	no	0	10	1	1
	yes	6	7	1	6
Total number		194	822	3777	4803

Source: Authors' calculations based on Bloomberg.

The largest percentage of Eurobonds with covenants is observed in the markets of India, South Korea and China. The US is ahead of European countries (Table 9.1).

In all markets, the share of financial companies in the total issue volume of corporate Eurobonds with and without covenants is largest in the period from 2014 to 2019.

Considering the period from 2014 to 2018, in Germany the largest number of Eurobonds with covenants were issued in 2014, 2015 and 2018, in India in 2014 and 2015, in South Korea the distribution is about equal except for 2016, and in China in 2017 and 2018. The number of corporate Eurobonds with and without covenants is shown in Table 9.2. Considering industry specifics, we see that covenants are a mechanism of risk reduction.

For almost all the countries under consideration, the yield of initial placement for bonds with covenants is higher than for those without covenants (source: authors' calculations based on Bloomberg). It can be assumed that restrictions serve as a signal of risk, which causes requirements for a higher return rate for creditors. However, a more accurate assessment will be given on the basis of econometric analysis.

Significance of covenants: Comparing the Eurobond market of S. Korea with Germany

Based on the previous studies and our own considerations, we perform a regression analysis to identify the significance of the influence of covenants on corporate Eurobonds on the yield of initial placement, taking into account control variables.

The analysis is performed using a sample of two markets: developed (Germany) and emerging (South Korea). These countries are selected due to the highest availability of data on yields of initial placement in the Bloomberg database. In the framework of this chapter, all non-financial sectors are considered, due to the special nature of the activities of financial companies which should be analyzed separately. The dependent variable is the yield of initial placement (*yield*). The following factors are selected as control variables:

- *Maturity* is the time to maturity (number of years);
- *Size* is the logarithm of total assets of an issuer in the previous year;
- *Sector* is the issuer's sector dummy;
- *Year* is the year of issue (1 for 2014, 2 for 2015, etc.);
- *Public status* is the dummy of public companies (0 is no, 1 is yes);
- *Country* is the country of issue (0 is South Korea, 1 is Germany).
- *Covenants* is a dummy variable: 1 for bond issues with covenants, 0 for issues without covenants.

In the first step, we find the correlation coefficients among the factors to evaluate the possibility of including them simultaneously in one model. Then we build an OLS regression, and the results are shown in Table 9.3. We perform the Breusch–Pagan and White tests in order to check the presence of heteroskedasticity in the model residuals.

With the inclusion of covenants, the initial placement yield is lower, and for South Korea it is lower than for Germany. This suggests that the inclusion of covenants in loan agreements reduces the cost of debt in the markets of Germany and South Korea. The larger the company and the longer the maturity of Eurobonds, the lower the yield of initial placement. For non-public companies, debt is more expensive.

Our empirical research for the Eurobond market of China and India

In 2015–2019, the average annual growth rates of the economies of India and China, as well as the growth rates of the volume of outstanding corporate bond

Table 9.3 The results of the regression analysis

Variable	*The coefficient*
maturity	0.0884***
covenants	-1.1809
dummy_country (Germany)	2.1671*
non-public	1.1105***
year dummies	
2 (2015)	-0.6354***
3 (2016)	-1.3329***
4 (2017)	-0.6919**
5 (2018)	-1.5361***
size	-0.6599***
constant	7.0723***
Sector dummies	yes
R^2	0.347
N	111
aic	435.475
bic	446.313

Significance levels: * p <10%, ** p <5%, *** p <1%

markets in these countries, were high. The purpose of our study is to reveal the effect of covenants on the yield of initial placement of Eurobonds in India and China.

We test the following *hypothesis:* covenants have a significant negative effect on the yield of the initial placement on corporate bonds of India and China.

A negative effect of covenants was revealed by Chava and Jarrow (2004), Reisel (2004), Ju and Wei (2005), and Bradley and Roberts (2004).

As a dependent variable, we use the yield of initial placement of Eurobonds (in dollars). The list of covenants under consideration is given in Table 9.4.

In line with previous papers on the research topic, we select the following financial indicators of issuers as control variables:

Logarithm of assets (ln_Assets). We assume a negative direction of influence: the larger the company, the lower the risk of default, and therefore the lower the yield of a corporate Eurobond.

Assets to equity (Assets_to_Equity). We assume a positive direction of influence: the higher the level of debt burden, the higher the risks of investment and the higher the yields of corporate Eurobonds.

YTM of GB of the same maturity (in dollars, YTM_GB). We assume that the higher the yield of a GB which is a proxy of the risk-free rate, the higher the yield of a corporate Eurobond.

Logarithm of maturity (ln_Dur). We assume that the higher the maturity, the higher the yield of a corporate Eurobond.

ROE. We assume that higher ROE indicates a better financial position for the company, and therefore lower yields on Eurobonds can be expected.

Table 9.4 Share of the largest issues of corporate Eurobonds for which covenants are established

Type of covenants	*Share of Eurobond issues with covenants, %*	
	China	*India*
Limitation on Indebtedness	33	48
Limitation on Subsidiary Debt	20	25
Limitation on Liens	100	99
Limitation on Restricted Payments	31	17
Limitation on Investments	29	10
Limitation on Payment Restrictions Affecting Restricted Subsidiaries	31	21
Limitations on Transactions with Affiliates	31	23
Limitation on Business Activities	29	30
Limitation on Sale of Assets	47	44
Limitation on Sale/Leaseback	33	13
Merger Restrictions	82	41
Change of Control	60	96
Cross Default	73	97
Rating Trigger	5	18
Collective Action Clause	56	93
Designation of Restricted and Unrestricted Subsidiaries	33	15
Limitation on Layering	31	15
Covenant Suspension/Fall-Away	33	41
Events of Default	98	99
Financial Covenants	18	28
Others	15	1
Number of issues	55	71

Source: Cbonds, Eikon Refinitiv, authors' calculations.

We test the following multivariate linear regression model for the dependence of Eurobond yields on covenants and financial indicators of the issuer:

$$\begin{aligned} YTM &= \alpha + \beta_{1,1} * Covenant_1 + \ldots + \beta_{1,N} * Covenant_N + \beta_{2,1} \cdot \ln\_Assets + \\ &+ \beta_{2,2} \cdot Assets\_to\_Equity + \beta_{2,3} \cdot YTM\_GB + \beta_{2,4} \cdot \ln\_Dur + \beta_{2,5} \cdot ROE + \varepsilon \end{aligned} \tag{9.1}$$

where *YTM* is the dependent variable, $Covenant_1, \ldots, Covenant_N$ are covenants (Table 9.4).

We also test multivariate linear regression models with the total number of covenants established for the Eurobond as an independent variable. The variables are included in the model taking into account the multicollinearity matrix.

In order to form a sample, we initially select the 100 largest issues of corporate Eurobonds of India and China placed in the period from 2014 to 2019 (source: Cbonds). The issuer financial indicators for the previous year

Table 9.5 Descriptive characteristics for the sample of the largest Indian corporate Eurobonds

	YTM	*Ln_Dur*	*Ln_Assets*	*Assets_to_ Equity*	*ROE*	*YTM_GB*
Min	2.9	0.83	6.69	1.81	0.01	2.42
Max	12	3.40	11.88	10.82	0.61	7.13
Mean	5.25	1.92	9.72	4.26	0.12	4.25
St. Dev.	1.65	0.45	1.38	2.68	0.11	1.52
Number of obs	71					

Source: Cbonds, Eikon Refinitiv, authors' calculations.

Table 9.6 Descriptive characteristics for the sample of the largest Chinese corporate Eurobonds

	YTM	*Ln_Dur*	*Ln_Assets*	*Assets_to_ Equity*	*ROE*	*YTM_GB*
Min	1.89	0.78	0.15	7.16	0.02	2.77
Max	9.73	4.33	3.69	12.52	0.30	4.33
Mean	4.96	2.93	1.73	11.64	0.18	3.47
St. Dev.	2.40	1.04	0.68	0.93	0.08	0.37
Number of obs	55					

are taken from the Eikon Refinitiv database. Due to omissions in the data on covenants and on financial indicators of issuers in case of non-public companies, as well as clearing the sample from extremal values, the final sample consists of 71 observations for Indian Eurobonds and 55 observations for the Chinese market.

The descriptive statistics for the dependent and control variables for the largest Indian and Chinese corporate Eurobonds are presented in Tables 9.5 and 9.6, respectively.

Tables 9.5 and 9.6 provide information on covenants established for the largest issues of corporate Eurobonds under consideration. From Table 9.6, it follows that in China, the issuers of largest corporate Eurobond issues set limitation on liens (100%), covenants of events of default[1] (98%), and merger restrictions (82%). In India, the Eurobond issuers most frequently set limitation on liens (99%), covenants of events of default (99%) and cross default [2] (97%).

The calculation results are presented in Table 9.7. We note that for most covenants the statistical significance of their effect on the dependent variable is not high. For both China and India, the total number of covenants established for corporate Eurobonds has a positive effect on the yield of initial placement. For India, this factor is significant at the 5% level. We conclude that for the emerging Eurobond markets of China and India, the establishment of covenants is a signal

Table 9.7 Results of calculations on the sample of the largest issues of Chinese and Indian Eurobonds

	China, ytm				*India, ytm*		
	(1)	*(2)*	*(3)*	*(4)*	*(5)*	*(6)*	*(7)*
Num_of_ covenants		0.055			0.116**		
		(0.062)			(0.047)		
Financial_ covenants	-1.153**						
	(0.473)						
Merger restrictions			-0.006				
			(0.417)				
Limitation of indebtedness			0.799				
			(0.506)				
Cross_default				-0.135		-0.958	
				(0.325)		(1.071)	
Limitation of payment				0.731			
				(0.782)			
Rating trigger							-0.419
							(0.457)
Collective action clause							-0.487
							(0.692)
YTM_GB	0.193	0.102	0.190	0.103	0.167	0.195*	0.185
	(0.147)	(0.152)	(0.157)	(0.149)	(0.115)	(0.118)	(0.121)
Ln_Dur	0.517**	0.525**	0.520**	0.499**	-0.985**	-0.999**	-1.007**
	(0.277)	(0.239)	(0.233)	(0.240)	(0.389)	(0.397)	(0.412)
Ln_Assets	-0.503***	-0.495***	-0.486***	-0.463***	-0.163	-0.259*	-0.414***
	(0.152)	(0.161)	(0.181)	(0.162)	(0.160)	(0.148)	(0.135)
Assets_to_Equity	0.555***	0.409***	0.447***	0.423***	-0.029	-0.028	-0.032
	(0.050)	(0.085)	(0.039)	(0.076)	(0.026)	(0.027)	(0.027)
ROE	-0.249	1.732			-4.644***	-5.793***	-5.245***
	(2.216)	(2.531)			(1.601)	(1.740)	(1.688)
Constant	6.497***	6.466***	6.499***	6.690***	7.687***	10.459***	11.426***
	(1.808)	(1.901)	(2.048)	(1.991)	(1.975)	(1.939)	(1.765)
Number of obs	55	55	55	55	71	71	71
R^2 adjusted	0.844	0.828	0.833	0.828	0.398	0.316	0.273

Significance levels: * $p < 10\%$, ** $p < 5\%$, *** $p < 1\%$

of an unfavourable financial position of the issuer rather than an opportunity to reduce the yield of initial placement.

For the Chinese Eurobond market, financial covenants have a significant negative effect on the yield of initial placement (Table 9.7). For the Indian market, this effect is not observed. For the Chinese market, a negative impact on the yield of initial placement is also exerted by merger restrictions, cross-defaults, and covenants of events of default. For the Indian market, cross-defaults, rating trigger, collective action clauses, covenants of events of default, and restrictions on transactions with affiliates have a negative impact on the yield of initial placement. These results are in line with the conclusions of Chava and Jarrow (2004), Reisel (2004), Jun and Wei (2005), and Bradley and Roberts (2004).

For the Indian Eurobond market, the yield of initial placement is significantly positively affected by the limitation on indebtedness, limitation on subsidiary debt, merger restriction and covenant suspension. For the Chinese market, a rating trigger significantly positively affects the dependent variable. Our explanation is that these covenants primarily signal investors about the unfavourable financial situation of the issuer. These results contradict Chava and Jarrow (2004), Reisel (2004), Ju and Wei (2005), and Bradley and Roberts (2004), but are in line with the conclusion of Tanigawa and Katsura (2014), who reveal a positive effect for the bonds rated A, BBB, BB and B in the Japan market.

For both the markets under consideration, the yield to maturity on GBs has a stable positive effect on the yield on initial placement of corporate Eurobonds. Impact of the size of the company is significantly negative (the principle of 'too big to fail'). The higher the ROE, the lower the yield of initial placement, but this effect is statistically significant only for the Indian market. For the Chinese market, the debt burden, as well as the maturity, has a significant positive effect on the yield of initial placement.

Conclusions

In this chapter, we test the influence of covenants on the cost of debt of Eurobond issuers in emerging and developed markets. For the Eurobond markets of S. Korea and Germany, the results of our regression analysis are the following: with the inclusion of covenants, the initial placement yield is lower. Therefore covenants in loan agreements reduce the cost of debt in the markets of Germany and South Korea. Comparing Germany and S. Korea, we come to the conclusion that covenants are more significant for S. Korea. On the one hand, S. Korea has got a developed exchange bond market; on the other, it is a 'transitional' country between developed and developing, so investors require more protection.

We also reveal the effect of covenants on the yield of initial placement for the largest Eurobond issues in India and China. For both China and India, the total number of covenants established for corporate Eurobonds has a positive effect on the yield of initial placement. We conclude that for the emerging Eurobond markets of China and India, the establishment of covenants is a signal of an unfavourable financial position of the issuer rather than an opportunity to reduce the yield of initial placement.

For the Chinese Eurobond market, financial covenants have a significant negative effect on the yield of initial placement. For the Chinese market, a negative impact on the yield of initial placement is also exerted by merger restrictions, cross-defaults, and covenants of events of default. For the Indian market, cross-defaults, rating trigger, collective action clauses, covenants of events of default, and restrictions on transactions with affiliates have a negative impact on the yield of initial placement. However, the statistical significance is not high.

Notes

1 Covenants of events of default are conditions, the violation of which is a trigger for the occurrence of a default on a bond (for example, non-payment of the principal amount of debt).
2 If the company has other debt obligations, then default on these obligations means cross-default on the current bond issue.

References

Bazzana, F., Broccardo, E. (2013). The covenant threshold in public and private debt. *Banca Impresa Società*, 32(1): 3–24. DOI: https://doi.org/10.1435/73808

Bradley, M., Roberts, M. R. (2004). The structure and pricing of corporate debt covenants. 6th Annual Texas Finance Festival. DOI: https://dx.doi.org/10.2139/ssrn.585882

Chava, S., Jarrow, R. A. (2004). Bankruptcy prediction with industry effects. *Review of Finance*, 8(4), 537–569. DOI: https://doi.org/10.1093/rof/8.4.537

Chava, S., Purnanandam, A. (2010). Is default risk negatively related to stock returns?. *The Review of Financial Studies*, 23(6), 2523–2559. DOI: https://doi.org/10.1093/rfs/hhp107

Isem, J., Porteous, D. (2005). Commercial banks and microfinance: Evolving models of success (No. 33458, pp. 1–8). Washington, DC: The Word Bank.

Ju, J., Wei, S. J. (2005). Endowment versus finance: a wooden barrel theory of international trade (No. 5-123). Washington, DC: International Monetary Fund.

Reisel, N. (2004). On the value of restrictive covenants: An empirical investigation of public bond issues. Working paper, Rutgers University.

Tanigawa, Y., Katsura, S. (2014). Covenants and collateral in Japanese corporate straight bonds: choice and yield spread. World Finance Conference Working Paper.

Part 3

If the default is tomorrow

10 If the default is tomorrow

Factors influencing corporate bond recovery rates

Introduction

The outstanding volume of corporate bonds (CB) in developing countries is growing at a faster pace compared to the CB market of developed countries, where the real returns (nominal rate minus inflation) are getting closer to zero, and developing countries are demonstrating attractive investment opportunities.

As demonstrated in the monograph of Teplova and Sokolova (2018), the volume of the CB market in developing countries increased from 2006 to June 2018 from 2.8 to 12.9 tn USD. The share of CB of developing countries in the total volume of outstanding CB on the global market increased from 11.2% to 31.7%. Investment in CB of developing countries entails high risk.

According to the review of S&P Global Fixed Income Research and S&P Global Market Intelligence's Credit Pro (2019), in 2018 there were 82 defaults on bonds in the global market, which was 14% less than in 2017. Despite the decrease in the amount of defaults, the volume of the debt which defaulted in 2018 was 131.65 bn USD, which was 26% above the indicator in 2017. The average volume of debt per company that defaulted increased to 1.6 bn USD (from 1.1 bn USD in 2017), which even surpassed the values of the 2009 crisis (1.4 bn USD) after the Lehman Brothers bankruptcy.

All the companies that defaulted in 2018 had BB+ rating and below at the beginning of the year, of which 74% were assigned to the category CCC/C. For the first time in over 38 years, during which S&P had conducted a study of defaults, CB with speculative grade rating constituted the majority of all issuers.

Most of the previous papers on the current topic are focused on the CB defaults of companies in developed countries and review a wide sample of companies of different sectors. Papers that study the determinants of the CB recovery rates in developing countries are practically absent (Mili et al., 2018).

The aim of Chapter 10 is to reveal the determinants of the CB recovery rate of both developed and developing countries. We analyze the influence of bond issue characteristics, the issuer's financial conditions and macroeconomic variables. The originality of our research is that, first, compared to previous papers, we consider an extended sample of CB from developing countries with a focus on Russia. For example, Mili et al. (2018) consider only three issues of rouble CB that defaulted.

Second, a distinguishing feature of our research is a comparative analysis of the factors that significantly influence the recovery rate in developing and developed countries. Third, Chapter 10 is focused on the bonds of financial companies which occupy a high share in many developing countries. For example, among the rouble CB issued in 2008–2018, the share of banks and financial institutions made up 54%. The share among Asia's emerging markets is 35%, in Latin America 36% (source: calculated by authors according to Bloomberg database).

Review of methods to calculate the recovery rate in the case of default

The recovery rate shows the amount of money that an investor can expect to be returned after the issuer's default. The definition contains the possibility of different approaches in the quantitative evaluation of this rate. Let us review them in detail.

The economic approach in calculating recovery rate. In accordance with Basel II, the loss given default (LGD) is calculated as the ratio of expected loss (EL) to the exposure at default (EAD)[1]:

$$LGD = EL \,/\, EAD \tag{10.1}$$

In accordance with Basel II and III, the recovery rate (RR) is calculated as[2]:

$$RR = 1 - LGD = 1 - EL \,/\, EAD \tag{10.2}$$

Formula (2) can be represented as the ratio of the discounted cash flows of recovery payments minus collection costs to the exposure at default (EAD):

$$RR = \frac{1}{EAD} \cdot \sum_{t=1}^{T} \frac{(RP_t - C_t)}{(1 - r)^t} \tag{10.3}$$

The disadvantages of this approach are: firstly, due to the difficulty of accessing the recovery payments, since they can be realized both in cash or non-cash form; secondly, due to the difficulty of assessing direct and indirect collection costs; and thirdly, due to the choice of an appropriate discount rate, especially for longer time horizons.

The market approach in calculating the recovery rate. This approach is based on the assumption that the market takes into account the uncertainty concerning future recovery cash flows, the evaluation of costs and the discount rate. All expectations are reflected in the market price. Thus the market price is the benchmark for calculating the bond recovery rate in the case of default (Guo et al., 2008).

In the market approach, the recovery rate can be calculated using several methods. The first is the ratio of market price after the default to the bond nominal value:

$$RR_d = B_d / F \tag{10.4}$$

where RR_d recovery rate, B_d is bond market value after the default, F is nominal value.

This method is employed by Moody's; the market price is taken 30 days after the default, which is due to the 30-day grace period of payments after the due date of coupon payments.

The disadvantage of this method is the potential problem of the incomparability of recovery rates of various bonds, because the bond market price is determined not only by its nominal value, and it can start to decrease long before the default happens.

The second method is the ratio of the market price after the default to the risk-free government bond price. The advantage of such a method is that it incorporates current macroeconomic variables into the price of a risk-free bond. The issue of using this approach lies in the difficulty of choosing the corresponding bond of the same maturity, especially in cross-country comparisons.

The third method is the ratio of market price after the event of default to the market price before the default:

$$RR_d = B_d / B_{d-} \tag{10.5}$$

where RR_d is recovery rate, B_d is bond market price after the default, and B_{d-} is bond market price before the event of default.

The advantage of this approach is that it is based on market quotes before and after the default; that is, it takes into account investor expectations. In our paper we employ this approach in calculating the recovery rate.

Review of previous researches on the determinants of recovery rate

The recovery rate is influenced by various groups of factors: the loan characteristics, the issuer's financial condition, and macroeconomic variables (Table 10.1).

Most papers focus on the corporate US market. Altman and Kishore (1996) find that the key determinants of CB recovery rates are the seniority of debt issues and the company's industry. Credit rating has no significant influence on the recovery rate. Hanson and Shuermann (2004) reach the same conclusion in regard to the leading role of debt seniority as a determinant of the recovery rate.

Acharya et al. (2007) conduct an analysis of factors that influence the recovery rate in the US market in 1982–1999. The volume of the bond issue significantly

Table 10.1 Traditionally considered determinants of the recovery rate

Factor	*Research papers*
Bond issue characteristics	
Seniority of debt issues	Altman and Kishore (1996), Hanson and Shuermann (2004), Mora (2015)
Secured/unsecured issue	Rösch and Scheule (2014), Mora (2015), Mili et al. (2018)
Volume of the bond issue	Acharya et al. (2007)
Credit rating	Rösch and Scheule (2014)
Firm-level factors	
Industry	Altman and Kishore (1996)
Leverage	Acharya et al. (2007)
Assets	Jankowitch et al. (2014), Mora (2015)
Age	Rösch and Scheule (2014)
Q Tobin	
Net income margin	Mora (2015)
Macroeconomic factors	
S&P 500 return rate	Acharya et al. (2007), Mora (2015)
GDP growth	Acharya et al. (2007), Rösch and Scheule (2014), Tobback et al. (2014), Mili et al. (2018)
Inflation	Rösch and Scheule (2014), Tobback et al. (2014), Qi and Zhao (2011)
Treasury bill interest rate	Mora (2015), Qi and Zhao (2011)
Unemployment rate	Tobback et al. (2014)

positively affects the recovery rate. Companies with higher leverage demonstrate lower recovery rates. The significance of macroeconomic variables decreases with the inclusion of industry variables.

Jankowitch et al. (2014) study the determinants of recovery rates among 818 US bonds from 259 issuers in 2002–2010. The authors conclude that the issuer's asset size significantly and positively affects the recovery rate. Market and industry-average levels of the recovery rate are the most significant factors influencing the recovery rate.

Rösch and Scheule (2014) discover factors that can forecast the probability of default and the recovery rate in the US bond market from 1982 to 2009. The sample includes 1653 defaults. The recovery rate is computed as the ratio of the bond price 30 days after the default to its nominal value. The authors conclude that the lower the bond's credit rating, the higher the probability of default and the lower the recovery rate. If the bond issue is a subordinated or unsecured loan, the recovery rate decreases. The influence of firm characteristics and GDP growth is also significant.

Mora (2015) reveals the significance of the influence of different types of bond security, the industry of the issuer, and a number of macroeconomic variables on the recovery rate. The sample includes 4222 bonds defaulted during 1978–2008. The author reveals a significant positive influence of the dummies of secured and senior bonds, and net income margin. Companies in pro-cyclical industries are characterized by lower recovery rates during turmoils. The market index return has a positive significant influence on the recovery rate.

Varma and Cantor (2005) study the influence of various types of defaults including bankruptcies in accordance with the US Code 7 and 11, on the recovery rate in the US market. They demonstrate that the recovery rate significantly depends on the type of default: the most negative influence on recovery rate was bankruptcies under Code 7.

Tobback et al. (2014) reveal the determinants of the recovery rates of over 987 CB in the US market in 1984–2011. The original conclusion is that there is a negative relationship between the lagged GDP growth rate and the recovery rate. The authors attribute this to the fact that during periods of high economic activity lenders tend to provide loans to borrowers with high risk for much higher interest rates, and during economic slowdowns these loans default. Inflation is also negatively related with recovery rate.

Qi and Zhao (2011) study the determinants of the recovery rate on US bank loans and bonds for a long time period from 1985 to 2008. The authors reveal a significant negative influence of three-month T-Bills and a positive influence of stock index returns on the recovery rate.

Some papers consider developed and developing markets (Mili et al., 2018). Mili et al. (2018) conclude that the recovery rate increases if bonds are senior, and this effect is more pronounced in developing markets. The larger the company and the lower the leverage, the higher the recovery rate for both emerging and developed markets. The recovery rate positively correlates with GDP growth rate, and the power of its influence is double for developed markets.

The most widely used method to study the determinants of recovery rates is a regression analysis. OLS regressions are used by Acharya et al. (2007), Qi and Hao (2011), Jankowitch et al. (2014), and Mora (2015). Researchers also use the following methods of regression analysis: logit and probit models (Chava et al. 2011), models with random and fixed effects (Rösch and Scheule, 2014), and generalized method of moments (Mili et al., 2018).

In recent times there has been a surge in the number of studies in which researchers use machine learning algorithms alongside regression models. Qi and Zhao (2011) compare the precision of different models and conclude that decision forests and neural networks possess higher forecasting power compared to linear regressions.

Yao et al. (2015) reveal that non-parametric models beat out-of-sample regressions in terms of precision in the US bond market. The best model in the quality of forecast precision for senior bonds is the SVR-model, and for other bonds the least squared support vector regression (LV-SVR) models are preferable. Loterman et al. (2012) build and test 24 parametric and non-parametric models of recovery rate evaluation. They reveal that non-parametric models (SVR and neural networks) provide better results than regression models.

In our paper we consider three groups of variables: macroeconomic factors, firm-level factors and bond characteristics. The majority of previous literature is focused on the US market (Yao et al., 2015; Tobback et al., 2014; Mora,

2015: Varma and Cantor, 2005). Comparatively little research has been done on developing markets (Mili et al., 2018). In our research, we close this gap.

Hypotheses of our research

We put forward and empirically test a number of hypotheses. The first group of hypotheses deal with the influence of bond issue characteristics on the recovery rate.

Hypothesis 1.1. Secured bonds have a higher recovery rate in the case of default.

As demonstrated by Rösch and Scheule (2014) and Mora (2015) for the US market, the presence of collateral significantly increases the recovery rate. Mili et al. (2018) also reveal a significant positive influence of collateral in both developed and developing markets.

Hypothesis 1.2. Senior bonds have a higher recovery rate in the case of default.

Senior bonds provide privileged rights over the issuer's assets. Altman and Kishore (1996), Hanson and Shuermann (2004), and Varma and Cantor (2005) demonstrate for the US market that bond seniority is one of the most significant determinants of the recovery rate.

The second group of hypotheses concern the influence of the issuer's financial indicators.

Hypothesis 2.1. The initiation of a bankruptcy of the issuer decreases the bond recovery rate. This effect is more pronounced in emerging markets.

Antonova (2013) reveals the significant influence of initiating bankruptcy procedure on the recovery rate of rouble CB. Similar conclusions are made by Varma and Cantor (2005) for the US market. We propose that due to the high risks in emerging markets the recovery rate will be less than in developed markets.

Hypothesis 2.2. The larger the company, the higher the bond's recovery rate in the case of default.

We assume that it is easier for larger companies to attract financing (including from the government) in a crisis (the principle of 'too big to fail'). As demonstrated by Mora (2015), Jacobs and Karagozoglu (2007), and Jankowitch et al. (2014), company size positively influences the recovery rate.

Hypothesis 2.3. A high leverage decreases the recovery rate for bonds.

As shown in Varma and Cantor (2005) for the US market and in Mili et al. (2018) on a sample of both developed and developing countries, companies with higher leverage demonstrate lower recovery rates in the case of default. The same conclusions are obtained by Mili et al. (2018) and Jankowitsch et al. (2014) in regard to the default barrier indicator. We assume that for higher leverage, the owners of lower seniority bonds accept higher risks and the recovery rate for this debt is lower.

Hypothesis 2.4. The share of highly liquid assets in the total assets has a significant influence on the recovery rate.

Under highly liquid assets we understand cash and its equivalents, and company's short-term investments. We suppose that the influence of this factor can be multi-directional. On the one hand, a large share of cash and equivalents in the assets is a sign of low asset management efficiency. On the other hand, a high share of highly liquid assets reflects the company's ability to repay investors in the case of default, and in the case of banks it means compliance with the requirements of the Basel Committee on liquidity. As demonstrated by Qi and Zhao (2011) for the US bank loans and bond market, the higher the share of cash in the total assets, the higher the recovery rate.

The third group of hypotheses deal with the influence of macroeconomic and institutional variables on the recovery rate in the case of default.

Hypothesis 3.1. The higher the index of law supremacy, the higher the recovery rate.

Compliance with legislation in general improves the protection of bondholder rights in particular. As demonstrated by Mili et al. (2018), a favourable institutional environment had a positive effect on the bond recovery rate in developed and emerging markets, including a reduction in information asymmetry during bankruptcy proceedings.

Hypothesis 3.2. In the event of a crisis in the economy, the recovery rate reduces.

We measure the state of the macroeconomic environment on the basis of the real GDP growth rate, inflation, and unemployment. We assume that the higher the GDP growth rate, the lower the inflation rate, and the lower the unemployment rate, the higher the recovery rate. In the event of a crisis, it is more difficult for companies to attract financing and pay off creditors. As demonstrated by Rösch and Scheule (2014) for the US market, a higher GDP growth rate increases the recovery rate. Tobbak et al. (2014) find a significant negative impact of inflation. Bellotti and Crook (2014) by using UK market data, reveal a significant negative effect of unemployment on the recovery rate of loans to individuals.

The list of variables and the expected direction of their influence are given in Table 10.2.

Table 10.2 Variables of our study

Variable	*Description*	*Expected direction of influence*
recovery rate	Dependent variable: recovery rate calculated by the market method at bond prices 3–4 months before default and 30 days after default (for more details see the section 'Description of the sample')	
bankruptcy	Dummy variable, equal to 1 if the company initiated bankruptcy proceedings, 0 – otherwise	-
senior	Dummy variable, equal to 1 in the case of seniority of the bond issue, 0 – otherwise	+
secured	The dummy variable, equal to 1 if the bond is secured, 0 – otherwise	+
ln_tot_assets	Company size, defined as the logarithm of total assets	+
Liq_assets_to_Assets	The share of highly liquid assets (cash, cash equivalents and short-term investments) in total assets, %	+ / -
Liq_assets_to_Debt	The ratio of highly liquid assets to debt, %	+ / -
Debt_to_Assets	Debt to asset ratio, %	-
def_bar	The default barrier, determined by the formula: (Short-term Debt + ½*Long-term Debt) / Total Assets	-
LTD_to_Assets	The ratio of long-term debt to assets, %	-
LTD_to_Debt	The share of long-term debt in total debt, %	-
rule_of_law	The World Bank Rule of law index, measured on a scale from -2.5 to 2.5, where -2.5 is the minimum, 2.5 is the maximum	+
unemployment	Unemployment rate, %	-
inflation	Inflation rate, % per annum	-
GDP	Real GDP growth rate, % per annum	+

Research methodology

In our research, we test linear regression models of the following form:

$$RecoveryRate = \alpha + \sum \beta_{1,i} bond\_characteristic_i + \\ + \sum \beta_{2,j} financial\_indicator_j + \sum \beta_{3,k} macro\_indicator_k + \varepsilon \tag{10.6}$$

where *RecoveryRate* is the recovery rate, *bond_characteristic* is one or several characteristics of the bond issue, *financial_indicator* is one or several financial indicators of the issuer, *macro_indicator* is one or several macroeconomic variables of the country of the issuer (refer to the variables description in Table 10.2).

Model testing is carried out both throughout the sample and individually by sub-samples of bonds in developed and emerging markets.

Variables are included in the regression models with account of the correlation matrix. We do not assume the presence of endogeneity in the model, since the financial indicators of issuing companies and macroeconomic indicators are obtained the year before default.

Description of the sample

The initial sample includes bonds of banks and financial institutions of developed and emerging markets which defaulted in 2008–2018. The data sources are Cbonds, Bloomberg, and Eikon Refinitiv. The peak of defaults occurred during the crisis of 2008: about 1200 defaults in 2008 and about 200 in 2018.

The specific choice of banks and financial institutions as an industry for consideration is due to the large share of bonds of these companies in the emerging capital markets. According to the Cbonds database, in Russia from 2008 to 2018, 4608 bond issues were placed in the domestic market, of which 54% are bonds of banks and financial institutions. In comparison, over the same period, 495 bond issues were placed in Kazakhstan, of which 67% are issues of financial sector companies. In emerging markets in Asia, 35% of bond issues are in the financial sector (source: Eikon Refinitiv, authors' calculations).

Further, for each bond issue from the initial sample, we check the availability of data on quotes before the default and 30 days after it. The sample is reduced to 508 bond issues. The next step is to look for financial indicators of the issuing companies and the characteristics of bond issues on the basis of Bloomberg, Capital IQ and SPARK. It is found that for 34% of the companies in the sample, the necessary indicators for calculation are absent in these databases. Thus the sample is reduced to 333 bonds of 121 issuers.

The resulting sample includes a number of bond issues by the same companies. Using financial indicators of the same company for a large set of different bond issues could potentially lead us to sampling bias. To solve this problem, the data is processed: bonds of the same issuer are included in the sample only if one of the following conditions is met: 1) at least one year passed between the defaults on various issues, 2) or different issues defaulted at one time, but they have different security or seniority. As an example of the latter situation, we consider two bond issues of Peresvet JSCB, defaults on which occurred in 2016, and the recovery rates are 30.5% and 81.5%.

The final sample contains 142 bond issues, including 70 bond issues of companies in emerging markets (Russia, Azerbaijan, Argentina, Brazil, Indonesia, Kazakhstan, China, Mexico, Panama, Poland, Ukraine, South Africa) and 72 issues of companies in developed market (USA, Australia, Austria, United

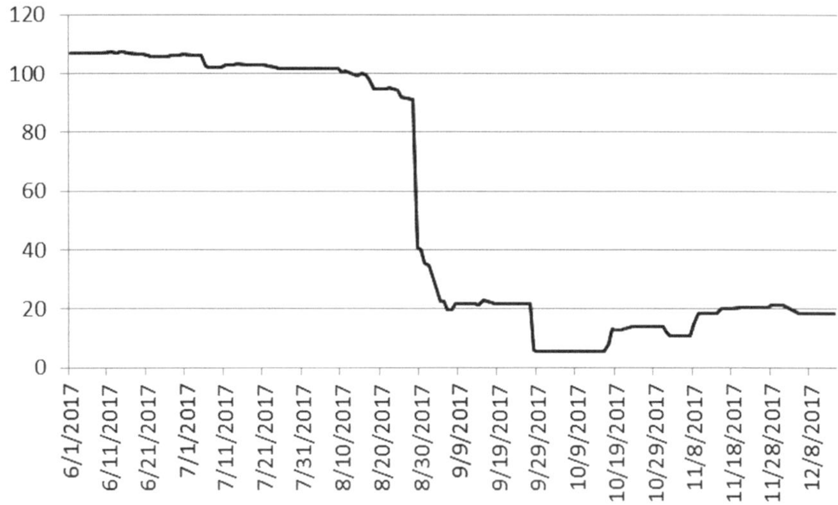

Figure 10.1 Dynamics of closing price on Eurobonds of Bank FC Otkritie, 10% 26 April 2019, USD, Berlin stock exchange.

Source: Cbonds.

Kingdom, Hong Kong, Greece, Denmark, Israel, Ireland, Iceland, Italy, Canada, Netherlands, New Zealand, Portugal, Switzerland, Japan).

Guo (2008) shows that bond prices start to decline well before the default date. To calculate the return rates, we consider bond prices 3–4 months before the event of default in order to level out possible price hikes. As an illustrative example, we show the dynamics of prices for Otkritie Bank Eurobonds, 10% April 26, 2019, USD (Figure 10.1). Significant price hikes were on August 28, 2017, when the Bank of Russia announced the reorganization of the bank, and a few days before this date, on August 24, 2017. The default date according to Cbonds is October 31, 2017. In this case, if one calculates the rate of return on the prices of Eurobonds one month before default, it would be incorrect.

Descriptive statistics on the recovery rate are presented in Table 10.3. The average recovery rates in developed and emerging markets are almost the same: 55.99% and 55.26%, respectively (Table 10.3). Figure 10.2 shows a histogram of the distribution of the recovery rate for our sample. We conclude that there is a high probability of a recovery rate of either 90–100% or 0–10% of the invested funds: 41% and 28%, respectively. The probability of a recovery rate from 20 to 90% of the invested funds does not exceed 31% in total (Figure 10.2). Our histogram is close to the histogram of the distribution of losses for defaults in the US market, constructed by Qi and Zhao (2011).

Descriptive statistics for independent variables are shown in Table 10.4. From Table 10.4 we can conclude that issuers in developed and emerging markets in

Table 10.3 Descriptive statistics on the recovery rate, %

	Full sample		*Emerging markets*		*Developed markets*	
	Mean	*Standard deviation*	*Mean*	*Standard deviation*	*Mean*	*Standard deviation*
Recovery_rate	55.63	37.71	55.26	38.24	55.99	37.45

Source: Authors' calculations on 142 observations.

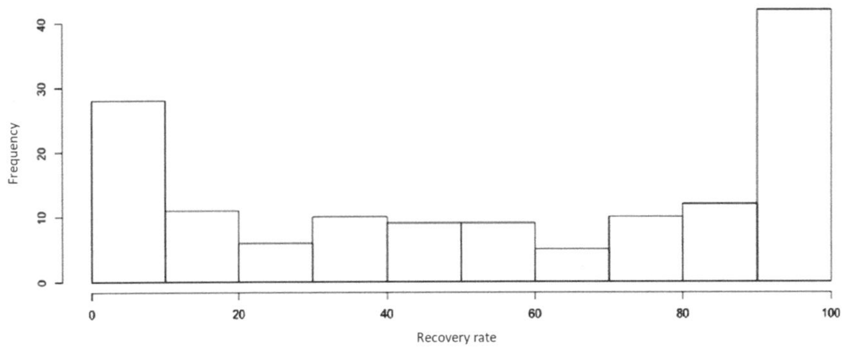

Figure 10.2 Probability distribution of the rate of return on bonds. The sample of our study.

our sample differ considerably in terms of the amount of total assets. In emerging markets, the debt burden is higher, on average; the ratio of debt to total assets is 0.55, while in developed markets it is 0.46. Emerging markets are characterized by significantly higher inflation rates – an average of 8.76% per year, while for developed markets it is 2.23%. There are low levels of the development of institutional environment: on average, the rule of law index is -0.51, while for developed countries the values stand at 1.45 (according to the World Bank scale from -2.5 to +2.5). Note that the average GDP growth rates for the samples of developed and developing markets coincide: 1.2% per year (Table 10.4), which we explain by the relatively large share of bond issues from the Russian Federation (about 50%) and the recession in the Russian economy in 2014–2016.

Results

Table 10.5 presents the results of calculations for the full sample of bonds. Variables of bankruptcy, the presence of collateral, the seniority of bond issues, the rule of law index and unemployment rate have a significant impact on the recovery rate.

The initiation of bankruptcy proceedings decreases the recovery rate on the company's bonds. In all model specifications, this variable is significant at 1% level

Table 10.4 Descriptive statistics: mean values of independent variables

	Full sample	*Emerging markets*	*Developed markets*
ln_tot_assets	8.21	6.90	9.57
Debt_to_Assets	0.51	0.55	0.46
LTD_to_Assets	0.35	0.41	0.29
Liq_assets_to_Assets	0.21	0.18	0.23
Liq_assets_to_Debt	1.71	2.59	0.86
ln_amt_issued	18.58	18.16	18.99
rule_of_law	0.48	-0.51	1.45
unemployment	6.89	6.97	6.82
inflation	5.45	8.76	2.23
GDP	1.20	1.19	1.20

(Table 10.5). The conclusion is consistent with the results of Antonova (2013) for the Russian market and Varma and Cantor (2005) for the US market.

For senior bond issues, the recovery rate rises, which is consistent with the conclusions of Altman and Kishore (1996), and Mora (2015) on the US market. This variable has a positive effect in all model specifications, but the statistical significance is not always high.

Our findings are often not surprising. The presence of collateral is a significant (at 1–5% level) factor that increases the recovery rate of bonds (Table 10.5). The conclusion is consistent with the results of Rösch and Scheule (2014), and Mora (2015) for the US market. The share of long-term debt in total assets negatively affects the recovery rate after default. Varma and Cantor (2005) on the US market and Mili et al. (2018) on a sample of developed and developing markets reach a similar conclusion with respect to the indicator of financial leverage.

Country and institutional factors are important. The rule of law index significantly positively (at 1–5% level) affects the recovery rate. A similar conclusion is obtained by Mili et al. (2018) for a sample of 600 bonds from developed and emerging markets.

The size of the company, measured as a logarithm of its total assets, has a positive effect on the recovery rate, although the statistical significance is not very high (Table 10.5). A conclusion about the positive effect of company size is also obtained by Jankowitsch et al. (2014), and Rösch and Scheule (2014) for the US market.

The original conclusion, which contradicts the initial hypothesis, is that the unemployment rate significantly and positively (at the 10% level) affects the recovery rate (Table 10.5). This conclusion contradicts the results of Bellotti and Crook (2014) for the UK market, but is consistent with the results of Tobback et al. (2014) for the US market. A possible explanation is that in an unfavourable economic situation (high unemployment), both lenders and borrowers tend to control risks more tightly. Judicial authorities and bankruptcy trustees are more careful in finding and returning the withdrawn assets.

Table 10.5 Calculations results on the full sample of bonds

	1	*2*	*3*
bankruptcy	-29.760***	-30.444***	-29.866***
	(6.176)	(6.192)	(6.260)
senior	23.557***	22.239	21.410
	(6.968)	(14.718)	(14.890)
secured	25.560***	25.109**	24.624**
	(8.438)	(11.311)	(11.393)
rule_of_law	8.440***	7.846***	8.022**
	(2.825)	(2.841)	(3.157)
LTD_to_Assets		-14.954	-15.398
		(9.329)	(9.886)
unemployment	1.293*	1.236*	1.239*
	(0.694)	(0.693)	(0.698)
subordinated		-4.612	-5.840
		(15.489)	(15.594)
ln_tot_assets			0.036
			(1.180)
Liq_assets_to_Assets			-12.526
			(12.377)
Constant	35.315***	43.451***	46.413**
	(9.101)	(16.580)	(20.461)
Observations	142	142	142
R^2	0.253	0.268	0.274
Adjusted R^2	0.225	0.230	0.224
Breusch–Pagan test, BP	6.7905	8.5958	11.063
(p-value)	(0.2367)	(0.283)	(0.2714)

Significance levels: * p <10%, ** p <5%, *** p <1%

The Breusch–Pagan test shows lack of heteroscedasticity in the constructed regression models (Table 10.5), and thus the resulting model is built on homogeneous observations and has a constant dispersion.

Table 10.6 presents the results of calculations for developed and emerging markets separately. For developed markets, the initiation of bankruptcy, the seniority of the bond issue, the ratio of highly liquid assets to debt, and the GDP growth rate have a significant impact on the recovery rate. For emerging markets, the set of the most significant determinants of the recovery rate changes: the fact of initiating bankruptcy proceedings, the availability of collateral and the size of the company are important.

Initiating bankruptcy proceedings reduces the bond recovery rate for default, both for a subsample of developed markets and a subsample of emerging markets (Table 10.6). The conclusion is consistent with the results of Antonova (2013), and Varma and Cantor (2005). We note that the fact of bankruptcy initiation is significant at the 1% level for both developed and emerging markets, but the regression coefficient of this factor for the sample of bonds from emerging markets is higher than for the developed ones.

Table 10.6 Results of calculations for the sub-samples of bonds of developed and emerging markets

	Developed markets		*Emerging markets*	
	1	*2*	*3*	*4*
bankruptcy	-24.057***	-24.292***	-40.324***	-37.566***
	(8.449)	(8.620)	(9.210)	(9.562)
senior	27.547***	23.561**	18.751	17.790
	(8.490)	(9.393)	(11.681)	(12.001)
secured	14.047	10.072	29.374**	29.586**
	(10.828)	(11.821)	(12.372)	(12.823)
Liq_assets_to_Debt	5.141*	5.693		
	(2.992)	(3.645)		
Liq_assets_to_Assets				-11.332
				(16.332)
ln_tot_assets	-1.836		2.443*	1.803
	(1.785)		(1.407)	(1.643)
Debt_to_Assets	0.768			
	(20.545)			
LTD_to_debt				4.456
				(12.695)
rule_of_law		1.150		6.243
		(9.520)		(8.194)
GDP	-3.810***	-3.735**		
	(1.416)	(1.472)		
unemployment				0.606
				(0.902)
Constant	52.607***	70.893**	28.701*	31.356
	(8.982)	(27.846)	(16.601)	(23.050)
Observations	72	72	70	70
R^2	0.294	0.307	0.362	0.386
Adjusted R^2	0.240	0.219	0.323	0.305

Significance levels: * $p < 10\%$, ** $p < 5\%$, *** $p < 1\%$

For a sample of bonds from developed markets, the seniority of bond issues has a significant positive effect on the recovery rate (Table 10.6), which is consistent with the results of Altman and Kishore (1996), and Mora (2015) for the US market. The seniority factor loses its statistical significance for emerging market bonds, although the regression coefficient remains positive.

On the contrary, it is essential for emerging markets to provide collateral for bonds: this factor has a significant positive (at the 5% level) effect on the recovery rate after the default (Table 10.6). For developed markets, this factor preserves the direction of influence, but loses its statistical significance. Our conclusion differs from the results of Rösch and Scheule (2014) and Mora (2015) on the US market; in these studies, the availability of collateral is a significant factor.

Another difference is that for developed market bonds, the company size negatively affects the recovery rate (significance is not high), while for emerging markets the size effect is positive and significant at 10% level. This result contradicts the findings of Jankowitch et al. (2014) on the positive impact of asset size in the US market but is consistent with the results of Acharya et al. (2007) on the insignificance of the issuer's amount of assets. We attribute this paradoxical relationship in developed markets to the poor financial condition of many large companies during the 2008–2009 crisis, and to accepting higher risks by larger companies. In emerging markets, the principle of 'too big to fail' is more pronounced.

For companies in developed markets, we conclude that the higher the ratio of highly liquid assets (cash, cash equivalents and short-term investments) to debt, the higher the recovery rate (at the 10% level). For emerging markets, this factor has no significant effect.

For companies in emerging markets, we obtain the following relationship: the larger the share of long-term debt in total debt, the higher the bond recovery rate in the case of default (Table 10.6). A similar relationship is revealed by Jankowitsch et al. (2014).

For emerging market bonds, a higher share of highly liquid assets in the total assets reduces the recovery rate, although the statistical significance of this factor is not very high (Table 10.6). This result contradicts the findings of Qi and Zhao (2011) on the US market. Our explanation is that, firstly, in emerging markets, the inflation rate is higher, and cash and cash equivalents are depreciating faster, and secondly, short-term investment involves higher risks for emerging markets.

The higher the real GDP growth rate, the lower the recovery rate in the event of default on the bonds of companies in developed markets (the factor is significant at the 1% level). This result contradicts the findings of Rösch and Scheule (2014) on the positive impact of GDP growth on the recovery rate but is consistent with the findings of Tobback et al. (2014). Our explanation: as a factor of influence, we consider the GDP growth rate with a lag of one year. In favourable macroeconomic conditions, borrowers and lenders take more risks, which after a while leads to an increase in defaults and a reduction in the recovery rate. For bonds in emerging markets, GDP growth does not have a significant impact on the recovery rate.

The rule of law index has a positive effect on the recovery rate, which is in line with the findings of Mili et al. (2018), but for samples of developed and developing markets separately, the statistical significance of this factor is not high. Thus, differences in the institutional environment between clusters of developed and developing markets are significant, and within these clusters, cross-country differences in the rule of law index do not have a decisive influence on the rate of return.

Similarly, unlike the entire sample, the unemployment rate does not significantly affect the recovery rate when considering samples of developed and developing markets separately (Table 10.6).

Conclusion

For the first time, we reveal and compare the determinants of the bond recovery rate for defaults for developed and emerging markets with the consideration of an extended sample of rouble CB. Hypotheses on the effects of the characteristics of bond issues, financial indicators of the issuer and macroeconomic indicators are tested on the basis of multivariate linear regression models, as in most previous studies on the research topic: Acharya et al. (2007), Qi and Zhao (2011), Jankowitch et al. (2014), and Mora (2015). Although the market method for calculating the recovery rate is generally acceptable, we see a certain simplification of this approach, especially if low-liquid bonds of emerging markets are included in the sample.

When testing hypotheses for the full sample of bond issues, we obtain both the expected results and original conclusions. The bankruptcy initiation dummy has a significant negative effect on the rate of return. The dummy variables of bond seniority and collateral have a significant positive effect. The statistical significance of the impact of the company size and its debt burden is not high, but the direction of influence is as expected: the larger the company, the higher the recovery rate; the higher the share of long-term debt in total assets, the lower the recovery rate.

The role of the institutional environment is important: the rule of law index has a positive effect on the recovery rate. The paradoxical result is that the higher the unemployment rate, the higher the recovery rate. We explain this, firstly, by the fact that the unemployment rate is included in the models with a lag of one year, and secondly, by the fact that in an unfavourable economic situation lenders, borrowers, and other participants are more careful in controlling refunding and restructuring of the issues.

When testing hypotheses on bonds of developed and emerging markets separately, we reveal a number of differences. Bankruptcy initiation reduces the recovery rate for both samples, but the strength of this factor is higher for emerging markets. In developed markets, the seniority of bond issues has a significant positive effect on the recovery rate, but this factor is not significant for emerging markets. Conversely, in emerging markets, collateral for bonds plays a key role, while in developed markets this factor loses its significance. The effect of company size and the share of long-term debt in total debt is significant only for emerging markets. For developed markets, the influence of the ratio of highly liquid assets to debt is significant; in emerging markets this factor is not significant. In developed markets, the original conclusion is that the higher the growth rate of real GDP, the lower the recovery rate. Optimism in the market reduces the vigilance of participants and efforts to return funds. In addition, our paper considers the lagged GDP growth rate. In favourable macroeconomic conditions, borrowers and lenders take more risks, which after a while lead to an increase in defaults and a reduction in the recovery rate.

Notes

1 An Explanatory Note on the Basel II IRB Risk Weight Functions, 2005.
2 An Explanatory Note on the Basel II IRB Risk Weight Functions, 2005.

References

Acharya, V. V., Bharath, S. T., Srinivasan, A. (2007). Does industry-wide distress affect defaulted firms? Evidence from creditor recoveries. *Journal of Financial Economics*, 85: 787–821. DOI: https://doi.org/10.1016/j.jfineco.2006.05.011

Altman, E. I., Brady, B., Resti, A., Sironi, A. (2005). The link between default and recovery rates: Theory, empirical evidence and implications. *Journal of Business*, 78: 2203–2227. DOI: https://doi.org/10.1086/497044

Altman, E. I., Kishore, V. M. (1996). Almost everything you wanted to know about recoveries on defaulted bonds. *Financial Analysts Journal*, 52: 57–64. DOI: https://doi.org/10.2469/faj.v52.n6.2040

Antonova, E. N. (2013). Estimation of the rate of return on corporate bonds of Russian issuers. Thesis for the degree of PhD. 155 p. (in Rus.)

Bellotti, T., Crook, J. (2014). Retail credit stress testing using a discrete hazard model with macroeconomic factors. *Journal of the Operational Research Society*, 65(3), 340–350. DOI: https://dx.doi.org/10.1057/jors.2013.91

Chava, S., Stefanescu, C., Turnbull, S. (2011). Modeling the loss distribution. *Management Science*, 57(7): 1267–1287

Covitz, D. M., Han, S. (2005). An empirical analysis of bond recovery rates: Exploring a structural view of default. *SSRN Electronic Journal*, 1–45. DOI: https://dx.doi.org/10.2139/ssrn.675987

Elkamhi, R., Jacobs, K., Pan, X. (2014). The cross section of recovery rates and default probabilities implied by credit default swap spreads. *Journal of Financial and Quantitative Analysis*, 49: 193–220. DOI: https://doi.org/10.1017/S0022109014000088

Guo, X., Jarrow, R. A., Lin, H. (2008). Distressed debt prices and recovery rate estimation. *Review of Derivatives Research*, 11: 171–204. DOI: https://doi.org/10.1007/s11147-009-9029-2

Hanson, S., Schuermann, T. (2006). Confidence intervals for probabilities of default. *Journal of Banking & Finance*, 30(8), 2281–2301. DOI: https://doi.org/10.1016/j.jbankfin.2005.08.002

Jacobs, M., Karagozoglu, A. K. (2007). Understanding and Predicting Ultimate Loss-Given-Default on Bonds and Loans. Risk Analysis. DOI: https://doi.org/10.3905/jfi.2011.21.1.006

Jankowitsch, R., Nagler, F., Subrahmanyam, M. G. (2014). The determinants of recovery rates in the US corporate bond market. *Journal of Financial Economics*, 114: 155–177. DOI: https://doi.org/10.1016/j.jfineco.2014.06.001

Loterman, G., Brown, I., Martens, D., Mues, C., Baesens, B. (2012). Benchmarking regression algorithms for loss given default modeling. *International Journal of Forecasting*, 28: 161–170. DOI: https://doi.org/10.1016/j.ijforecast.2011.01.006

Mili, M., Sahut, J. M.,Teulon, F. (2018). Modeling recovery rates of corporate defaulted bonds in developed and developing countries. *Emerging Markets Review*, 36(C): 28–44. DOI: https://doi.org/10.1016/j.ememar.2018.03.001

Mora, N. (2015). Creditor recovery: The macroeconomic dependence of industry equilibrium. *Journal of Financial Stability*, 18: 172–186. DOI: https://doi.org/10.1016/j.jfs.2015.04.004
Rösch, D., Scheule, H. (2014). Forecasting probabilities of default and loss rates given default in the presence of selection. *The Journal of the Operational Research Society*, 65(3): 393–407. DOI: https://doi.org/10.1057/jors.2012.82
Qi, M., Zhao, X. (2011). Comparison of modeling methods for Loss Given Default. *Journal of Banking and Finance*, 35: 2842–2855. DOI: https://doi.org/10.1016/j.jbankfin.2011.03.011
S&P Global Market Intelligence's Credit Pro (2019) Rating Transition, Default, and Recovery Rate Analytics. www.spglobal.com. https://spglobal.com/marketintelligence/en/solutions/creditpro-
Teplova, T. V., Sokolova, T. V. (2018). Research fields of bond markets. INFRA-M. Russia, Moscow. (In Rus.) ISBN 978-5-16-014988-2
Tobback, E., Martens, D., van Gestel, T., Baesens, B. (2014). Forecasting loss given default models: Impact of account characteristics and the macroeconomic state. *Journal of the Operational Research Society*, 65: 376–392. DOI: https://doi.org/10.1057/jors.2013.158
Varma, P., Cantor, R. (2005). Determinants of recovery rates on defaulted bonds and loans for North American corporate issuers. *The Journal of Fixed Income*, 14: 29–44. DOI: https://doi.org/10.3905/jfi.2005.491110
Yao, X., Crook, J.,Andreeva, G. (2015). Support vector regression for loss given default modelling. *European Journal of Operational Research*, 240: 528–538. DOI: https://doi.org/10.1016/j.ejor.2014.06.043

11 Determinants of corporate bond defaults

The role of corporate governance in emerging markets

Introduction

According to a review by S&P Global Fixed Income Research and S&P Global Market Intelligence's Credit Pro (2019), in 2016–2018, in the global market, there was a tendency towards an increase in the volume of debts on which a default was declared, and the average amount of debt per one company that defaulted was significantly growing. In 2018–2019, the volume and number of defaults on CBs in China's largest market are growing sharply: in 2016–2017, the volume of unfulfilled obligations was 25–30 bn yuan ($3.5–4 bn), then in 2018 and January–November 2019, 120 bn yuan (about $17 bn). Problems with non-payment of debt in China began from the banking sector and spread across a wide range of industries in the non-financial sector.

Defaults affect the interests of a wide range of stakeholders: owners, creditors, management and employees of a company. The growth of defaults, especially on debt obligations of large companies, can lead to socio-economic instability.

A significant factor affecting the probability of default and the performance of companies is the quality of corporate governance (Cao et al., 2015; Ali et al., 2018a). At the same time, most of the previous studies on this research topic focus on the financial indicators of issuers and macroeconomic factors (Rösch and Scheule, 2014; Guo and Bruneau, 2014; Han and Zhou, 2014). Mostly, previous studies consider developed markets (Ali et al., 2018a; Cao et al., 2015; Schultz et al., 2017).

The aim of our study is to analyze the impact of corporate governance indicators on the probability of default on corporate bonds of companies in developed and developing markets. The novelty of our research is that it focuses on corporate governance factors and on identifying their non-linear effects. Unlike previous papers, we compare the results for developed and emerging markets.

The sample includes companies from a wide range of industries in the non-financial sector that defaulted in 2008–2019. Data is collected from information and analytical databases Bloomberg, Eikon Refinitiv, Cbonds, and from company websites. The research methodology is testing probit models.

Previous studies

The researchers distinguish the following groups of factors influencing the probability of default: 1) financial indicators of the issuer, 2) corporate governance factors, 3) macroeconomic indicators (Table 11.1).

Rösch and Scheule (2014) identify factors predicting the probability of default on corporate bonds in the US bond market. They reveal the important role of bond credit rating, firm industry and of dummy variables of subordinated and unsecured bonds.

Guo and Bruneau (2014) study the impact of 162 macroeconomic factors on default risk for the US and the Eurozone markets and find that the most significant factors for both samples are production volume and unemployment rate.

Han and Zhou (2014) conclude that an increased activity of informed market participants indicates an increased probability of default. The probability of default is negatively related to the return on the issuer's stocks, the S&P 500 index and short-term government bonds.

Cao et al. (2015) for the US market from 1998 to 2005 conclude that the small size of the BD, the high percentage of independent directors and female directors, as well as the low share of institutional investors in the firm equity capital reduce the risk of default.

Table 11.1 Traditionally considered determinants of the probability of default

Factor	*Research papers*
Financial firm-level factors and industry	
Industry	Rösch and Scheule (2014), Agrawal and Maheshwari (2018)
Leverage	Schultz et al. (2017), Ali et al. (2018a)
Assets	Rösch and Scheule (2014), Schultz et al. (2017)
Q Tobin	Rösch and Scheule (2014)
EBITDA margin	
Corporate governance	
Board of directors (BD) size	Cao et al. (2015), Schultz et al. (2017), Ali et al. (2018a)
Percent of independent directors	Cao et al. (2015)
Percent of female directors	
Remuneration of the top managers	Schultz et al. (2017), Ali et al. (2018a)
Ownership structure	Cao et al. (2015), Schultz et al. (2017)
Macroeconomic factors	
S&P 500 return rate	Guo and Bruneau (2014)
GDP growth	
Inflation	
Interest rates	Guo and Bruneau (2014), Han and Zhou (2014)
Unemployment rate	
Liquidity in the bond market	Chen et al. (2018), Javadi and Mollagholamali (2018)
Yield curve slope	Javadi and Mollagholamali (2018)

Ali et al. (2018a) also consider default in terms of corporate governance quality in the Australian market and find that high quality of corporate governance reduces the probability of default. Rapidly growing companies carry increased default risks, while increased liquidity reduces this risk.

Agrawal and Maheshwari (2018) associate the risk of default with the firm industry. The sample includes 135 companies which defaulted in the period 2000–2011, and 135 company analogues by size which did not declare default. The authors conclude that the industrial beta coefficient is positively correlated with the probability of default.

Based on a review of previous studies, we also distinguish three groups of factors that can influence the probability of default (Table 11.1). We note that the study of the impact of corporate governance factors is the subject of a relatively small number of papers (Ali et al., 2018a; Cao et al., 2015; Schultz et al., 2017), which primarily focus on developed markets. In our study, we close this gap.

Research hypotheses

The following hypotheses are tested in our study:

Hypothesis 1. The percentage of women on the Board of Directors (BD) and the Management Board is related to the probability of default by a non-linear U-dependence.

We assume that with an increase in the percentage of women on the BD and the Management Board, the probability of default first decreases, and then it begins to increase. On the one hand, as shown by Ali et al. (2018b) for the Australian market, the higher the percentage of women in the BD, the lower the probability of default. A similar conclusion is obtained by Cao et al. (2015) for the US market. Faccio et al. (2016) for the markets of the EU countries reveal that firms with women-CEO are characterized by lower values of financial leverage, ROA volatility and the probability of default. On the other hand, Berger et al. (2014) show that banks with a high percentage of women in the BD take more risk. Ahern and Dittmar (2012) reveal a negative effect of the percentage of women in the BD on firm performance.

Owen and Temesvary (2017) show that there is a non-linear U-shaped relationship between the gender composition of American banks' BD and their performance, measured by the ratio of operating income to operating expenses and ROA. We attribute this to the fact that female members of the BD and the Management Board pursue a more conservative policy, characterized by the adoption of a lower level of risk, which, to a certain level, reduces the probability of default, but further affects the profitability of companies, the implementation of promising investment projects, etc.

Hypothesis 2. The higher the number of members of the BD audit committee, the less the probability of default.

The BD audit committee provides control over the annual and financial reporting and accounting as a whole, as well as the work of external auditors. The activities of the audit committee are aimed at reducing financial risks, and therefore we assume a negative impact of the size of this committee on the probability of default. In particular, Platt and Platt (2012) for the US market reveal a negative effect of the number of members of the audit committee on the probability of default. Ali et al. (2018a) for the Australian market show that a better audit system reduces the probability of default.

Hypothesis 3. For companies where the CEO is the Chairman of the BD, the probability of default is higher.

The fact that one person occupies the both positions of the CEO and the Chairman of the BD can lead to an increase in opportunistic behaviour of the CEO, and an increase in agent conflicts between managers and owners, and managers and creditors. CEOs holding the position of Chairman of the BD are inclined to take riskier decisions and actions in their personal interests, since in this case the controlling functions of the BD are limited (Malmendier and Tate, 2009). Tang (2017) for a sample of the US IT companies shows that CEO duality significantly negatively affects firm performance, as measured by total shareholder return. Bebchuk et al. (2011) show that if the CEO is the Chairman of the BD, then his or her share in the total remuneration of the top-5 managers increases. The authors reveal significant negative effects of the influence of the CEO's share in managerial remuneration (as a measure of CEO power) on the investment attractiveness of the company (measured by Tobin Q) and return on assets (ROA). As shown by Lehlou et al. (2014) for US public companies, the 'duality' of the CEO increases the probability of default.

Hypothesis 4. The larger the size of the BD, the lower the probability of default.

A larger number of the BD members are able to exercise more effective control over the activities of managers, thereby smoothing out the problem of agent conflicts. As shown by Anderson et al. (2004) for the US market, companies with large BD are characterized by lower cost of borrowed financing, i.e. creditors regard the risks of these companies as lower. A similar conclusion about a decrease in the cost of debt financing with an increase in the size of BD in the Russian market is obtained by Teplova and Sokolova (2019). As shown by Lehlou et al. (2014) for US public companies, the probability of default is lower for companies with large BD.

Hypothesis 5. The authority duration of the BD non-linearly (U-shaped) affects the probability of default.

We assume that at first, with an increase in the authority duration of the BD, the probability of default decreases, since the increased experience of the BD members and their coordinated actions to monitor and control the functioning of the company play a favourable role. After a certain optimal authority duration, the irremovability of members of the BD leads to the fact that they can make more risky decisions, which positively affects the probability of default.

In line with the previous papers on this research topic, we include the following control variables in the regression models:

- *Return on assets (ROA)*. We assume that the higher the ROA, the lower the probability of default, since companies with high ROA operate more efficiently. The conclusion about the negative relationship of ROA with the probability of default is obtained by Ali et al. (2018a) for the Australian market.
- *The share of total debt in assets*. We assume that the higher the debt burden, the higher the probability of default. Ali et al. (2018a) reveal a significant positive effect of financial leverage on the probability of default for the Australian market, and Cao et al. (2015) find the same relationship for the US market.
- *Long-term debt ratio*. We assume a positive relationship between this indicator and the probability of default. Javadi and Mollagholamali (2018) for the US market reveal that the risk of default increases with the share of short-term debt. The authors attribute this effect to the difficulties of prolonging or repaying large short-term debt, increased liquidity risks, as well as losses of shareholders in case of prolongation of debt.
- *Net working capital ratio*, characterizing the financial stability and liquidity of the corporate bond issuer. Atman (1968) and Shumway (2001) reveal a negative impact of this indicator on the probability of default for the US market.
- *Real GDP growth rate*: we assume that the lower this indicator, the higher the probability of default. The GDP growth rate reflects the entire macroeconomic situation in a country. Rösch and Scheule (2014) show that with an increase in GDP growth, the probability of default of US companies decreases.
- *Dummy of a developed/emerging market*. We assume that in countries with developed markets the macroeconomic situation is more stable, and inflation and interest rates are lower; therefore the probability of default is less than for emerging markets.

Research methodology. Description of the variables

Revealing the determinants of the probability of default (P) of an issuer of LCY corporate bonds is performed on the basis of the following probit model:

$$P = \int_{-\infty}^{x^T\beta} \Phi(Z)dZ \qquad \Phi(Z) = \frac{1}{\sqrt{2\pi}} e^{-Z^2/2} \tag{11.1}$$

Table 11.2 Description of the variables of our study

Variable	*Description*	*Expected direction of influence*
Default	The dependent dummy variable, taking the value 1 in case of default and 0 otherwise	
Indicators of corporate governance		
board_duration	The authority duration of the BD (in years)	-
board_duration2	The square of *board_duration*	+
board_size	The number of the BD members	-
ceo_duality	The dummy variable taking the value 1, if the CEO is the Chairman of the BD, and 0 otherwise	+
ln_prct_fem_exec	The percent of women on the Management Board	-
ln2_prct_fem_exec	The square of *ln2_prct_fem_exec*	+
ln_prct_fem_board	The percent of women on the BD	-
ln2_prct_fem_board	The square of *ln2_prct_fem_board*	+
membrs_audit	The number of members of the BD audit committee	-
Control variables: financial indicators of bond issuers		
ltd_td	The share of long-term debt in the total debt, %	-
Roa	Return on assets, %	-
td_ta	The share of the total debt to the total assets	+
wc_ta	The coefficient of net working capital	-
Macroeconomic variables		
Developed	The dummy variable taking the value 1 in case of a developed market and 0 otherwise	-
gdp_growth	Annual real GDP growth, %	-

$$Z = \beta_0 + \sum_k \beta_{1,k} \cdot CorpGov_k + \sum_j \beta_{2,j} \cdot ControlVar_j + \varepsilon \tag{11.2}$$

where $CorpGov_k$ are corporate governance indicators, $ControlVar_j$ are control variables (see Table 11.2), and $\beta\beta_{01\ldots,kj}$ that's right: β_1 and β_2 are the estimated coefficients of the regression model.

To evaluate the model, the maximum likelihood method is used.

Descriptive statistics

The sample of our study includes LCY corporate bond issuers from developed and developing countries, which were defaulted in 2008–2019, as well as financially stable companies. We consider public companies, due to the fact that financial and non-financial information in the databases is more fully disclosed. As for the industry affiliation of bond issuers, only companies belonging to the non-financial sector are included in the sample, because the set of key indicators for analyzing the financial statements of companies in the financial and non-financial sectors varies significantly.

We consider only cases of actual default; in the Bloomberg and Eikon Refinitiv databases, which are characterized by the most comprehensive disclosure of information on the global securities market, there is no data on technical defaults. Additional sources of information on financial and non-fundamental indicators of companies and defaults on corporate bonds are Cbonds, Capital IQ and official websites of bond issuers.

We note that in developed markets, defaults do not always result in companies leaving the market. Our sample also includes companies that defaulted but went through a restructuring process: for example, American Airlines defaulted in 2011, but it is currently operating successfully. On the contrary, in emerging markets, in most cases, the fact that a default is declared leads to the company leaving the market. An example is the Russian company Transaero.

In general, for developed and emerging markets in 2008–October 2019, 1164 companies (including 482 non-financial and 682 financial companies) declared default on 3127 LCY corporate bond issues (source: Bloomberg, authors' calculations, see Tables 11.3 and 11.4). In developed countries, during the reporting period, there were 415 cases of default on corporate bonds of non-financial companies, of which 64% were American companies, and 11% were German. The peak of defaults occurred in 2008, due to the global financial crisis of 2007–2008. Bursts of defaults were observed in 2012–2013 in the USA and in South Korea, and in 2018 in China. The latter is due to the tightening of monetary policy, the fight against shadow banking and rising interest rates in China, and this state policy continues in 2019.

Table 11.3 Statistics on defaults on corporate bonds of companies in emerging markets in 2008–2019

	Number of issuers defaulted on corporate bonds			*Number of corporate bond issues defaulted*
	Non-financial companies	*Financial companies*	*Total*	
China	36	37	73	207
Russia	10	13	23	56
Brazil	4	5	9	14
India	7	1	8	25
Poland	4	3	7	48
Montenegro	0	6	6	6
Mexico	4	1	5	12
Other countries	2	2	4	19
Total	67	68	135	387

Source: Bloomberg, authors' calculations

Table 11.4 Statistics on defaults on corporate bonds of companies in developed markets in 2008–2019

	Number of issuers defaulted on corporate bonds			*Number of corporate bond issues defaulted*
	Non-financial companies	*Financial companies*	*Total*	
USA	266	576	842	2375
Germany	46	1	47	74
Israel	13	5	18	18
Canada	16	1	17	23
UK	14	3	17	20
Luxembourg	13	0	13	31
Japan	9	3	12	29
S. Korea	11	1	10	70
Liechtenstein	0	6	6	6
Other countries	28	7	35	105
Total	415	614	1029	2740

Source: Bloomberg, authors' calculations.

The final sample includes a significantly smaller number of observations, due to the lack of data on corporate governance indicators and financial statements one year before the default, as well as frequent cases of default on several issues of corporate bonds of one issuer within one year. The sample includes observations on only one issue of corporate bonds, the first one, for which a default was declared. In total, the sample includes 109 public companies in the non-financial sector that defaulted on CB in LCY in the period under review in 34 developed and emerging countries. Due to the exclusion of many observations and the lack of data in the databases, there is a skewness in the sample under consideration.

In addition, the sample includes financially stable companies similar to those defaulted by the following criteria: 1) the company is also an issuer of corporate bonds, 2) the company belongs to the same country and industry. In total, the sample includes 188 financially stable companies – analogues.

Our sample covers a wide range of industries (see Figure 11.1).

Descriptive statistics on the sample, including financial and non-fundamental indicators of issuers, are presented in Table 11.5.

Research results

The calculation results are presented in Tables 11.6–11.8. We note that for the vast majority of the significant explanatory variables, the direction of influence is the same for the whole sample and for the samples of companies in developing and developed markets.

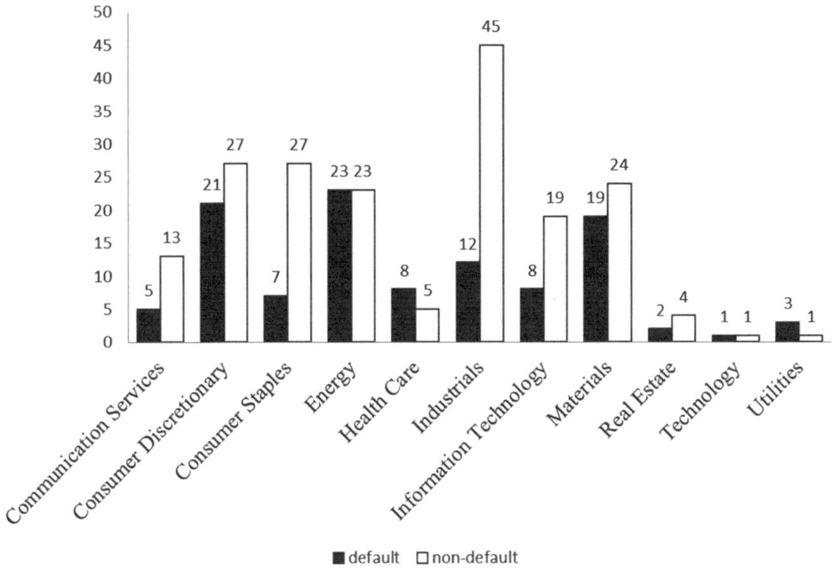

Figure 11.1 Industry affiliation of companies in our sample

Table 11.5 Descriptive statistics on the sample

Variable	*Obs*	*Mean*	*Std. Dev.*	*Min*	*Max*
default	297	0.357	0.480	0	1
board_size	297	8.178	3.221	0	20
members_audit	241	2.747	1.469	0	8
ceo_duality	284	0.363	0.482	0	1
board_duration	271	7.063	3.224	0	20
board_duration_2	271	60.236	52.468	0	400
ln2_prct_fem_board	277	1.400	1.512	0	5
ln_prct_fem_board	277	4.237	4.970	0	21.3
ln2_prct_fem_exec	263	1.333	1.601	0	4.5
ln_prct_fem_exec	263	4.330	5.581	0	21.3
td_ta	293	0.331	0.239	0	1
ln_fncl_lev	272	1.114	0.760	0.025	4.511
Roa	291	-0.020	0.170	-0.5	0.3
ltd_td	282	0.609	0.344	0	1
wc_ta	297	0.088	0.272	-0.5	0.8
gdp_growth	297	1.641	2.853	-4.8	8.17
rule_of_law	296	0.885	0.911	-0.792	2.038
ddeveloped	297	0.613	0.488	0	1

Our hypothesis about a U-shaped dependence of the probability of default on the percentage of women in the BD and the Management Board is confirmed (Tables 11.6–11.8). For all the samples, the signs of the explanatory variables of the percentage of women in the BD and the Management Board are negative, and when squared, they are positive. At the same time, statistical significance at the 5–10% level is observed only for the percentage of women on the Management Board and its square for the whole sample of companies. For other variables, the statistical significance is not high.

Our results regarding the non-linear effect of the gender composition of the BD on the probability of default coincide with the conclusions of Owen and Temesvary (2017) for the US market. The result regarding the non-linear effect of the gender composition of the Management Board is original; the authors of previous papers did not investigate this topic.

In emerging markets, the duality of CEO plays a significant role in increasing the likelihood of default, which is consistent with our hypothesis (Table 11.8). If we consider the whole sample of companies (Table 11.6), then the direction of influence of this factor also remains positive, but the statistical significance is not high. The result is consistent with the findings of Lehlou et al. (2014) for US public companies.

The influence of the size of the BD on the probability of default is negative for the three samples, but it is significant at a 5% level only for the whole sample and for the sample of companies in developed markets (Tables 11.6–11.8). The result is consistent with the findings of Teplova and Sokolova (2019) in the Russian market, and Lehlou et al. (2014) in the US market. For emerging markets (Table 11.8), the size of the BD is not critical to increase the risk of default. We attribute this result to the relatively low quality of corporate governance in emerging markets.

The number of members of the BD audit committee negatively affects the probability of default; the result is stable for the three samples (Tables 11.6–11.8). This result is consistent with the findings of Platt and Platt (2012) for the US market, and Ali et al. (2018a) for the Australian market.

We obtained an original result that the influence of the authority duration of the BD is stable, positive and significant for all three samples (Tables 11.6–11.8). We explain this by the fact that the higher the authority duration of the BD members, the higher the risks they take and the lower the effectiveness of decisions.

For most of the control variables, the expected conclusions are obtained. Thus the impact of ROA is consistently negative and significant at a 1–5% level for the sample of all companies and companies in developed markets (Tables 11.6–11.8), which is consistent with the findings of Ali et al. (2018a) for the Australian market. In emerging markets, the significance of ROA is not high.

The influence of the debt burden, measured by the share of debt in assets, is negative and significant at a 1–5% level for the three considered samples (Tables 11.6–11.8). The result is consistent with the findings of Ali et al. (2018a) for the Australian market and Cao et al. (2015) for the US market.

Table 11.6 The results for the whole sample of companies

	(1)	*dy/dx*	*(2)*	*dy/dx*	*(3)*	*dy/dx*
Log likelihood	-74.67737		-75.21324		-76.85056	
Number of obs	216	216	216	216	216	216
_cons	-1.9794*** (0.6951)		-1.5066*** (0.4948)		-1.4846*** (0.496)	
board_duration	0.2652* (0.1481)	0.0999* (0.0557)	0.1307*** (0.0474)	0.0493*** (0.018)	0.1376*** (0.0476)	0.0519*** (0.0181)
board_duration2	-0.0093 (0.0098)	-0.0035 (0.0037)				
board_size	-0.1185** (0.0514)	-0.0446** (0.0195)	-0.1258** (0.0509)	-0.0475** (0.0193)	-0.1373*** (0.0524)	-0.0518*** (0.0198)
ceo_duality	0.3333 (0.2489)	0.1256 (0.0936)	0.3002 (0.2445)	0.1133 (0.0922)	0.2879 (0.2432)	0.1086 (0.0918)
ln2_prct_fem_exec	0.2377** (0.1191)	0.0895** (0.045)	0.2282** (0.1167)	0.0861* (0.0441)		
ln_prct_fem_exec	-0.814* (0.4166)	-0.3067* (0.1573)	-0.7799* (0.409)	-0.2943* (0.1546)		
ln2_prct_fem_board					0.0354 (0.1)	0.0134 (0.0378)
ln_prct_fem_board					-0.0397 (0.337)	-0.015 (0.1272)
members_audit	-0.1366 (0.0977)	-0.0515 (0.0368)	-0.1473 (0.0965)	-0.0556 (0.0364)	-0.1761* (0.0969)	-0.0665* (0.0365)
ltd_td	-0.8349* (0.4503)	-0.3145* (0.1723)	-0.8493* (0.449)	-0.3205* (0.1721)	-0.7548* (0.4417)	-0.2849* (0.1685)
Roa	-2.6462*** (0.8738)	-0.997*** (0.3357)	-2.6802*** (0.8711)	-1.0114*** (0.3349)	-2.6111*** (0.8564)	-0.9856*** (0.3295)
td_ta	3.2557*** (0.7552)	1.2266*** (0.2921)	3.2761*** (0.7542)	1.2363*** (0.2919)	3.1091*** (0.7433)	1.1735*** (0.2857)
wc_ta	0.5156 (0.5432)	0.1943 (0.2052)	0.551 (0.539)	0.2079 (0.2039)	0.453 (0.5281)	0.171 (0.1997)
ddeveloped	0.5122* (0.2898)	0.193* (0.1091)	0.538* (0.2884)	0.203* (0.1086)	0.4675* (0.2841)	0.1765* (0.1069)
gdp_growth	0.2927*** (0.0523)	0.1103*** (0.0204)	0.2913*** (0.0524)	0.1099*** (0.0203)	0.2979*** (0.0509)	0.1124*** (0.0197)

Significance levels: * p <10%, ** p <5%, *** p <1%

Table 11.7 The results for the sample of companies in developed markets

	(1)	*dy/dx*	*(2)*	*dy/dx*	*(3)*	*dy/dx*
Log likelihood	-44.86486		-45.69948		-46.31964	
Number of obs	110	110	110	110	110	110
_cons	-1.3805 (1.216)		-0.2263 (0.757)		-0.0484 (0.7742)	
board_duration	0.399* (0.2402)	0.1393* (0.082)	0.132* (0.0742)	0.0465* (0.0254)	0.137* (0.0786)	0.048* (0.0266)
board_duration2	-0.0176 (0.015)	-0.0061 (0.0052)				
board_size	-0.1285 (0.0849)	-0.0449 (0.0291)	-0.1615* (0.0832)	-0.0568** (0.0284)	-0.1893** (0.0898)	-0.0663** (0.0301)
ceo_duality	0.0141 (0.3314)	0.0049 (0.1157)	-0.0333 (0.3249)	-0.0117 (0.1143)	-0.2017 (0.3232)	-0.0706 (0.1128)
ln2_prct_fem_exec	0.2781 (0.1742)	0.0971 (0.0602)	0.2242 (0.1653)	0.0789 (0.0577)		
ln_prct_fem_exec	-1.07* (0.6029)	-0.3735* (0.2079)	-0.8856 (0.5721)	-0.3116 (0.1995)		
ln2_prct_fem_board					-0.2575 (0.1817)	-0.0902 (0.0622)
ln_prct_fem_board					0.7869 (0.5688)	0.2755 (0.1947)
members_audit	-0.0149 (0.1332)	-0.0052 (0.0465)	-0.0392 (0.1297)	-0.0138 (0.0455)	-0.0893 (0.1431)	-0.0313 (0.0496)
ltd_td	-1.2746* (0.6619)	-0.4449* (0.2341)	-1.3218** (0.6758)	-0.4651* (0.2399)	-1.1558* (0.6549)	-0.4046* (0.2328)
Roa	-2.36** (0.981)	-0.8238** (0.3531)	-2.4782** (0.989)	-0.872** (0.3584)	-2.3751** (0.9617)	-0.8315** (0.3464)
td_ta	2.5806*** (1.0045)	0.9008** (0.3655)	2.6449*** (1.0167)	0.9306** (0.3721)	2.4844** (0.9759)	0.8698** (0.3558)
wc_ta	0.4978 (0.9199)	0.1738 (0.3228)	0.7354 (0.9066)	0.2587 (0.3217)	0.4757 (0.892)	0.1666 (0.3145)
gdp_growth	0.3399*** (0.1229)	0.1186*** (0.0413)	0.3501*** (0.1266)	0.1232*** (0.0426)	0.2669** (0.1206)	0.0934** (0.0414)

Significance levels: * $p < 10\%$, ** $p < 5\%$, *** $p < 1\%$

Table 11.8 The results for the sample of companies in emerging markets

NumCalc	*(1)*	*dy/dx*	*(2)*	*dy/dx*	*(3)*	*dy/dx*
Log likelihood	-23.5377		-23.53927		-23.39957	
Number of obs	106	106	106	106	106	106
_cons	-2.7034** (1.3384)		-2.6502*** (0.9331)		-2.5076*** (0.9225)	
board_duration	0.183 (0.3392)	0.0703 (0.1305)	0.1645** (0.0782)	0.0633** (0.0312)	0.1499* (0.0771)	0.0578* (0.0307)
board_duration2	-0.0013 (0.0239)	-0.0005 (0.0092)				
board_size	-0.1269 (0.0972)	-0.0488 (0.0377)	-0.1272 (0.0971)	-0.0489 (0.0377)	-0.1016 (0.0922)	-0.0392 (0.0357)
ceo_duality	1.1464** (0.5613)	0.4407** (0.2112)	1.1374** (0.536)	0.4373** (0.2018)	1.1307** (0.514)	0.436** (0.1937)
ln2_prct_fem_exec	0.1353 (0.204)	0.052 (0.0786)	0.1382 (0.1972)	0.0531 (0.0759)		
ln_prct_fem_exec	-0.2954 (0.7606)	-0.1136 (0.2928)	-0.3045 (0.7428)	-0.1171 (0.2859)		
ln2_prct_fem_board					0.2219 (0.2114)	0.0856 (0.0827)
ln_prct_fem_board					-0.5876 (0.7358)	-0.2266 (0.2871)
members_audit	-0.3421 (0.2446)	-0.1315 (0.0937)	-0.3394 (0.2388)	-0.1305 (0.0915)	-0.3108 (0.2391)	-0.1199 (0.0919)
ltd_td	-0.0871 (0.7744)	-0.0335 (0.2986)	-0.0836 (0.7716)	-0.0321 (0.2975)	0.0587 (0.8111)	0.0226 (0.3124)
Roa	-3.6791 (3.0231)	-1.4144 (1.1788)	-3.7196 (2.9308)	-1.4301 (1.1428)	-3.7981 (3.0851)	-1.4645 (1.2112)
td_ta	4.0343*** (1.5182)	1.5509*** (0.5829)	4.0143*** (1.4698)	1.5434*** (0.5656)	3.3387** (1.6901)	1.2874** (0.6424)
wc_ta	-0.4824 (1.2362)	-0.1854 (0.4726)	-0.4739 (1.2235)	-0.1822 (0.4679)	-0.3952 (1.0035)	-0.1524 (0.385)
gdp_growth	0.363*** (0.0884)	0.1395*** (0.0355)	0.3624*** (0.0876)	0.1394*** (0.0353)	0.3481*** (0.0811)	0.1342*** (0.0329)

Significance levels: * $p < 10\%$, ** $p < 5\%$, *** $p < 1\%$

The share of the long-term debt in the total debt negatively affects the probability of default; this factor is significant at 10% for the whole sample and for the sample of companies in developed markets.

We obtain an unexpected result regarding the positive impact of GDP growth on the probability of default, which contradicts the conclusions of Rösch and Scheule (2014). We attribute this to the fact that explanatory variables are considered with a time lag: one year before the default. In a period of higher GDP growth, companies are over-optimistic about their growth prospects and are more prone to risk, attract more debt financing, which further leads to an increase in the probability of default.

For the sample of all companies, the dummy of belonging to a developed market has a positive effect on the probability of default. We attribute this to the fact that in developed countries it is easier for medium and even small companies to enter the bond market and attract financing at low interest rates. At the same time, such companies do not properly monitor and control the risks they take, and they overestimate their growth opportunities in the context of low GDP growth in developed countries.

Conclusions

For the first time, we perform an analysis of the determinants of defaults on corporate bonds of companies in the non-financial sector in developed and developing markets and compare the findings for the different samples. The time period is from 2008 to 2019. We use probit models to identify the determinants of the probability of defaults.

We obtain an original conclusion about the non-linear U-shaped dependence of the probability of default on the percentage of women in the BD and the Management Board. We attribute this to the fact that female members of the BD and the Management Board pursue a more conservative policy, characterized by the adoption of a lower level of risk, which, to a certain level, can reduce the likelihood of default, but further adversely affects the profitability of companies and the implementation of promising investment projects.

We also obtain an original result that the influence of the authority duration of the BD is stable, positive and significant for all the three samples. We attribute this to the fact that the higher the authority duration of the BD members, the higher the risks they take and the lower the effectiveness of decisions.

For emerging markets, the fact that one person occupies both positions of CEO and Chairman of the BD plays a significant role in increasing the likelihood of default, which corresponds to our hypothesis.

The influence of the size of the BD on the probability of default is negative and significant at the 5% level for the whole sample of companies and for the sample of companies in developed markets. For emerging markets, this factor is not significant. We attribute this result to the relatively poor quality of corporate governance in emerging markets.

The number of members of the BD audit committee negatively affects the probability of default; the result is stable for the three samples.

We understand the limitations of some conclusions of our study due to a relatively small sample size. As areas of further research, we note the need to expand the sample and to take into account such determinants of default probability as the size and industry of the bond issuer.

References

Agrawal, K., Maheshwari, Y. (2018). Efficacy of industry factors for corporate default prediction. *IIMB Management Review*, 31: 71–77. DOI: https://doi.org/10.1016/j.iimb.2018.08.007

Ahern, K., Dittmar, A. K. (2012). The changing of the boards: The impact on firm valuation of mandated female board representation. *The Quarterly Journal of Economics*, 127(1): 137–197. DOI: https://doi.org/10.1093/qje/qjr049

Ali, S., Liu, B., Su, J. J. (2018a). Does corporate governance quality affect default risk? The role of growth opportunities and stock liquidity. *International Review of Economics and Finance*, 58: 422–448. DOI: https://doi.org/10.1016/j.iref.2018.05.003

Ali, S., Liu, B., Su, J. J. (2018b). Women on board: Does the gender diversity reduce default risk? 9th Conference on Financial Markets and Corporate Governance. SSRN: https://ssrn.com/abstract=3109256

Anderson, R. C., Mansi, S. A., Reeb, D. M. (2004). Board characteristics, accounting report integrity, and the cost of debt. *Journal of Accounting and Economics*, 37(3): 315–342. DOI: https://doi.org/10.1016/j.jacceco.2004.01.004

Bebchuk, L. A., Cremers, K. J. M., Peyer, U. C. (2011). The CEO pay slice. *Journal of Financial Economics*, 102: 199–221. DOI: https://doi.org/10.1016/j.jfineco.2011.05.006

Berger, A. N., Kick, T., Schaeck, K. (2014). Executive board composition and bank risk taking. *Journal of Corporate Finance*, 28: 48–65. DOI: https://doi.org/10.1016/j.jcorpfin.2013.11.006

Cao, Z., Leng, F., Feroz, E. H., Davalos, S. V. (2015). Corporate governance and default risk of firms cited in the SEC's Accounting and Auditing Enforcement Releases. *Review of Quantitative Finance and Accounting*, 44: 113–138. DOI: https://doi.org/10.1007/s11156-013-0401-9

Chen, H., Cui, R., He, Z., Milbradt, K. (2018). Quantifying liquidity and default risks of corporate bonds over the business cycle. *Review of Financial Studies*, 31(3): 852–897. DOI: https://doi.org/10.1093/rfs/hhx107

Faccio, M., Marchica, M., Mura, R., (2016). CEO gender, corporate risk-taking, and the efficiency of capital allocation. *Journal of Corporate Finance*, 39: 193–209. DOI: https://doi.org/10.1016/j.jcorpfin.2016.02.008

Guo, L., Bruneau, C. (2014). Macroeconomic variables and default risk: An application of the FAVAR model. *Revue d'Economie Politique*, 124(5): 817–857. DOI: https://doi.org/10.3917/redp.245.0817

Han, S., Zhou, X. (2014). Informed bond trading, corporate yield spreads, and corporate default prediction. *Management Science*, 60(3): 675–694. DOI: https://doi.org/10.1287/mnsc.2013.1768

Javadi, S., Mollagholamali, M. (2018). Debt market illiquidity and correlated default risk. *Finance Research Letters*, 26: 266–273. DOI: https://doi.org/10.1016/j.frl.2018.02.002

Lehlou, S., Tebourbi, I., Bouslimi, L. (2014). Internal governance mechanism and default probability: Evidence from US public firms. *International Journal of Corporate Governance*, 5(1–2). DOI: https://doi.org/10.1504/IJCG.2014.062351

Malmendier, U., Tate, G. (2009). Superstar CEOs. *Quarterly Journal of Economics*, 124: 1593–1638. DOI: https://doi.org/10.1162/qjec.2009.124.4.1593

Owen, A. L., Temesvary, J. (2017). The performance effects of gender diversity on bank boards. MPRA Paper No. 80078.

Platt, H., Platt, M. (2012). Corporate board attributes and bankruptcy. *Journal of Business Research*, 65(8), 1139–1143. DOI: https://doi.org/10.1016/j.jbusres.2011.08.003

Rösch, D., Scheule, H. (2014). Forecasting probabilities of default and loss rates given default in the presence of selection. *The Journal of the Operational Research Society*, 65: 393–407. DOI: https://doi.org/10.1057/jors.2012.82

Schultz, E. L., Tan, D. T., Walsh, K. D. (2017). Corporate governance and the probability of default. *Accounting and Finance*, 57: 235–253. DOI: https://doi.org/10.1111/acfi.12147

Shumway, T. (2001). Forecasting bankruptcy more accurately: A simple hazard model. *The Journal of Business*, 74(1): 101–124. DOI: https://doi.org/10.1086/209665

Taffler, R.J. (1982). Forecasting company failure in the UK using discriminant analysis and financial ratio data. *Journal of Royal Statistical Society*, 145(3): 342–358. DOI: https://doi.org/10.2307/2981867

Tang, J. (2017). CEO duality and firm performance: The moderating roles of other executives and blockholding outside directors. *European Management Journal*, 35(3): 362–372. DOI: https://doi.org/10.1016/j.emj.2016.05.003

Teplova, T., Sokolova, T. (2019). Surprises of corporate governance and Russian firms debt. *Journal of Economics and Business*, 102 (March–April): 39–56. DOI: https://doi.org/10.1016/j.jeconbus.2018.10.001

Xing, K., Yang, X. (2019). Predicting default rates by capturing critical transitions in the macroeconomic system. *Finance Research Letters*. Published online. DOI: https://doi.org/10.1016/j.frl.2019.02.007

Part 4

Forecasting the dynamics of the bond market

12 Sanction shock and the SSA Caterpillar method

Forecasting the market dynamics

A brief description of the SSA Caterpillar method

Singular spectral analysis (SSA) is designed to detect the key components of time series, to smooth out, and to forecast the dynamics of time series. It allows researchers to consider not only linear trends but also periodic fluctuations, and to suppress noise.

Using this method to reconstruct (to smooth out) the past values of time series involves the following stages (Loskutov et al., 2009):

1. Constructing a trajectory matrix.
   Based on the initial single-dimension time series $(x_i)_{i=1}^{N}$ we form *L*- dimensional embedding vectors (Loskutov et al., 2009):

$$x_t = (x_{t-L+1}\ x_{t-L+2}\ \dots\ x_t)^T,\ t = L, L+1, \dots, N. \tag{12.1}$$

   Then we make a transition to the multidimensional series: with the embedded vectors we construct a trajectory matrix *X* with *L x (N-L+1)* dimensions (Loskutov et al., 2009):

$$X = \begin{pmatrix} x_1 & x_2 & \dots & x_p & \dots & x_{N-L+1} \\ x_2 & x_3 & \dots & x_{p+1} & \dots & x_{N-L+2} \\ \dots & \dots & \dots & \dots & \dots & \dots \\ x_L & x_{L+1} & \dots & x_{2L-1} & \dots & x_N \end{pmatrix} \tag{12.2}$$

2. Singular decomposition.
   For the trajectory matrix *X* we construct a covariance matrix *C* (Loskutov et al., 2009):

$$C = \frac{1}{N-L+1} XX^T \tag{12.3}$$

Let us denote: $\lambda_1 \geq \lambda_2 \geq \ldots \geq \lambda_L$ are the eigenvalues of matrix C, Λ is the matrix of eigenvalues, $V^1, V^2, \ldots, V^L$ are the eigenvectors of matrix C, and $V = (V^1, V^2, \ldots, V^L)$ is the matrix of eigenvectors. Then we obtain the following equation (Loskutov et al., 2009):

$$\Lambda = V^T C V \tag{12.4}$$

3. Transition to the principal components.
   We construct a matrix of the transition to the main components of Υ (Danilov, Jiglyavsky, 1997; Loskutov et al., 2009):

$$\Upsilon = V^T X = (\Upsilon_1, \Upsilon_2, \ldots, \Upsilon_L) \tag{12.5}$$

Matrix X can be decomposed into its principal components (Danilov, Jiglyavsky, 1997; Loskutov et al., 2009):

$$X = V^1 \Upsilon_1 + V^2 \Upsilon_2 + \ldots + V^L \Upsilon_L \tag{12.6}$$

which is equivalent to:

$$X = W_1 + W_2 + \ldots + W_L \tag{12.7}$$

where $W_k = V^k \Upsilon_k = V^k (V^k)^T X$ (Loskutov et al., 2009).

By considering r maximal eigenvalues $\lambda_1 \geq \lambda_2 \geq \ldots \geq \lambda_r$ and corresponding matrices $W_1, W_2, \ldots, W_r$, we can smooth out matrix X and eliminate noises which are the fast-changing components (Danilov, Jiglyavsky, 1997; Loskutov et al., 2009):

$$X \approx \tilde{X} = W_1 + W_2 + \ldots + W_r \tag{12.8}$$

4. SSA- smoothing (reconstructing past values)
   We need to apply diagonal averaging over the smoothed component of $\tilde{X}$ in order to restore the initial time series (Loskutov et al., 2009; Danilov, Jiglyavsky, 1997):

$$\tilde{x}_s = \begin{cases} \dfrac{1}{s} \sum_{i=1}^{s} \tilde{x}_{i,s-i+1}, & 1 \leq s \leq L \\ \dfrac{1}{L} \sum_{i=1}^{L} \tilde{x}_{i,s-i+1}, & L \leq s \leq N - L + 1 \\ \dfrac{1}{N - s + 1} \sum_{i=1}^{N-s+1} \tilde{x}_{i+s-N+L-1,N-L+2-i}, & N - L + 1 \leq s \leq N \end{cases} \tag{12.9}$$

Forecasting time series values with the help of the SSA Caterpillar method for p moments in the future implies the sequential application of the forecasting operation for one moment p times (Loskutov et al., 2009).

Let us describe the process of forecasting x_{N+1} based on the known values of $x_1, x_2, ..., x_N$. Consider r maximum eigenvalues of matrix C and their respective eigenvectors $V^1, V^2, ..., V^r$. Let us construct a subspace $S(P)$ for which these eigenvectors form the basis (Loskutov et al., 2009):

$$S(P) = \sum_{i=1}^{r} p_i V^i \tag{12.10}$$

where p_i $(i=1,...,r)$ are parameters.

Any column of matrix X can be decomposed by bases $V^1, V^2, ..., V^r$. A set of parameters $P^k = (p_1^k, p_2^k, ..., p_r^k)$ corresponds to the column X^k (Loskutov et al., 2009):

$$X^k = \sum_{i=1}^{r} p_i^k V^i = S(P^k) \tag{12.11}$$

Now we need to find the column $X^{N+1} = S(P^{N+1})$. Denote following (Danilov and Jiglyavsky, 1997; Loskutov et al., 2009):

$$Z = \begin{pmatrix} v_1^1 & v_1^2 & \dots & v_1^r \\ v_2^1 & v_2^2 & \dots & v_2^r \\ \dots & \dots & \dots & \dots \\ v_{L-1}^1 & v_{L-1}^2 & \dots & v_{L-1}^r \end{pmatrix} \tag{12.12}$$

$$Z^* = (v_L^1, v_L^2, ..., v_L^r) \tag{12.13}$$

$$\tilde{P} = \begin{pmatrix} \tilde{p}_1^{N+1} \\ \tilde{p}_2^{N+1} \\ \dots \\ \tilde{p}_1^{N+1} \end{pmatrix} \tag{12.14}$$

$$Q = \begin{pmatrix} x_{N-L+2} \\ x_{N-L+3} \\ \dots \\ x_N \end{pmatrix} \tag{12.15}$$

Then the vector of parameters $\tilde{P}$ can be determined from the system of equations (Danilov and Jiglyavsky, 1997; Loskutov et al., 2009):

$$Z\tilde{P} = Q \quad (12.16)$$

$$\tilde{P} = (Z^T Z)^{-1} Z^T Q \quad (12.17)$$

The forecast for x_{N+1} is done via the formula (Danilov and Jiglyavsky, 1997; Loskutov et al., 2009):

$$x_{N+1} = Z^* \tilde{P} \quad (12.18)$$

The results of reconstructing and forecasting the dynamics of stock and bond indices by using the SSA Caterpillar method

We present and compare the dynamics of actual versus estimated values of stock and bond index time series, including indices of the Russian market, on the basis of the SSA Caterpillar method. The period is from December 31, 2009 to January 1, 2019. This period encompasses the recovery period of both developed and developing economies after the global financial crisis of 2008–2009, the Eurozone debt crisis in 2010–2012, and the period of increased volatility in the global commodity market of 2014–2016.

On the interval from December 31, 2009[1] to April 6, 2018 we conduct a reconstruction of the past indices values by smoothing out the initial time series based on the SSA Caterpillar method, and on the interval from April 9, 2018 to January 1, 2019, the same method is used to estimate the forecast values of the indices. The separation date between the reconstruction and the forecast is the 6th of April 2018. It was chosen in connection with the adoption of a new package of sanctions by the EU and the USA against the largest Russian companies and their managers. Another package of anti-Russian sanctions was adopted on April 9, 2018. Thus the quality of the forecast using the SSA Caterpillar method in terms of external shocks can be assessed using the stock and bond indices of the Russian market.

Figure 12.1 shows the average absolute deviations of the reconstructed values from the actual ones for the considered stock and bond indices 2011–2017. From Figure 12.1 we can see that the largest average deviations are characteristic for the stock indices of MSCI Russia and MICEX. We attribute this to the fact that stock indices are more volatile than bond indices. Nevertheless, the average deviations for MSCI Russia and MICEX indices are 1.4% and 1%, respectively, which indicates a good quality of reconstructing the past dynamics of stock indices. For all considered bond indices, the average absolute deviations of the reconstructed values from the actual values do not exceed 0.7%, and the

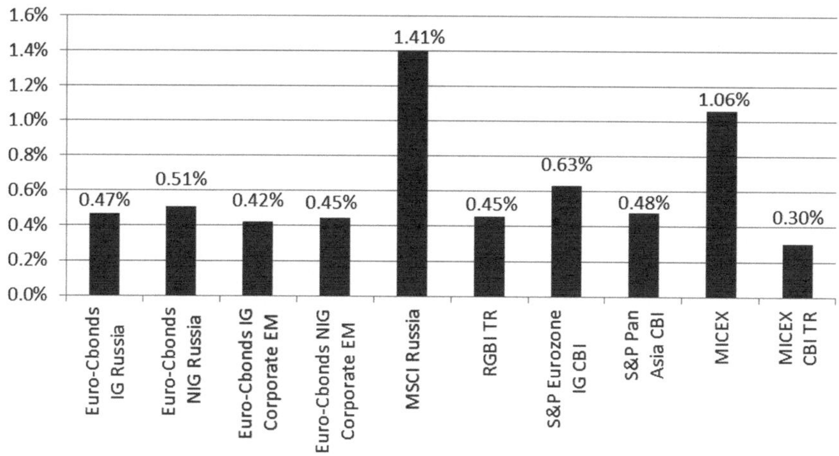

Figure 12.1 Average absolute deviations of reconstructed values from actual values for the considered stock and bond indices during 2011–2017, %.

Note. The Euro-Cbonds IG Russia, Euro-Cbonds IG Corporate EM, Euro-Cbonds NIG Corporate EM indices are calculated from 2015, so for these the deviation calculation period is from 2015 to 2017.

Source: S&P, Cbonds, TR Eikon, authors' calculations.

minimum average deviation of 0.3% is demonstrated by the rouble-denominated MICEX CBITR index (Figure 12.1).

In Figure 12.2 average deviations of the reconstructed index values from the actual ones are presented for 2010–2017. For the stock indices of the Russian market MSCI Russia and MICEX, the average deviations reached their maximum in 2011 (1.9% and 1.5% respectively) during the debt crisis in the Eurozone, while during the crisis for the Russian economy in 2014–2015, deviations were slightly smaller (1.7% and 1.2%, respectively). For most bond indices, peak deviations were observed in 2014–2015, but they did not exceed 1.1%. Thus it can be stated that during the periods of increased volatility in financial markets, the SSA Caterpillar method demonstrates a lower quality of reconstructing the past dynamics of the indices.

Figures 12.3–12.5 show that the forecast estimates on average correspond to the actual dynamics of the index values only for the MICEX (Figure 12.3). For the dollar-denominated Russian stock market index MSCI Russia, rouble-denominated corporate (CB) and government bond indices (MICEX CBI TR and RGBI TR), indices of corporate Eurobonds of Russian issuers with investment and non-investment ratings (Euro-Cbonds IG Russia – Figure 12.4; Euro-Cbonds NIG Russia) actual values are lower than the forecast estimates.

In comparison, during the same period (from April 9, 2018, to January 1, 2019), forecast estimates of bond indices of some developing and developed

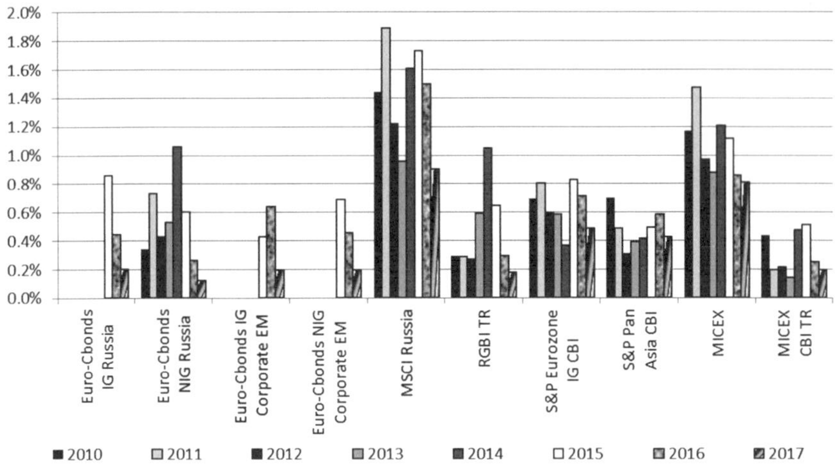

Figure 12.2 Dynamics of the corporate bonds index of issuers from Asian countries (S&P Pan Asia CBI).

Source: S&P, authors' calculations.

Figure 12.3 Dynamics of the Moscow Exchange Stock Index (MICEX).

Source: TR Eikon, authors' calculations.

Figure 12.4 Dynamics of the corporate Eurobonds index of Russian issuers with an investment rating (Euro-Cbonds IG Russia).

Source: Cbonds, authors' calculations.

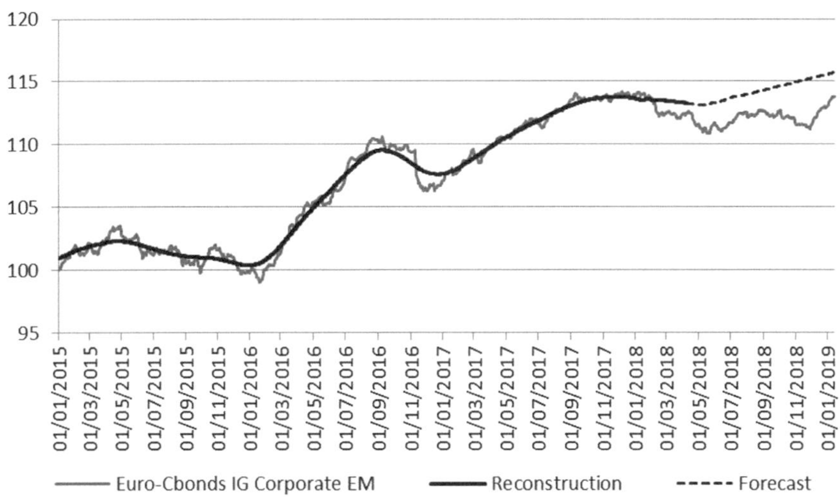

Figure 12.5 Dynamics of the corporate Eurobond index of issuers with investment ratings from developing countries (Euro-Cbonds IG Corporate EM).

Source: Cbonds, authors' calculations.

countries are obtained. Forecasts are made on the dynamics of corporate Eurobonds indices of issuers with investment and non-investment ratings from developing countries (Euro-Cbonds IG Corporate EM – Figure 12.5; Euro-Cbonds NIG Corporate EM), CB index of issuers with investment rating from the Eurozone (S&P Eurozone IG CBI), and CB index of issuers from Asian countries (S&P Pan Asia CBI). For these indices, the actual values are lower than the forecast estimates.

Table 12.1 presents the average deviation of the forecast values from the actual values for the considered stock and bond indices within 30, 60 and 100 trading days (starting from April 9, 2018). S&P Pan Asia CBI index and the rouble-denominated MICEX CBITR index demonstrate the lowest deviations between the forecast values and the actual ones (on average 0.6%) over the period of 30 trading days. Corporate Eurobonds indices of issuers from developing countries with non-investment and investment rating have slightly higher deviations: 0.9% and 1.3%, respectively. The maximum deviation is demonstrated by MSCI Russia index – 8.8% (Table 12.1), that is, for this index, the forecast quality is low. Deviations of more than 3% are also demonstrated by the Euro-Cbonds IG Russia and Euro-Cbonds NIG Russia indices: 3.9% and 4.5%, respectively (Table 12.1).

For 60 trading days, there are no significant changes in the quality of forecasts and the composition of the 'leader' and 'anti-leader' indices of the rating. The minimal deviation is observed for MICEX CBITR and S&P Pan Asia CBI – 1 and 1.4%, respectively (Table 12.1), which indicates a good quality of forecasts for these indices. As for the valuation period of 30 trading days, last place in terms of deviations is occupied by the MSCI Russia stock index – 8.4% (Table 12.1). Deviations of more than 3% are observed for three more indices – Euro-Cbonds IG Russia and Euro-Cbonds NIG Russia, and S&P Eurozone IG CBI.

Finally, for a period of 100 trading days, the picture changes slightly, and the first two places in terms of deviations are occupied by the Euro-Cbonds IG Corporate EM and the MICEX Russian stock market index: 1.6% and 1.8%, respectively (Table 12.1). Thus, even for a longer evaluation period, the forecast quality of the dynamics of these indices is quite high. MSCI Russia index again shows the maximum deviation – 8.5%. The other five bond indices demonstrate a deviation of more than 3% (Table 12.1). Thus, for longer periods, the quality of forecast decreases, and it is preferable to use the SSA Caterpillar method to predict the index dynamics for periods of 30 and 60 trading days.

The question then arises as to what explains the overvaluation of the bond indices forecast estimates for countries that did not have sanctions imposed by the United States and the EU on April 6–9, 2018. One possible explanation is the market reaction to the increase in the US Federal Reserve rate as part of reverting the Quantitative Easing programme. There was a clear upward trend in the rates of yield on one-year US government bonds in April–September, 2018; it can be assumed that on the bond markets of other countries yields were rising, and bond prices, on the contrary, were decreasing.

By using statistical methods, we test the hypothesis about the effect of one-year and ten-year US government bonds (Treasuries) yields on the value of

Table 12.1 Estimation of deviations of stock and bond indices forecast values from actual ones. Factors affecting the magnitude of deviations

Stock or bond index	*The duration of the period (trading days) upon which the assessment is made, starting from April, 9, 2018*	*The average deviation of the predicted value from the actual one, %*	*The correlation coefficient of the forecast deviation with 10-year US Treasury yield*	*The correlation coefficient of the forecast deviation with 1-year US Treasury yield*
Euro-Cbonds IG Russia (USD)	30	3.88	**-0.50**	**-0.51**
	60	3.66	-0.21	-0.42
	100	3.88	-0.25	0.22
Euro-Cbonds NIG Russia (USD)	30	4.48	0.42	0.38
	60	4.43	0.48	0.10
	100	3.99	0.32	-0.29
Euro-Cbonds IG Corporate EM (USD)	30	1.33	**0.90**	**0.92**
	60	1.60	**0.56**	**0.93**
	100	1.55	0.46	0.38
Euro-Cbonds NIG Corporate EM (USD)	30	0.92	**0.73**	**0.78**
	60	1.96	0.07	**0.82**
	100	2.63	-0.25	**0.79**
MSCI Russia (USD)	30	8.76	**-0.85**	**-0.92**
	60	8.37	**-0.66**	**-0.50**
	100	8.49	-0.49	-0.08
S&P Eurozone IG CBI (USD)	30	2.20	**0.86**	**0.88**
	60	4.11	0.18	**0.81**
	100	5.09	-0.04	**0.83**
S&P Pan Asia CBI (USD)	30	0.57	**0.76**	**0.78**
	60	1.41	-0.11	**0.71**
	100	3.44	-0.25	**0.89**
MICEX CBI TR (RUB)	30	0.60	**0.80**	**0.84**
	60	1.00	0.01	**0.80**
	100	1.82	-0.27	**0.82**
RGBI TR (RUB)	30	2.07	-0.04	-0.06
	60	2.75	-0.28	**0.56**
	100	4.12	-0.35	**0.77**
MICEX (RUB)	30	1.85	**0.81**	**0.86**
	60	1.78	**0.62**	0.30
	100	1.79	0.45	0.04

Note: In bold are the correlation coefficients that exceed 0.5 in absolute terms.

the deviation for the considered stock and bond indices. Table 12.1 shows the corresponding correlation coefficients for valuation periods of 30, 60 and 100 trading days. It can be seen that the rates of return on annual Treasuries have high and positive correlation coefficients (above 0.5) with most of the considered indices, and these dependencies are most pronounced for periods of 30 and 60 trading days. Therefore, for 30 trading days, the correlation coefficients between the yield of one-year Treasuries and Euro-Cbonds IG Corporate EM, S&P Eurozone IG CBI, MICEX, MICEX CBI TR, Euro-Cbonds NIG Corporate EM, S&P Pan Asia CBI indices are not less than 0.78 (Table 12.1). For the Euro-Cbonds NIG Russia index, the correlation coefficient is positive, but is significantly lower at only 0.38. For the RGBITR index, a strong correlation is not present on the 30-day interval, but on the 60-day interval, the correlation coefficient is 0.56 (Table 12.1).

The exception is the dollar-valued MSCI Russia stock index, which is negatively correlated with the yield of one-year Treasuries. The correlation coefficient is -0.92 for 30 days and -0.5 for 60-day period for this index. Thus, an increase in the Fed rate contributed to a decrease in the deviation of the forecast values from the actual ones, despite the fact that the MSCI Russia index is an outsider in the quality of forecasts for the 30, 60 and 100 days: forecast values exceed the actual values on average by 8–9%. We attribute this to the fact that the introduction of anti-Russian sanctions by the United States and the EU played a decisive role in the dynamics of the MSCI Russia index, and stock prices of Russian companies in dollar terms fell significantly due to the external shock.

It should be noted that the correlation coefficients between the yield of ten-year Treasuries and the deviations, as a rule, are lower compared to those for one-year Treasuries. Bond indices are more sensitive to the dynamics of the short-term interest rates of US Treasuries.

Varying the length of the embedded vector

Let us analyze the accuracy of forecasts of stock and bond indices provided that the length L of the embedded vector x is varied over a 30-day time period starting April 9, 2018: L = 10, 21, 63, 126 and 252 trading days, which corresponds to calendar periods of two weeks, one month, one quarter, one half-year and one year. For all forecasts, we use the first ten eigenvectors. Table 12.2 shows the results of the accuracy of the forecasts for each index under consideration and the value of L.

In Figure 12.6, we present forecasting errors averaged over the considered indices over the 30-day period by the length L of the embedded vector. We can conclude that for the forecast period under consideration, the optimal value of the length L is 126 trading days, i.e. one half-year: for this value L, the forecasting error averaged over stock and bond indices is the smallest (Figure 12.6). The highest average forecasting error is typical for a length L of 10 days.

In Figure 12.7, we visualize forecasting errors in the 30-day periods for each index. Based on Table 12.2 and Figure 12.7, we can conclude that the highest forecasting error is observed for the stock index of the Russian market MSCI Russia; it ranges from 5.213% (at L = 126) to 9.311% (at L = 252). The lowest forecasting errors are observed for Euro-Cbonds IG Corporate EM bond indices

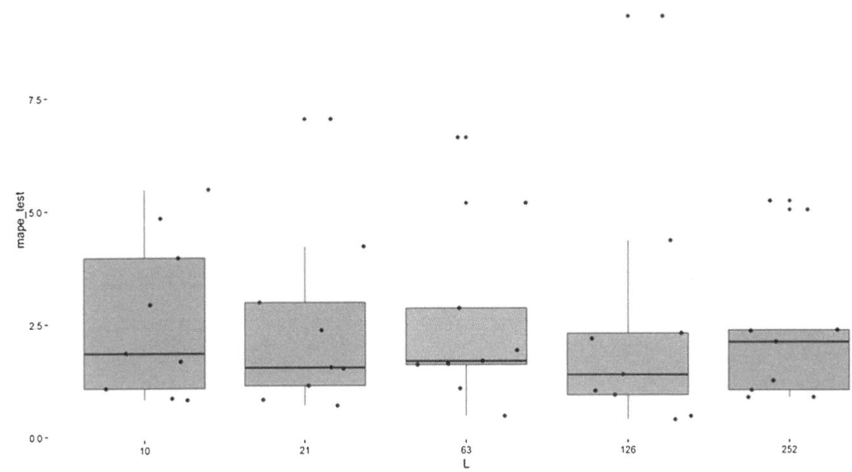

Figure 12.6 Averaged forecasting errors in the 30-day period depending on the length L of the embedded vector.

Table 12.2 Estimates of the accuracy of forecasts with varying parameter L for each index under consideration for the 30-day forecast period

Index	*L=10*	*L=21*	*L=63*	*L=126*	*L=252*
S&P_Pan_Asia_CBI	0.813	0.812	1.602	0.438	0.848
S&P_Eurozone_IG_CBI	4.845	2.355	2.845	0.901	2.347
RGBI_TR	1.852	1.502	1.589	2.278	2.084
MSCI_Russia	5.485	7.037	6.622	9.311	5.213
Micex_CBI_TR	1.066	1.12	1.054	1.362	0.849
Euro-Cbonds_NIG_Corporate_EM	1.669	1.529	1.675	0.995	1.012
Euro-Cbonds_IG_Corporate_EM	0.844	0.682	0.448	0.365	1.21
Euro-Cbonds_NIG_Russia	3.962	4.211	5.171	4.329	5.015
Euro-Cbonds_IG_Russia	2.924	2.976	1.909	2.163	2.325

(from 0.365% at L = 126 to 0.448% at L = 63) and the S&P Pan Asia CBI index (from 0.438% at L = 126 to 1.602% at L = 63).

Then we consider the accuracy of the forecasts of stock and bond indices provided that the length L of the embedded vector x is varied over a 180-day time period starting April 9, 2018: L = 10, 21, 63, 126 and 252 trading days. The 180-day forecast period is further divided into 30-day windows, and we will forecast and evaluate the forecast accuracy on each such window separately, and then we consider the averaged estimates for 6 windows. For all forecasts, we use the first 10 eigenvectors. Table 12.3 shows the results of the forecast accuracy for each index under consideration and the value of L.

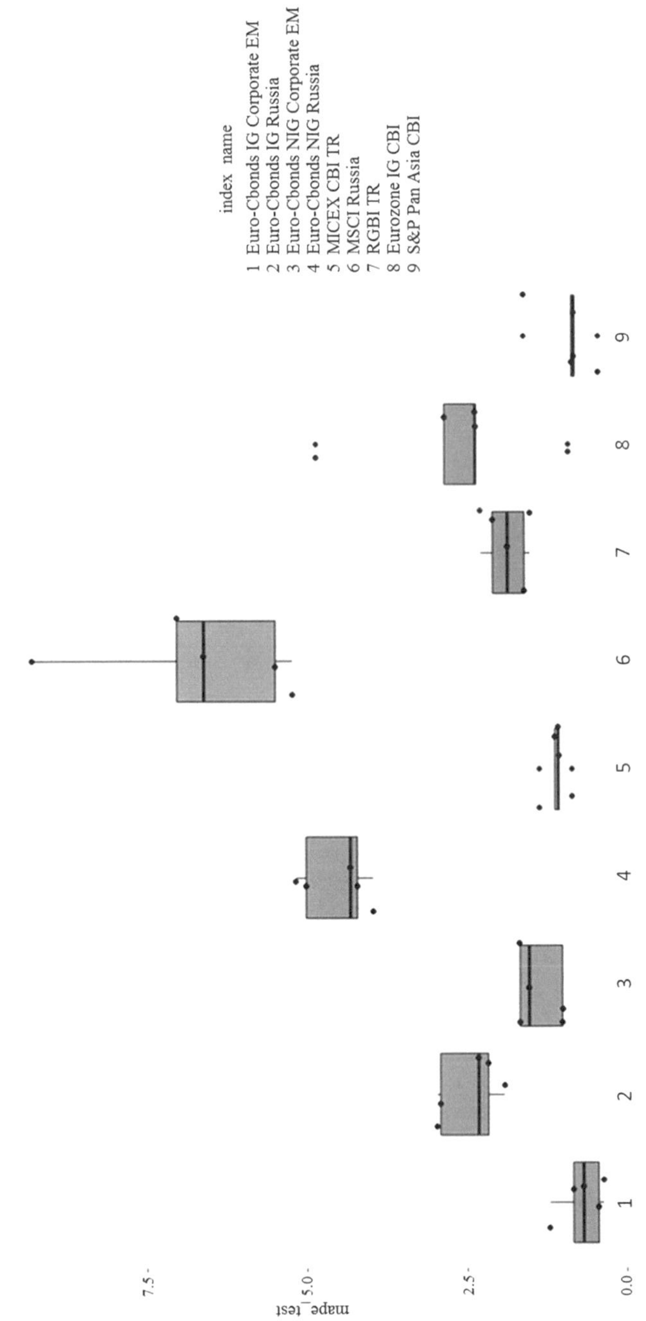

Figure 12.7 Forecasting errors in the 30-day period by different indices.

Table 12.3 Estimates of the accuracy of forecasts with varying parameter L for each index under consideration for a forecast period of 180 days (the window length is 30 days)

Index	*L=10*	*L=21*	*L=63*	*L=126*	*L=252*
S&P_Pan_Asia_CBI	2.593	0.864	1.004	0.782	1.593
S&P_Eurozone_IG_CBI	4.006	1.54	1.765	1.175	1.279
RGBI_TR	1.258	0.948	1.036	1.433	1.702
MSCI_Russia	11.737	3.786	4.236	5.388	4.434
Micex_CBI_TR	1.002	0.617	0.938	0.879	0.641
Euro-Cbonds_NIG_Corporate_EM	1.683	0.944	1.293	1.214	2.377
Euro-Cbonds_IG_Corporate_EM	0.791	0.469	0.449	0.814	0.637
Euro-Cbonds_NIG_Russia	10.019	1.222	2.247	1.678	1.879
Euro-Cbonds_IG_Russia	1.191	0.981	1.108	1.325	1.518

We also estimate forecasting errors averaged over the considered indices on the 180-day period (with a window length of 30 days) depending on the length L of the embedded vector. For the forecast period under consideration, the optimal value of the length L is 21 trading days, i.e. one calendar month: for this value of L, the forecasting error averaged over stock and bond indices is the smallest. The highest average forecasting error is typical for a length L of 10 days.

Based on Table 12.3, we conclude that the highest forecasting error is observed for the stock index of the Russian market MSCI Russia; it ranges from 3.786% (at L = 21) to 11.737% (at L = 10). The lowest forecasting errors are observed for Euro-Cbonds IG Corporate EM bond index (from 0.449% at L = 63 to 0.814% at L = 126) and the MICEX CBI TR index (from 0.617% at L = 21 to 1.002% at L = 10). For example, in Figure 12.8 we present actual and forecasted values for the Euro-Cbonds IG Corporate EM Index (L = 63 days).

Varying the number of the eigenvectors

Now we analyze the accuracy of forecasts of stock and bond indices varying the number of the eigenvectors of the matrix C ($C = \frac{1}{N-L+1} XX^T$) over the 30-day period starting from April 9, 2018, with L = 21 and 126. The number of the eigenvectors for the singular decomposition of the trajectory matrix is determined based on the value of the eigenvalues and is from 5 to 8 for different indices. We estimate the forecasting errors averaged over the considered indices over the 30-day interval depending on the length L of the embedded vector. The optimal value of the length L, minimizing the average error, is 21 trading days. We conclude that, as for the case of 10 eigenvectors, the highest forecasting error is observed for the stock index of the Russian market MSCI Russia. It is 4.647% (if L = 21) and 6.394% (if L = 126). The lowest forecasting errors, as before, are observed for the Euro-Cbonds IG Corporate EM bond index (0.852% if L = 21

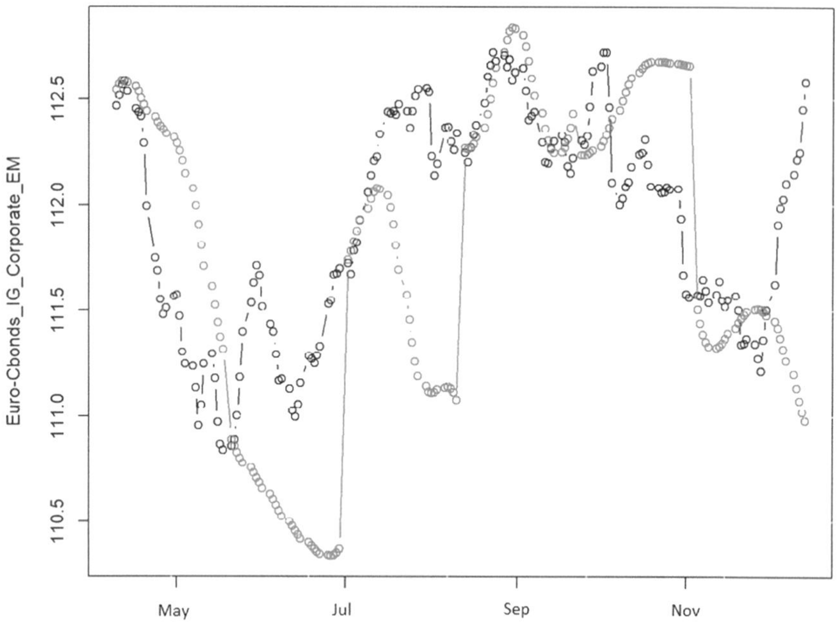

Figure 12.8 Actual and forecasted values of Euro-Cbonds IG Corporate EM Index (L = 63 days) on the 180-day period.

and 1.228% if L = 126) and the S&P Pan Asia CBI index (0.555% if L = 26 and 1.518% if L = 126).

Note

1 Some indices considered in this section only started to be calculated in 2015; for these the period of reconstruction of past values begins in 2015.

References

Loskutov, A. Y., Kozlov, A. A., Khakhanov, Y. M. (2009). Entropy and time series forecast in the theory of dynamical systems. *Izv. universities* "PND", 17(4): 98–113. In Russian.

Danilov, D. L. Zhiglyavsky, A. A. eds. (1997). The main components of the time series: "Caterpillar-SSA". St. Petersburg: Presscom. 119–123. In Russian.

13 Modelling and forecasting systemic risk on the bond market

Introduction

The relationship between an asset's risk and its expected return is one of the most widely studied subjects in financial economics. A fundamental study on this topic was conducted by Sharpe (1964) and Lintner (1965), who developed the capital asset pricing model (CAPM).

According to the CAPM model, the expected risk premium for investors over the risk-free rate is proportional to the systematic risk of the asset. The systematic risk of a security is determined by the beta coefficient, which is calculated as a covariance between the return on a diversified market portfolio and the return of an asset divided by the variance of the market portfolio return. In the CAPM model, the value of the beta coefficient is assumed to be constant. A number of subsequent papers have demonstrated that volatility of asset returns is not constant, and as a result, the beta coefficient changes over time (Fabozzi and Francis, 1978).

Variability of systematic risk requires applying dynamic models to estimate the beta coefficient as part of an iterative portfolio optimization. Dynamic beta modelling is performed through various methods, such as Markov models, GARCH models, Kalman filter, models of stochastic volatility, and semi-parametric models.

The goal of this paper is to compare various approaches to estimating and forecasting dynamic beta using indices of government and corporate bonds of the Russian market.

The results for the bond market are compared with the results for the stock indices of emerging markets.

Literature review

There are several econometric methods for constructing dynamic beta. Fabozzi and Francis (1978) use the Kalman filter to determine the beta coefficient in the random walk process. Groenewold and Fraser (1999) also model the beta coefficient using the Kalman filter on the monthly data of the Australian stock market from December 1979 to February 1994. Beta coefficients are also evaluated using recursive and rolling regressions. It has been proved that beta coefficients are non-stationary. He and Kryzanowski (2008) consider the Kalman filter as a blending of the random walk process and mean reversion.

An alternative way to build a beta coefficient is to use GARCH models. The pioneers in implementing this method on the stock market are Bollersev et al. (1988), and Engle and Rodrigues (1989). They consider one-dimensional GARCH models that reflected the dynamics of market volatility or the volatility of an individual security.

In order to estimate the beta, we must take into account the evolution of a covariance between two assets over time. As a solution, multidimensional GARCH models with in-built asymmetry are introduced. Choudhry and Wu (2008) use multidimensional GARCH, BEKKGARCH, GARCH-GJR, GARCH-X models to estimate the daily beta coefficients of 20 British companies from January 1989 to December 2003. The results are also compared to the results on the base of the Kalman filter. In each case, the Kalman filter has greater or equal accuracy in estimating profitability in the CAPM model.

Lie, Brooks and Fama (2000) compare the results of building daily dynamic beta on the shares of 15 financial companies in Australia using a Kalman filter and a GARCH model. The Kalman filter shows smaller error in the prediction of profitability when estimating the beta coefficient.

Li (2003) also compare the accuracy of yield predictions using beta coefficients, constructed using the GARCH model and the Kalman filter. The authors evaluate the beta coefficients of the New Zealand industrial sectors from January 1997 to August 2002. The author shows that, in-sample, the stochastic volatility model and the Kalman filter demonstrate the highest accuracy (the mean square errors are 1.2540 and 1.2894, respectively), while the GARCH model shows the lowest accuracy (the mean square error is 1.5483). Other results are obtained from out-of-sample tests: the mean square error of the GARCH model is the smallest (1.1021), which demonstrates its superiority over the other models. The mean square error of the Kalman filter is the highest (1.1681; source: Li, 2003).

The stochastic volatility model (SV) is also one of the popular methods for constructing beta coefficients. Yu (2002) finds that, based on the daily return on assets of the 40 largest New Zealand companies from January 1980 to December 1998, the SV model turns out to perform better than GARCH in out-of-sample predictions.

Johansson (2009) compares beta estimates from the SV and GARCH multidimensional models based on the weekly MSCI index data for 27 developing and 3 developed countries from December 1994 to December 2006. In most cases, the SV model performs better than the GARCH model.

Another way to build dynamic beta coefficients is to use semi-parametric models. Hastie and Tibshirani (1993) consider regression models with coefficients as smooth functions of other variables. Esteban and Orbe-Manadaluniz (2010) use semi-parametric models to build beta coefficients in the Spanish stock market. The non-parametric approach is used by Eisenbeiss, Kauermann and Semmler (2007) on the daily yield data of indices of the German industrial sectors. The data is taken for the period from April 1991 to March 2003. The results of building the model are compared with the beta coefficients obtained using the CAPM. The mean square error of the GCV dynamic model for all sectors is lower than that of the CAPM, which indicates the superiority of the non-parametric approach in the accuracy of the forecast before estimating the constant beta.

Another method for evaluating dynamic beta is to use Markov chains. Mergner and Bulla (2008) review the Markov switching model and compare it with other popular methods on monthly data in Europe from April 1986 to December 1993 in- and out-of-sample. In-sample, the best result by the mean square error is demonstrated by the Kalman filter (0.178), and the worst result is shown by the OLS model (0.289). The Markov switching model is inferior to the Kalman filter. Out-of-sample the best result is demonstrated by the Kalman filter (the mean square error is 0.191), while the worst result is shown by the Markov switching model (0.210; source: Mergner and Bulla, 2008).

Based on the results of analyzing previous papers, it can be concluded that in most cases the Kalman filter is superior to the other approaches for in-sample tests. Few papers are devoted to comparing semi-parametric models, but Asaturov (2017) reveals smaller error in estimating beta by semi-parametric regression with a uniform nuclear function in the in-sample period for Russian companies' stocks. GARCH models work better in out-of-sample beta predictions. More advanced GARCH approaches (for example, GARCH with built-in asymmetry of correlation) can provide higher accuracy in prediction of the beta coefficient to estimate returns in comparison with the CAPM.

Research hypotheses

Based on the previous literature, we test the GARCH dynamic conditional correlation model (GARCH-DCC), the GARCH model with asymmetric conditional correlation (GARCH-G-DCC), models with asymmetric conditional correlation and volatility in dynamics (GARCH-AG-DCC), the Kalman filter, semi-parametric regressions and rolling regression for government and corporate bond indices of the Russian market.

The beta calculation is carried out over two periods – in-sample to estimate the current yield at the current time and out-of-sample to forecast one step further. We put forward the following hypotheses:

Hypothesis 1: The best model in terms of in-sample estimation accuracy of the bond indices' beta coefficients is the Kalman filter.

Hypothesis 2: The best model in terms of out-of-sample prediction accuracy of bond indices' beta coefficients is the GARCH model with the built-in asymmetry in conditional volatility.

For the first time, semi-parametric regressions and asymmetric GARCH models are tested to build dynamic beta using Russian bond market data.

Methodology for calculating dynamic beta coefficients

Dynamic models for estimating beta coefficients

Asset returns are calculated by the following formula:

$$r_t = 100 * ln\left(\frac{ind_t}{ind_{t-1}}\right) \tag{13.1}$$

where ind_t is the index value at time t.

Classical regression

The classical regression is as follows:

$$R_t = \alpha + \beta * R_{m,t} + \varepsilon_t, \varepsilon_t N(0, \sigma^2) \tag{13.2}$$

where R_t is an asset return at moment t; $R_{m,t}$ is a diversified market portfolio return at moment t; ε_t is the error term with zero mean and constant variance.

Alpha and beta coefficients are calculated using the least-squares method. The beta coefficient formula is:

$$\beta = \frac{Cov(R_t, R_{m,t})}{D(R_{m,t})} \tag{13.3}$$

where $Cov(R_t, R_{m,t})$ is the covariance between the asset return and the market portfolio; $D(R_{m,t})$ is the variance of the market portfolio return.

The beta coefficient is a measure of the sensitivity of a security to a market portfolio. The higher the value of beta, the higher the volatility of an asset in relation to the market, and therefore the higher the risk. The value of beta obtained using formula 2 is used in the CAPM model of Sharpe (1964).

Out-of-sample beta coefficients are estimated by rolling regression.

The Kalman filter

The Kalman filter evaluates the state of the system over time and builds a space-state model using a system of observation and state equations. The market model for an asset return on the base of the Kalman filter is as follows:

$$R_t = \alpha_t + \beta_t * R_{m,t} + \varepsilon_t, \beta_t = \beta_{t-1} + \eta_t, \alpha_t = \alpha_{t-1} + u_t \tag{13.4}$$

$$\varepsilon_t N(0, \sigma_\varepsilon^2), \eta_t N(0, \sigma_\eta^2), u_t N(0, \sigma_u^2) \tag{13.5}$$

where ε_t, η_t, u_t are random and independent error terms; α_t, β_t represent state transition equations; R_t, $R_{m,t}$ represent the observation model.

Faff, Hillier and Hillier (2000) estimate the beta random walk process, which is constructed using the formulas:

$$\begin{cases} y_t = Z_t * x_t + d_t + \omega_t \\ x_t = M_t * x_{t-1} + c_t + S_t * \upsilon_t \end{cases} \tag{13.6}$$

$$\omega_t N(0,\ \sigma^2_{\omega}),\ \upsilon_t N(0,\ Q_t) \tag{13.7}$$

$$\text{where } y_t = R_t,\ Z_t = (1R_{m,t}),\ x_t = \begin{pmatrix} \alpha_t \\ \beta_t \end{pmatrix}, \tag{13.8}$$

$$M_t = S_t \begin{pmatrix} 1 & 0 \\ 0 & 1 \end{pmatrix},\ \sigma^2_{\omega} = \sigma^2_{\omega},\ \upsilon_t = \begin{pmatrix} \eta_t \\ u_t \end{pmatrix},\ Q_t = \begin{pmatrix} \sigma^2_{\eta} & 0 \\ 0 & \sigma^2_{u} \end{pmatrix} \tag{13.9}$$

Denote:

$$b_t = E_t(x_t), b_{t\vee t-1} = E_{t-1}(x_t), P_t = E_t((b_t - x_t) * (b_t - x_t)^T) \tag{13.10}$$

The Kalman filter is described by the following system of equations:

$$\begin{cases} b_{t\vee t-1} = M_t * b_{t-1} + c_t \\ P_{t\vee t-1} = M_t * P_{t-1} * M_t^T + S_t * Q_t * S_t^T \\ y_{t\vee t-1} = Z_t * b_{t\vee t-1} = d_t \\ v_t = y_t - y_{t\vee t-1} \\ F_t = Z_t * P_{t\vee t-1} + Z_t^T + H_y \\ b_t = b_{t\vee t-1} + P_{t\vee t-1} * Z_t^T * F_t^{-1} v_t \\ P_t = (I_m - P_{t\vee t-1} * Z_t^T * F_t^{-1} * Z_t) * P_{t\vee t-1} \end{cases} \tag{13.11}$$

Unknown parameters are estimated using the maximum likelihood method:

$$L(\lambda) = \frac{-1}{2} * T * \ln(2\pi) - \frac{1}{2} \sum \left(\ln(F_t) + \frac{v_t^2}{F_t} \right) \tag{13.12}$$

At the first stage the initial values are set as following: $\alpha_t = 0$ and $\beta_t = 1$.

Multidimensional GARCH class models

To calculate dynamic beta, we apply the GARCH-DCC model described by Engle (2002) and the GARCH-A-DCC reviewed by Capiello, Engle and Sheppard (2006).

The GARCH-DCC model, the GARCH-G-DCC and GARCH-AG-DCC are also applicable. The GARCH-AG-DCC model is well suited for studying the asymmetry of volatility response and asset correlation during negative shocks.

According to multidimensional GARCH models, the equations of returns are as follows:

$$R_t = c + \varepsilon_t, R_{m,t} = c_m + \varepsilon_{m,t}, \varepsilon_t \vee Infrm_{t-1} N(0, D_t \rho_t D_t) \quad (13.13)$$

where c, c_m are the expected value of a security and portfolio; ε_t, $\varepsilon_{m,t}$ are error terms; $Infrm_{t-1}$ is information at moment t; D_t is the diagonal matrix of conditional deviations of asset and portfolio returns; ρ_t is the matrix with conditional correlation of asset and portfolio returns.

The diagonal matrix is determined as follows:

$$D_t = \begin{pmatrix} \sqrt{h_{m,t}} & 0 \\ 0 & \sqrt{h_t} \end{pmatrix} \quad (13.14)$$

where $h_{m,t}$, h_t are conditional dispersions of portfolio and asset balances at time t.

The matrix with conditional correlations looks as follows:

$$\rho_t = \begin{pmatrix} 1 & p_{m,t} \\ p_{m,t} & 1 \end{pmatrix} \quad (13.15)$$

where $p_{m,t}$ is conditional dispersion of portfolio and asset balances at time t.

The formula for calculating the matrix of conditional correlations in the DCC model is presented below:

$$\rho_t = diag(S_t)^{\frac{-1}{2}} S_t diag(S_t)^{\frac{-1}{2}} \quad (13.16)$$

$$S_t = (1 - \alpha - \delta)\acute{S}\, \alpha u_{t-1} u_{t-1}{'} + \delta S_{t-1} \quad (13.17)$$

$$\acute{S} = E(u_t u_t{'}), \alpha + \delta < 1, \alpha > 0, \delta > 0, \quad (13.18)$$

where u_t are error terms ε_t after normalization; S_t is a normalized residual covariance matrix; α and δ are parameters that detect an increase in the correlation between the asset and the portfolio in the case of fluctuations with the same sign.

In the equation of correlation inside the GARCH model with built-in asymmetry of the conditional correlation (GARCH-A-DCC), the following formula is used:

$$S_t = (1 - \alpha - \delta)\acute{S} - \gamma\acute{K} + \alpha u_{t-1}u_{t-1}' + \delta S_{t-1} + \gamma\eta_{t-1}\eta_{t-1}' \quad (13.19)$$

$$\acute{K} = E(\eta_t\eta_t'), \alpha + \delta + \gamma > 1, \alpha > 0, \delta > 0, \gamma > 0, \quad (13.20)$$

where $\eta_t = [u_t < 0]u_t$ equals u_t if $u_t > 0$, otherwise 0; $\acute{K}$ is an unconditional covariance matrix.

The formula for calculating the conditional variance of the asset and market portfolio in the GARCH model is presented by Bollerslev (1988):

$$\begin{cases} \sigma_t^2 = c_1 + k_1\varepsilon_t^2 + \tau_1\sigma_{t-1}^2 \\ \sigma_{m,t}^2 = c_2 + k_2\varepsilon_{m,t}^2 + \tau_2\sigma_{m,t-1}^2 \end{cases} \quad (13.21)$$

Glosten, Jaganathan and Runkle (1993) consider the GARCH-G model with the asymmetry of conditional volatility over time:

$$\begin{cases} \sigma_t^2 = c_1 + k_1\varepsilon_t^2 + \lambda_1\varepsilon_t^2[\varepsilon_t < 0] + \tau_1\sigma_{t-1}^2 \\ \sigma_{m,t}^2 = c_2 + k_2\varepsilon_{m,t}^2 + \lambda_2\varepsilon_{m,t}^2[\varepsilon_{m,t} < 0] + \tau_2\sigma_{t-1}^2 \end{cases} \quad (13.22)$$

$$\lambda_1, \lambda_2 > 0 \quad (13.23)$$

where λ_1, λ_2 are parameters that take into account the asymmetry in volatility shocks. With negative values ε_t the value in front of the coefficient equals 0. In the case of the significance of the coefficients, this demonstrates higher volatility of the asset in the case of negative shocks.

Conditional covariance is calculated as:

$$h_{m,t} = p_{m,t}\sigma_t\sigma_{m,t}, \quad (13.24)$$

where σ_t is an asset's conditional standard deviation; $\sigma_{m,t}$ is portfolio return's conditional standard deviation; $p_{m,t}$ is conditional correlation between the asset and the portfolio.

An asset's dynamic beta is calculated as following:

$$\beta_t = \frac{h_{m,t}}{\sigma_{m,t}^2} \quad (13.25)$$

The estimation of the GARCH model's unknown parameters is done using maximum likelihood estimation:

$$L = \frac{-1}{2}\sum_{t=1}^{T}(2\log(|D_t|)) + \log(|\rho_t|) + \varepsilon_t'\rho_t^{-1}\varepsilon_t \quad (13.26)$$

In addition to models with a normal distribution of residuals, the same GARCH models are used, the residuals of which have a Student's distribution. As a result, we compare the accuracy of estimation and prediction of beta coefficients among six models of the GARCH class.

Semi-parametric models

Semi-parametric models have recently gained popularity in scientific research. Their feature is that they do not require the knowledge of the model's functional form. Such models can be used in the case of an unknown dependence of the parameters that are included in the linear model.

Hastie and Tibshirani (1993) consider regression models with coefficients as smooth functions of other variables:

$$R_t = \alpha_t + \beta_t * R_{m,t} + \varepsilon_t, \tag{13.27}$$

$$\alpha_t = f\left(\frac{t}{T}\right),\ \beta_t = g\left(\frac{t}{T}\right),\ \varepsilon_t N(0,\sigma_\varepsilon^2) \tag{13.28}$$

where t is a moment in time; T is the sample size; α_t, β_t are coefficients, defined as functions with unknown forms and time as their argument.

The relationship between the coefficients as a function of time is studied by Esteban and Orbe-Manadaluniz (2010). The target function for evaluation of the coefficients is proposed in the following way:

$$\min_{(\alpha_t,\beta_t)} \sum_{z=1}^{T} K_{t,z}^{h}(R_z - \alpha_t - \beta_t * R_{m,z})^2, \tag{13.30}$$

where $K_{t,z}^{h} = h^{-1}K\left(\frac{t-z}{Th}\right)$ is a weighting function, called the kernel; h is the width of the window.

The window width serves as a smoothing parameter, upon which the accuracy of the model depends and which determines the size of the subsample. Esteban and Orbe-Manadaluniz (2010) make the choice of the width of the window through cross-validation. Too small a width can make the results non-interpretable. Too large a width of the window, on the other hand, will make the estimates the same for the entire period.

The resulting formula for estimating the coefficients is presented below:

$$(\alpha_t,\beta_t)' = \left(\sum_{z=t-1}^{t-Th} K_{t,z}^{h} X_z X_z'\right)^{-1} \sum_{z=t-1}^{t-Th} K_{t,z}^{h} X_z R_z \tag{13.31}$$

where $X_z = (1 R_{m,z})'$; R_z is an asset return; Th is the size of the subsample.

The kernel function assigns more weights to the observations that are the closest to the considered time instant t, while with a larger time gap the values of the weight of the observations decrease.

The degree of smoothing of the coefficient function depends on the type of the kernel function. In the case of a uniform function, an equal weight is assigned to observations in a subsample. The Gauss kernel assigns more weights to the observations on the 'tails' of the distribution than the Epanechnikov kernel.

The Gauss kernel function is represented by the formula:

$$K\left(\frac{t-z}{Th}\right) = \frac{1}{\sqrt{2\pi}} exp\left(\frac{-1}{2} * \left(\frac{t-z}{Th}\right)^2\right) \tag{13.32}$$

The Epanechnikov kernel function looks as follows:

$$K\left(\frac{t-z}{Th}\right) = \begin{cases} \frac{3}{4}\left(1-\left(\frac{t-z}{Th}\right)^2\right), -1 \leq \left(\frac{t-z}{Th}\right) \leq 1 \\ 0 \; else \end{cases} \tag{13.33}$$

The uniform kernel function looks as follows:

$$K\left(\frac{t-z}{Th}\right) = \begin{cases} \frac{1}{2}, \; -1 \leq \left(\frac{t-z}{Th}\right) \leq 1 \\ 0 \; else \end{cases} \tag{13.34}$$

In this paper we consider models with all three types of kernel functions for in-sample and out-of-sample data.

Choosing the most accurate model

As a measure of the estimation accuracy and forecast, the formula for calculating the mean square error (MSE) is used. The quality of the models will be checked when evaluating beta in-sample and predicting the dynamic coefficients out-of-sample.

At the in-sample period, the formula looks as follows:

$$MSE = \frac{\sum_{t=1}^{T}(R_t - R_t)^2}{T} \tag{13.35}$$

where T is the sample size; $\hat{R}_t$ is the in-sample asset return estimate.

At the out-of-sample period the formula is as follows:

$$MSE = \frac{\sum_{t=1}^{T} (R_{t+t\vee t} - R_t)^2}{T} \tag{13.36}$$

where $\hat{R}_{t+1\vee t}$ is the asset return's predicted value at the moment t+1.

A smaller value of the MSE indicates a better accuracy of the model estimation and forecast.

Study sample

The construction of beta coefficients is performed on the basis of weekly returns of government and corporate bonds indices in Russian market. The MSCI index is chosen as the market portfolio, and the yield of three-month US bonds is chosen as the risk-free rate. The data source is the Cbonds database.

The period from January 2010 to December 2015 is considered as the sample and contains 313 observations. Internal sampling is used to estimate beta coefficients. The out-of-sample period includes the period from January 2016 to December 2018, upon which the one step ahead beta coefficient forecast is built. The out-of-sample period consists of 157 observations. The first 50 observations in-sample are used to evaluate the dynamic beta on the base of semi-parametric models and are not included in the comparison.

To compare the results on the Russian bond market with the results on the stock markets, MSCI indices of 18 developing countries are also considered, including Mauritius, Colombia, Botswana, Lebanon, Peru, Thailand, Tunisia, Indonesia, Sri Lanka, Morocco, Jordan, the Philippines, Egypt, Nigeria, India, Vietnam, Pakistan, Bangladesh, and Kenya.

The results of modelling the dynamic beta coefficients

Beta estimation for the Russian bond market indices in-sample

Following Mergner and Bulla (2008) and Asaturov (2017), all models are assigned a rank from 1 to 11 in such a way that the worst value in the beta estimation is assigned the maximum value of 11. According to the results presented in Table 13.1 and Figure 13.1, for corporate and government rouble bond indices, GARCH models demonstrate the best results on the in-sample period; in particular, the model with the asymmetry of conditional correlation and volatility in the dynamics (GARCH-AG-DCC). The worst results in the accuracy of beta estimates are shown by semi-parametric models.

On the contrary, the results for the developing countries stock markets demonstrate the advantage of in-sample semi-parametric models. For example, for 12 out of 18 developing countries' stock indices, the semi-parametric model with

Table 13.1 Rouble bond indices: comparing the mean square error (MSE) values of in-sample models

	Government bonds	*Corporate bonds*
GARCH-AG-DCC	2.086	7.169
GARCH-DCC	2.086	7.169
GARCH-G-DCC	2.086	7.169
Kalman Filter	2.090	7.183
GARCH-AG-DCC (t-stat.)	2.086	7.168
DCC-GARCH (t-stat.)	2.086	7.168
GARCH-G-DCC (t-stat.)	2.086	7.168
Semi-parametric model (Gauss kernel)	2.092	7.188
Semi-parametric model (Uniform kernel)	2.092	7.188
Semi-parametric model (Epanechnikov kernel)	2.092	7.187
Rolling regression	2.092	7.188

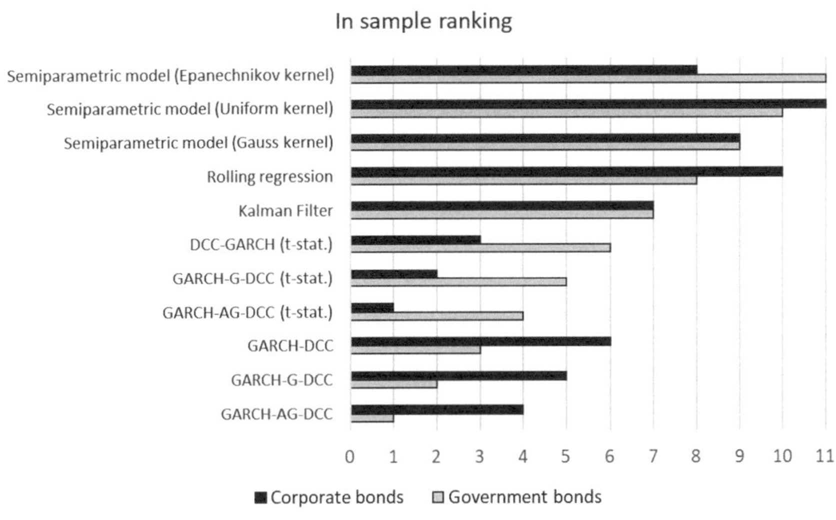

Figure 13.1 Indices of rouble bonds: comparison of the rank of models in-sample.

the Epanechnikov kernel function has the highest accuracy. For 4 out of 18 stock indices, the Kalman filter has the best results. According to the average rank, semi-parametric regressions also demonstrate the highest accuracy of estimation (Figure 13.2).

Despite the fact that most of the previous studies in this topic show the superiority of the Kalman filter in terms of the accuracy of in-sample estimates, Hypothesis 1 is rejected for the Russian bond market.

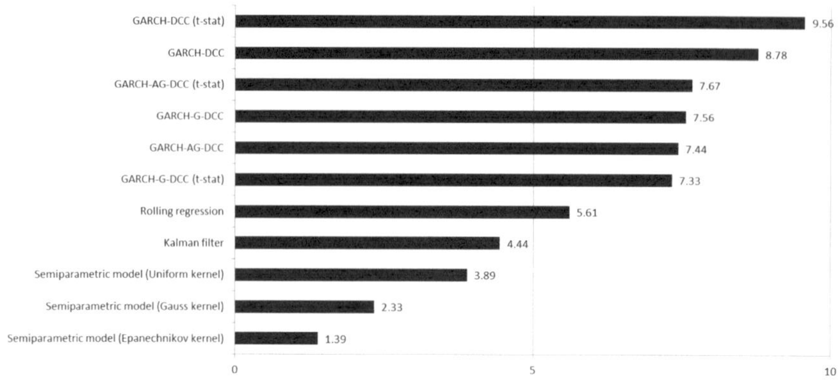

Figure 13.2 Stock indices of developing countries: comparison of average rank of models in-sample[1].

Table 13.2 Rouble bond indices: comparing the mean square error (MSE) values of out-of-sample models

	Government bonds	*Corporate bonds*
GARCH-AG-DCC	3.210	4.008
GARCH-DCC	3.230	4.103
GARCH-G-DCC	3.210	4.007
Kalman Filter	3.059	4.424
GARCH-AG-DCC (t-stat.)	3.220	4.005
DCC-GARCH (t-stat.)	3.247	4.101
GARCH-G-DCC (t-stat.)	3.220	3.990
Semi-parametric model (Gauss kernel)	2.855	3.616
Semi-parametric model (Uniform kernel)	2.870	3.625
Semi-parametric model (Epanechnikov kernel)	2.832	3.602
Rolling regression	3.573	4.577

Russian bond market indices out-of-sample beta coefficients forecast

As suggested by the results presented in Table 13.2 and Figure 13.3, for the indices of corporate and government rouble bonds, semi-parametric models – in particular, the model with the Epanechnikov kernel – demonstrate the best results in the out-of-sample period. Rolling regression shows the worst results in accuracy for government bonds and the Kalman filter for corporate bonds, followed by GARCH models.

On the contrary, for the stock indices of developing countries considering out-of-sample period, the GARCH models show the best estimates for 8 out

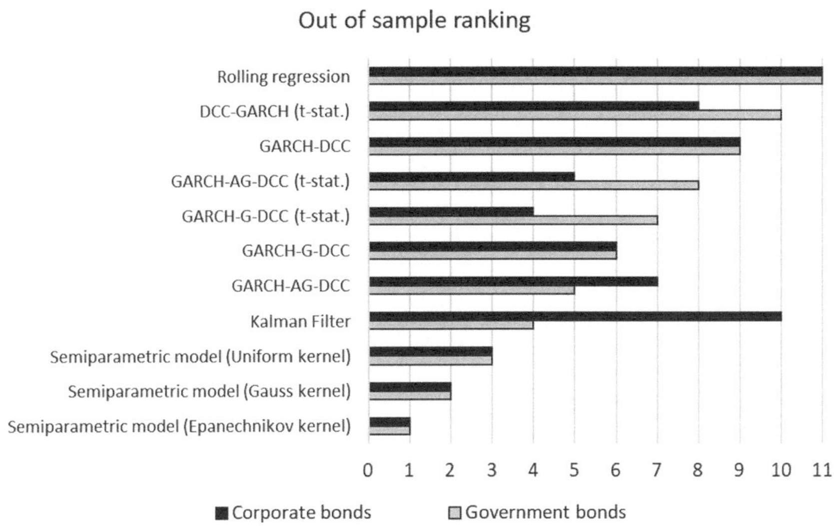

Figure 13.3 Indices of rouble bonds: comparison of ranks of models out-of-sample.

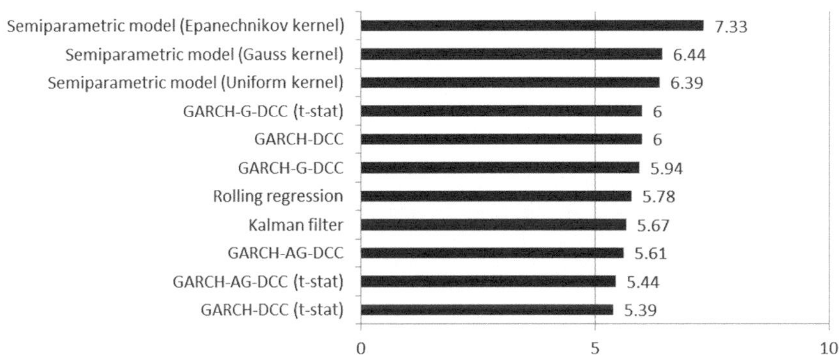

Figure 13.4 Stock indices in developing countries: comparing middle rank of models out-of-sample.

of 18 markets, and semi-parametric models do so for 7 out of 18 markets. The Kalman filter does not provide higher accuracy for any of the markets under consideration. During the out-of-sample period, the models show a significant narrowing of the scatter of average ranks, and the leaders are the GARCH-DCC and the model with asymmetry in the conditional correlation and volatility in the dynamics (GARCH-AG-DCC) (Figure 13.4).

Thus the out-of-sample results for stock and bond market indices of developing countries are contrasting: if semi-parametric models are more optimal in accuracy for the bond markets, then GARCH models are better for the stock markets. For bond markets, the alternative hypothesis is rejected.

Conclusion

In this chapter we evaluate various approaches to modelling the bond indices beta coefficients in the Russian market: GARCH models, Kalman filter, semi-parametric regressions, and rolling regression.

Based on a review of previous studies on the topic of research, we hypothesize that the Kalman filter will have the highest accuracy of the beta estimate in-sample and that the GARCH models will have the highest predictive power out-of-sample. According to the results of testing various approaches for corporate and government rouble bond indices during the period from 2010 to 2018, neither hypothesis is confirmed.

It is revealed that for the in-sample period (from 2010 to 2015) on the Russian bond market, GARCH models are the most accurate; in particular, the model with asymmetry of conditional correlation and volatility in the dynamics (GARCH-AG-DCC). For the out-of-sample period (from 2016 to 2018), semi-parametric models – in particular, the model with the Epechnikov kernel – allow a better forecast.

For comparison, in the emerging stock markets, the opposite results are obtained: if the use of semi-parametric models are optimal for the in-sample period, then for the out-of-sample one the GARCH models perform better.

Note

1 Stock fund results are provided by Abdulkadyrov, student of National Research University Higher School of Economics (Russia).

References

Asaturov, K. G. (2017). Intertemporal systematic risk: Definition of determinants and portfolio optimization: PhD thesis. HSE, Moscow. In Russian.

Bollersev, T., Engle, R. F., Wooldridge, J. M. (1988). A capital asset pricing model with time-varying covariances. *Journal of Political Economy*, 96: 116–131. DOI: https://doi.org/10.1086/261527

Capiello, L., Engle, R. F., Sheppard, K. (2006). Asymmetric dynamics in the correlations of global equity and bond returns. *Journal of Financial Econometrics*, 4: 537–572. DOI: https://doi.org/10.1093/jjfinec/nbl005

Choudhry, T., Wu, H. (2008). Forecasting ability of GARCH vs Kalman filter method: Evidence from daily UK time-varying beta. *Journal of Forecasting*, 27: 670–689. DOI: https://doi.org/10.1002/for.1096

Eisenbeiss, M., Kauermann, G., Semmler, W. (2007). Estimating beta-coefficients of German stock data: A non-parametric approach. *The European Journal of Finance*, 13(6): 503–522. DOI: https://doi.org/10.1080/13518470701201405

Engle, C., Rodrigues, A. (1989). Tests of international CAPM with time-varying covariances. *Journal of Applied Econometrics*, 4: 119–138. DOI: https://doi.org/10.1002/jae.3950040203

Engle, R. F. (2002). Dynamic conditional correlation: A simple class of multivariate generalized autoregressive conditional heteroscedasticity models. *Journal of Business and Economics Statistics*, 20(3): 339–350. DOI: https://doi.org/10.1198/073500102288618487

Esteban, M. V., Orbe-Manadaluniz, S. (2010). A nonparametric approach for estimating betas: The smoothed rolling estimator. *Applied Economics*, 42: 1269–1279. DOI: https://doi.org/10.1080/00036840701721257

Fabozzi, F., Francis, J. (1978). Beta as a random coefficient. *Journal of Financial and Quantitative Analysis*, 13: 101–116. DOI: https://doi.org/10.2307/2330525

Faff, R. W., Hillier, D., Hillier, J. (2000). Time-varying beta risk: An analysis of alternative modeling techniques. *Journal of Business Finance and Accounting*, 27: 523–554. DOI: https://doi.org/10.1111/1468–5957.00324

Glosten, L. R., Jaganathan, R., Runkle, R. (1993). On the relation between the expected value and the volatility of the nominal excess return on stocks. *Journal of Finance*, 48(5): 1779–1801. DOI: https://doi.org/10.1111/j.1540–6261.1993.tb05128.x

Groenewold, N., Fraser, P. (1999). Time-varying estimates of CAPM betas. *Mathematics and Computers in Simulations*, 48: 531–539. DOI: https://doi.org/10.1016/S0378–4754(99)00033–6

Hastie, T., Tibshirani, R. (1993). Varying-coefficient models. *Journal of the Royal Statistic Society*, Series B (Methodology), 55(4): 757–796. DOI: https://doi.org/10.1111/j.2517–6161.1993.tb01939.x

He, Z., Kryzanowski, L. (2008). Dynamic betas for Canadian sector portfolios. *International Review of Financial Analysis*, 17: 1110–1122. DOI: https://doi.org/10.1016/j.irfa.2007.08.001

Johansson, A. C. (2009). Stochastic volatility and time-varying country risk in emerging markets. *The European Journal of Finance*, 15(3): 337–363. DOI: https://doi.org/10.1080/13518470802466006

Li, X. (2003). On unstable beta risk and its modelling techniques for New Zealand industry portfolios. Massey University Commerce. Working Paper 03.01.

Lie, F., Brooks, R., Fama, R. (2000). Modelling the equity beta risk of Australian financial sector companies. *Australian Economic Papers*, 39: 301–311 DOI: https://doi.org/10.1111/1467–8454.00093

Lintner, J. (1965). Valuation of risk assets and the selection of risk investments in stock portfolios and capital budgets. *Review of Economics and Statistics*, 47: 13–37. DOI: https://doi.org/10.1016/B978–0-12–780850–5.50018–6

Mergner, S., Bulla, J. (2008). Time-varying beta risk of pan-European industry portfolios: A comparison of alternative modeling techniques. *European Journal of Finance*, 14(8): 771–802. DOI: https://doi.org/10.1080/13518470802173396

Sharpe, W. (1964). Capital asset prices: A theory of market equilibrium. *Journal of Finance*, 19: 425–442. DOI: https://doi.org/10.1080/13518470802173396

Yu, J. (2002). Forecasting volatility in the New Zealand Stock Market. *Applied Financial Economics*, 12(3): 193–202. DOI: 10.1080/09603100110090118

Part 5

ETFs and portfolio investment

14 A new tool for an investor in the bond market

Corporate bond ETF

Introduction

This chapter discusses financial products based on bonds (bond portfolios) and shows the characteristics of their exchange behaviour. Tracking bond behaviour began in the 1970s (Table 14.1) in the US (bond market boom). A decade later, the first collective investment fund for the bond index appeared. The first exchange-traded funds (ETFs) appeared only in 2002. Now they occupy a worthy place in the financial asset market. The importance of the emergence of ETFs is due to the fact that many bonds of the US market and the global market are traded in the over-the-counter (OTC) market. Very often, transactions are possible only with large packages (10–100 thousand US dollars). Bond ETFs provide both less lottery (the share of the iShares Core U.S. Aggregate Bond ETF fund was quoted at $110 in 2017) and high liquidity. If in 2002 the iShares provider listed only four bond ETFs (Treasuries and corporate bonds with investment ratings), then by 2019 there are more than 320 bond ETFs with more than $540 billion of assets under management (AUM) in the US market.

From 2006 to 2009 ETFs on government bonds (GBs) prevail. As of 2017, ETFs on GBs lose to funds on IG credit and aggregate (source: Richardson, 2018).

Some ETFs do not formally copy the index; the managers include only selected bonds in the portfolio (for example, they do not include all bonds of the high-yield (HY) index). An example of this practice is the exclusion of companies with large debt burdens. This is due to an attempt to reduce a priori high risk of HY bonds.

At etfdb.com, one can find a large number of bond ETFs and choose an acceptable one, including HY bonds. The brightest representatives of this segment of the financial market are the following ETFs:

- iShares Core US Aggregate Bond (AGG) includes US government and highly reliable corporate bonds in its portfolio and is characterized by low volatility.
- SPDR Barclays High-Yield Bond ETF (JNK) includes HY bonds of the US market in its portfolio.

Table 14.1 Timeline of development of products based on bonds in the US market

Year	*Event*
1973	Lehman Brothers: First total return bond index
1983	Wells Fargo: First bond index fund
1987	Lehman Brothers: Bond-level index prices
1999	Electronic trading of U.S./Euro government bonds
2002	First bond ETF. TRACE: Publicly disseminated traded corporate bond prices
2004	CDX launched
2005	iTRAZZ launched in Europe / Asia
2013	TRACE: MBS traded prices
2014	TRACE: 144A prices
2019	More than 320 bond ETFs

Source: Compiled by the authors based on Richardson (2018).

Table 14.2 Bond ETFs and commissions

Fund name	*Fund commission, %*
Xtrackers Low Beta High-Yield Bond ETF (HYDW)	0.2
IShares Edge High-Yield Defensive Bond ETF (HYDB)	0.35
Goldman Sachs Access High-Yield Corporate Bond ETF (GHYB)	0.35
Xtrackers Low Beta High-Yield Bond ETF (HYDW)	0.2
IShares Edge High-Yield Defensive Bond ETF (HYDB)	0.35
Goldman Sachs Access High-Yield Corporate Bond ETF (GHYB)	0.34

Source: etfdb.ru.

- ProSharesUltraShort20+ Year Treasury (TBT): the portfolio opens short positions on the US Treasury bonds with long maturity (more than 20 years) with a double leverage (i.e. if the bonds in the base portfolio fall by 1%, then the fund's portfolio aims to show a growth of 2%)
- iShares JPMorgan USD EmergMarkets Bond (EMB) includes government bonds of emerging markets (China, India, Brazil, Russia, etc.) in its portfolio.

Some examples of the bond ETFs modus operandi are shown in Table 14.2. The commission fees are relatively low, which makes ETFs attractive for investors (Table 14.2). All these funds are young and do not have a long history of returns for comparative analysis. The maximum drops over the past two years were as follows: HYDW – 2.07% (compared to the Bloomberg Barclays US Corporate Bond Market Index – 2.99%), HYDB 'lost in the moment' – 4.84%, and GHYB – 4.08%.

Description of the variables

We examine a number of different ETFs in the US. The objective is to identify the features of the ETF time series correlation on bond market segments. The emphasis is to distinguish the characteristics of the high-yield bond ETFs volatility dynamics from the volatility dynamics of other types of ETFs. The following securities are considered (Table 14.3):

We check for the stationarity of each time series on the basis of the Dickey–Fuller test, and reduce them to a stationary form.

Figure 14.1 shows the graphical analysis of the time series.

From Figure 14.1 we can see that some companies have similar trends, but it is impossible to reveal aggregate trends for all the ETFs under study. For example, BKLN, HYG, HYS, and BSJK have quite similar trends. At first glance, these funds do not have common characteristics, so one of our goals is to reveal common features of these time series.

Correct econometric models are based on the first difference time series due to their stationarity. The unstable dynamics of time series volatility requires further analysis and constructing ARCH and GARCH volatility models.

The models of the time series

To further model volatility, it is necessary to evaluate the significance of the dependent variable lag, as well as to assess the heteroskedasticity of the residuals (the main condition for using GARCH models).

ARIMA type model

Models of the ARIMA type (p, d, q) consist of three key components: p is the number of lags of the model of the AR group, q is the number of lags of the model of the MA group, d is the level of the model difference to bring the dependent variable to a stationary form. Thus, we obtain a model of the following form (Box and Jenkins, 1970):

$$\Delta y_t = \alpha_1 \Delta y_{t-1} + \dots + \alpha_p \Delta y_{t-p} + \varepsilon_t + \theta_1 \varepsilon_{t-1} + \dots + \theta_q \varepsilon_{t-q} \qquad (14.1)$$

Let us review the models and the residuals in detail for two ETF time series: *BKLN* is *Invesco Senior Loan ETF* and *HYG* is *iShares iBoxx USD High-Yield Corporate Bond ETF.*

BKLN – Invesco Senior Loan ETF

To determine the lag value in the ARIMA model, we consider the correlogram of the first time series difference (Figure 14.2).

Note that second lags of the dependent variable are significant, so we consider the ARIMA model (2, 1, 2). The results of the model are presented in Table 14.4.

All the variables turn out to be significant. Therefore we can carry out further analysis based on this model.

We will test for the presence of ARCH processes in residuals. The result is presented in Table 14.5:

Table 14.3 Description of dependent variables

Ticker	*Name*	*Description*	*Issuer*	*Issue volume, $bn*	*Issue date*
BKLN	Invesco Senior Loan ETF	Fixed Income: U.S. - Corporate, Broad-based High-Yield Floating Rate	Invesco	$4.4	March 3, 2011
FTSE	First Trust Enhanced Short Maturity ETF	Fixed Income: U.S. - Broad Market, Broad-based Short-Term	First Trust	$4.77	August 5, 2014
PFF	iShares Preferred and Income Securities ETF	Fixed Income: U.S. - Corporate, Preferred	Blackrock	$16.46	March 26, 2007
PGX	Invesco Preferred ETF	Fixed Income: U.S. - Corporate, Preferred Investment Grade	Invesco	$5.36	January 31, 2008
HYG	iShares iBoxx USD High-Yield Corporate Bond ETF	Fixed Income: U.S. - Corporate, Broad-based High-Yield	Blackrock	$17.51	April 4, 2007
HYS	PIMCO 0–5 Year High-Yield Corporate Bond Index ETF	Fixed Income: U.S. - Corporate, Broad-based High-Yield Short-Term	AllianZ-score	$1.41	June 16, 2011
BSJK	Invesco Bullet Shares 2020 High-Yield Corporate Bond ETF	Fixed Income: U.S. - Corporate, Broad-based High-Yield Short-Term	Invesco	$1.1	September 24, 2013

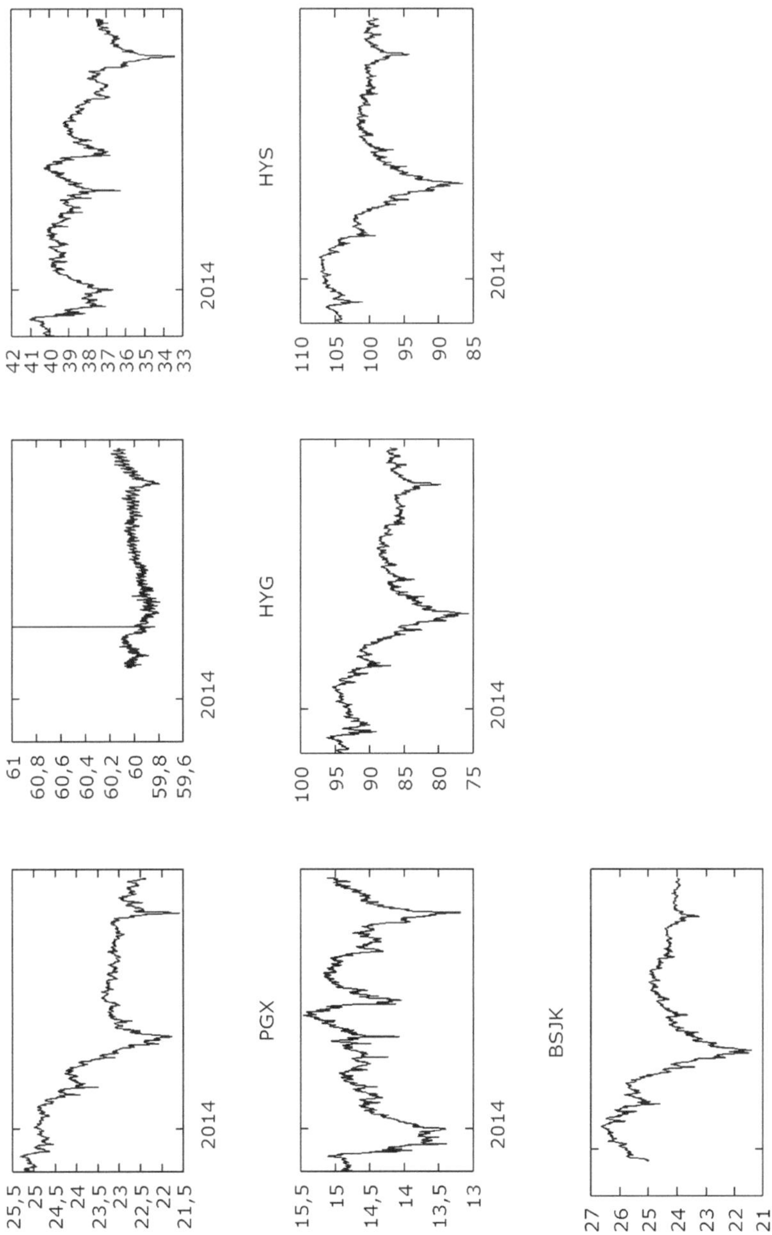

Figure 14.1 The dynamics of the ETFs market quotes.

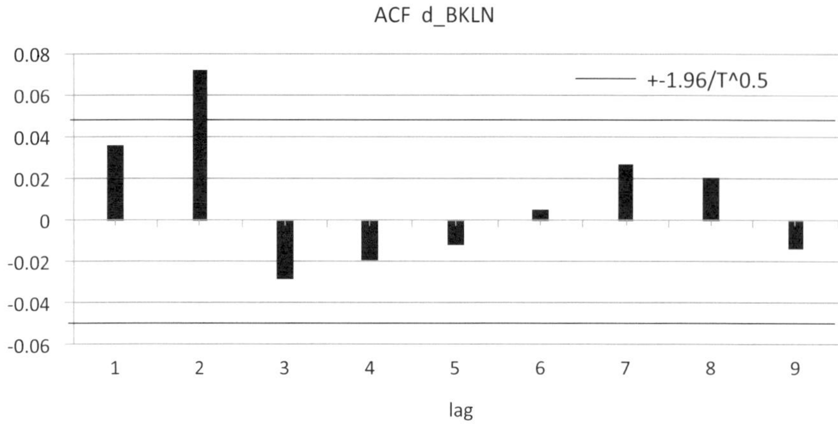

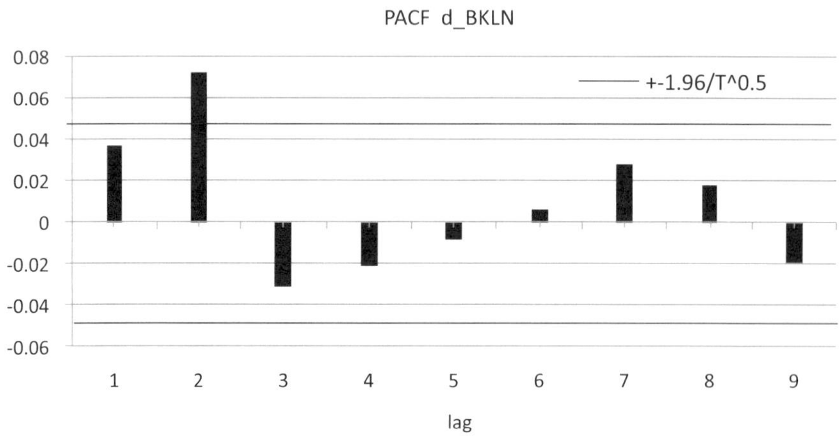

Figure 14.2 ACF and PACF graphs of the first difference for BKLN.

Table 14.4 ARIMA for ETF BKLN

	Coefficient	*Std. error*	*Z-score-score*	*p-value*	
Const	−0.00153174	0.00117327	−1.306	0.1917	
phi_1	1.07250	0.0325512	32.95	<0.0001	***
phi_2	−0.927998	0.0331173	−28.02	<0.0001	***
theta_1	−1.03460	0.0266412	−38.83	<0.0001	***
theta_2	0.925813	0.0425367	21.77	<0.0001	***
Mean	−0.001527	Std. dev.		0.046901	
Mean error	1.81e-07	Std. error		0.046559	
Log-likelihood	2816.515	Akaike criterion		−5621.030	
SchwartZ-score criterion	−5588.368	Hannan-Quinn criterion		−5608.941	

Significance levels: * p <10%, ** p <5%, *** p <1%

Table 14.5 Test result for the presence of ARCH processes

	Coefficients	*Std. error*	*t-statistics*	*p-value*	
Alpha (0)	0.00115597	0.000174615	6.620	0.0000	***
Alpha (1)	0.383784	0.0242396	15.83	0.0000	***
Alpha (2)	-0.0266859	0.0259590	-1.028	0.3041	
Alpha (3)	0.0345254	0.0259531	1.330	0.1836	

Significance levels: * p <10%, ** p <5%, *** p <1%

Table 14.6 ARIMA for ETF HYG

	Coefficient	*Std. error*	*Z-score*	*P-value*	
const	−0.00431072	0.00650016	−0.6632	0.5072	
phi_1	0.436046	0.164791	2.646	0.0081	***
phi_3	0.347385	0.148479	2.340	0.0193	**
theta_1	−0.379431	0.159488	−2.379	0.0174	**
theta_3	−0.445136	0.144661	−3.077	0.0021	***
Mean	−0.004260	St. Dev.		0.333547	
Mean std.error	9.17e-06	Std. error		0.331151	
Log-likelihood	-536.2355	AIC		1084.471	
Schwartz criterion	1117.133	HQIC		1096.559	

Significance levels: * p <10%, ** p <5%, *** p <1%

Null hypothesis: no ARCH processes

Test statistics: LM = 263458, p-value = P (Chi-squared (5) > 263458) = 7.10618e-055

The heteroskedasticity test and the test for the presence of ARCH processes in residuals indicate the presence of a GARCH-type model. Thus, we build such a model for ETF BKLN.

HYG – iShares iBoxx USD High-Yield Corporate Bond ETF

Based on the analysis of the correlogram of the first difference in the ETFHYG time series, we construct a regression model with significant 1 and 3 lags in both parts of the ARIMA model (Table 14.6).

We test for the presence of ARCH processes in residuals:

Test statistics: LM = 180.977, p-value = P (Chi-square (5) > 180.977) = 3.30903e-037

This ETF is also considered in further econometric modelling of the residuals volatility.

Other ETFs

For other funds including Invesco Senior Loan ETF (BKLN), First Trust Enhanced Short Maturity ETF (FTSE), iShares Preferred and Income Securities

ETF (PFF), Invesco Preferred ETF (PGX), PIMCO 0–5 Year High-Yield Corporate Bond Index ETF (HYS), we also reveal ARCH processes. We conclude that it is reasonable to construct GARCH-type models.

Volatility modelling

GARCH models are based on the conditional variance dynamics. Independent variables are the lag values of the squared residuals of the model, as well as the lag values of the variance itself. GARCH (p, q) models have the following form (Bollerslev, 1986):

$$h_t = var(\varepsilon_t) = \alpha_0 + \alpha_1\varepsilon_{t-1}^2 + \ldots + \alpha_p\varepsilon_{t-p}^2 + \beta_1 h_{t-1} + \ldots + \beta_q h_{t-q} \quad (14.2)$$

Coefficients α_i represent volatility, and β_i represent its correlation with past values. Our next step is to build a GARCH model. To simplify our analysis, we try to construct the simplest and most accessible form of the model (the most preferred form is GARCH (1,1)).

To construct the residual dynamics, we consider the correlation values between the quotes, or the stationary series in the form of the first difference of quotes, and their past values. In this section we show detailed construction for *Invesco Senior Loan ETF* and *iShares iBoxx USD High-Yield Corporate Bond ETF*.

BKLN – Invesco Senior Loan ETF

To model the residuals volatility from ARIMA of the first difference ETF BKLN, we will use the GARCH model, which will include 1 and 2 lags of the first difference of the dependent variable (Table 14.7).

We note that all the variables are significant, and therefore we can evaluate the volatility dynamics of this ETF compared to other series in the sample. Also, based on this model, due to the significance of the dependent variable lags, it is

Table 14.7 GARCH for ETF BKLN

	Coefficient	*Std. error*	*Z-score*	*P-value*	
const	−0.00172232	0.000871044	-1.977	0.0480	**
d_BKLN_1	−0.0487283	0.0272929	-1.785	0.0742	*
d_BKLN_2	0.0703446	0.0262242	2.682	0.0073	***
alpha(0)	7.55061e-05	2.58546e-05	2.920	0.0035	***
alpha(1)	0.124465	0.0232268	5.359	<0.0001	***
beta(1)	0.842742	0.0316299	26.64	<0.0001	***
Mean	−0.001541	St. Dev.		0.046896	
Log-likelihood	3037.815	AIC		-6061.631	
Schwartz criterion	-6023.533	HQIC		-6047.530	

Significance levels: * p <10%, ** p <5%, *** p <1%

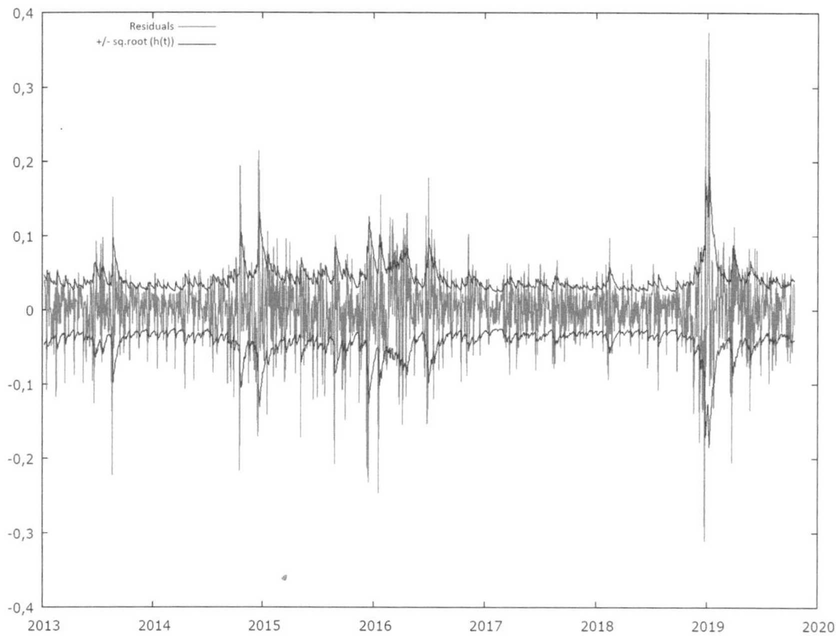

Figure 14.3 Dynamics of actual and estimated residuals.

possible to forecast the future dynamics of BKLN quotes considering the confidence interval, which is dependent on past data.

Based on Figure 14.3, the current model repeats the residuals' dynamics without outliers. Therefore, we can use this GARCH model to further analyze the ETF volatility.

HYG – iShares iBoxx USD High-Yield Corporate Bond ETF

When we build a model for the HYG series, the first lag turns out to be insignificant, so for the next step it is necessary to exclude insignificant variables and analyze a better model. The results are presented in Table 14.8.

Since all the variables turn out to be significant, we can further analyze the volatility of quotes based on this model, which is also confirmed by the dynamics of the residuals.

Summary of the volatility modelling

We present the results in a summary Table 14.9 for a comparative analysis.

The ETF quotes are not explicitly correlated with volatility. However, we can draw some conclusions about the relationship between the dynamics of the ETF quotes and the volatility.

Table 14.8 GARCH for ETF HYG after excluding insignificant variables

	Coefficient	*Std. error*	*Z-score*	*P-value*	
const	0.00135986	0.00614029	0.2215	0.8247	
d_HYG_3	−0.0688951	0.0261744	−2.632	0.0085	***
alpha(0)	0.00452278	0.000953260	4.745	<0.0001	***
alpha(1)	0.162707	0.0218829	7.435	<0.0001	***
beta(1)	0.802248	0.0238470	33.64	<0.0001	***
Mean	−0.004179	St. Dev.		0.333758	
Log-likelihood	−339.1281	AIC		690.2562	
Schwartz criterion	722.9076	HQIC		702.3417	

Significance levels: * $p < 10\%$, ** $p < 5\%$, *** $p < 1\%$

Table 14.9 Summary of the volatility models results

Ticker	*Name*	*Alpha(0)*	*Alpha(1)*	*Beta(1)*	*Order of lags*	*Excluded lags for the GARCH part*
BKLN	InvescoSenior Loan ETF	0.00007***	0.124***	0.8427***	1 and 2	No
FTSE	First Trust Enhanced Short Maturity ETF	0.00049***	0.983***	0.0169	1	No
PFF	iShares Preferred and Income Securities ETF	0.00326***	0.2127***	0.592***	1	Yes
PGX	InvescoPreferred ETF	0.00045***	0.1676***	0.6351***	No	Yes
HYG	iShares iBoxx USD High-Yield Corporate Bond ETF	0.00452***	0.1627***	0.8022***	3	Yes
HYS	PIMCO 0–5 Year High-Yield Corporate Bond Index ETF	0.00371***	0.1671***	0.7909***	No	No
BSJK	Invesco BulletShares 2020 High-Yield Corporate Bond ETF	0.000101**	0.14415***	0.8408***	2 and 4	Yes

Significance levels: * $p < 10\%$, ** $p < 5\%$, *** $p < 1\%$

Firstly, in the US, the interdependence of several ETFs is evident, regardless of how complex and similar are their structure. However, most ETFs with similar dynamics relate to high-yield portfolios, which implies a strong influence of external factors on companies and portfolios.

Secondly, based on a graphical analysis, the high-yield ETFs have a higher error volatility, while in models of variance, the coefficient in front of the lagged residual variance is slightly higher than for portfolios that adhere to other strategies.

Thirdly, there is no significant correlation in the dynamics of ETF volatility. ETF providers in the US correctly diversify their portfolios.

Fourthly, in some ETFs, the relationship between current and lagged values turns out to be a consequence of the influence of volatility and residuals' variance, which caused exclusion of some lags in the final model.

Comparison of the ETF dynamics with a portfolio of T-bills with different maturities

The Dickey–Fuller test results at a 95% significance level for T-bills ETFs, with different maturities, are shown in Table 14.10.

According to one of the modifications of the Dickey–Fuller test, the series is significant at a 95% level. Therefore we carry out a correlation analysis at the series level for various time intervals. We consider the correlation for each year (Table 14.11).

The correlation signs switch depending on the calendar year; however, for almost all ETFs the correlation is quite strong. Let us conduct a graphical analysis for some ETFs.

Table 14.10 Dickey–Fuller test results for T-bills ETF at row level

	Test statistics	*p-value*	*Conclusion*
Without a constant	-1.96533	0.04727	stationary
With a constant	-0.429548	0.9019	non-stationary
With a constant and a trend	-2.11386	0.5375	non-stationary

Table 14.11 Results of correlation analysis at the series level

	BKLN	*FTSE*	*PFF*	*PGX*	*HYG*	*HYS*	*BSJK*
2019	-0.15131	-0.47819	-0.54083	-0.52777	-0.43818	-0.36132	-0.23086
2018	-0.8336	0.459607	0.309538	0.49852	0.551165	0.514328	0.500287
2017	0.794695	-0.65251	-0.28549	-0.69624	-0.31369	-0.20968	-0.52156
2016	-0.87607	-0.59474	-0.15941	-0.08245	-0.92476	-0.94616	-0.9406
2015	0.69231	0.480825	0.368725	-0.35216	0.628128	0.665968	0.728488

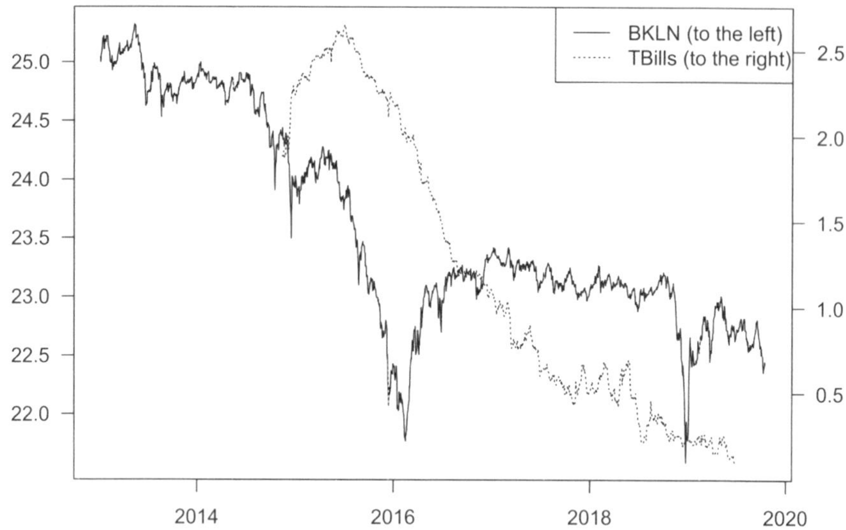

Figure 14.4 ETF BKLN and T-bills dynamics.

Figure 14.4 shows the dynamics of ETF BKLN and T-bills. In 2015, a strong positive relationship was observed between these series; moreover, in the first half of the year there was simultaneous growth of both portfolios. Further, for most of the year 2016 there was a strong negative correlation, especially in the second half of the year. For the next two years, the relationship is also visible and strong, but by 2019 the correlation is weakening and there is a discorrelation.

The relationship between ETF FTSE and T-bills is not as significant as between BKLN and T-bills; it is mainly characterized by the presence of a general trend and remains approximately constant, regardless of the year (Figure 14.5).

When analyzing the correlation between ETF PGX and T-bills (Figure 14.6), we note that this relationship has become significant only for the last three years; however, it has the characteristics of a market general trend.

The correlation of risk-free government bonds and ETF PFF is relatively low, compared with other ETFs. A strong negative relationship between ETF HYG and T-bills was observed in 2015 and 2016, but in 2018–2019 the correlation weakened. We obtain a similar conclusion with respect to ETF HYS and T-bills. By 2015, we see a strong positive correlation between BSJK ETFs and government bonds. At the start of 2016, the high-yield portfolio reversed the trend, which led to a change in the correlation sign. By 2019, correlation values are falling.

Thus, for the majority of the ETFs, at certain points in time, there was a strong correlation with government bonds. At the end of 2018, these correlations changed. More precise estimates are obtained for stationary series of the first differences (Table 14.12).

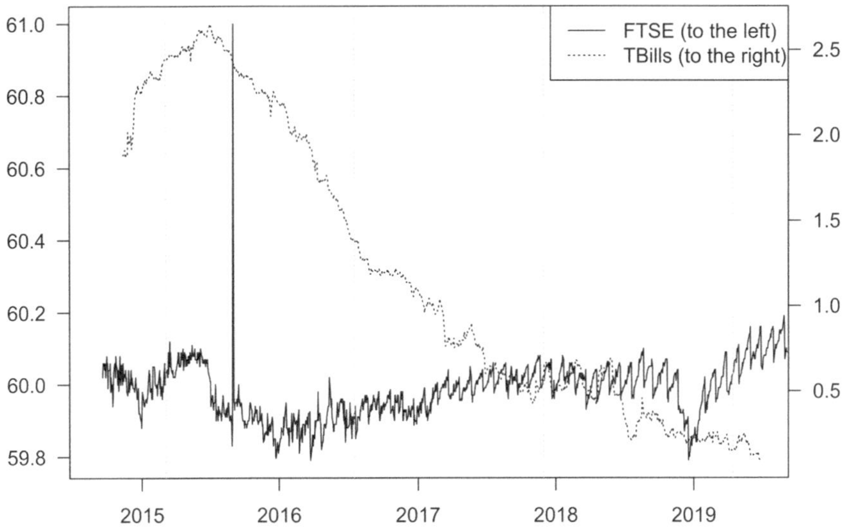

Figure 14.5 Dynamics of ETF FTSE and T-bills.

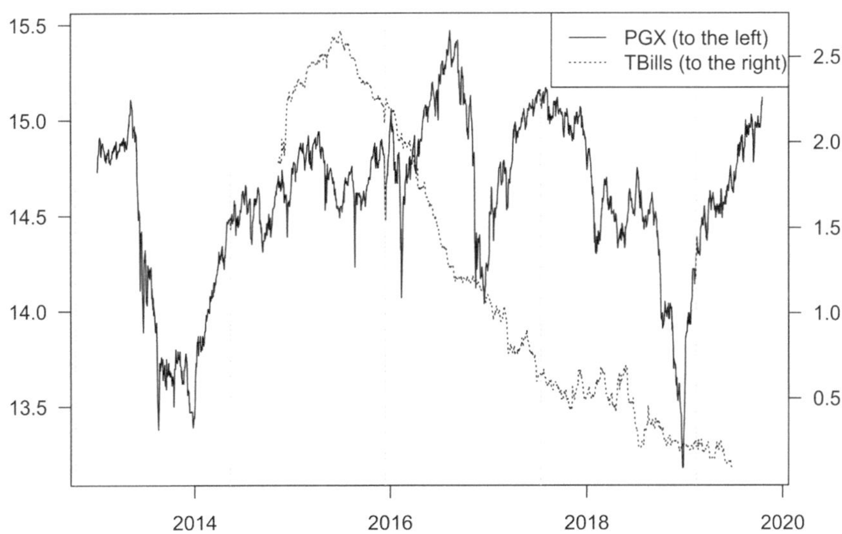

Figure 14.6 Dynamics of ETF PGX and T-bills.

Table 14.12 Results of correlation analysis for the first differences

	BKLN	*FTSE*	*PFF*	*PGX*	*HYG*	*HYS*	*BSJK*
2019	-0.01909	-0.02438	0.028002	-0.03882	0.10525	0.111066	0.004358
2018	-0.04711	-0.00454	-0.04905	-0.06927	-0.10004	-0.11134	-0.08998
2017	-0.02441	-0.03721	-0.01869	0.00956	-0.12139	-0.12537	-0.03003
2016	-0.09848	-0.08628	-0.1743	-0.15983	-0.11543	-0.11468	-0.12328
2015	-0.04659	-0.03621	-0.0823	-0.07843	0.002153	0.026314	-0.00729

Table 14.12 shows that the correlation coefficients of the first differences are near zero, i.e. the correlation between the dynamics of ETFs and T-bills is false and is associated exclusively with trends in financial markets. This allows us to build diversified portfolios of various ETFs, including high-risk ones.

Calculations based on the R package

We also apply the R packages to find the optimal parameters of ARIMA models in terms of their predictive ability. We use the function *auto.arima of the package forecast*[1]. This function, based on the Hyndman and Khandakar algorithm (2008), selects the optimal parameters according to the AIC criterion (the smaller, the better). We analyze the interaction of time series based on the Var (p) model and test the stability of the relationship based on Granger-causality. We conclude that the built-in R functions allow us to obtain more optimal values, compared to the approach based on the selection of parameters according to the significance of their coefficients.

An overview of trends on emerging market bond ETFs

Emerging market bond ETFs are unique exchange-traded investment funds aimed at generating additional income from investing in the government and corporate bonds of emerging economies. These funds, due to their peculiarity, combine both the characteristics of bond ETFs in general and the characteristics of more traditional equity ETFs of emerging markets, so we evaluate their state and further development in these two directions.

We note the growth of the number of emerging market bond ETFs from 21 in 2015 to 70 in the beginning of 2020 (source: Bloomberg). If we consider the net cash inflows of these funds, there is no clear trend to growth (Figure 14.7).

From 2015 to 2019, the average annual inflow to emerging market bond ETFs was $24.8 bn (source: Bloomberg). Figure 14.2 shows the total net cash inflow to these funds, which at the end of Q4 2019 was $15.8 bn. This is 18 times less than the previous peak in Q2 2017, when the inflow was $294 bn and is 26.6 times less than the maximum value of cash inflow in Q1 2018, when emerging market bond ETFs attracted more than $420 bn (source: Bloomberg). In general, in terms of cash inflows, there is no clear trend indicating a systematic

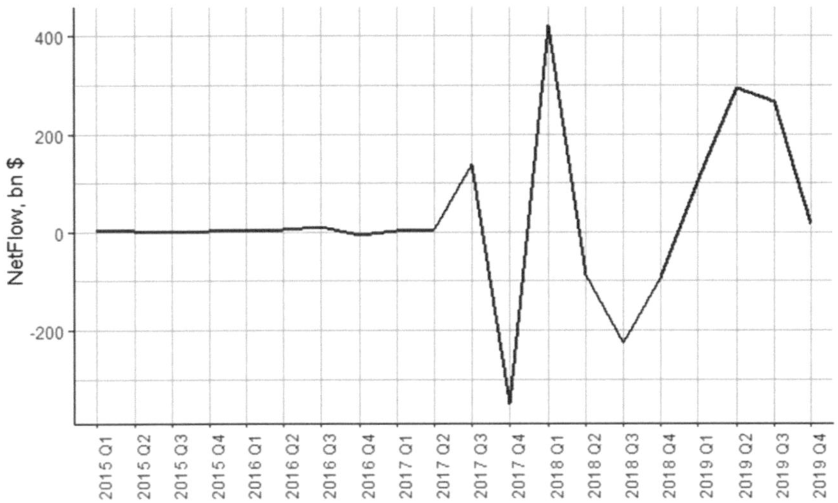

Figure 14.7 The total net cash flow of emerging market bond ETFs.
Source: Bloomberg.

increase, but there is a sharp increase in volatility after Q2 2019; for example, the standard deviation of the inflow after the second half of 2017 was $231 bn, and before the second half of 2017 it was only $4.6 bn (source: authors' calculations based on Bloomberg). This observation gives us an interesting picture: over the past two and a half years, the number of ETFs has grown, but this did not affect the increase in cash inflows.

If we consider the breakdown of the inflows to all equity and bond ETFs by developing economy, then, in general, the list of the top-10 countries by inflow in 2019 coincided with that of over the past three years (Figures 14.8 and 14.9). In 2019, Brazil, India, Saudi Arabia, Mexico, Colombia, and Vietnam remained the leaders by the inflow of funds. A noticeable difference in Figures 14.3 and 14.4 appears for China and Taiwan, and it is undoubtedly associated with the epidemic of coronavirus, as well as the trade war between the US and China. Over the past three years, China attracted $23.5 bn (first place), but the outflow over 2019 alone was $6.8 bn (source: authors' calculations based on Bloomberg).

According to etf.com, JPMorgan USD Emerging Markets Sovereign Bond ETF (15.33%), Invesco Emerging Markets Sovereign Debt ETF (14.94%) and Vanguard Emerging Markets Government Bond ETF (12.56%) are the top three emerging bond ETFs in 2019 (Table 14.13).

If we consider the emerging market bond ETF as a segment of the global bond ETF market, then we can conclude that this segment is currently experiencing rapid growth, which, according to expert opinion, will also continue in 2020. In March 2019, in the US the total NAV of bond funds reached $1 tn[2].

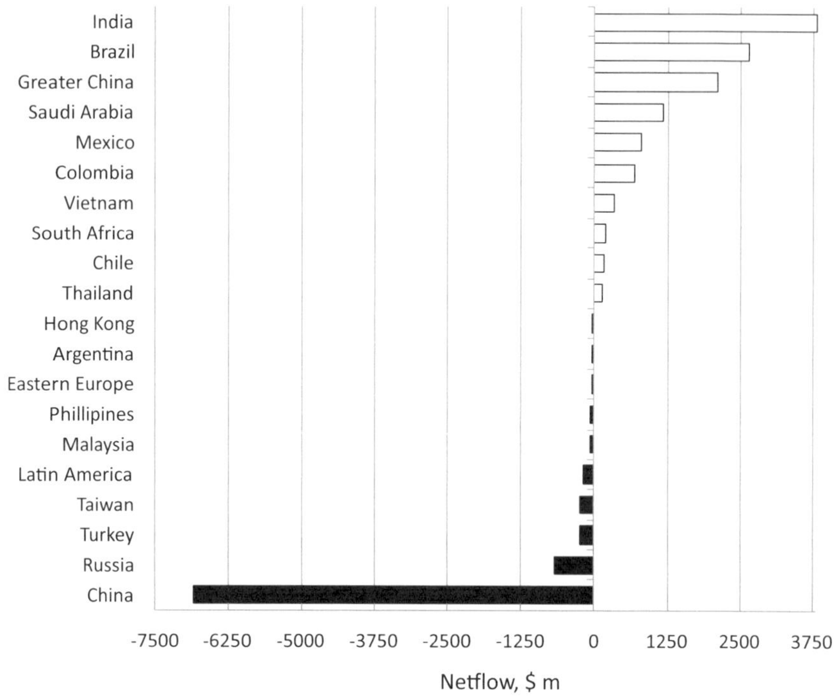

Figure 14.8 Top 10 emerging economies by inflow to equity and bond ETFs in 2019. Source: Bloomberg.

In an interview with the Wall Street Journal, the president of the world's largest investment company BlackRock. Inc, Robert S. Kapito, said that currently only about 1% of all bonds in the world are collected in ETF portfolios, which opens the door to about $100 tn of bonds, due to which he expects the bond ETF market to increase to $4 tn in the next five years, which will occupy a third of the entire ETF market by 2023[3].

We highlight several reasons for the growing popularity of bond ETFs. One of the most important reasons is the increase in liquidity in the bond market. Usually, bonds are traded in the OTC market, and some bonds may not be traded for days or even months, while the value of bond ETFs changes every 15 seconds[4].

We also consider a change in the preferences of market participants to be an important factor in the growth of bond ETFs. According to S. Sachs, head of Goldman Sachs Asset Management, the transition from active to passive management is a key factor in the growth of bond ETFs. According to a study by Greenwich Associates of institutional investors in the US, in 2018, 60% of respondents said that they used bond ETFs in their strategies, while in 2017 this indicator was only 20%[5]. J. Schneider, the managing director of PIMCO

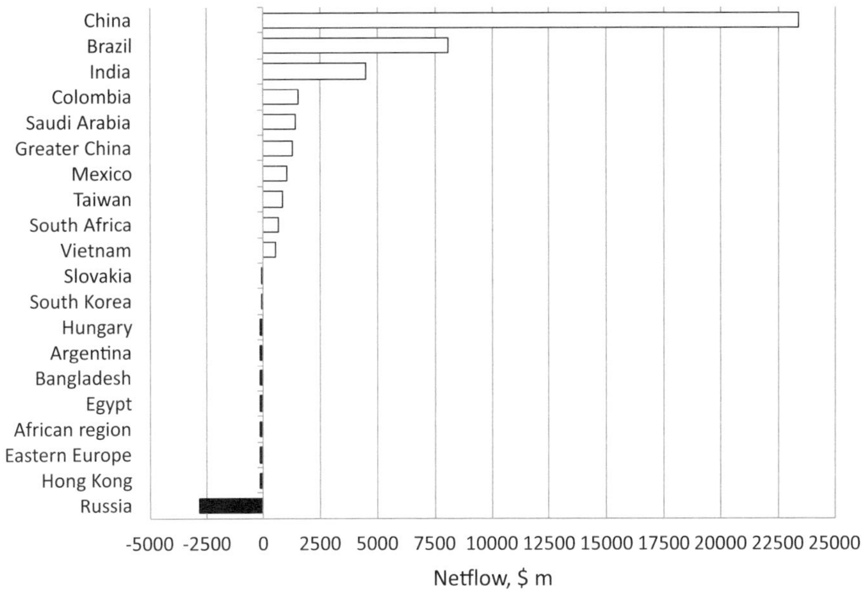

Figure 14.9 Top-10 emerging economies by inflow to equity and bond ETFs in 2017–2019. Source: Bloomberg.

investment company, explained this phenomenon by a desire of investors to find safer investments after the increased volatility in the stock market in 2018[6].

The influence of the relatively low fees is controversial. Although bond ETFs are a cheaper solution for debt financial strategies than stand-alone bond issues, P. Sleep, senior manager at Seven Investment Management, argues that the most liquid bond ETFs are still more expensive than similar funds with active management: the largest ETFs of high-yield bonds, emerging market bonds and convertibles require 50 basis points as fees, while cheaper active funds exist[7].

Macroeconomic and political factors play a significant role defining the inflows to equity and bond ETFs. For example, in 2019 one of the key factors was the manifestation of the beginning of the 'first phase' of the agreement between China and the US after a protracted trade war between these two countries. According to Bloomberg, in the second week of December 2019 alone, US ETFs attracted more than $1.15 bn, which is eight times more the $141 m attracted a week earlier.

In 2019–2020, emerging market ETFs reacted strongly to the coronavirus epidemic in China. As of February 7, 2020, net inflows into US ETFs of emerging markets were $122 m, while in the previous week there was an outflow of $2.5 bn, which was associated with investor worries about a negative impact of the epidemic on global growth[8]. Partly, this growth in inflows was due to the

Table 14.13 List of emerging market bond ETFs with the best result in 2019

Fund	*Return rate, %*	*Net assets value (NAV), $ m*	*Rank by return rate*	*Rank by NAV*
JPMorgan USD Emerging Markets Sovereign Bond ETF	15.33	93,71	1	12
Invesco Emerging Markets Sovereign Debt ETF	14.94	3600	2	3
Vanguard Emerging Markets Government Bond ETF	12.56	1840	3	4
iShares JP Morgan USD Emerging Markets Bond ETF	12.48	16040	4	1
iShares J.P. Morgan EM Corporate Bond ETF	12.31	224,96	5	9
WisdomTree Emerging Markets Corporate Bond Fund	11.81	37,53	6	14
Invesco BulletShares 2024 USD Emerging Markets Debt ETF	11.45	16,05	7	18
VanEck Vectors Emerging Markets High-Yield Bond ETF	11.36	388,43	8	8
SPDR DoubleLine Emerging Markets Fixed Income ETF	10.88	88,19	9	13
VanEck Vectors Emerging Markets Aggregate Bond ETF	10.60	15,26	10	19

Source: etf.com.

growth of the Chinese stock market, because the Central Bank decided to maintain liquidity. In general, most emerging market ETFs ended 2019 positively after the largest losses in 2018 over the past three years.

Table 14.14 shows inflows of US investors' money to equity and bond ETFs by regions from February 2019 to January 2020. The Asian ETF market demonstrated the highest outflow of $-7 bn (or -11% of the total regional NAV). The greatest contribution to this outflow was the Chinese market, due to the macroeconomic factors described above. The Eastern European ETF market was also characterized by a decrease in investment attractiveness and an outflow of investors' money. On the contrary, the Central and South America region demonstrated the highest inflow in the equity and bond ETF market which was $1.6 bn (or +13% of the total regional NAV; Table 14.14).

Table 14.15 shows inflows to the top-10 (by NAV) emerging bond market ETFs and the return rates in 2017–2019. These ETFs do not demonstrate unique trends.

Table 14.16 shows the portfolio structure of the top-3 (by NAV) emerging bond market ETFs by country as of the end of February 2020. From Table 14.4

Table 14.14 Inflows of US investors' money to equity and bond ETFs by regions, February 2019–January 2020

Region	*Inflow (or outflow), $ m*	*Inflow (outflow) to the total NAV, %*
Asia	- 6 929	-11
China	- 6 819	-5
India	3 613	32
Hong Kong	-760	-3
S. Korea	508	1
Singapore	298	11
Thailand	145	14
Philippines	-30	-10
Malaysia	-54	-6
Africa and Middle East	486	30
Central and South America	1 558	13
Eastern Europe	-969	-37
Russia	-845	-44

Source: Authors' calculation based on Bloomberg.

we can conclude that the portfolio structure of these ETFs is widely diversified not only by countries, but also by geographical region.

An alternative to these strategies may be investing in LCY bonds. Last year, iShares J.P. Morgan EM Local Currency Bond ETF (LEMB) showed results below the benchmark, and the return rate was only 6.7%[9].

A significant factor is the growing interest of investors, caused primarily by high return rates, high liquidity, and the low management fees of bond ETFs. Market sentiment regarding portfolio diversification will depend on the monetary policy of the US and the biggest countries.

Emerging market bond ETFs are highly sensitive to changes in macroeconomic and institutional factors. In 2018–2019 the trade war between the US and China had a serious impact on the bond ETFs, then in 2020 the coronavirus and country isolation play the key role. The policy of central banks regarding key rates is also an important factor.

Considering developing countries, an investment attractive area is bonds of some 'exotic countries', for which there are refinancing programmes supported by the IMF.

Conclusions

We note that in terms of choosing ARIMA parameters, the built-in R functions allow us to obtain more optimal values, compared to the approach based on the selection of parameters according to the significance of their coefficients. Using the specification of the most appropriate GARCH (1,1) model with a normal

Table 14.15 Inflows to the top-10 (by NAV) emerging bond market ETFs and the return rates in 2017–2019

Ticker	*Name*	*Segment (Fixed Income, Emerging Markets)*	*Issuer*	*Expense ratio, %*	*AUM, Jan. 2020, $bn*	*Net flows, $ m*			*Annual return rate, %*	
						2017	*2018*	*2019*	*Average in 2017–2019*	*2019*
EMB	iShares JP Morgan USD Emerging Markets Bond ETF	Government, Non-LCY	Blackrock	0.39	16.06	3821.25	3393.54	137.89	6.16	12.93
EMLC	VanEck Vectors J.P. Morgan EM Local Currency Bond ETF	Government, Treasury	VanEck	0.3	4.44	2114.85	628.40	82.81	3.37	4.75
PCY	Invesco Emerging Markets Sovereign Debt ETF	Government, Non-LCY	Invesco	0.5	3.57	1152.37	-971.40	-404.25	6.48	15.24
VWOB	Vanguard Emerging Markets Government Bond ETF	Government, Non-LCY	Vanguard	0.3	1.81	63.60	152.73	484.60	6.33	12.86
EBND	SPDR Bloomberg Barclays Emerging Markets Local Bond ETF	Government, Treasury Investment Grade	State Street Global Advisors	0.3	1.05	293.13	270.91	360.80	4.03	5.6
LEMB	iShares J.P. Morgan EM Local Currency Bond ETF	Government, Treasury Investment Grade	Blackrock	0.3	0.54	-7.47	143.74	137.85	1.91	1.66
EMHY	iShares Emerging Markets High-Yield Bond ETF	Broad Market, Broad-based High-Yield	Blackrock	0.5	0.44	555.23	-338.00	88.47	4.74	9.22
HYEM	VanEck Vectors Emerging Markets High-Yield Bond ETF	Corporate, Broad-based High-Yield	VanEck	0.4	0.39	39.27	-81.61	65.72	5.58	11.01
CEMB	iShares J.P. Morgan EM Corporate Bond ETF	Corporate, Broad-based	Blackrock	0.5	0.22	30.23	-9.38	105.51	5.91	11.91
ELD	WisdomTree Emerging Markets Local Debt Fund	Broad Market, Broad-based	Wisdom Tree	0.55	0.18	-31.73	1.77	-3.27	3.96	7.81

Source: etf.com.

Table 14.16 Portfolio structure of the top-3 (by NAV) emerging bond market ETFs by country, as at February 28, 2020

Country rank	*EMB: iShares JP Morgan USD Emerging Markets Bond ETF*		*PCY: Invesco Emerging Markets Sovereign Debt ETF*		*EMLC: VanEck Vectors J.P. Morgan EM Local Currency Bond ETF*	
	Country	*Share in the ETF portfolio (%)*	*Country*	*Share in the ETF portfolio (%)*	*Country*	*Share in the ETF portfolio (%)*
1	Mexico	5.65	China	2.74	Brazil	9.98
2	Indonesia	4.95	Poland	2.71	Indonesia	8.52
3	Turkey	4.11	Chile	2.70	Mexico	8.28
4	Qatar	3.97	Peru	2.70	Thailand	8.26
5	Philippines	3.69	Philippines	2.67	Poland	6.87
6	Saudi Arabia	3.69	Paraguay	2.67	S. Africa	6.86
7	Brazil	3.54	Panama	2.67	Russia	5.80
8	Colombia	3.47	Indonesia	2.67	Colombia	4.53
9	Russia	3.41	Croatia	2.67	Peru	3.25
10	S. Africa	3.02	Mexico	2.66	Romania	2.98
	Others	60.5	Others	73.14	Others	34.67

Source: Authors' calculations based on etf.com.

distribution is reasonable, since this model gives high-quality forecasts of the volatility of individual ETFs. In the future, it is possible to expand the study in the direction of multivariate GARCH modelling to analyze the simultaneous interaction of the volatility of some ETFs on the volatility of other ETFs.

We conclude that the correlation of risk-free GBs and ETF PFF is relatively low, compared with other ETFs. A strong negative relationship between ETF HYG and T-bills was observed in 2015 and 2016, but in 2018–2019 the correlation weakened. We obtain a similar conclusion with respect to ETF HYS and T-bills. By 2015, we see a strong positive correlation between BSJK ETFs and GBs. At the start of 2016, the high-yield portfolio reversed the trend, which led to a change in the correlation sign. By 2019, correlation values fell. This allows investors to build diversified portfolios of various ETFs, including high-risk ones.

We also reveal trends concerning emerging market bond ETFs. The number of emerging bond ETFs rapidly grows, and their portfolio structure is widely diversified by geographical region. From 2015 to 2019, the average annual inflow to emerging market bond ETFs was $24.8 bn (source: Bloomberg), but there is no clear trend to the growth of this inflow.

We highlight several reasons for the growth of popularity of bond ETFs. These are: increase in liquidity in the bond market; transition from active to passive management; and the desire of investors to find safer investments after increased volatility in the stock market in 2018. Macroeconomic and political factors play a significant role defining the inflows in equity and bond ETFs.

Notes

1 To know more details about the package, please see: https://github.com/robjhyndman/forecast.
2 Flood, C. (2019, December 2). Bond ETFs outshine equity rivals in 2019. Retrieved from Financial Times: https://app.ft.com/content/3295b03a-3535-4cb1-a456-23588 ae7b61c.
3 Henderson, R. (2019, April 24). Landmark for exchange traded bond funds as assets crash through $1tn: Fixed income. Retrieved from Financial Times: www.ft.com/content/a01564ba-37d5-11ea-a6d3-9a26f8c3cba4.
4 Ibid.
5 Loder, A. (2019, July 1). Bond exchange-traded funds pass $1 trillion in assets. Retrieved from WSJ: www.wsj.com/articles/bond-exchange-traded-funds-pass-1-trillion-in-assets-11561986396.
6 Mellow, C. (2020, January 3). Emerging market bond investors now have to look harder for higher yield. Retrieved from Barrons: www.barrons.com/articles/emerging-market-bond-investors-now-have-to-look-harder-to-find-higher-yield-51578098232.
7 Nauman, B. (2019, October 7). Bond investors weigh merits of ETFs. Retrieved from Financial Times: www.ft.com/content/600ba5d4-cff0-11e9-b018-ca4456540ea6.
8 Oyamada, A. (2020, February 12). Emerging market ETF insights. Retrieved from www.bloomberg.com.
9 Smith, M. (2020, February 12). ETFs boost liquidity for off-the-run high-grade bonds, BofA says. Retrieved from www.bloomberg.com.

References

Bollerslev, T. (1986). Generalized autoregressive conditional heteroskedasticity. *Journal of Econometrics*, 31(3): 307–327. DOI: https://doi.org/10.1016/0304-4076(86)90063-1

Box, G. E. P., Jenkins, G. M. (1970). Time Series Analysis Forecasting and Control. Holden-Day, San Francisco.

Hyndman R. J, Khandakar Y (2008). Automatic time series forecasting: The forecast package for R. *Journal of Statistical Software*, 27.

Richardson, S. (2018). Big Data in Fixed Income Markets? AQR Capital Management, LLC. URL: https://www.ipfos.eu/wp-content/uploads/2018/11/AQR-Big-Data-in-FI-Markets-vPrint.pdf

15 Portfolio investment in emerging bond markets

Trends and determinants

The determinants of portfolio investment flows: what the results of previous studies say

Waqas et al. (2015) analyze the impact of macroeconomic factors on the volatility of foreign portfolio investment (FPI) inflows to South Asian countries (China, India, Pakistan and Sri Lanka). The period of the study is from 2000 to 2012. FPI volatility is simulated using the GARCH model. The authors conclude that the higher the inflation rate, stock index return and economic growth rate, the lower the volatility of FPI inflow. The authors attribute this to the fact that the ability to obtain high returns and macroeconomic stability attracts foreign investors. A larger FDI inflow stimulates FPI inflow and reduces its volatility. The depreciation of the national currency reduces the volatility of FPI inflows only for the Chinese market.

Garg and Dua (2014) reveal determinants of FPI inflow into India from 1995 to 2011. The authors analyze the determinants of both FPI inflow as a whole and its components: foreign institutional investment flows (FIIS) and investment in ADR and GDR. The analysis is based on the Autoregressive Distributed Lag approach. It is revealed that the return rate of the national stock index has a significant positive effect on the inflow of FPI and FIIS. If the return rate of the Emerging market MSCI Index increases, the inflows of FPI and FIIS to India decline, due to the substitution effect: foreign investors choose other markets. The difference in interest rates in the national and global markets has a significant positive impact on FPI and FIIS; the authors explain this by an increased investment attractiveness of debt securities of Indian issuers. The inflow of FPI and FIIS is positively affected by the growth rate of the industrial production index and is negatively affected by the volatility of the exchange rate. The decrease in co-movement between the national and global stock market indices leads to an increase in portfolio investment, as investors seek to diversify risks.

Ahmad et al. (2015) investigate the determinants of FPI inflows to China from 2000 to 2010. Testing the hypotheses about the significance of the influence of macroeconomic factors is carried out on the basis of multivariate regression models. The authors find that the most significant factor positively affecting the inflow of FPI is the volume of external debt. The authors attribute this to the fact that attracting external loans improves the infrastructure and productivity of companies, which further increases the investment attractiveness of the national financial market. Other significant determinants are GDP growth and FDI inflow. The appreciation of the national currency increases the investment attractiveness of securities from the point of view of global investors.

Al-Smadi (2018) reveals the determinants of FPI inflows to the Jordanian market from 2000 to 2016 using multivariate regression models and the Granger test. The results show the positive impact of GDP growth and the negative impact of inflation. Macroeconomic stability increases the investment attractiveness of the national financial market. Creditworthiness measured as the ratio of international reserves to imports positively affects the dependent variable. The opportunity to diversify risks also increases the inflow of FPI. The significance of institutional factors is revealed. The lower the quality of government regulation and the higher the level of corruption, the lower the inflow of FPI.

Pala and Orgun (2015) analyze the impact of a wide range of macro-indicators and financial market development indicators on the inflow of FPI into Turkey from 1998 to 2012. The authors rank the factors by the significance of the influence and find that the most significant positive influence is exerted by the level of interest rates, gross national income and current account balance.

Bhatta et al. (2018) construct an original measure of biases in foreign bond allocations. The sample includes 54 developed and emerging markets from 2000 to 2012. Multifactor linear regression models reveal that foreign investors tend to invest more in bond markets characterized by bigger size (measured as private debt to GDP), higher real return rates, less volatility of exchange rates, and the higher level of investors' rights protection. Non-economic factors also play an important role. The foreign biases between two bond markets are higher if the countries are geographically close to each other and have a common official language. Investors tended to decrease their bond allocations during the sovereign debt crisis in Europe in 2009–2011.

Most of the previous papers analyze the period from before the beginning of the 2000s to 2012–2014 (Bhatta et al., 2018; Pala and Orgun, 2015; Ahmad et al., 2015; Garg and Dua, 2014) or focus on one market or geographical region. Unlike them, we take into account a longer period from 2007 to 2018 and consider a cross-country sample of 14 emerging bond markets. The originality of our paper is that we analyze the determinants of FPI inflows in debt securities, while previous studies are mostly devoted to FPI inflows as a whole, without dividing them into the stock and bond markets (Pala and Orgun, 2015; Al-Smadi, 2018; Waqas et al., 2015). In accordance with the conclusions of the previous studies, we consider a set of factors characterizing financial market development, macroeconomic environment and the quality of institutions. Our contribution is taking into account non-linear effects of factors characterizing the size of the national stock and bond market.

Testing hypotheses about the impact of macroeconomic and institutional factors on flows in debt instruments

We put forward the following hypotheses:

The *first group* of hypotheses regards the impact of country-level factors on FPI inflows in debt instruments.

Hypothesis 1.1. FPI inflow in debt instruments (% of GDP) increases in conditions of macroeconomic stability.

We measure macroeconomic stability by the size of the economy, the rate of economic growth, inflation and the depreciation of the national currency. We assume that the larger the GDP, the higher the real GDP growth rate, the lower the inflation rate and the lower the percentage change of the national currency against the US dollar, the greater the investment attractiveness of government and corporate bond markets and, accordingly, the higher FPI inflow to debt instruments. As shown by Garg and Dua (2014) for the Indian market and Ahmad et al. (2015) for the Chinese market, the economic growth rate and the national currency exchange rate are significant determinants of portfolio investment. Al-Smadi (2018) reveals the significant impact of economic growth and inflation for the Jordanian market. Pala and Orgun (2015), for the Turkish market, reveal a positive relationship between the FPI inflow and the size of the economy. Unlike these studies, we focus on the FPI inflow into debt instruments and consider a cross-country sample.

Hypothesis 1.2. If the size of the national market of government and corporate bonds is relatively small, then its increase significantly positively affects FPI inflow to debt instruments (% of GDP). On the contrary, if the size of the national bond market is relatively large, its further increase significantly negatively affects FPI inflow to debt instruments (% of GDP).

We assume that if the size of the national bond market is relatively small, its increase makes it more attractive for foreign investors looking to find high yields and diversify risks (Al-Smadi, 2018). Bhatta et al. (2018) using a sample of developed and developing economies until 2012 reveal that the ratio of private debt to GDP is a significant determinant of foreign biases in bond allocations. Unlike Bhatta et al. (2018), we consider government and corporate publicly-traded debt and exclude bank loans from consideration.

On the contrary, if the size of the national bond market is relatively large, we assume that its further increase leads to a decrease of bond yields while opportunities for risk diversification do not change significantly. Therefore the FPI inflow decreases.

Hypothesis 1.3. If the size of the national stock market is relatively small, then its increase significantly negatively affects FPI inflow to debt instruments (% of GDP). On the contrary, if the size of the national stock market is relatively large, its further increase significantly positively affects FPI inflow to debt instruments (% of GDP).

We assume that equity and debt markets in developing countries are substitutes. If the national stock market grows, then global investors invest more funds in it, and this negatively affects the FPI inflow into debt instruments. This hypothesis is original, and in previous papers it has not been tested.

Hypothesis 1.4. FPI inflow into debt instruments (% of GDP) positively depends on the quality of institutions.

We consider such proxies for the quality of institutions as political stability, trade, investment and finance freedom. In previous studies on this research topic, the significance of institutional factors was revealed. Al-Smadi (2018) for the Jordanian market shows that the lower the quality of government regulation and the higher the level of corruption, the lower the inflow of FPI. Bhatta et al. (2018), using a cross-country sample, reveal that the level of investor rights protection positively affects foreign bond allocation.

Hypothesis 1.5. FPI inflow into debt instruments (% of GDP) positively depends on real interest rates.

A higher level of real interest rates attracts global investors taking into account negative real interest rates in developed bond markets. Pala and Orgun (2015) for Turkey's market shows that one of the most significant positive factors influencing FPI inflow is the level of interest rates. Garg and Dua (2014) come to an analogous conclusion for the Indian market.

The *second group* of hypotheses regards the impact of global factors on FPI inflows into debt securities.

Hypothesis 2.1. FPI inflow into debt instruments (% of GDP) positively depends on the return rate of the S&P 500 index.

We assume that the higher the return rate of the S&P 500 index, the more the optimism of global investors and the higher their risk taking. If the S&P 500 grows, then global investors look for high return rates in all markets including emerging bond markets.

Hypothesis 2.2. FPI inflows into debt instruments (% of GDP) negatively depend on the US VIX volatility index.

We assume that during periods of increasing uncertainty in the global financial market, investors reduce allocations in emerging debt markets due to risk aversion. Bhatta et al. (2018) show that investors decreased their foreign bond allocations during the sovereign debt crisis in Europe in 2009–2011.

To control regional effects, we introduce a dummy variable of Asian countries. We assume that the Asian bond markets were attractive for foreign investors in 2007–2018 due to the dynamic development and liberalization of capital flow movements.

The list of variables of our study is shown in Table 15.1.

Testing of the above hypotheses is carried out on the basis of panel data regression models with random effects:

$$y_{i,t} = \alpha + \beta \cdot X_{i,t} + u_i + \varepsilon_{i,t} \tag{15.1}$$

where $y_{i,t}$ is the dependent variable (Table 15.1), i is the country, t is the year, $X_{i,t}$ is the vector of explaining variables (Table 15.1), u_i are individual effects, and $\varepsilon_{i,t}$ is the error term.

Given a potential endogeneity of the variables, we also try to use the system generalized method of moments to test the above hypotheses (GMM-Sys models). This method was developed by Arellano and Bond (1991), Arellano and Bover (1995), and Blundell and Bond (1998):

$$y_{i,t} = \alpha \cdot y_{i,t-1} + \beta_0 \cdot X_{i,t} + \mu_i + \varepsilon_{i,t} \tag{15.2}$$

$$y_{i,t} - y_{i,t-1} = \alpha \cdot (y_{i,t-1} - y_{i,t-2}) + \beta_0 \cdot (X_{i,t} - X_{i,t-1}) + \varepsilon_{i,t} - \varepsilon_{i,t-1} \tag{15.3}$$

with additional conditions of the moment:

$$\begin{aligned} E[(y_{i,t-s} - y_{i,t-s-1})(\mu_i + \varepsilon_{i,t})] = 0, \quad s = 1 \\ E[(X_{i,t-s} - X_{i,t-s-1})(\mu_i + \varepsilon_{i,t})] = 0, \quad s = 1 \end{aligned} \tag{15.4}$$

where μ_i are country effects.

The descriptive statistics on the sample

The sample includes 168 observations on 14 emerging countries for 2007–2018. We consider the following countries: Brazil, China, Czechia, India, Indonesia, Malaysia, Mexico, Philippines, Poland, Russia, S. Africa, S. Korea, Thailand, and Turkey. These countries are characterized by relatively large or rapidly growing bond markets. The descriptive statistics are shown in Table 15.2.

Table 15.1 Description of variables of our study

Variable	*Description of the variable*	*Direction of influence*	*Source*
fpi_debt_inflow	The dependent variable: the FPI inflow into debt instruments (% GDP)		IMF
fpi_equity_inflow	The FPI inflow into equity instruments (% GDP)	-	IMF
real_interest_rate	Real interest rate (%) measured based on the average nominal yield of 10-year local currency government bonds and inflation rate	+	Authors' calculations based on investing.com and World Bank
lngdp	Logarithm of GDP	+	World Bank
ln_gov_bonds	Logarithm of the volume of outstanding government bonds to GDP	+	Bloomberg, Asian Bonds Online
ln_gov_bonds_2	The square of *ln_gov_bonds*	-	
ln_corp_bonds	Logarithm of the volume of outstanding corporate bonds to GDP	+	
ln_corp_bonds_2	The square of *ln_corp_bonds*	-	
ln_stock_market	Logarithm of the stock market capitalization (in % of GDP)	-	World Bank
ln_stock_market_2	The square of *ln_stock_market*	+	
gdp_growth	Real GDP annual growth rate, %	+	
inflation	Inflation annual rate, %	-	
exchange_rate	Change in the national currency exchange rate to the US dollar for the year,%	-	Bloomberg
political_stability	Index of political stability (-2.5 is the minimum, +2.5 is the maximum)	+	Worldwide governance indicators
sp500	S&P 500 Index return rate for the year, %	+	Bloomberg
vix	US VIX index averaged for the year	-	
dummy_asia	Dummy variable: 1 – if the country is in Asia, 0 – otherwise	+	
year dummies	Dummy variables of years	+ / -	

Table 15.2 The descriptive statistics on the sample

Variable	*Obs*	*Mean*	*Std. Dev.*	*Min*	*Max*
fpi_debt_inflow	168	1.12	1.69	-4.49	6.87
fpi_whole_inflow	168	1.41	2.20	-9.13	8.79
fpi_equity_inflow	168	0.29	1.08	-4.64	3.39
real_interest_rate	168	0.02	0.02	-0.06	0.08
lngdp	168	27.40	1.01	25.73	30.24
gdp_growth	168	4.06	3.18	-7.8	14.2
inflation	168	4.50	3.15	-0.9	16.3
ln_stock_market	168	4.06	0.68	2.7	5.9
exchange_rate	168	-0.03	0.12	-0.43	0.33
ln_gov_bonds	168	3.78	0.62	1.7	4.7
ln_corp_bonds	168	2.84	0.96	-0.4	4.4
political_stability	168	-0.39	0.75	-2.01	1.11
vix	168	19.80	6.20	11.03	32.24
sp500	168	0.06	0.17	-0.38	0.30
trade_freedom	168	76.47	7.78	44.2	88.0
invest_freedom	168	49.91	16.62	20	80
finance_freedom	168	53.99	14.48	20	80
dummy_asia	168	0.5	0.5	0	1

The results of our empirical study

The results of testing regressions with random effects are presented in Table 15.3. The results of testing GMM-models regarding the influence of independent variables are similar to the results of the regressions with random effects, but Sargan tests showed the relatively low quality of GMM-models. Therefore the regression models with random effects are more relevant.

Our hypotheses regarding the non-linear effects of the size of the markets of government bonds and stocks on the FPI inflow in debt securities have been confirmed (Table 15.3). The influence of the size of the government bond market is described by a parabola with branches down: if this market is relatively small, then with its increase the FPI inflow (in % of GDP) also increases. We attribute this to the fact that the development of a relatively small bond market increases its attractiveness for foreign investors looking for opportunities to diversify risks and obtain high returns. On the contrary, a too-large bond market no longer provides significant additional opportunities for risk diversification, but, as a rule, is characterized by lower return rates, which reduces the FPI inflow (in % of GDP). A similar dependence is observed for the corporate bond market, but in most specifications of the regression models, the square of the size of the corporate bond market is not statistically significant. We conclude that for the corporate bond market the dominant effect is an increase in FPI inflow (in % of GDP) with an increase in the size of the bond market. This result is in accordance with Bhatta et al. (2018), who revealed that private debt to GDP significantly positively affects foreign biases in bond allocations for a sample of developed and

Table 15.3 The results of the regression analysis

	Dependent variable: FPI inflow to debt instruments				*Dependent variable: whole FPI inflow*
	1	*2*	*3*	*4*	*5*
exchange_rate	1.7618 (1.2784)	0.6921 (1.4643)	0.281 (1.4498)	2.1332* (1.101)	0.6931 (1.4641)
ln_gov_bonds	4.2023** (1.9822)	3.635* (2.0272)	1.8771 (2.1717)		3.6354* (2.0268)
ln_gov_bonds_2	-0.6546** (0.2952)	-0.5432* (0.2986)	-0.2775 (0.3244)		-0.5433* (0.2985)
ln_stock_market	-5.3559** (2.5645)	-8.5322*** (2.6866)	-7.3399*** (2.7375)		-8.5365*** (2.6861)
ln_stock_market_2	0.661** (0.2941)	0.9789*** (0.3096)	0.8593*** (0.3142)		0.9794*** (0.3095)
ln_corp_bonds	0.8149* (0.4834)	0.7673 (0.4739)	0.8054* (0.4701)	1.3976*** (0.5372)	0.7674 (0.4738)
ln_corp_bonds_2	-0.1574 (0.0963)	-0.0892 (0.0963)	-0.0958 (0.0943)	-0.2969** (0.1167)	-0.0892 (0.0962)
lngdp		4.5988 (6.1433)			4.6003 (6.1421)
lngdp_2		-0.0865 (0.1111)			-0.0866 (0.1111)
political_stability	0.3119 (0.1961)	0.2654* (0.201)	0.2101 (0.2156)	0.5839* (0.3241)	0.2655 (0.2009)
invest_freedom	0.0107 (0.0112)	0.002 (0.0144)		0.002 (0.0144)	
trade_freedom			0.0357 (0.0259)		
real_interest_rate				8.004 (6.8375)	
sp500	2.4801*** (0.8781)	13.6503** (6.634)	16.8893** (6.8162)		13.6493** (6.6327)
fpi_equity_inflow	0.0613 (0.1438)	-0.0743 (0.1438)	-0.0631 (0.1429)	0.2921** (0.1248)	
dummy_asia	-0.1987 (0.3664)	0.1987 (0.3661)	0.1862 (0.3809)	-0.1609 (0.5315)	0.199 (0.366)
_cons	4.0301 (5.855)	-49.0874 (84.6829)	9.1169 (6.4216)	-0.0547 (0.7631)	-49.1008 (84.6667)
year dummies	no	yes	yes	no	yes
Wald	44.07	89.21	81.98	25.58	251.03
R-square overall	0.221	0.384	0.378	0.108	0.637
Observations	168	168	168	168	168

Significance levels: * p <10%, ** p <5%, *** p <1%

developing economies. Unlike the government bond market, the influence of the size of the stock market on FPI inflow is described by a parabola with branches up (Table 15.3). We explain this by the fact that in developing economies there is competition between national stock and bond markets. A growing national stock market attracts more funds from global investors, and this negatively affects the FPI inflow into debt instruments. This hypothesis has not been tested in previous studies.

The FPI inflow is not determined by the size of the economy. The influence of the logarithm of GDP is positive, but not significant (Table 15.3). Pala and Orgun (2015), for the Turkish market, revealed a positive significant influence of the size of the economy on the FPI inflow. The higher the real interest rates on government bonds, the higher the FPI inflow. This conclusion coincides with the results of Garg and Dua (2014) for the Indian market. An appreciation of the national currency against the US dollar leads to an increase in the FPI inflow (Table 15.3). This result coincides with the conclusion of Ahmad et al. (2015) for the Chinese market. The influence of inflation is negative, but the statistical significance is not high. The negative influence of inflation was earlier revealed by Al-Smadi (2018) for the Jordanian market.

Such institutional factors as the indices of political stability, investment freedom and trade freedom positively affect the FPI inflow (Table 15.3); the direction of their influence is stable, but only political stability is statistically significant in some model specifications. Our results regarding the quality of institutions coincide with the conclusions of Al-Smadi (2018) and Bhatta et al. (2018), but they considered other proxies: the quality of government regulation, the level of corruption, and investor rights protection.

If the S&P 500 index increases, then the FPI inflow into debt securities of emerging markets also increases (Table 15.3). The influence of this factor is significant at the 5% level. Our explanation is that S&P 500 growth is an indicator of investor optimism.

The influence of a country belonging to the Asian region is unstable and insignificant (Table 15.3). We also reveal stable and significant negative inflow of dummies for 2009, 2013 and 2014.

To check the stability of the results, we analyze the impact of the above factors on the whole FPI inflow (into equity and debt securities in total). The results are presented in Table 15.3. For most factors, the direction of the influence and significance coincide with the results for the FPI inflow into debt securities.

Conclusions

We perform an empirical study to reveal the determinants of portfolio investment in the debt securities of emerging markets. Previous studies are mostly devoted to FPI inflows as a whole, without dividing them into the equity and debt markets. We consider the period from 2007 to 2018 and a cross-country sample of 14 emerging bond markets. We analyze the influence of national and global factors characterizing financial market development, the macroeconomic environment, and the quality of institutions. Our contribution is to take into account the non-linear effects of the size of the national stock and bond markets. To test the hypotheses, we apply panel data regressions with random effects.

The influence of the size of the government bond market on the FPI inflow is described by a parabola with branches down. We attribute this to the fact that the development of a relatively small bond market increases its attractiveness for foreign investors looking for opportunities to diversify risks and obtain high return rates. On the contrary, a too-large bond market is characterized by lower return rates, which reduces the FPI inflow (in % of GDP). For the corporate bond market the dominant effect is an increase in FPI inflow (in % of GDP) with an increase in the size of the bond market. The influence of the size of the stock market on the FPI inflow is described by a parabola with branches up. We explain this by the fact that in developing countries there is competition between national stock and bond markets.

The higher the real interest rates on government bonds, the higher the FPI inflow. The appreciation of the national currency against the US dollar leads to an increase in the FPI inflow. The influence of inflation is negative.

We reveal a positive influence of the indices of political stability, investment freedom and trade freedom, and the most significant factor is political stability.

If the S&P 500 index increases, then the FPI inflow to debt securities of emerging markets also increases. Our explanation is that S&P 500 growth is an indicator of investor optimism.

References

Ahmad, F., Draz, M. U., Yang, S. C. (2015). Determinants of foreign portfolio inflows: Analysis and implications for China. *Asian Journal of Finance and Accounting*, 7(2): 66–77. DOI: https://dx.doi.org/10.2139/ssrn.2542610

Al-Smadi, M. (2018). Determinants of foreign portfolio investment: The case of Jordan. *Investment Management and Financial Innovations*, 15(1): 328–336. DOI: https://doi.org/10.21511/imfi.15(1).2018.27

Arellano, M., Bond, S. (1991). Some tests of specification for panel data: Monte Carlo evidence and an application to employment equations. *Review of Economic Studies*, 58: 277–297. DOI: https://doi.org/10.2307/2297968

Arellano, M., Bover, O. (1995). Another look at the instrumental-variable estimation of error-components. *Journal of Econometrics*, 68: 29–52. DOI: https://doi.org/10.1016/0304-4076(94)01642-D

Bhatta, B., Marshall, A., Thapa, C. (2018). Foreign bias in bond portfolio investments: The role of economic and non-economic factors and the impact of the global financial and sovereign debt crises. *The European Journal of Finance*, 24(7–8): 654–681. DOI: https://doi.org/10.1080/1351847X.2017.1343199

Blundell, R. W., Bond, S. R. (1998). Initial conditions and moment restrictions in dynamic panel data models. *Journal of Econometrics*, 87: 115–143. DOI: https://doi.org/10.1016/S0304-4076(98)00009-8

Garg, R., Dua, P. (2014). Foreign portfolio investment flows to India: Determinants and analysis. *World Development*, 59: 16–28. DOI: https://doi.org/10.1016/j.worlddev.2014.01.030

Pala, A., Orgun, B. O. (2015). The effect of macroeconomic variables on foreign portfolio investments: An implication for Turkey. *Journal of Business, Economics and Finance*, 4(1): 108–126.

Waqas, Y., Hashmi, S. H., Nazir, M. I. (2015). Macroeconomic factors and foreign portfolio investment volatility: A case of South Asian countries. *Future Business Journal*, 1: 65–74. DOI: https://doi.org/10.1016/j.fbj.2015.11.002

Part 6

Anomalies in the bond markets

16 Calendar effects in emerging bond markets

Introduction

Timing is one of the controversial issues in the development of investment strategies and trading in the financial markets. One point of view states that it is enough to buy securities with a certain periodicity (for example, each month), and that will be more attractive compared to waiting for successful moments. But there is another point of view, which argues that there are systematic deviations of the financial asset prices from fair values and investors should exploit these patterns. One of the popular research topics is calendar anomalies. Among them, there are the effects of the day of the week, month of the year, the beginning and end of the month and holidays (for example, the New Year's rally on the stock market). For example, the stock market reveals the existence of anomalies on Monday (lower daily yield, Cross, 1973), January, October (extremely volatile and unprofitable months for investors), the end of the year (increases in stock prices), and the end of the day. However, we cannot say for sure that these observations are true for all asset classes, market segments and national markets. For example, the effect of Tuesday was revealed for the stock markets of France, Japan, Australia, and Italy (Jaffe and Westerfield, 1985). Moreover, previously identified anomalies fade over time. One of the possible explanations is that with an increase in market capitalization and an improvement in the skills of the participants, information efficiency increases, information spreads faster and is better processed, and more and more robots are eliminating deviations from fair levels by using arbitrage strategies.

Literature review

One of the first studies on the US bond market was done by Johnston et al. (1991). They consider the weekly seasonal effects on the returns of futures on long-term Treasury bonds, short-term Treasury bonds and Treasury bills (T-bonds, T-notes, T-bills). The authors do not find an effect of the day of the week for T-notes futures, but they identify two distinct patterns in futures on T-bonds: a negative effect of Monday and a positive effect of Tuesday. Futures on

T-bills also have a positive effect of Tuesday. However, the significance of the day of the week effect predominantly depends on the study time period.

As a research object, authors can also consider various indices. For example, they can be the daily prices of emerging economy stock market bond indices: emerging market bond index (EMBI+) and Morgan Stanley Capital international index for emerging countries (MSCI EM).

More recent studies reach opposite conclusions: Polwitoon and Tawatnuntachai (2008) show that these anomalies persist, while Nippani and Arize (2008) show that in developed markets, some of these effects disappear or lose strength.

One feature of Nippani and Arize (2008) is the identification of calendar anomalies in the entire corporate bond market and in two sectors: industry and utilities. They use the Dow Jones bond indices (DJBD), the Dow Jones Industrial Bonds Index (DJBID), and the Dow Jones Index of Utility Shares and Bonds (DJBUD) for analysis. The data includes daily returns of these indices for the period from January 1, 1982 to April 5, 2002. The null hypothesis is as follows: there is no 'weekend effect' / 'Monday effect', 'end of the year effect'. The model is defined as:

$$R_t = \beta_0 + \beta_1 MON + \varepsilon_{it} \tag{16.1}$$

where R_t is the daily return of the index (DJBD, DJBID, DJBUD) on the day t, β_0 is a constant, $\beta_1 MON$ is a dummy variable, which equals 1, if it is Monday, and 0 in otherwise, and ε_{it} is an error term.

The model of Keim (1987) and Brusa et al. (2003) is:

$$R_t = \beta_0 + \beta_1 \text{DMON}_t + \beta_1 \text{DJAN}_t + \beta_1 \text{DMON} * \text{DJAN}_t + \varepsilon_{it} \tag{16.2}$$

where R_t is daily index returns on day t, DMON_t is a dummy variable, which equals 1 if it is Monday, and 0 otherwise. DJAN_t is a dummy variable, which equals 1 if the day t is one of the 5 trading days in January, and 0 otherwise. DMON*DJAN_t is a dummy variable, which is equal to 1 if day t is Monday and is within one of the first 5 trading days in January, and 0 otherwise.

Based on the Connolly model (Connolly, 1989), Nippani and Arize (2008) reveal that the returns on Mondays are considerably less than the average return for the rest of the week, but not for all periods for each of the indices (Table 16.1).

Table 16.1 Results for Connolly's (1989) model

Connolly (1989) model	*The Monday effect*
DJBD	Observed in 2 out of 3 subperiods
DJBID	Observed in 2 out of 3 subperiods
DJBUD	Observed in 1 out of 3 subperiods

Table 16.2 Results for Keim (1987) and Brusa et al. (2003) models: 3 out of 3 subperiods

Keim (1987) and Brusa et al. (2003)	*End of the year effect*
DJBD	Observed in 3 out of 3 subperiods
DJBID	Observed in 3 out of 3 subperiods
DJBUD	Observed in 2 out of 3 subperiods

Table 16.3 Results for Keim (1987) and Brusa et al. (2003) models: 1 out of 3 subperiods

Keim (1987) and Brusa et al. (2003)	*End of the year effect*
DJBD	Observed in 1 out of 3 subperiods
DJBID	Observed in 1 out of 3 subperiods
DJBUD	Observed in 0 out of 3 subperiods

Nippani and Arize (2008) also reveal an end of the year effect, based on the significance of the coefficients before DJAN t (Table 16.2).

The last conclusion of Nippani and Arize (2008) is that the returns on Mondays at the beginning of the year are not different from returns at the beginning of the week in other months (Table 16.3).

Though it seems that there should be a difference in market anomalies among industries, the authors cannot prove it. There is less evidence of an end of the year effect in the index of utility companies compared to the index of industrial companies.

The study on the stock and bond market of Kenya shows some specifics. Murigu (2013) examines the daily bond prices of 11 firms that traded on the Nairobi Stock Exchange (NSE) and were included in the exchange index for the period from January 2009 to December 2013 (5 years). The null hypothesis is that there is no significant relationship between the day of the week and bond yields. The alternative hypothesis: there is a significant relationship between the day of the week and bond yields. The authors use a rather simple method of OLS. They show that Tuesday has the highest yield compared to any other day of the week, and this day is also the most volatile. Wednesday, on the contrary, has the lowest yield. This conclusion is not confirmed for the stock market. Onyuma (2009), who studied stock returns on the Kenyan market for the period 1980–2006, argues that Monday has the lowest returns and Friday provides the highest returns. Monday's yield is more volatile than for other days of the week.

Compton et al. (2013) conducted the first study of the month effect on the Russian stock and corporate bond market. The data includes RTS dollar index and MICEX Rouble index weighted by market capitalization, as well as RuxCbonds and CBITR bond indices. The study period is from January 1, 2003 to December 31, 2008. The null hypothesis is the absence of the 'January effect', 'the end of the month effect', or the 'weekend (or Monday) effect' for the bonds and stocks of Russian issuers. The researchers used the least-squares method, where dummies are the explanatory variables, each of which corresponds to an observation for a specific day of the week or month of the year. The authors show that Russian bonds demonstrate unusually high yields in the first months of the year, which is not observed in the Russian stock market. A significant end of the month effect is observed both in the Russian stock and corporate bond markets.

Khanthavit (2016) analyzed the day of the week effect on the Thailand corporate bond market from Friday, June 15, 2007 to Friday, March 18, 2016 (2142 observations). The null hypothesis is about equal average returns for five working days. The object of the study is corporate bonds of the Thai Bond Market Association, as well as risk-free instruments. The conclusion is that the bonds under consideration show a high positive Friday yield, but the effects of the day of the week are significant only for some bonds.

Methodology of our research

We study whether there is any dependence between the bond yield and a time interval (day, week or month). The hypothesis is tested by the OLS method. The feature of the model is the presence of dummies as explanatory variables. We regress the asset returns on a constant and on dummy variables. Our linear multifactor regression model is:

$$\Delta I_j = \beta_{0j} + \sum_{k=1}^{n} \beta_{kj} \, D_{kj} + \varepsilon_j \tag{16.3}$$

where ΔI_j is the return of asset j over a certain period, n is the number of months in a year or days in a week, ε_j is the standard error, and D_{kj} is the dummy variable, indicating the time period (that is, the month or the day of the week). $D_{kj} = 1$ if the data is from period k, and $D_{kj} = 0$ otherwise. β_{kj} is the coefficient before the dummy, which reflects the presence or absence of a relationship between the returns in the base period and other periods. The variable β_{0j} shows the average return of the base period, which is excluded from the regression to avoid interdependence among regressors.

Thus, to test the hypotheses on data for the days of the week, the model has the following specification, where the base period is Monday:

$$R_{it} = \alpha_i + \beta_{2i} D_{2i} + \beta_{3i} D_{3i} + \beta_{4i} D_{4i} + \beta_{5i} D_{5i} + \varepsilon_{it} \tag{16.4}$$

That is, if the observation corresponds to Tuesday, then $D_{2i}=1$, $D_{3i}=D_{4i}=D_{5i}=0$. The other days of the week are defined identically.

The model for analyzing monthly returns with January as a base period is as follows:

$$R_{it} = \alpha_i + \beta_{2i}D_{2i} + \beta_{3i}D_{3i} + \beta_{4i}D_{4i} + \beta_{5i}D_{5i} + \beta_{6i}D_{6i} + \beta_{7i}D_{7i} + \ldots + \beta_{12i}D_{12i} + \varepsilon_{it} \quad (16.5)$$

If the observation corresponds to January, then $D_{2i}=1$, $D_{3i}=D_{4i}=\ldots=D_{12i}=0$. The other months of the year are defined identically.

We compute daily returns as:

$$\Delta I = \frac{P_t - P_{t-1}}{P_{t-1}} * 100 \quad (16.6)$$

where P_t is the price of the security on day t, P_{t-1} is the price of a security on day t-1 (the previous day), and ΔI is the return on a security over one day. We consider the closing prices on the trading days.

A similar formula is used to calculate the monthly returns of securities. Only now the variable P_t reflects the price of a security in month t, P_{t-1} is the price of the security on month t-1 (the previous month), and ΔI is the return of a security over one month.

Then we estimate OLS regression coefficients by using the STATA program. To identify their significance, we consider the value of t-statistics and the corresponding p-value. If the p-value is less than 5%, the coefficient is considered significant.

The data

Our study is based on historical prices of bond indices, ETFs, and government and individual corporate bonds of the Russian market.

For the study, we select the bonds of 'blue chip' companies, leading in economic and financial indicators in the Russian market (Table 16.4). These include the corporate bonds of Sberbank of Russia PJSC, VTB Group, Gazprom PJSC, MTS, Lukoil, Nornickel, and NOVATEK. We also include bonds issued by the Government of Russian Federation (OFZ). In addition, to obtain more accurate, comprehensive results, the analysis is conducted on the Moscow Exchange indices based on government and corporate bonds (RGBI, RUCBITR), as well as ETFs issued by FinEx and Sberbank (IE00B7L7CP77, RU000A1000F9). All information for the study of monthly returns is taken for the period 2014–2019. For daily anomalies, we also use data on securities for the periods 2015–2019 and 2017–2019.

An automated Dickey–Fuller unit root test is used for each time series by using the STATA program. They all turn out to be stationary at a 5% significance level, which means that an OLS regression method is applicable.

Table 16.4 Securities that form the sample of our study

Type of security	*Issuer*	*ISIN*	*Period*
Government bond index	MOEX	RU000A0JQV61	January 16, 2014 – April 2, 2019
Corporate bond index	MOEX	RU000A0JPT17	April 30, 2013 - May 17, 2019
ETF	Sberbank Asset Management JSC	RU000A1000F9	January 25, 2019 - May 17, 2019
ETF	FinEx	IE00B7L7CP77	April 30, 2013 - May 17, 2019
Corporate bonds	VTB Capital S.A.	XS0842078536 RU000A0JV3Q3 XS0810596832	January 2, 2014 - April 25, 2019 January 3, 2014 - April 23, 2019 December 26, 2014 - April 24, 2019
Corporate bonds	Sberbank of Russia PJSC	RU000A0JWUE9 RU000A0JXRW5	September 30, 2016 - April 23, 2019 May 30, 2017 - April 16, 2019
Corporate bonds	Gazprom PJSC	XS0316524130 XS0191754729	January 1, 2014 - April 2, 2019
Corporate bonds	Rosneftegaz JSC	RU000A0JX355	December 23, 2016 - April 26, 2019
Corporate bonds	Lukoil	XS0919504562	January 2, 2014 - April 9, 2019
Corporate bonds	MTS	RU000A0ZYWY5	March 7, 2018 – April 26, 2019
Government bonds	The Government of the Russian Federation	RU000A0JTG59 RU000A0JSMA2 RU000A0JXQF2 RU000A0JPLH5 RU000A0JRTL6	April 1, 2013 - May 24, 2019 March 1, 2013 - May 24, 2019 May 3, 2017 - April 9, 2019 January 1, 2014 - April 9, 2019 January 6, 2014 - April 8, 2019
Corporate bonds	Nornickel	XS0982861287	January 1, 2014 - April 23, 2019
Corporate bonds	NOVATEK	XS0864383723	January 16, 2014 - April 2, 2019

In addition, we conduct tests for heteroskedasticity and autocorrelation. If these properties exist, the estimates obtained by OLS will not be effective (they will not have the smallest dispersion in comparison with other estimates). That is, standard errors will be overestimated, and the values of t- and F-statistics will be underestimated, confidence intervals will be too wide. In other words, according to the test results, it is possible to erroneously conclude that the model parameter is insignificant, when it is significant. Therefore, to obtain the correct results, it is necessary to get rid of these signs, if they are observed.

We test for heteroskedasticity using the White test, carried out by the functions 'estatimtest, white'. If heteroskedasticity is detected, then a correction is performed using the robust function. Also, the Durbin–Watson statistics are obtained using the 'estatedwatson' function. It allows one to reveal the presence of a residual autocorrelation. In case of autocorrelation, the function 'praisereg..., corc' is used to correct the data.

The results of our study

It should be noted that not all of the securities under consideration show both effects. For some bonds only an anomaly of the day of the week is observed, for others, that of the month of the year.

The effect of the day of the week

The government security that shows the day of the week effect is the Moscow Exchange RGBI index: Tuesday's yield is lower than that of other days of the week at a significance level of less than 1% (Figure 16.1, Table 16.5). ETF on government securities issued by Sberbank (RU000A1000F9) does not show significant results.

The effect of the day of the week is demonstrated by bonds issued by VTB, Gazprom, Rosneft, Lukoil, MTS, as well as ETF issued by FinEx (IE00B7L7CP77). We reveal a general pattern: most securities have the lowest yield on Tuesday and the largest yield on Wednesday (Figure 16.2).

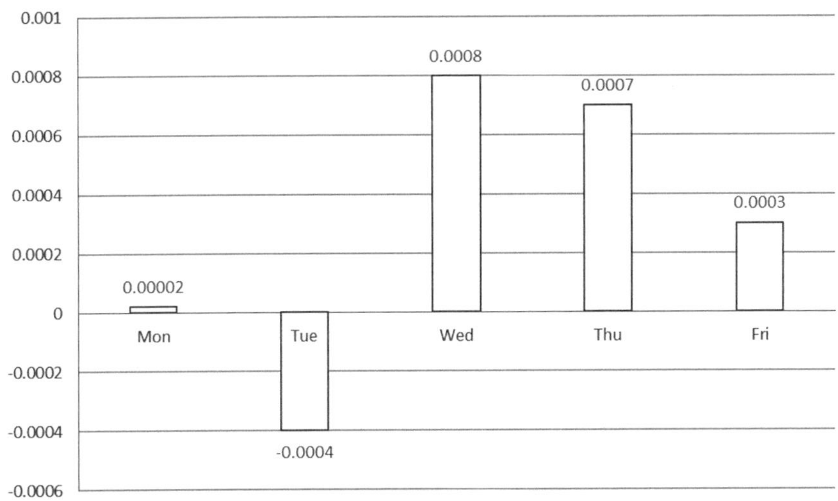

Figure 16.1 RGBI mean return rate by days of the week.

Table 16.5 Mean return rates by days of the week

	RGBI	*RUCBITR*	*FXRB*	*SBER*
Monday	0.00002	0.000530508	-0.0004	-0.000944
Tuesday	-0.0004	0.000180762	-0.0008	0.000145
Wednesday	0.0008	0.000151904	0.0019	-0.000507
Thursday	0.0007	0.000327620	0.0007	0.001146
Friday	0.0003	0.000486337	0.0003	0.002561

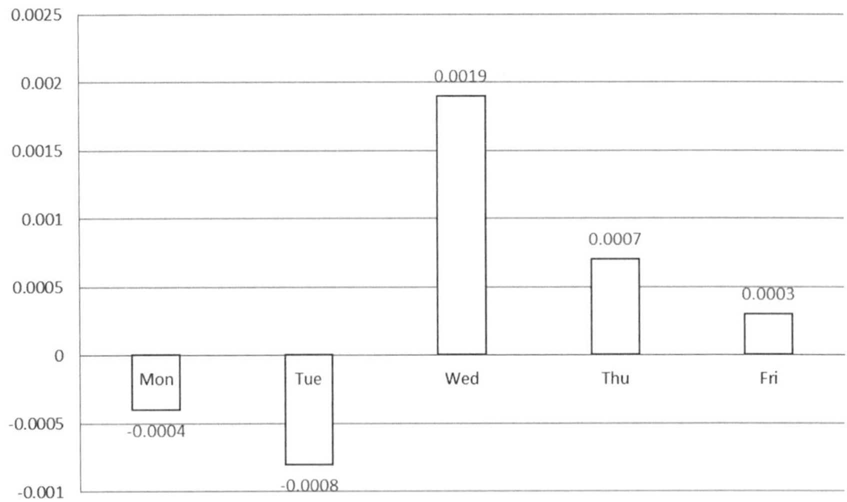

Figure 16.2 FXRB mean return rate by days of the week.

For example, FinEx ETF (IE00B7L7CP77) demonstrates a clear relationship between Wednesday, Monday, and Tuesday: Wednesday's yield is higher than that of Monday and Tuesday. VTB Eurobonds with a maturity in 2022 also have the lowest yield on Tuesday compared to other days of the week. Historical data on VTB Eurobonds (2024) shows that Wednesdays and Mondays are better days for an investor than Tuesdays. As for Gazprom Eurobonds with a maturity in 2037, Tuesdays and Mondays are the least profitable. Rosneft security earns more on Fridays than on Mondays. Lukoil is also the least attractive for earnings on Tuesdays and Mondays, but most attractive on Wednesdays. The conclusion on the MTS bond is that Thursday is better than Tuesday or Friday.

Based on the generalized findings, we can conclude that in the Russian bond market, Tuesday is the least profitable day of the week and Wednesday is the most profitable.

Table 16.6 Mean return rates by months of the year

	RGBI	*RUCBITR*	*FXRB*
January	0.0062	0.0045	-0.0080
February	0.0130	0.0126	-0.0072
March	0.0171	0.0115	0.0330
April	0.0138	0.0120	0.0083
May	0.0059	0.0080	0.0139
June	0.0023	0.0072	0.0194
July	0.0030	0.0061	0.0098
August	-0.0060	0.0008	0.0021
September	0.0179	0.0079	0.0078
October	0.0083	0.0046	-0.0095
November	-0.0014	0.0040	0.0117
December	-0.0048	0.0057	-0.0034

The effect of the calendar month

Almost all the securities under consideration show the presence of month of the year anomalies (Table 16.6). However, the results are contradictory.

For example, the MOEX index of government bonds tends to have a low yield in January, while this effect is not detected for most corporate bonds.

As for other securities, January is consistently worse than April for OFZs with a maturity in December 11, 2019 (RU000A0JTG59), according to the OLS estimates. A similar result is obtained for OFZ with a maturity in July 20, 2022 (RU000A0JSMA2). OFZ 26222 (RU000A0JXQF2) shows that January is worse than August. For OFZ with a maturity in July 19, 2023 (RU000A0JPLH5) September is the least profitable month of the year. OFZ maturing in July 23, 2026 (RU000A0JRTL6) shows that October is better than January, April, August, and September.

Thus four of the six securities reveal that January is the least profitable month for the investor. The Moscow Exchange Corporate Bonds Index (RUCBITR) identifies August as the worst month of the year (Figure 16.3). In addition, this month is a loss for Gazprom, with a repayment period in 2037, and for NOVATEK. Securities of VTB and Sberbank Eurobonds, MTS and Nornickel show different results.

The term 'January effect' is traditionally understood as the existence of the highest profitability in this month for the stock market. However, the opposite effect is revealed for the Russian government bond market.

Conclusions

As in the stock market, there are calendar anomalies in the bond market. They are identified in the American market (Johnston et al., 1991; Nippani and Arize, 2008), in the market of Thailand (Khanthavit, 2016) and others. In this chapter,

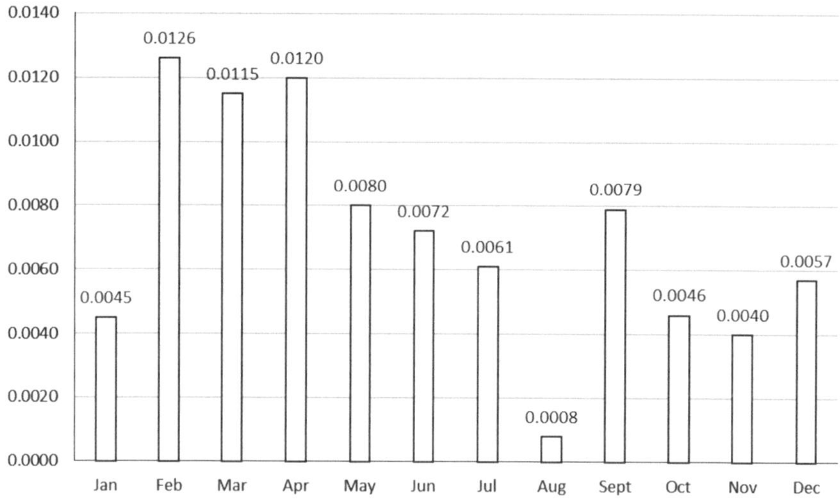

Figure 16.3 RUCBUTR mean return rates by months.

we show the basic techniques for identifying calendar effects and reveal their presence in the emerging Russian market. We explain the presence of these effects by taxation rules, accumulated coupon income, and the actions of institutional investors. We conclude that in the Russian bond market, Tuesday is the least profitable day of the week and Wednesday is the most profitable. January is the least profitable month for the investor.

References

Brusa, J., Liu, P., Schulman, C. (2003). The weekend and 'reverse' weekend effects: An analysis by month of the year, week of the month, and industry. *Journal of Business Finance and Accounting*, 30(5-6): 863–890. DOI: https://doi.org/10.1111/1468-5957.05386

Compton, W., Kunkel, R. A., Kuhlemeyer, G. (2013). Calendar anomalies in Russian stocks and bonds. *Managerial Finance*, 39(12): 1138–1154. DOI: https://doi.org/10.1108/MF-03-2013-0067

Connolly, R. A. (1989). An examination of the robustness of the weekend effect. *Journal of Financial and quantitative Analysis*, 24(2), 133–169. DOI: https://doi.org/10.2307/2330769

Cross, F. (1973). The behavior of stock prices on Fridays and Mondays. *Financial Analysts Journal*, 29(6): 67–69. DOI: https://doi.org/10.2469/faj.v29.n6.67

Jaffe, J. F., Westerfield, R. (1985). The week-end effect in common stock returns: The international evidence. *Journal of Finance*, 40(2): 433–454. DOI: https://doi.org/10.1111/j.1540-6261.1985.tb04966.x

Johnston, E. T., Kracaw, W. A., McConnell, J. J. (1991). Day-of-the-week effects in financial futures: An analysis of GNMA, T-Bond, T-Note, and T-Bill Contracts. *Journal of Financial and Quantitative Analysis*, 26(1): 23–44. DOI: https://doi.org/10.2307/2331241

Keim, D. (1987). Daily returns and size-related premiums: One more time. *Journal of Portfolio Management*, 13: 41–47.

Khanthavit, A. (2016). Day-of-the-week effects in Thailand's corporate-bond market. *Catalyst*, 13(1): 86–95.

Murigu, P. W. (2013). Day of the week effect and bond market returns at the Nairobi securities exchange. Thesis. University of Nairobi.

Nippani, S., Arize, C. A. (2008). U.S. corporate bond returns: A study of market anomalies based on broad industry groups. *Review of Financial Economics*, 17(3): 157–171. DOI: https://doi.org/10.1016/j.rfe.2007.02.007

Onyuma, S. O. (2009). Day-of-the-week and month-of-the-year effect on the Kenyan stock market returns. *Eastern Africa Social Science Research Review*, 25(2): 53–74. DOI: https://doi.org/ https://doi.org/10.1353/eas.0.0009

Polwitoon, S., Tawatnuntachai, O. (2008). Emerging market bond funds: A comprehensive analysis. *The Financial Review*, 43(1): 51–84. DOI: https://doi.org/10.1111/j.1540-6288.2007.00186.x

17 Which investment strategy is profitable in the bond market?

Reverse or momentum? What about risk?

Introduction

Factor strategies or investment styles (also called smart beta strategies) are well known in the stock market. But a number of hedge funds also use them for the bond market to form bond portfolios. There are also academic studies of factor strategies in the bond market, comparing by the 'risk–return' criterion such popular anomalies as the higher return rates on securities of relatively undervalued issuers and higher return rates of portfolios of low-volatility assets, and the selection of securities in the portfolio on the base of the criterion of momentum (inertial movement, that is, the selection of exclusively 'past winners'). Typical selection strategies and questions arising, on setting criteria for one or another factor, are demonstrated on the AQR hedge fund cube of decision-making (Richardson, 2018) with three projections: 1) strategy selection (criteria for selecting bonds in a portfolio), 2) strategy design selection (i.e. justification of periods of tracking past results, the proportion of bonds in the sample that will be included into the portfolio and others), and 3) selection of the time of entry and exit (timing).

Richardson (2018) comes to the conclusion that the more strategies the investor has in his arsenal, the more parameters are used and tested for building strategies (the choice of strategy design is important, as shown by Teplova and Mikova (2019) for the stock market) and higher individual portfolio management skills (for example, choosing the right time to open or close a position, i.e. timing), the more profitability this investor can earn.

The momentum strategy implies the advantage of a portfolio of bonds with the highest price growth for the previous period (this can be a month or a quarter, usually a period of up to one year) with respect to bonds that showed the worst result in cumulative return rate from price changes (past loser). Carry strategy can be realized through the purchase of bonds with the highest observed yield (YTM) and the sale of bonds with the lowest YTM (this is an extremely simplified representation of the carry). The value strategy is traditionally based on market multiples (PE, MVBV, EVEBITDA). A low-risk strategy implies the selection of assets (in this review, bonds) in the portfolio with the lowest YTM volatility or the lowest drawdown for a certain previous period (this period is determined as part of the strategy design selection).

An interesting result of the AQR hedge fund study (Richardson, 2018): US bonds of value firms (with low market multiples) provide the maximum result according to the 'risk-return' criterion: Sharpe ratio is equal to 2. Second place is occupied by the strategy of low volatility. Selection on the principle of carry is more acceptable for emerging market bonds. If an investor builds a combined strategy (which the AQR hedge fund itself sells to its customers, for which a commission is taken), then the Sharpe ratio will increase to 2.5 (Richardson, 2018). The study claims that this is true for other types of bonds. This effect is achieved by reducing risks due to different behaviour of factor strategies during different phases of the business cycle. A private investor can build a similar strategy, through factor ETFs that are available in the US market. Another option is to build a portfolio according to the principles shown below.

There is a tendency for both individual and institutional investors to use momentum strategies more frequently in their activities (Antonacci, 2013). Professional interest in the results of past investment in financial markets is high (Kaminsky et al., 2004; Haan and Kakes, 2011). Kaminsky et al. (2004) confirm the significance of using arbitrage momentum strategies by mutual funds in Latin America. Based on the analysis of the portfolio structure of 13 Latin-American mutual funds, the authors conclude that managers systematically buy winners and sell losers. Momentum investment strategies are also applied by Korean national equity funds (Kim and Wei, 1999). Haan and Kakes (2011) compare the choice of Dutch institutional investors between the classic momentum strategy and the 'against the market' strategy.

Previous research

Initially the paradox of creating a profitable trade strategy on past winners and losers was demonstrated in the US stock market (De Bondt and Thaler, 1985; Jegadeesh and Titman, 1993). Jegadeesh and Titman (1993) prove the existence of price anomalies in terms of the paradox of profitability of the momentum strategy (its idea is based on the inertia of asset price movement) and the momentum strategy reversal, or the strategy of return to an average return rate level (past winners are overestimated due to the excess reaction of investors and, subsequently, their return rate is falling, making it possible to invest in past losers). The authors show that opening a long position on relative winners and a short position on losers can bring excess returns within the range from 1% to 12%, while the dynamics of the excess return rate curve tends to attenuate and completely disappear after six months. Research on other stock markets, including developing ones, appeared in the first decade of the 21st century. Their focus was on revealing interesting patterns in the behaviour of prices of high and low liquid stocks and of large and small companies.

Moskowitz et al. (2012) were the first to compare the results of investment according to the trend (time-series) momentum strategy using a wide set of securities. The authors confirm the possibility of predicting return rates on 58 asset classes: stock indices, currency pairs, futures and forward contracts for the delivery of goods, and government bonds within the period from one to twelve months. Geczy and Samonov (2015) consider the cross-section momentum effect on six asset classes of the US market on long-term series (215 years) and conclude the existence of an excess momentum return rate for all asset classes except commodities. Asness et al. (2013) also compare results for five asset classes from 1972 to 2011. The originality of their paper is in the juxtaposition of two elements of factor investment: the momentum effect and the value effect.

Despite revealing the effects of trend dynamics in many markets, the portfolio momentum effect (cross-section momentum) is of particular interest. The stock market formed this line of research.

Several interesting investment strategies considering both investor behaviour and return rate behaviour patterns have been offered for the bond market in recent years. For example, in financial media (Wall Street Journal[1], Forbes[2]), in open access materials of investment companies and funds (RBC Global Asset Management[3], Nuveen Asset Management[4]) one can find reference to 'rolling down the curve' strategy as the maturity date is approaching. The strategy suggests opening a long position on the issuer's second by maturity bond a few months before the redemption of the same issuer's first, by maturity, bond. The given strategy is based on the supposition that the money released by redemption of a short bond by the issuer is automatically allocated to the following by maturity bond, provided that the investor is confident in the issuer and in the general economic situation.

The first research analyzing the bond market with an attempt to reveal the momentum effect appeared relatively recently, in the middle of the 2000s. Gebhardt et al. (2005) initiate the research of this phenomenon in the US corporate bond market. January 1973–December 1996. Luu and Yu (2012) consider momentum as risk hedging.

Pospisil and Zhang (2010) also consider the US bond market. They conclude that the momentum strategy on the sample of investment grade bonds is more profitable (the yield is 0.53% per month, and the standard deviation of yield is 3.18%) compared to the 'against the market' strategy. The results of the momentum strategy are positive even assuming model adjustment for transaction costs. Testing a similar model on top-rated bonds demonstrates the opposite results: the reversal is more profitable.

Jostova et al. (2013) investigate the problem from a different perspective: the bonds of investment (81.67% of the sample) and non-investment (18.33%) grades are analyzed independently (9709 firms from 1973 to 2011). The authors conclude that the losers' strategy brought 0.53%, the winners' one 0.9%. The momentum effect is non-significant from 1973 to 1990, and it is significant from 1991 to 2011. Portfolio return rates increase nearly monotonically: from 0.32% for P1 to 0.91% for P10. The return rate increases over the course of time. The authors investigate if the obtained excess return rate covers systematic risk using the model by Fama and French (1993). The hypothesis of covering systematic risk is rejected. Including credit risk in the analysis, by means of checking several hypotheses, the authors find the following consistent pattern: the worse the credit rating of the bond, the higher the possibility of its inclusion in the winners'/losers' portfolio (74.83% of the bonds with D credit rating are included in P1 or P10 portfolios, compared to 11.61% of the bonds with A+ bonds). These observations make it possible to reveal correlation between credit rating and momentum effect, whereby the authors divide the bonds into quantiles according to credit rating, using the conditional momentum strategy. The decile portfolios are created inside each quantile, and the further procedures remain unchanged. The momentum effect of non-investment grade bonds is 1.21% and 1.92% in the periods 1973–1990 and 1991–2011 respectively. There is no momentum effect on investment grade bonds. The momentum effect of non-investment grade bonds increases over the course of time, which can be explained by the decline of the average credit rating of the portfolio. The bonds of private firms represent a larger share of the momentum effect than the bonds of public companies.

Geczy and Samonov (2015) analyze 47 stock indices, 48 currencies, 43 government bond indices, 76 commodities, and 301 global sectors on a monthly basis in the period from 1800 to 2014. The authors reveal that the momentum effect is significant for all the considered assets and their combinations, except the commodity market.

Asness et al. (2013) consider two strategies based on momentum effect and value investing. The sample is based on monthly statistics from January 1972 to July 2011 and includes the indicators of several countries, such as the US, Canada, UK, the countries of Continental Europe and Japan. The authors conclude that, in most cases, excess return take place both in applying momentum strategy and in the case of value effect. However, non-significant values of excess return are received on some portfolios, particularly on bonds.

Our research: investigating momentum anomaly in the Russian market

Further we present methodology, data and the results of testing the Russian market of government bonds for momentum anomaly. The bond market is ahead of the stock market in volume of raising external capital. For example, in 2016, raising by means of rouble bond issues by Russian non-financial companies is 1329 bn Rub against the negligible raising through the stock market (only 25 bn Rub in 2015; in peak 2007 it was 411 bn Rub). By trading volume the bond market ranks second after stocks in the domestic market.

Hypothesis

We investigate the possibility of building profitable momentum strategy on rouble government bonds. We investigate the influence of liquidity of bond issues, as well as the significance of macroeconomic factors in explaining the identified anomaly.

Data

The sample consists of weekly historical values of total monthly return rate (1) of corporate bonds of 303 domestic companies listed on the Moscow exchange (MOEX) in the period from January 15, 2010 to April 1, 2016.

$$r_{i,t} = \frac{(p_{i,t} + AI_{i,t} + Coupon_{i,t}) - (P_{i,t-1} + AI_{i,t-1})}{P_{i,t-1} + AI_{i,t-1}} \tag{17.1}$$

where $r_{i,t}$ is total monthly return rate, $P_{i,t}$ is the bond price at the end of the month, $AI_{i,t}$ is the accumulated coupon income at the end of the month, and $Coupon_{i,t}$ is the coupon paid in the period of $[t\text{-}1;t]$.

Weekly values of the total return rate are calculated based on daily statistics of bond weighted average prices, coupon yield and accumulated coupon income (ACI)[5]. In initial time-series, there are omissions in data resulting in development of the methodology on restoring the omitted values. Restoring of omitted data is made for the weighted average price and ACI using the same procedure: the previous value of the corresponding indicators is used instead of the omitted value, regardless of the length of the omitted values interval.

Using such a filter allows avoiding wrong calculation of a part of excess return, if it could not be received because of lack of trades on a particular trading day.

Besides, the existence of omitted values in the sample makes it possible to place liquid bonds into a separate group. We classify a bond as a liquid one if the number of successive omitted values of quotations in the initial sample does not exceed 5 trading days; otherwise a security belongs to the group of non-liquid financial instruments. The list of liquid securities is represented by 25 corporate bonds, the average daily Bid-Ask on which is 0.89% of par value, and the median indicator of spread reaches 0.5%, which is illustrative of low liquidity of the bond market compared to 'blue chips' of the stock market (Table 17.1). Thus, for example, the relative Bid-Ask spread for May 2016 of the stocks of Gazprom PJSC[6] and Lukoil PJSC[7] is estimated at less than 0.01%, compared to the Bid-Ask spread indicators on the bonds of these companies (0.29% and 0.61% correspondingly). The average volume of liquid bonds emission slightly exceeds 5 bn Rub, given that the state is among the owners in four of the companies only.

Table 17.1 Composition of portfolios from 2010 to 2016

Period	*2010*	*2011*	*2012*	*2013*	*2014*	*2015*	*2016*
Number of bond issues, pcs	167	190	208	226	226	228	228
Number of liquid bonds in the sample, pcs	16	12	9	10	10	12	12
Number of bond issues not meeting the requirement of liquidity, pcs	151	178	199	216	216	216	216

The test procedure on momentum effect existence is initially made across the entire sample. The same procedure is further applied to liquid bonds. In both sub-samples, the number of companies pretending to being included in one of the portfolios – winners or losers – varied depending on the bonds listed in the exchange in the relevant period (Table 17.1).

Strategies

The following strategies are tested in our study:

1) The classical momentum strategy based on the methodology by Jegadeesh and Titman (1993), implying opening a long position on relative past winners and opening a short position on losers;
2) The classical reversal strategy (a reversal or upstream one) implying opening a long position on losers and a short one on winners;
3) The modified or 'partial' strategy implying opening only a long position on past relative winners;
4) The modified procedure of reversal strategy implying opening a long position on past relative losers.

We estimate the investment results according to a standard design of strategies (for example, in accordance with Jegadeesh and Titman, 1993; Jostova et al., 2013) in order to obtain comparable conclusions, and search the best strategy by varying analysis windows and percentiles, both by the return rate maximization criterion and by the risk minimizing criterion.

The specifics of strategies developing (using the algorithm of searching for three time windows) allows us to make some essential conclusions. First, the estimation of excess return obtained according to the results of classical strategies (strategies 1 and 2) allows comparing the values of abnormal return rate to the results of similar tests in the American market of corporate bonds. Secondly, the modified strategies provide for the possibility of using the elaborated model in the Russian market whose activity is regulated by restrictions on short selling. Before January 14, 2016 the quarterly list of liquid securities permitted for margin trading on the Moscow exchange was formed according to the Order of the FFMS of Russia No. 06-25/pz-n dated March 7, 2006, On Approval of Regulation on Criteria of Securities Liquidity[8].

As the sampling period of our research is synchronized with the validity period of the stated Order, it is reasonable to consider the scenario in which opening short positions on corporate bonds is impossible (strategies 3 and 4).

Results

For each of the four strategies we build 217 portfolios (weekly opening of the investment position on the entire analysis period considered). The period of monitoring the historical bond yield varies from 1 to 12 months (this is the monitoring period or the period for ranking portfolios), the time lag (skipping investment activity) changes from 0 to 8 weeks, and the investment period (holding a portfolio) takes on values from 1 to 12 months. Besides, we consider different percentiles for including the bonds in 'extreme' portfolios – relative winners and losers. The analysis is built on comparison of percentiles according to value 10%, 20%, 30%, and 50%. Therefore, changing the combination of three windows of the investment strategy and four percentiles, the comparative analysis is built by 6480 strategies. Brokers and stock exchange commissions in this research are not included in the analysis. Adjustment of the results for benchmark yield does not take place.

A) Classical procedure of momentum investment (arbitrage portfolio)

The results of the classical momentum strategy (strategy 1) built on the entire sample of 303 Russian bonds in the MOEX, with standard parameters (traditionally used in previously made researches – 16 strategies) of the monitoring period (3, 6, 9, and 12 months), of the time lag (0 months), of the investment period (3, 6, 9, and 12 months), with winners' and losers' decile portfolios (the first and the last 10% of the sample) are presented in Table 17.2. The general conclusion is that momentum strategy in the Russian bond market is unprofitable. The same conclusion is confirmed on the rest of the percentiles (20%, 30%, 40%, and 50%): all the strategies demonstrate statistically significant, but unprofitable results. Profitable strategies are the upstream ones: long positions should be opened on past losers and short ones on past winners, and such

Table 17.2 Average monthly return rate of arbitrage portfolios (Win-Los) built on the entire sample of corporate bonds

Monitoring period, months	*Investment period, months*	*Win-Los yield, %*	*t-statistics Win-Los*
3	3	-11.07%	66.70***[9]
	6	-2.54%	26.04***
	9	-3.01%	42.69***
	12	-1.99%	33.16***
6	3	-6.68%	34.25***
	6	-1.79%	17.41***
	9	-2.48%	28.04***
	12	-0.84%	14.23***
9	3	-9.01%	49.80***
	6	-2.79%	25.95***
	9	-2.37%	37.79***
	12	-1.99%	31.28***
12	3	-7.87%	38.45***
	6	-1.19%	12.29***
	9	-2.67%	32.88***
	12	-1.00%	16.07***

Significance levels: * p <10%, ** p <5%, *** p <1%

investment will bring significant positive returns. Average yields of the stated strategies (3/0/3, 3/0/6[10] etc.) will be positive at 1% level of significance (Table 17.2).

Nevertheless, the investor can take profit from momentum investment extending the period of portfolio building and changing the lag length. The acceptable results on the return rate are received in case of the momentum strategy with the monitoring period of 12 months, the time lag of 3 weeks and the investment period of 3 months (12/0,75/3), with the 10% criterion of selecting 'extreme' portfolios. Average monthly yield of such a strategy is 2.28%. The most profitable strategy developed on the entire sample brings monthly income of 8.71% (t-stat = 68.12***). Provided that the strategy is characterized by the following parameters: the monitoring period of historical yield is 11 months, the time lag is 2 months, and the investment is made within the following 4 months (Table 17.3). The average monthly return rate of winners' portfolio is 7.18%, and the return rate of losers' portfolio is negative and comprises -1.53%. The unique character of the results of this strategy is that it brings positive return rates on all the portfolios on the whole perspective of the analysis, which is not often obtained in the market of other financial instruments (Figure 17.1). All the portfolios of this strategy design demonstrate positive return rates, and their average return rate is 8.71% per month.

We also consider the results of the best strategy according to t-statistics value. When using this criterion, the best reversal strategy brings a monthly return rate of 11.59%.

Investment within a month after the 12-month selection of the worst and of the best on the 'against the trend' strategy provides for maximum monthly return rate (30%). We note that it is a hypothetical return rate that could be earned by opening short positions. It is impossible to ensure real investment on this strategy (there are no possibilities of margin trading on corporate bonds in Russia). The rest of the indicators of the strategies considered are presented in Table 17.3.

Table 17.3 The results of the most profitable, the best by t-statistics momentum strategy and of the reversal strategy for the entire sample of corporate bonds[11]

	Momentum strategy		*The most profitable reversal strategy*
	The most profitable	*The best by t-statistics*	
Formation period, months	11	10	12
Time lag, months	2	0	0
Investment period, months	4	3	1
Decile (the share of Win and Los, included in the portfolio), %	10%	40%	10%
Monthly return rate of Win-Los (Los-Win for the reversal), %	8.71%	11.59%	30.07%
t-statistics	68.12***	171.66***	72.50***

Significance levels: * p <10%, ** p <5%, *** p <1%

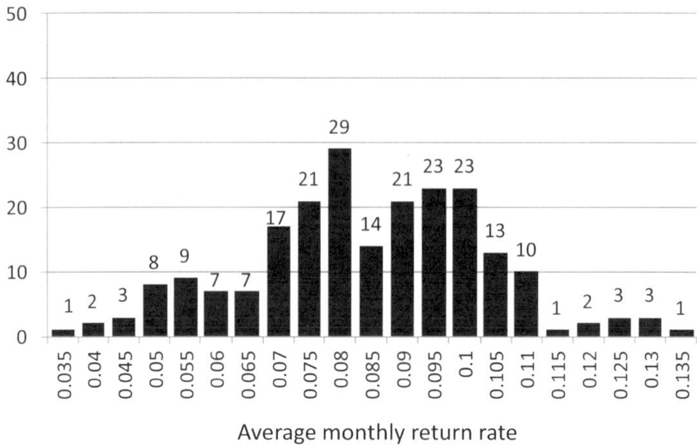

Figure 17.1 Distribution of portfolios by average monthly return rate for the most profitable strategy built on the sample of Russian bonds.

On the sample of liquid bonds, the standard design of momentum strategies also shows negative yield. The return rates are lower than on the entire sample.

The selection of the best strategy is performed in a similar way to the entire sample. In contrast to the results on the entire sample, the return rates obtained on liquid bonds for the most part are not significant at the acceptable levels of significance. Besides, the maximum statistically significant monthly return rate turns out to be lower and comprised 1.16%, compared to 2.28% of monthly return rate on the entire sample. The best strategy on liquid bonds brings the lowest return rate of 6.31% against 8.71%. Against-the-market strategies demonstrate the best results.

B) Modified strategy (without short positions)

Due to restriction on margin bond trading in the Russian market, the results of the modified momentum strategy implying opening long positions only are of practical interest. This strategy is better adapted to the realities of the domestic market, and that is why the findings can be used for development of real trade strategies.

The first stage of the analysis does not meet expectations: as in the case with the classical momentum strategy, when using standard parameters of the strategy design (the monitoring period is 3, 6, 9, 12 months, the time lag is 0 months, the investment period is 3, 6, 9, 12 months, the parameter of decile portfolios is 10% of the sample), negative indicators of return rate are obtained on the entire sample. Our conclusions remain the same: the reversal momentum effect is functioning in the Russian market.

Investment in past winners on the sample of solely liquid corporate bonds also causes lossmaking results.

Comparison to the results of similar researches

In most of the modern researches, the nature of the momentum effect is studied in the American market. The papers focused on government and corporate bonds are in roughly equal proportions. Due to the absence of other similar researches, the only available variant is comparing the results to the conclusions stated in the papers on the American market.

Unlike our research, almost all the authors use the unaltered approach by Jegadeesh and Titman (1993): in the research papers of Kim (2012) and Jostova et al. (2013), all the considered models apply the 6/1/6 strategy with formation of winners' and losers' portfolios as 10% of the entire sample. Pospisil and Zhang (2010) vary the length of the observation and the investment periods, and the rest of the variables are similar to the standard ones. Inclusion of the search algorithm in our analysis allows comparing the assessment criteria (return rate and risk), as well as testing the result sustainability.

Monthly return rate obtained in the Russian market is higher in relation to possible results obtained in the American market: 8.71% as against maximum 0.59%. In general, the higher return rate in the Russian market can be explained firstly by the higher country risk and, secondly, by currency of securities, i.e. the Russian rouble against the US dollar.

To reveal possible correlations between the return rate of the best strategy and the real situation in the Russian economy and, particularly, in the financial market, we conduct an analysis of factors influencing the profitability of momentum strategies. Presumably, explanatory variables are:

- *Inflation rate*[12]. Possibility of obtaining positive return rate is provided due to an increase in prices in the economy, but not to internal reasons or momentum effect.
- *Return rate of IFX-Cbonds index.* The index is calculated on the basis of 30 most liquid corporate bonds issued in roubles and being not less than 5% of total market capitalization. Overlapping of the market winners list and the largest and liquid issues is possible.
- *Return rate of MICEX index.* The consideration of this parameter is stipulated by the possibility of slower reaction of the corporate bond market to changes in the economy affecting the stock performance.
- *Yield of mid-term and short-term GKO-OFZ bonds.* It is assumed that the high yield in the corporate bond market is caused either by the low yield in the government bond market regarded as an alternative investment instrument or, on the contrary, by their growth, which can be explained by synchronicity of government and corporate bond market sectors. Resultant dependence is stipulated by prevalence of one of the stated dependences in the given period.

- *Yield of one-year and 10-year state bonds.* The justification of these factors' inclusion is similar to the previous paragraph.
- *Foreign capital inflows/outflows to the funds investing in the Russian securities.* As corporate bonds are one of the most attractive investment instruments, it is assumed that there is a direct correlation between the yield and this indicator. The research includes absolute values of inflows/outflows and the cumulative results.

To reduce non-stationarity of time-series, all the variables are transformed by means of calculation of absolute increases. According to the results of the checkup test, all the series are found to be stationary on the Dickey–Fuller test.

As a result of the correlation analysis, significant dependences are not found. Maximal correlation is reached on the variables of 'return rate of the best momentum strategy' and 'return rate of MICEX index' and represented -0.0903, which is not enough to claim the existence of correlation between the indicators (Table 17.4).

The nature of dependence between the analyzed variables is also tested by construction of sliding correlations with the calculation period of six months (24 weeks); the Granger causality test is made (from one to five lags). According to the results of the sliding correlations analysis, significant correlations in regards to the market or to specific aspects of indicators are not identified: correlation of the return rate of the best momentum strategy (11/2/4, 10% percentile) with each of the considered variables is from -0.44 to +0.61, for the majority of variables, and negative correlation is increasing by the end of the reviewed period. The Granger test does not reveal any leading dependences of factors in relation to the stated return rate. However, the return rate of the best momentum strategy

Table 17.4 Correlations of return rate of the best momentum strategy and macroeconomic factors

Factor	*Variable*	*Correlation of return rate of the best momentum strategy and the factor*
Inflation in % to the previous period	cpi	-0.0176
Return rate of IFX-Cbonds index	ifx	0.0454
Return rate of MICEX index	micex	-0.0903
Yield of long-term GKO-OFZ bonds	ofzm	-0.0791
Yield of mid-term GKO-OFZ bonds	ofzl	-0.0240
Yield of one-year government bonds	oneg	-0.0551
Yield of 10-year government bonds	teng	-0.0099
Foreign capital inflows/outflows to the funds investing in the Russian securities, absolute value	fund	0.0176
Foreign capital inflows/outflows to the funds investing in the Russian securities, cumulative value	fundc	-0.0389

proves to be leading in relation to the inflation rate (5% level of significance) and to the MICEX index (10% level of significance).

The attempt to explain the return rate of momentum investment through retrograding to macroeconomic factors is unsuccessful. We conclude that the return rates of the strategies on the past investment results (momentum and reversal) in the Russian market should be accepted as anomalies, and not explainable by the dynamics of macroeconomic and financial indicators.

Recommendations to practitioners on selecting windows for developing the reversal strategy

As we conclude that realization of the reversal strategy (opening long positions on part losers) is reasonable in the Russian market, let us comment on the recommendations regarding design selection (Figures 17.2–17.4). The least dispersion of return rates across the reviewed strategies takes place in the case of the average monitoring period; the return rate in relation to the monitoring period is shifted to positive values. Return rate distribution depending on the lag is equal (Figure 17.3); it is shifted to negative values with the growth of the time lag. The highest dispersion of return rate is revealed on short investment periods (Figure 17.4); the risk of receiving negative return rate of momentum investment is reduced with the growth of the investment period.

Regression of momentum return rate to the stated factors shows acceptable results (at 1% level of significance), the determination coefficient is more than 0.3, and all the explanatory variables prove to be significant at 1% level. Such results indicate the significance of the stated factors for developing the reversal momentum strategy.

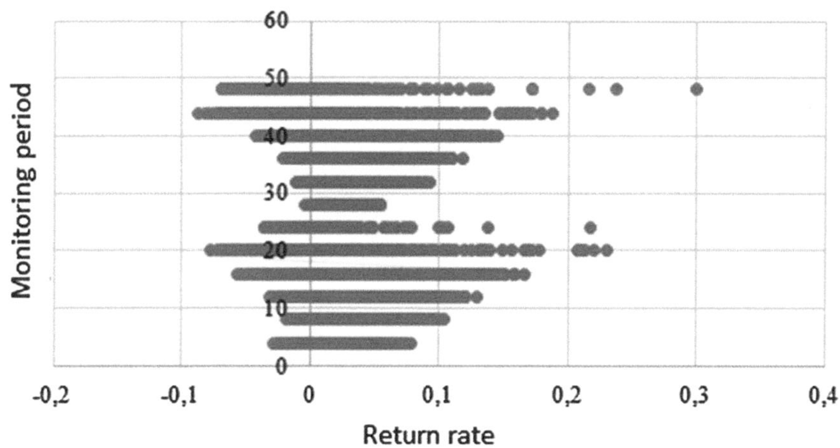

Figure 17.2 Correlation of the reversal momentum strategy return rate and the monitoring period.

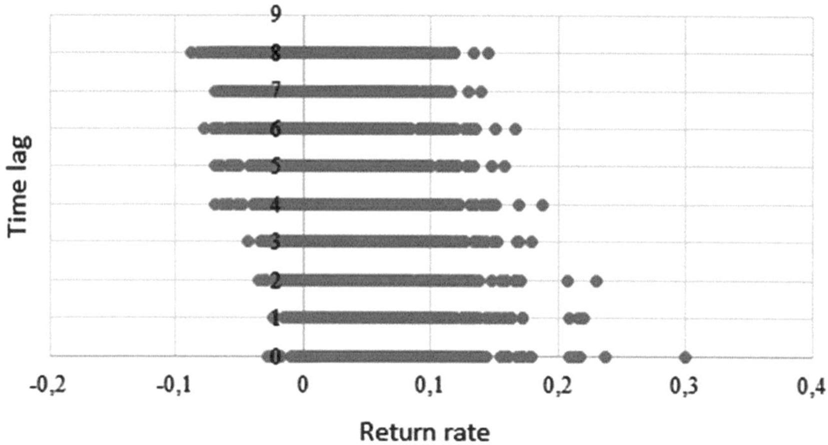

Figure 17.3 Correlation of the reversal momentum strategy return rate and the time lag.

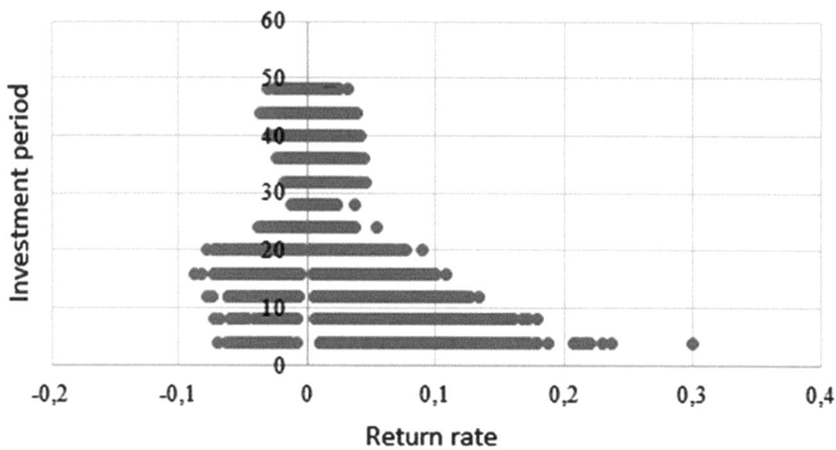

Figure 17.4 Correlation of the reversal momentum strategy return rate and the investment period.

Conclusions

According to the results of research of the Russian corporate bond market, we prove the anomaly in the yield behaviour when monitoring past investment results allows developing profitable trade strategies. The use of the standard design while developing strategies shows the existence of the reversal effect: the strategies with opening long investment positions on past relative losers and short positions on past winners are profitable. This general conclusion is consistent with the conclusions made by Jostova et al. (2013) for the American corporate bond market.

The best return rate results are also demonstrated by the strategy adopted for the Russian market conditions and providing opening solely long positions on losers. We explain the result by the fact that corporate bonds are highly attractive for the Russian institutional investors. In the period from 2013 to the first quarter of 2016, government and corporate bonds prevailed in investment structure of Pension Fund of the Russian Federation (PFRF) and Non-State Pension Fund (NSPF): by the end of the first quarter of 2016, the investment of PFRF in corporate bonds was 38.9% and the investment of NSPF was 42.6%. Such performance of indicators explains both significant trading volume on the considered instruments and the possibility of obtaining excess return in the corporate bond market. The policy of the Central Bank of the Russian Federation allowed earning approximately 3–5% of positive real yield at an annual rate in the bond market. Such a great demand for bonds created a situation of overestimation.

Our conclusion is consistent with the results of the researches in the American market, where the bonds of non-investment rating and of relatively low liquidity demonstrate such anomalies in price formation. In the Russian market, the impact of past investment results is demonstrated both by the entire sample of bonds and by the sample of low liquid bonds, the test results on which are more obvious.

Notes

1 Lin, C. (2013). Taking a trip down the yield curve. The Wall Street Journal, March 17. URL: www.wsj.com/articles/SB10001424127887324532004578362960303777092.
2 Proccer, M. (2013). One of the most profitable strategies in bond investing. Forbes, February 4. URL: www.forbes.com/sites/marcprosser/2013/02/04/one-of-the-most-profitable-strategies-in-bond-investing/#165902b216a0.
3 A simple strategy for boosting fixed income returns: Rolling down the yield curve. (2012). RBC Global Asset Management. URL: http://funds.rbcgam.com/pdf/di/articles/rbc-etfs-fixed-income-strategy_e.pdf.
4 Riding the yield curve in up and down markets. (2019). Nuveen. URL: www.nuveen.com/Home/Documents/Default.aspx?fileId=18769.
5 Data source: Cbonds Financial Information URL: http://ru.cbonds.info/. Accessed date: May 15, 2019.
6 Data source: Cbonds Group – Investfunds. URL: http://stocks.investfunds.ru/stocks/25/. Accessed date: May 15, 2019.
7 Data source: Cbonds Group – Investfunds. URL: http://stocks.investfunds.ru/stocks/7/. Accessed date: May 15, 2019.
8 The Archive of list of liquid securities // The Moscow Exchange. URL: http://moex.com/a3581. Accessed date: May 15, 2016.
9 From now on * 10% level of significance, ** 5% level of significance, *** 1% level of significance.
10 From now on the design of the strategy is defined as monitoring period/time lag of opening the investment position/investment period.
11 Win is the winners' portfolio, Los is the losers' portfolio, Win-Loss is the winners' return rate minus the losers' rate.
12 Monthly data; reduced to weekly data by means of restoring the missing values by using trend.

References

Asness, C. S., Moskowitz, T. J., Pedersen, L. H. (2013). Value and momentum everywhere. *The Journal of Finance*, LXVIII (3): 929–986. DOI: https://doi.org/10.1111/jofi.12021

Antonacci, G. (2013). Absolute momentum: A simple rule-based strategy and universal trend-following overlay. Available at SSRN: http://dx.doi.org/10.2139/ssrn.2244633

De Bondt, W. F. M., Thaler R. (1985). Does the stock market overreact? *The Journal of Finance*, 40(3): 793–805. DOI: https://doi.org/10.1111/j.1540-6261.1985.tb05004.x

Fama, E. F., French, K. R. (1993). Common risk factors in the returns on stocks and bonds. *Journal of Financial Economics*, 33, 3–56. DOI: https://doi.org/10.1016/0304-405X(93)90023-5

Gebhardt, W. R., Hvidkjaer, S., Swaminathan, B. (2005). Stock and bond market interaction: Does momentum spill over? *Journal of Financial Economics*, 75: 651–690. DOI: https://doi.org/10.1016/j.jfineco.2004.03.005

Geczy, C. C., Samonov, M. (2015). 215 years of global multi-asset momentum: 1800–2014. URL: http://papers.ssrn.com/sol3/papers.cfm?abstract_id=2607730

Haan, L., Kakes, J. (2011). Momentum or contrarian investment strategies: Evidence from Dutch institutional investors. *Journal of Banking and Finance*, 35(9): 2245–2251. DOI: https://doi.org/10.1111/j.1540-6288.2007.00186.x

Jegadeesh, N., Titman, S. (1993). Returns to buying winners and selling losers: Implications for stock market efficiency. *The Journal of Finance*, 48(1): 65–91. DOI: https://doi.org/10.1111/j.1540-6261.1993.tb04702.x

Jostova, G., Nikolova, S., Philipov, A., Stahel, C. W. (2013). Momentum in corporate bond returns. *The Review of Financial Studies*, 26(7): 1649–1693. DOI: https://doi.org/10.1093/rfs/hht022

Kaminsky, G., Lyons, R., Schmukler, S. (2004). Managers, investors, and crises: Mutual fund strategies in emerging markets. *Journal of International Economics*, 64(1): 113–134. DOI: https://doi.org/10.1016/S0022-1996(03)00075-8

Kim, D. (2012). Cross-asset style momentum. *Asia-Pacific Journal of Financial Studies*, 41(5): 610–636. https://doi.org/10.1111/j.2041-6156.2012.01084.x

Kim, W., Wei, S. -J. (1999). Offshore investment funds: Monsters in emerging markets? NBER Working Paper; No. 7133.

Luu, B. V., Yu, P. (2012). Momentum in government-bond markets. *The Journal of Fixed Income*, 22(2): 72–79. DOI: https://doi.org/10.3905/jfi.2012.22.2.072

Moskowitz, T. J., Ooi, Y. H., Pedersen, L. H. (2012). Time series momentum. *Journal of Financial Economics*, 104: 228–250. DOI: https://doi.org/10.1016/j.jfineco.2011.11.003

Pospisil, L., Zhang, J. (2010). Momentum and reversal effects in corporate bond prices and credit cycles. *Journal of Fixed Income*, 20(2): 101–115. DOI: https://doi.org/10.3905/jfi.2010.20.2.101

Richardson, S. (2018). Big Data in Fixed Income Markets? AQR Capital Management, LLC. URL: https://www.ipfos.eu/wp-content/uploads/2018/11/AQR-Big-Data-in-FI-Markets-vPrint.pdf

Teplova, T.V., Mikova, E.S. (2019). Investments on market inefficiencies and behavioral bias INFRA-M. Russia, Moscow. (In Rus.) ISBN: 978-5-16-016043-6

Part 7

Analytical and information databases: algorithms of work

18 Eikon Refinitiv, Bloomberg and Cbonds databases for solving research problems

The description of the algorithms is presented in Tables 18.1–18.11.

Table 18.1 Searching and analyzing data on outstanding bonds for a given date (present or past)

The algorithm in Eikon Refinitiv	*The algorithm in Bloomberg*	*The algorithm in Cbonds*
1. Press the  button, in the drop-down menu choose *Search Tools*, then *Government & Corp Bonds*. 2. In the new window *Government and Corporate Bond Search* set the parameters of filtering the list of bonds (by pressing the *Edit Filter* button beside the name of the required column). For example, you can choose the following parameters: *Issuer Type = Corporate* (for corporate bonds); *Asset Status Include Issued* (for currently outstanding bonds) or choose *Issued and Expired/Matured* (to include bonds that were outstanding in the past); *Issuer Contains the issuer name* (if you need to find data on one or more issuers; for example, *Gazprom* for PAO GAZPROM and its subsidiaries); *Principal Currency Include Currencies* (for example, *US Dollar* and *Russian Rouble*); *Issue Date Before of Equal to* (for example, December 31, 2016 for bonds, issued until the end of 2016);	1. In the command line indicate *SRCH* function to work with bonds. 2. Set the bond filtering parameters. For example, you can set the following parameters: *Asset Classes = Corporates* (for corporate bonds); *Security Status Include Active* (to show only currently outstanding bonds) or choose *Active, N/A and Matured* (to show all bonds, incl. outstanding in the past); *Issuer Name Include names of the issuers* (if we need to find data for one or several issuers; for example, *GAZPRU* for PAO Gazprom); *Currency Include currency* (examples: *USD, RUB*); *Issue Date Less Than* Date in the MM/DD/YYYY format (example: December 31, 2016 for bonds issued before 2016);	1. In the left menu go to section *Bonds→Bond search.* 2. Set the parameters of bond filtration. For example, you can choose the following columns: *Country* of the bond issuer; *Sector* (sovereign, municipal or corporate); *Issue market* (Domestic or International); *Currency*; *End of placement to* (Example: December 31, 2016 for bonds issued before this date); *Maturity from* (Example: December 31, 2016 means bonds that matured after 2016, in conjunction with the previously mentioned filter by the end of placement, we get bonds that were outstanding on the date in the past).

Table 18.1 Cont.

The algorithm in Eikon Refinitiv	*The algorithm in Bloomberg*	*The algorithm in Cbonds*
Maturity After or Equal to (for example, December 31, 2016 for bonds that are matured after the end of 2016, in conjunction with the above-mentioned filter *Issue Date* you obtain bonds that were outstanding on the chosen date in the past); *Country of Borrower* is the country of the actual borrower. It allows us to find Eurobonds (even if they are issued via SPV). *Country of Issue* is the market where the Eurobonds are traded (for Eurobonds the value is *Eurobond Markets*); *Country of Incorporation* is the country of the bond issuer; this filter in conjunction with *Country of Issue* allows you to find bonds of national corporations that are traded on the local market. 3. For the list of bonds, it is possible to set the displayed columns by clicking beside the *Add/Remove Columns* field. For example, you can pick the following columns to be displayed: *Issuer* is the name of the issuer; *Ticker* is a unique ID of the issuer; *ISIN* is a bond's international security identification number; *Preferred RIC* is the bond's unique code from Eikon; *Coupon* is the coupon rate; *Issue Date* is the date of initial placement; *Maturity* is the date of maturity; *Principal Currency* is the bond's currency; *Amount Issued* is the issue volume. 4. To export the list of bonds in Excel, choose the menu item → *Export All.*	*Maturity Greater Than* Date in MM/DD/YYYY format (Example: 12/31/2016 for bonds that are matured after 2016, together with the filter by *Issue Date* you obtain bonds that were outstanding in the past); *Country of Risk* – the country of the issuer. This filter lets us to find not only bonds on local market, but also Eurobonds (even if they were issued with the help of SPV). 3. After setting the bond data filtration parameters click *Results* button. You will get a list of bonds. 4. On the *Results* tab you can edit the displayed columns by choosing the menu item *Settings→Edit Columns.* For example, you can choose the following columns: *Issuer Name* – the name of the issuer; *Ticker* is a unique ID of the issuer; *Bloomberg ID* is a bond's Bloomberg database ID; *ISIN* is the bond's international security identification number; *Series* is the series of the bond; *Coupon* is the coupon rate; *Issue Date* is the date of the first placement; *Maturity* is the bond maturity date; *Currency* is the bond currency; *Amount Issued* is the volume of the issue. To return to the list of bonds, click *<Menu> to Return.* 5. To export the list of bonds in Excel, choose the menu item *Actions→ Export to Excel.*	3. After setting the filtration parameters click *Search.* A list of bonds will be displayed. 4. For the list of bonds, you can set the displayed columns by choosing the menu item *Show/Hide column.* For example, you can choose following columns: *Issuer;* *Issue volume;* *Coupon rate;* *Frequency of coupon payments;* *Currency;* *ISIN;* *Issue status, i.e. Outstanding* or *Matured.* Press the *Apply* button to update the list of bonds. 5. To export the list of bonds in Excel, click *Excel.*

Table 18.2 Searching and analyzing data on new bond issue placements

The algorithm in Eikon Refinitiv	*The algorithm in Bloomberg*	*The algorithm in Cbonds*
1. Click , in the drop-down menu, choose *Search Tools*, then *Government & Corp Bonds*. 2. In the new window *Government and Corporate Bond Search* set the filter parameters of the bonds list (by clicking *Edit Filter* beside the name of the required column). Like the algorithm mentioned above (for outstanding bonds), you can choose the following parameters: *Issuer Type*; *Asset Status*; *Issuer Contains* the name of the issuer; *Principal Currency Include* bond currency; *Issue Date Between Date1 and Date2* (Example: January 1, 2016 and December 31, 2016 accordingly – for bonds, issued in 2016); *Country of Borrower;* *Country of Issue*; *Country of Incorporation.* 3. For the list of bonds, you can edit the list of displayed columns by clicking beside the *Add/Remove Columns* field. 4. To export the list of bonds in Excel, choose the menu item → *Export All.*	1. In the command line indicate the function *SRCH* to work with the list of bonds. 2. Set the filtration parameters (the key filter is *Issue Date*). Like in the previous algorithm (for outstanding bonds), you can edit the following parameters: *Asset Classes*; *Issuer Name Include* the name of the issuer, *Currency Include* bond currency; *Issue Date in the Range of Date1 and Date2* in MM/DD/YYYY format (Example: January 1, 2016 and December 31, 2016 accordingly – for bonds, issued in 2016); *Country of Risk.* 3. After setting the filtration parameters, click *Results.* You will get the list of bonds. 4. On the *Results* tab you can edit the displayed columns by choosing the menu item *Settings→Edit Columns.* 5. To export the list of bonds in Excel, choose the menu item *Actions→ Export to Excel.*	1. In the left menu go to the section *Bonds→ Bond search.* 2. Set the bond filtration parameters (the key parameter is *End of placement*). Like the previous algorithm (for outstanding bonds), you can choose the following parameters: *Country*; *Industry*; *Issuer* contains the name of issuer; *Currency*; *End of placement from* Date1 *to* Date2. 3. After setting bond filtration parameters, click *Search.* The list of bonds will be displayed. 4. To edit the displayed columns, choose the menu item *Show / hide columns.* 5. To export the list of bonds in Excel, click *Excel.*

Table 18.3 Searching and analyzing data on matured bonds

The algorithm in Eikon Refinitiv	*The algorithm in Bloomberg*	*The algorithm in Cbonds*
The instruction is executed analogously to the previous one for new bond issues, but as the filtration parameters you should indicate: *Maturity Between* Date1 *and* Date2 (for example, January 1, 2016 and December 31, 2016 accordingly for bonds matured in 2016).	The instruction is executed analogously to the previous one for new bond issues, but as the filtration parameters you should indicate: *Maturity in the Range of* Data1 *and* Date2 in the MM/DD/YYYY format (for example, January 1, 2016 and December 31, 2016 accordingly for bonds matured in 2016).	The instruction is executed analogously to the previous one for new bond issues, but as the filtration parameters you should indicate: *Maturity from* Date1 *to* Date2.

Table 18.4 Searching and analyzing data on bond historic yields to maturity and yields at pricing

The algorithm in Eikon Refinitiv	*The algorithm in Bloomberg*	*The algorithm in Cbonds*
Above we presented instructions that allow you to export data of the bonds into Excel. Suppose that in the *A1* cell you have a bond ISIN, by which you need to export data on the bond YTM in 2017. To do so: 1. In Excel, go to *Thomson Reuters* tab, connect to Eikon by clicking *Login* and enter your login and password. 2. Based on ISIN obtain the bond RIC (a unique ID in TR Eikon), by entering the following formula in *A2* (or another cell): *=TR(A1;"TR.RIC";"CODE=ISIN NULL=BLANK")*` 3. Click *Build Formula* on *Thomson Reuters* tab. In the window *Formula Builder* set the parameters: - in the field *Instruments* reference to the cell *A2*, where the bond RIC is placed (by clicking ▦ beside *Instruments*); - click ▦ *Time Series* to display historic data; - in the left block *Category* choose *Yield to maturity*; - in the central block *Fields* click *Add* beside the variable *Timestamp* and *Close* (to load two columns – date and yield to maturity, accordingly); - to the right from the block *Parameters & Quick Functions* in the fields *Start* and *End* choose *January 1, 2017* and *December 31, 2017*. - click the *Insert* button.	Above we presented instructions that allow you to export data of the bonds into Excel. Suppose that in the cell *A1* you have a bond ticker, by which you need to get the bond YTM in 2017. The bond ticker should be indicated as a Bloomberg ID with the addition of *« Corp»*. For example, if *Bloomberg ID* is equal to *AP596774*, then you can use the following function to obtain the bond's ticker: *CONCATENATE(«AP596774»; «_ Corp»)*. Next: 1. In Excel go to the *Bloomberg* tab, choose *Function Builder*. 2. A field to enter a function's name will appear. Choose the function *BDH* to export historical data.`	To export the historical YTM: 1. In the left menu go to the section *Prices→By Trading Systems*. 2. Set the filtration parameters of bond quotes. You can set the following parameters: *Stock Exchange*; *Sector* of the issuer (sovereign, municipal or corporate); *Industry* of the issuer; *Issue market* (*Domestic bonds* or *International bonds*); *Currency of issue*; *Issue* (if you need to obtain information on one or several selected issues); *Search method*: *on a certain date* or *over a period of time* (in the last case you can get information for only one bond issue). *Trade date* or the period of trade; 3. Click *Search*. You will get the results. 4. In the list of bond quotes click *Search parameters* and choose *YTM (close)*. 5. To export data in Excel, click *Save in Excel format*. To export data on yield at pricing: 1. In the left menu choose *Bonds→Bond search*. 2. Set the filtration parameters (the detailed instructions are provided above).

(*continued*)

Table 18.4 Cont.

The algorithm in Eikon Refinitiv	*The algorithm in Bloomberg*	*The algorithm in Cbonds*
As an alternative, you can directly enter the following formula into an Excel cell: *=RHistory(A2;"YLDTOMAT.Timestamp; YLDTOMAT.Close";"START:01-Jan-2017 END:31-Dec-2017 INTERVAL:1D CONVERTCODE:YES";;"TSREPEAT:NO")* where *A2* refers to the cell with the bond RIC, *YLDTOMAT.Timestamp* and *YLDTOMAT.Close are* names (codes) of the date and YTM fields, *START* and *END* are the start and the end dates of the data to be exported, *INTERVAL* is the frequency of the data (in our example it is daily). To obtain the bond yield at pricing, let us review the following algorithm. Suppose you have already loaded the following data in Excel: Cell *C1* contains the bond's *ISIN*; *D1* contains *Issue Price* (in %); *E1* contains *Issue Date* (in DD.MM.YYYY format); *F1* contains *Maturity* (in DD.MM.YYYY format); *G1* contains *Coupon Rate* (in %). Then in the cell *I1* (or in another cell by the user's choice) you should add an additional formula to obtain the parameters of bond issue: *=TR(C1;"TR.ADF_BONDSTRUCTURE";;)* In the J1 cell add an additional formula for coupon rate parameters: *=TR(C1;"TR.ADF_RATESTRUCTURE";;)* And lastly, in the H1 enter the formula to calculate the bond yield of pricing: *=AdBondYield(D1;E1%;F1;G1%;I1;J1)*	3. Set the parameters of *BDH* function. As the first parameter set the *A1* cell in Excel, where you have the bond ticker, or you can manually enter the bond name. For example, «*GAZPRU 8.625 04/28/2034 REGS CORP*». The second parameter is the name (code) of the YTM variable in Bloomberg database: *YLD_YTM_MID*. The third and the fourth parameters of the *BDH* function are the start and the end dates of the period, for which you need to export data (in our example you should set *January 1, 2017* and *December 31, 2017* accordingly). Click *Ok*. As an alternative, you can directly enter the following formula in Excel: *=BDH(A1; «YLD_YTM_MID»; «01/01/2017»; «12/31/2017»)* where *A1* refers to the cell with the bond ticker. To obtain the bond yield at pricing, you should use the following function: *=BDP(A1;"YIELD_ON_ISSUE_DATE")* where *A1* refers to the cell with the bond ticker.	3. Click *Search*. The list of bonds will be displayed. 4. To set the list of displayed columns, choose the menu item *Show /Hide columns*. In the list of displayed columns, you should include the *Yield at pricing*. 5. To export the list of bonds in Excel, click *Excel*.

Table 18.5 Searching and analyzing data on defaults and recovery rates

The algorithm in Eikon Refinitiv	*The algorithm in Bloomberg*	*The algorithm in Cbonds*
To search data on defaults, you should open the list of bonds and fill in the required filters to limit the sample (for example, by country, issue date, currency etc.). The main principles of working with the list of bonds are explained above (refer to search algorithms of outstanding or new bond issues). Next in the list of bonds you should choose (with the help of *Add/Remove Columns* option) the column *Asset Status*. Filter by *Asset Status* column by the value *In Default*. To export the list of defaulted bonds, in Excel you should click →*Export All*. You can see the default date details for the chosen bond. To do so, you should click *Description* tab and in the section *Schedules & History* → *Asset Status History* look up the date of the status change to *In Default*. The recovery rate can be calculated based on the market approach by exporting to Excel the historic bond quotes after a certain period from the default date (for example, after 30 days). The algorithm of exporting historic bond quotes is analogous to historic YTM (see above).	To search for data on defaults, you should open the list of bonds and fill in the required filters to limit the sample (for example, by country, issue date, currency etc.). To display the defaulted bonds, you should set the filter in the field *Is Defaulted* (choose the option *Yes*). The main principles of working with the list of bonds are described above (see search algorithms for outstanding or new bond issues). To view and export the data by the default date, you should display the corresponding column. To do so, on the *Results* tab choose the menu item *Settings→Edit Columns*. Then with the help of *Add* button include *Default Date* in the list of displayed columns and click *<Menu> to Return*. To export the list of defaulted bonds, in Excel choose the menu item *Actions → Export to Excel*. The recovery rate can be calculated using the market approach by exporting to Excel the bond historic quotes after a certain interval from the default date (for example, after 30 days). The algorithm of exporting historic bond quotes is analogous to historic YTM (see above).	1. In the left menu go to the section *Bonds→ Defaults*. 2. Set the filtration parameters of bond defaults: *Country;* *Sector;* *Industry;* *Announcement date;* *Type of security* (domestic/ international bond); *Currency*; *Type of obligation* (covenant, coupon, buyback option, redemption); *Default type* (default, non-execution of put option, repurchase technical default, technical default). 3. Click *Search*. The results will be displayed. 4. Click *Excel* to export data. The recovery rate can be calculated using the market approach. The algorithm of exporting historic bond quotes is analogous to historic data on YTM (see above). The data for calculating the recovery rate by the classical method (considering the date and the volume of actual payments) is not provided in a structured way. It is displayed in the news, on the issuer page in the section *News and research*.

Table 18.6 Searching and analyzing data on bond issue covenants

The algorithm in Eikon Refinitiv	*The algorithm in Bloomberg*	*The algorithm in Cbonds*
The collection of covenants data is done manually on the base of the bond page and prospectus. To get to the bond page, in the list of bonds, double-click on the bond RIC (see the search algorithms for outstanding or new bonds). On the bond page, you should go to the *Description* tab, then in the *Covenants* section there will be information about the prospectus and the presence of covenants by type (but this information is not available for all issues).	The collection of covenants data is done manually on the base of the bond page and prospectus. To display only bonds whose prospectus is available, in the filtration parameters of the bonds list you should include *Has Prospectus* filter (value *Yes*). To go to the bond page, in the list of bonds, double-click on the bond row (see the search algorithms for outstanding or new bonds). In the displayed menu choose *DES*. On the bond page you should go to the *Bond Description* tab and in the left menu choose *Covenants*, to see the prospectus choose *CF Prospectus*.	The collection of covenants data is done manually on the base of the bond page and prospectus. 1. In the left menu go to the section *Bonds* → *Issue search*. 2. Set the parameters of filtration (detailed instructions are provided above). 3. Click *Search*. The list of bonds will be displayed. 4. In the list of bonds click the link with the bond name in the column *Security*. 5. On the bond page go to the section *Covenants*. Click *Excel* to export data. 6. In case of absence of the block *Covenants*, go to the tab *Issue* and in the section *Issue documents* download the prospectus.

Table 18.7 Searching and analyzing data on embedded call and put options

The algorithm in Eikon Refinitiv	*The algorithm in Bloomberg*	*The algorithm in Cbonds*
To search data on call and put embedded options you should open the list of bonds and enter the required filters to limit the search (for example, by country, issue date, currency etc.). The main principles of working with the list of bonds are described above (refer to search algorithms for outstanding or new bond issues). Then you should choose the columns to display (with the option *Add/Remove Columns*): *Callable* is the sign that embedded call option is provided (it is possible to filter the list by the values *Yes/ No*); *Next Call Date* is the date of the next call option; *Putable* is the sign that the bonds have the embedded put option (it is possible to filter the list by the values *Yes/No*); *Next Put Date* is the date of the next put option. To export the list of options with embedded options into Excel, click →*Export All.*	To search data on embedded call and put options, you should open the list of bonds, fill in the required filters to limit the sample (for example, by country, issue date, currency etc.). To display the defaulted bonds, set the filter by the field *Maturity Type* (choose the variable *Callable* and/or *Putable*). The main principles of working with the list of bonds are described above (see search algorithms for outstanding or new bond issues). To view and export data by the dates of the next call and put options, set the corresponding columns. To do so, on the *Results* tab choose the menu item *Settings→Edit Columns.* Then with the help of *Add* button include *Next Call Date* and/or *Next Put Date* to the list of displayed columns and click *<Menu> to Return.*	1. In the left menu go to the section *Bonds → Issue search.* 2. Set the parameters of filtration (detailed instructions are provided above). 3. Click *Search.* The list of bonds will be displayed. 4. To set the parameters of columns, choose the menu item *Show / Hide columns.* Choose *Offer date (call)* and *Offer date (put)* to be shown in the list of displayed bonds. 5. To export the list of bonds in Excel, click *Excel.*

Table 18.8 Searching and analyzing data on bond liquidity indicators

The algorithm in Eikon Refinitiv	*The algorithm in Bloomberg*	*The algorithm in Cbonds*
For example, let us review the search of the Bid-Ask spread. The algorithm of searching for the liquidity indicators is analogous to the previous algorithm of exporting the historic yield to maturity, but in the window *Formula Builder* you should select the following values: category *Bid* and the fields *Timestamp* and *Close* for the *Bid* price; category *Ask* and the fields *Timestamp* and *Close* for the Ask price. Then you can calculate the Bid-Ask spread as a difference between Ask and Bid prices.	For example, let us review the search of the Bid-Ask spread. The algorithm of searching for the liquidity indicators is analogous to the previous algorithm of exporting the historic yield to maturity, but in the function *BDH* instead of *YLD_YTM_MID* parameter you should indicate: *PX_Bid* for the Bid price; *PX_Ask* for the Ask price. Then you can calculate the Bid-Ask spread as a difference between Ask and Bid prices.	1. In the left menu go to the section *Prices→By Trading Systems.* 2. Set the parameters of filtration (analogous to the previous algorithm of exporting the historic yield to maturity). 3. Click *Search.* The results will be displayed. 4. In the list of quotes click *Search parameters* and choose the columns with liquidity variables for display (for example, *Bid-Ask spread, Daily trading volume, Number of trades, Volume in securities,* etc.). 5. To export the results in Excel, click *Save in Excel format.*

Table 18.9 Searching and analyzing data on the issuer's financials

The algorithm in Eikon Refinitiv	*The algorithm in Bloomberg*	*The algorithm in Cbonds*
If there is only one issuer: 1. In the search field fill in the company name or a part of it (for example, *GAZP* for PAO Gazprom) and click *Enter.* 2. In the drop-down menu with the list of companies' securities, choose the stock ticker of a public company (for example, *GAZP. MM* for stocks of PAO Gazprom) or the name of a private company (for example, *Agronova-L OOO* for «*Agronova-L*»). 3. The company page will be open. On the company page choose the menu item: *Financials→Income Statement* to display the income statement; *Financials→Balance Sheet* to display the balance sheet; *Financials→Cash Flow* to display the cash flow statement; *Financial→Ratios–Key Metrics* to display the key financial ratios. 4. On the displayed tab with the financial variables click *Download to Excel* to export. If you need to export data for a sample of issuers: 1. In Excel you should go to the tab *Thomson Reuters*, connect to Eikon by clicking the *Login* and enter the login and password. 2. If the issuer RIC is unknown, you can get the data based on the ISIN or the RIC of the bond. The references to certain cells are provided for an example.	If there is only one issuer: 1. In the command line fill in the company name or a part of it (for example, *GAZP* for PAO Gazprom). 2. In the drop-down menu with the list of companies' securities choose the stock ticker of a public company (for example, *GAZP RM Equity* for PAO Gazprom) or the ticker of a private company (for example, AGRNVA Corp for Agronova-L OOO). 3. In the menu with the list of functions for a company choose *Company Analysis→Financial Analysis.* The financial report and several financial indicators will be displayed. 4. Go to the tab with the required financial indicators, for example, *Key Stats* for the key financial indicators, *I/S* for the income statement, *B/S* for the balance sheet, *C/F* for the cash flow statement, *Ratios* for the financial ratios. 5. To export the whole tab, choose the top menu item *Output→Excel→Custom Report.* To export one financial indicator, double-click its row and the graphics of the indicator will be displayed. Then click on the right mouse's button, select *Copy / Export Option → Copy Data to Clipboard* and paste the data into Excel.	To find the issuer's financial report, you should: 1. In the left menu choose: *Issuers→ IFRS Reports.* 2. Set the search parameters: *Issuer.* *Balance sheet* or *Profit and loss account indicators* (for example, *Assets* or *Sales revenue*). *Period.* 3. Click *Search.* 4. To export the financial statements click *Save in Excel.*

(*continued*)

Table 18.9 Cont.

The algorithm in Eikon Refinitiv	*The algorithm in Bloomberg*	*The algorithm in Cbonds*
Let us put the ISIN in the *A1* cell. To get the bond RIC using the ISIN, you should enter the following formula in the *B1* cell: *=TR(A1;”TR.RIC”;”CODE=ISIN NULL=BLANK”)* To obtain the company's number code in the *C1* cell, you should enter the formula: *=TR(B1;”TR.FiIssuerOrganization”;)*	If you need to export financial indicators for a sample of issuers: 1. In Excel go to *Bloomberg tab*, choose *Function Builder*. 2. You will get a field to enter a function. Choose the function *BDH* to load the historical data. 3. Then set the parameters of *BDH*. The first parameter is the stock ticker (for example, it can be given as «*GAZP RM EQUITY*» or refer to the cell in Excel where that ticker is located).	
In the *D1* cell indicate the formula for obtaining the company's intermediate identifier: *=CONCATENATE(C1;”@orgid”)* At last, to get the issuer's RIC, enter the following formula in the *E1* cell: *=TR(D1;”TR.RIC”)* 3. Click *Build Formula* on the *Thomson Reuters* tab. In the *Formula Builder* window set the parameters: - In the *Instruments* field refer to the cell with the issuer's RIC by clicking beside the *Instruments* field (in the above example it is the *D1* cell); - click *Real Time and Fundamentals* to display the financial and non-fundamental variables; - to search for financial indicators, in the *Search Data Items* field enter the name of the indicator (for example, *Revenue*) and click *Enter*, or you can browse the fields by categories (see the *Category* block);	The second parameter is the name of the financial indicator (for example, for the revenue it is *SALES_REV_TURN*). The third and the fourth parameters of *BDH* are the start and end dates of the period, for which you should export the financial indicator (for example, you can set *January 1, 2010* and *January 1, 2017* accordingly). Click *Ok*. As an alternative, you can directly enter the following formula into the cell in Excel: *=BDH(A1;”SALES_REV_TURN”;”01/01/2010”;”01/01/2017”)*	

Table 18.9 Cont.

The algorithm in Eikon Refinitiv	*The algorithm in Bloomberg*	*The algorithm in Cbonds*
- in the *Fields* block click *Add* beside the required indicator (for revenue, *Total Revenue*); - in the *Parameters & Quick Functions* block, in the *Financial Period* field set the period, for example, *FY2017 for the year 2017* (to obtain time series of revenue over a period, put the check mark in the *Series* field, in the drop-down list choose *Start-End* and in the fields *From* and *To* set the corresponding dates). - click *Insert*. As an alternative, you can directly enter the following formula into Excel (for example, *F1* cell): *=TR($E1;"TR.TotalRevenue";"Period=FY2017";F1)* where *E1* refers to the cell with the company's RIC. In the below example you will load the revenues for a given company for 2017. As an example, we provide several formulas for loading other financial indicators: - for *EBIT* (adjusted by TR Eikon, i.e. cleaned from non-operational costs): *=TR(E1;"TR.NormalizedEbit";"Period=FY2017";G1)* - for long-term debt *=TR(E1;"TR.TotalLongTermDebt";"Period=FY2017";H1)* - for company assets: *=TR(E1;"TR.TotalAssetsReported";"Period=FY2017";I1)*	where *A1* is the reference to the cell with the company ticker. In the below example you will export the revenue of a given company during the period from January 1, 2010 to January 1, 2017. As an example, we also provide several formulas to export other financial indicators: - for *EBIT*: *=BDH(A1;"EBIT";"01/01/2010";"01/01/2017")* - for long-term debt *=BDH(A1;"BS_LT_BORROW";"01/01/2010";"01/01/2017")* - for the company assets: *=TR(E1;"BS_TOT_ASSET";"Period=FY2017";I1)*	

Table 18.10 Searching and analyzing the data on issuer company's non-fundamental variables (example of searching the data about the capital structure, the board of directors, and the management)

The algorithm in Eikon Refinitiv	*The algorithm in Bloomberg*	*The algorithm in Cbonds*
If there is only one issuer: 1. Execute the first two steps of the above algorithm to search for financial variables of the issuer. 2. On the company's page choose the necessary menu item: *Ownership→Shareholders Report* to display data on company's capital structure and its investors; *ESG→Officers* to display the information about the board of directors and the management. 3. On the displayed tab click *Download to Excel* for export. If you need to export data on a sample of issuers: 1. Execute the first two steps of the above algorithm to search for financial variables of the issuer in Excel. 2. Click *Build Formula* on the *Thomson Reuters* tab. Choose the parameters of corporate governance similarly to the algorithm of searching the financial variables described above and click *Insert*.	If there is only one issuer: 1. Execute the first two steps of the above algorithm to search for financial variables of the issuer. 2. In the menu with the list of functions for a company, choose *Company Analysis→Ownership Summary* to display the capital structure and the company investors. Then go to the tab *Current* or *Historical* to view the current or historical information. Or in the menu with the list of functions for the company choose *Company Overview*, then *Management Overview→Company Management* to display the information about the board and the management. Go to the tab *Executives* to view the information about the managers, the *Board* tab to view the information about the board, the *Committees* tab to view the information about the board committees. If you need to load data for a sample of issuers: 1. Execute the first two steps of the above algorithm to search for financial variables of the issuer in Excel. 2. Set the parameters of *BDH* function by indicating the required variables of corporate governance by analogy with the algorithm of searching the financial variables described above. As an alternative, in the Excel cell you can set the required formulas to download non-fundamental variables. For example, we give several formulas (in all formulas the first parameter *A1* is the reference to the ticker of the issuer company, for example, «*GAZP RM Equity*»):	The database does not provide non-fundamental variables.

Table 18.10 Cont.

The algorithm in Eikon Refinitiv	*The algorithm in Bloomberg*	*The algorithm in Cbonds*
As an alternative, in the Excel cell you can set the required formulas to load non-fundamental variables. For example, we give several formulas (in all formulas the first parameter *$A5* is the reference to the issuer company, the indicators are downloaded for 2015): - for the board size: *=TR(A5;"TR.BoardSize";"Period=FY2015";F5)* - for the percentage of women in the board *=TR(A5;"TR.AnalyticBoardFemale";"Period=FY2015";H5)* - for the attribute if the CEO is in the board of directors: *=TR(A5;"TR.CGCEOBoardMember";"Period=FY2015";G5)* - for the percentage of independent board members: *=TR(A5;"TR.AnalyticIndepBoard";"Period=FY2015";M5);* - for the attribute of having an audit committee with three or more people, including the financial expert: *=TR(A5;"TR.AnalyticAuditCommExpertise";"Period=FY2015";L5).* To find the full name of the CEO and his birth date (at the current date), you can use the following formula: *=TR(A5;"TR.OfficerName;TR.OfficerAge;TR.OfficerTitle";"CH:Fd RNK=R 1:R30 NULL= BLANK")*	- for the board size (at the end of 2015): *=BDH(A1;"NUMBER_OF_DIRECTORS_ON_BOARD";"31.12.2015";"31.12.2015")* - for the percentage of women in the board (at the end of 2015) *=BDH(A1;"NUMBER_OF_WOMEN_ON_BOARD";"31.12.2015";"31.12.2015")* - for the attribute if the CEO is in the board (at the end of 2015): *=BDH(A1;"SAME_PERSON_CEO_AND_CHMN";"31.12.2015";"31.12.2015")* - for the percentage of independent board members (at the current date): *=BDP(A1;"PCT_INDEPENDENT_DIRECTORS")* - for the board audit size (at the current date): *=BDP(A1;"SIZE_OF_AUDIT_COMMITTEE")* To find the CEO's age (at the end of 2015), use the formula: *=BDH(A1;"CHIEF_EXECUTIVE_OFFICER_AGE";" 31.12.2015";" 31.12.2015")* To display the types of investors and their shares in the capital structure (for example, the government, insurance companies, banks etc.) you should use the formula: *=BDS(A1;"PCT_ OWNERSHIP_TYP")*	

(*continued*)

Table 18.10 Cont.

The algorithm in Eikon Refinitiv	*The algorithm in Bloomberg*	*The algorithm in Cbonds*
As a result, it will display the data of 30 board members and managers of the company *(*formula parameter *RNK=R1:R30)*. Among them you can find the CEO in accordance with the field *Officer Title*. To find the name, the country, and the share of the major stockholder (for example, on December 29, 2015), use the following formula: *=TR(A5;"TAKE(TR. PctOfShares OutHeld,1); TAKE(TR.InvAddr Country,1)";"SDate=2015-12-29; RH:investorname")* To display the list of the 10 largest shareholders (for example, on 29.12.2015) use the following formula: *=TR(A5;"TAKE(TR.PctOfShares OutHeld,10)";"SDate=2015-12-29; RH:investorname")* To find the share of the government in the capital structure, use the following formula: *=TR(A5;"Sum (TAKE (TR. PctOfSharesO ut Held,100))";" SDate= 2015-12-29; TheInvestor Type=304")*		

Table 18.11 Searching and analyzing data on macroeconomic variables

The algorithm in Eikon Refinitiv	*The algorithm in Bloomberg*	*The algorithm in Cbonds*
1. Click , in the drop-down menu choose *Markets,* then *Economic Indicator.* 2. In the opened window choose the country in the field *Country,* for example, *Russia.* 3. In the field *Indicator* from the drop-down list, choose the macro variable, for example, *GDP growth (annual %)* for real GDP growth values. 4. The time series will be displayed, and they can be exported to Excel by clicking .	1. In the command line indicate *ECST.* 2. In the *Country* field choose the country, for example, *Russia.* 3. In the left panel there will be a list of macro variables. You must choose the variable, for example, the *National Accounts→Real GDP* for the real GDP growth, *Prices→Consumer Prices* for the inflation. 4. In the field *Range* choose the period, for example, Q1 2007–Q4 2017. 5. To export data, choose the row with the required variable. Click the right mouse button and from the menu choose *Export to Workbench.* 6. When the graph of the variable time series appears, choose the menu item *Export→ Data Table to Excel.*	1. In the left menu choose *Indices and statistics → Cbonds indices.* 2. Go to the tab *Archive, search, data export.* 3. In the field *Index type* choose the necessary variable, for example, *GDP, Interest rates, Inflation,* etc. 4. In the field *Indicators* choose the required macroeconomic variables. 5. Choose the period of the displayed data. 6. Click *Search.* The variables for the period will be displayed.

Index